DB2® Fundamentals Certification For Du...

DB2 Family Fundamentals Exam 512 Objective	*Where it's covered in this book . . .*
Section 1 of the Exam: Installation & Planning	
Ability to Install DB2 Universal Database, DB2 Clients & Developers Edition	Ch. 6 (Part II)
Knowledge of and ability to use the DB2 UDB GUI Tools and CLP	Ch. 8 (Part II)
Knowledge of concepts of Datawarehouse and OLAP Issues	Ch. 5 (Part II)
Knowledge of new V7.1 tools	Ch. 8 (Part II)
Section 2 of the Exam: Security and Instances	
Ability to describe the functionality of the Administration Server Instance (DAS)	Ch. 5 (Part II)
Ability to provide users with authority on DB objects	Ch. 10 (Part III)
Section 3 of the Exam: Creating and Accessing DB2 Databases	
Ability to create a DB2 database	Ch. 9 (Part III)
Ability to catalog a remote database or local database or DRDA	Ch. 7 (Part II)
Ability to use the DB2 GUI tools to create, access and manipulate DB2 objects	Ch. 8 (Part II)
Ability to create and access basic DB2 objects	Ch. 9 (Part III)
Section 4 of the Exam: SQL Usage	
Ability to start/end a unit of work	Ch. 12 (Part IV)
Given a DDL SQL statement, knowledge to identify results	Ch. 12 (Part IV)
Given a DML SQL statement, knowledge to identify results	Ch. 12 (Part IV)
Given a DCL SQL statement, knowledge to identify results	Ch. 10 (Part III)
Ability to use SQL to SELECT data from tables	Ch. 12 (Part IV)
Ability to use SQL to SORT or GROUP data	Ch. 12 (Part IV)
Ability to use SQL to UPDATE, DELETE, or INSERT data	Ch. 12 (Part IV)
Knowledge to identify the affect of a COMMIT or ROLLBACK statement	Ch. 12 (Part IV)
Knowledge to identify the scope of a COMMIT or ROLLBACK	Ch. 12 (Part IV)
Section 5 of the Exam: Database Objects	
Ability to demonstrate usage of DB2 data types	Ch. 9 (Part III)
Given a situation, ability to create a table	Ch. 9 (Part III)
Given a situation, knowledge to identify when referential constraints are used	Ch. 9 (Part III)
Knowledge to identify methods of data validation	Ch. 9 (Part III)
Knowledge to identify characteristics of a table, view, or index	Ch. 9 (Part III)
Knowledge of concepts of extenders	Ch. 9 (Part III)
Section 6 of the Exam: Database Concurrency	
Knowledge to identify factors that influence locking	Ch. 11 (Part III)
Ability to list the objects that locks can be obtained on	Ch. 11 (Part III)
Knowledge to identify scope of different types of DB2 locks	Ch. 11 (Part III)
Knowledge to identify factors affecting amount of locks that are used	Ch. 11 (Part III)
Knowledge to identify factors affecting the type of locks obtained	Ch. 11 (Part III)
Given a situation, knowledge to identify the isolation levels that should be used	Ch. 11 (Part III)

For Dummies: Bestselling Book Series for Beginners

DB2® Fundamentals Certification For Dummies®

Structured Query Language (SQL)

- **Data Control Language (DCL):** Used to provide access control to database objects (GRANT, REVOKE)
- **Data Definition Language (DDL):** Used to create, modify, or drop database objects (CREATE, DECLARE, ALTER, DROP)
- **Data Manipulation Language (DML):** Used to access or modify data (SELECT, INSERT, UPDATE, DELETE)

The Basics of SQL Syntax

Note: Words written in uppercase are part of the SQL syntax; the italicized words enclosed in angle brackets (< and >) represent values that you supply. Words or characters separated by vertical bars (|) represent valid choices. Material enclosed in square brackets ([and]) is optional.

To list all the rows in a table (the asterisk [*] means that all of the columns are to be returned):

```
SELECT * FROM <table>
```

To list a subset of rows from more than one table (this is a *join*; for a description of the various types of join, see "Joins Revisited" in Chapter 13, "The Rest of the SQL Story"):

```
SELECT * FROM <table_1>, <table_2> FETCH FIRST <n> ROWS ONLY
```

To list rows for a subset of columns: Restrict the result set by using a WHERE clause and predicates. Sort the result set by values in a specific column in ascending or descending order, using the ORDER BY clause:

```
"SELECT <col_1>, <col_2>, ... <col_n> FROM <table>
  WHERE <col_1>
  { = | <> | < | > | <= | >= | IS [NOT] NULL | [NOT] IN |
  [NOT] BETWEEN | [NOT] LIKE | [NOT] EXISTS }
  <[numeric_constant, 'string_constant']>
  ORDER BY <col_2> [ASC, DESC]"
```

To eliminate duplicate rows in a result set: Use the DISTINCT clause.

To assign a meaningful name to an expression or to any item in the select list: Use the AS clause.

To organize rows in a result set: Use the GROUP BY clause. Each group is represented by a single row in the result set:

```
SELECT <col_1>, <col_2>, ... <col_n> FROM <table>
  GROUP BY { (<col_1>, <col_2>, ... <col_n>) |
    GROUPING SETS (<col_1>, <col_2>, ... <col_n>) |
    ROLLUP (<col_1>, <col_2>, ... <col_n>) |
    CUBE (<col_1>, <col_2>, ... <col_n>) }
```

To retrieve results only for groups that satisfy a specific condition: Use the HAVING clause.

SQL Terms

Subquery: A SELECT statement that appears within a WHERE clause and feeds results to that WHERE clause.

Column functions: These operate on a set of values in a column (for example, SUM, AVG, MIN, MAX, COUNT).

Scalar functions: These operate on a single value to return another single value (for example, ABS, LENGTH, YEAR, MONTH, DAY, LCASE, UCASE).

Correlation names: Eliminate ambiguous references to identical column names from different tables. For example:

```
"SELECT t1.<col_1> FROM <table_1> t1
  WHERE t1.<col_1> < (SELECT AVG(t2.<col_1>) FROM <table_2> t2)"
```

Cheat Sheet $2.95 value. Item 0841-5.
For more information about Hungry Minds, call 1-800-762-2974.

For Dummies: Bestselling Book Series for Beginners

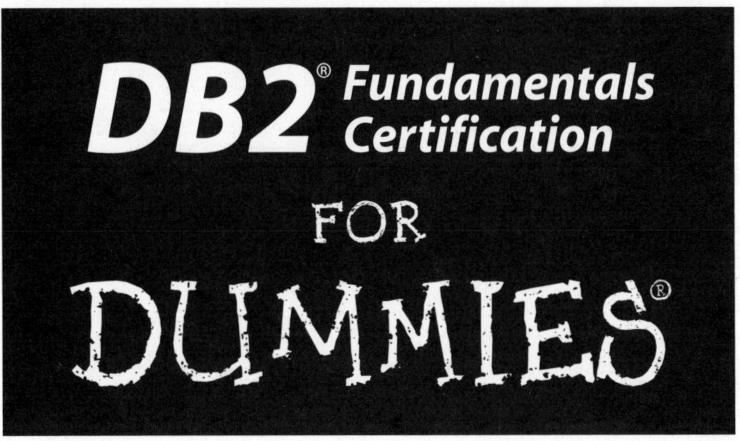

by Paul C. Zikopoulos, Jennifer Gibbs, and Roman B. Melnyk

Best-Selling Books • Digital Downloads • e-Books • Answer Networks • e-Newsletters • Branded Web Sites • e-Learning

New York, NY ◆ Cleveland, OH ◆ Indianapolis, IN

DB2® Fundamentals Certification For Dummies®

Published by
Hungry Minds, Inc.
909 Third Avenue
New York, NY 10022
www.hungryminds.com
www.dummies.com

Library of Congress Control Number: 2001089320

ISBN: 0-7645-0841-5

Printed in the United States of America

10 9 8 7 6 5 4 3 2 1

1O/SQ/QX/QR/IN

Distributed in the United States by Hungry Minds, Inc.

Distributed by CDG Books Canada Inc. for Canada; by Transworld Publishers Limited in the United Kingdom; by IDG Norge Books for Norway; by IDG Sweden Books for Sweden; by IDG Books Australia Publishing Corporation Pty. Ltd. for Australia and New Zealand; by TransQuest Publishers Pte Ltd. for Singapore, Malaysia, Thailand, Indonesia, and Hong Kong; by Gotop Information Inc. for Taiwan; by ICG Muse, Inc. for Japan; by Intersoft for South Africa; by Eyrolles for France; by International Thomson Publishing for Germany, Austria and Switzerland; by Distribuidora Cuspide for Argentina; by LR International for Brazil; by Galileo Libros for Chile; by Ediciones ZETA S.C.R. Ltda. for Peru; by WS Computer Publishing Corporation, Inc., for the Philippines; by Contemporanea de Ediciones for Venezuela; by Express Computer Distributors for the Caribbean and West Indies; by Micronesia Media Distributor, Inc. for Micronesia; by Chips Computadoras S.A. de C.V. for Mexico; by Editorial Norma de Panama S.A. for Panama; by American Bookshops for Finland.

For general information on Hungry Minds' products and services please contact our Customer Care Department within the U.S. at 800-762-2974, outside the U.S. at 317-572-3993 or fax 317-572-4002.

For sales inquiries and reseller information, including discounts, premium and bulk quantity sales, and foreign-language translations, please contact our Customer Care Department at 800-434-3422, fax 317-572-4002, or write to Hungry Minds, Inc., Attn: Customer Care Department, 10475 Crosspoint Boulevard, Indianapolis, IN 46256.

For information on licensing foreign or domestic rights, please contact our Sub-Rights Customer Care Department at 212-884-5000.

For information on using Hungry Minds' products and services in the classroom or for ordering examination copies, please contact our Educational Sales Department at 800-434-2086 or fax 317-572-4005.

For press review copies, author interviews, or other publicity information, please contact our Public Relations Department at 317-572-3168 or fax 317-572-4168.

For authorization to photocopy items for corporate, personal, or educational use, please contact Copyright Clearance Center, 222 Rosewood Drive, Danvers, MA 01923, or fax 978-750-4470.

About the Authors

Paul Zikopoulos, BA, MBA, is a Database Specialist with the IBM Global Sales Support team. He has more than five years of experience with DB2 and has written numerous magazine articles and books about DB2. Paul has written articles for such magazines as *Linux Journal*, *DB2 Update*, *DB2 Magazine*, *IDUG Solutions Journal*, any many more. Recently, Paul co-authored the books *DB2 For Dummies* (IDG Books Worldwide, Inc., September 2000) and *"A DBA's Guide to Databases on Linux"* (Syngress Media, April 2000). Paul is a DB2 Certified Advanced Technical Expert (DRDA and Cluster/EEE) and a DB2 Certified Solutions Expert (Business Intelligence and Database Administration). You can reach him at paulz_ibm@yahoo.com.

Jennifer Gibbs, Hon. BSC, is a DB2 Certified Advanced Technical Expert and a senior member of the DB2 Technical Support Team at the IBM Toronto Laboratory. She provides technical support to DB2 EE and EEE customers worldwide and is the Team Lead of the Database Administration Support Team. Jennifer held the Team Lead position on the former DB2 EEE Support Team and has experience as a Technical Advocate for several high profile DB2 UDB customers. You can reach her at jgibbs_ibm@hotmail.com.

Roman B. Melnyk, PhD, is a senior member of the DB2 Information Development team, specializing in database administration and DB2 utilities. During more than five years at IBM, Roman has written numerous books for the DB2 product library and other related materials. Most recently, Roman co-authored the book *DB2 For Dummies* (IDG Books Worldwide, Inc., September 2000). You can reach him at roman_b_melnyk@hotmail.com.

Dedication

Paul Zikopoulos: When I started this book, as with all that I have written, I wrote the dedication first — a kind of inspiration to keep the fire burning through the wee hours of each morning. This is what I wrote:

> For Scott Reid, one of the best friends (and the best man for my wedding) a guy could have. Scott loves to win. Over the years, Scott has taken more money from me than I would like to admit. Be it a bet on a squash game or that impossible putt on the 18th hole, this guy just refuses, or more likely is too cheap, to lose. Scott recently got into a fight with cancer. I am forever grateful that he loves to win.

Unfortunately, cancer proved to be a bigger physical opponent than we all expected. Scott passed away in the early morning of June 28th. It was a hot and sunny day the morning he passed — the kind when he would call to play a round of golf. When I got the call at 6:30 a.m., I knew it wasn't for golf. Up until this day, Scott somehow found a way to greet you with his warm smile, refreshing personality, and charm (I told you he refused to lose).

I didn't get to spend the time I deserved to have had with him this last year. Scott, you are every place that I go, and the lessons that you unknowingly teach have made me a better person.

Scott, I really miss you.

Jennifer Gibbs: For Brian, Mom, Dad, and Lee-Ann, my source of strength, encouragement, and comfort.

Roman B. Melnyk: I would like to dedicate this book to my wife, Teresa, and to my children, Rosemary and Joanna.

Authors' Acknowledgments

Paul Zikopoulos: Take a look at the figure below and ask yourself which segment is longer: Segment A, the one on the left that goes from < to > or segment B on the right, which goes > to <.

I know what you are thinking, "I've seen this trick before, it may look like segment B is longer, but they are both the same size. You think you are going to catch me with this? Cute, but, been there, done that."

Now I want you to take a string and measure segment B; then measure segment A. Surprised? In this example, segment A is actually longer! This is the opposite of the trick that you have likely seen in the past. In fact, segment A is 20 percent longer than segment B. You were so confident that you knew this so well, weren't you?

So what does this mean? I am thanking a piece of string for empowering me to write a book? No! The point is that many times we go through life thinking we know it all, or more than we do, only to find out there is 20 percent more to learn. I want to thank the members of my current team, mentors really, for starting to teach me that 20 percent more (each of them, so that makes like 100 percent more to learn) and making me feel like a novice to the database game: Bill Wong, George Baklarz, Kevin Street, Jim Stittle, and Glen Sheffield. One would be hard pressed to find a more talented group of database specialists (did I mention that I am glad they don't work for the competition?).

Finally, thanks to Roman (once again) and Jennifer for helping to make another idea into what you have in your hands right now. Your ideas and contributions bring this book to a much higher level than I could have imagined on my own.

Jennifer Gibbs: Special thanks to my fiancé, Brian Riberdy, for his patience and support and for reviewing all of my chapters for me; to my friends and family for dealing with my absence while working on this project, and to Lily Lugomirski for giving me the opportunity to write this book. Finally, thanks to Roman and Paul — it's been a pleasure.

Roman Melnyk: Many thanks to my wife, Teresa, and to my children, Rosemary and Joanna, for their wonderful support during the preparation of this book.

All of us: Thanks to Judith Escott, Les Chapman, and Susan Visser, all important players in the DB2 skills development program. Your personal dedication to educating the world on DB2 has made the market for this book (and many others) possible. Thanks for all your help and support along the way.

Kelly Masci, an Information Developer at the IBM Toronto Lab, wrote Chapter 2, "How to Get Certified and What's Available." Kelly was actually preparing for this exam while we were writing this book. Needless to say, we used her as a guinea pig. We are happy to say that she passed the exam and is well on her way to becoming a certified database geek.

Blair Adamache signed up at the last moment to be our technical editor. Blair is a seventeen-year veteran of the IBM Toronto Lab. His first SQL statement (written in 1986 using 10base, the predecessor to FoxPro) eventually led to a fulltime job in relational database technology at IBM, beginning in 1987. In his current role, Blair is a second line manager for the DB2 Service team, and it is his responsibility to ensure that customers receive the best support for their database in the business. Blair has many years of experience with customers through stints in marketing, development, and management. We can't tell you how privileged we were to have him help us out, and help us out he did. We all thank you, Blair.

We also want to thank Carole McClendon at Waterside Productions, who always seems to keep us busy writing books.

Finally, this book could not have become what it was without the hard work and dedication from the folks at Hungry Minds. When you write a book on your own personal time, it becomes something that motivates you and also a cloud over your head. Many sacrifices were made on both sides, and we really want to thank Susan Christophersen and Constance Carlisle for their dedication and ability to keep the project moving through the bumps. An excellent editing team.

Publisher's Acknowledgments

We're proud of this book; please send us your comments through our Hungry Minds Online Registration Form located at www.dummies.com.

Some of the people who helped bring this book to market include the following:

Acquisitions, Editorial, and Media Development

Project Editor: Susan Christophersen

Acquisitions Editors: Nancy Maragioglio, Stacee Ehman

Copy Editor: Susan Christophersen

Technical Editor: Blair Adamache

Editorial Manager: Constance Carlisle

Permissions Editor: Carmen Krikorian

Media Development Specialist: Travis Silvers

Media Development Coordinator: Marisa Pearman

Media Development Manager: Laura Carpenter

Media Development Supervisor: Richard Graves

Editorial Assistant: Amanda Foxworth

Production

Project Coordinator: Regina Snyder

Layout and Graphics: Amy Adrian, Joyce Haughey, Jackie Nicholas, Barry Offringa, Jill Piscitelli, Jacque Schneider, Julie Trippetti, Jeremey Unger

Proofreaders: Laura Albert, Susan Moritz, TECHBOOKS Production Services

Indexer: TECHBOOKS Production Services

Special Help

Nicole Laux

General and Administrative

Hungry Minds, Inc.: John Kilcullen, CEO; Bill Barry, President and COO; John Ball, Executive VP, Operations & Administration; John Harris, Executive VP and CFO

Hungry Minds Technology Publishing Group: Richard Swadley, Senior Vice President and Publisher; Mary Bednarek, Vice President and Publisher, Networking and Certification; Walter R. Bruce III, Vice President and Publisher, General User and Design Professional; Joseph Wikert, Vice President and Publisher, Programming; Mary C. Corder, Editorial Director, Branded Technology Editorial; Andy Cummings, Publishing Director, General User and Design Professional; Barry Pruett, Publishing Director, Visual

Hungry Minds Manufacturing: Ivor Parker, Vice President, Manufacturing

Hungry Minds Marketing: John Helmus, Assistant Vice President, Director of Marketing

Hungry Minds Production for Branded Press: Debbie Stailey, Production Director

Hungry Minds Sales: Roland Elgey, Senior Vice President, Sales and Marketing; Michael Violano, Vice President, International Sales and Sub Rights

◆

The publisher would like to give special thanks to Patrick J. McGovern, without whom this book would not have been possible.

◆

Contents at a Glance

Cartoons at a Glance

By Rich Tennant

The 5th Wave
By Rich Tennant
JERRY CRAMS FOR THE EMOTICON SECTION OF THE DB2 CERTIFICATION EXAM.
©RICHTENNANT
Oo-I know this one! It's...uh...
C'mon Jerry. Over 800 more to go.

page 7

The 5th Wave
By Rich Tennant
©RICHTENNANT

"Hold your horses! It takes time to build a database for someone with as many parts as you have."

page 45

The 5th Wave
By Rich Tennant
©RICHTENNANT

"Oh, Scarecrow! Without the database in your laptop, how will we ever find anything in Oz?"

page 401

The 5th Wave
By Rich Tennant
©RICHTENNANT

"I couldn't get this 'job skills' program to work on my PC, so I replaced the motherboard, upgraded the BIOS, and wrote a program that links it to my personal database. It told me I wasn't technically inclined and should pursue a career in sales."

page 221

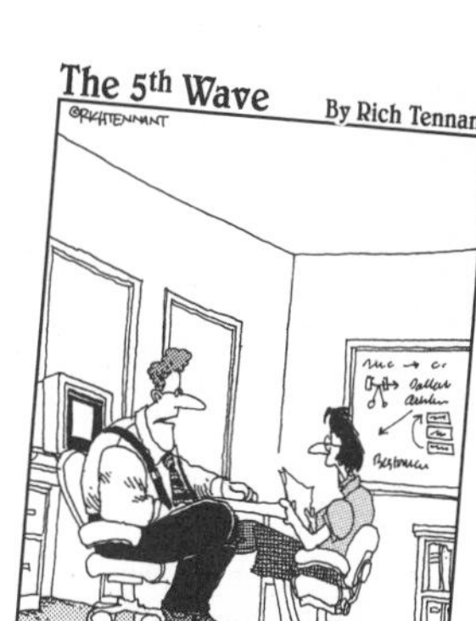

The 5th Wave
By Rich Tennant
©RICHTENNANT

"Our automated response policy to a large company-wide data crash is to notify management, back up existing data and sell 90% of my shares in the company."

page 335

Cartoon Information:

Fax: 978-546-7747

E-Mail: richtennant@the5thwave.com

World Wide Web: www.the5thwave.com

Table of Contents

Letter from Judith Escott, Worldwide Executive, Channel and Skills Development, Data Management, IBM

Today's computing environment is fast-paced, competitive, and dynamic. As computer professionals, one of the most effective ways to stay ahead of the technology curve and validate your skills is through certification. For employers, it increases your credibility and expertise, and for you, it represents a direct path to knowledge of the hottest technology in the market today, IBM DB2 Universal Database (DB2).

More than 20 years ago, relational database technology was invented in the IBM Research labs. IBM delivered the first commercially available database in the early 1980s. This invention created the unique ability to represent data in a simple tabular form, access it through the powerful SQL query language (also invented in the IBM Research labs), and make it readily available to the business community. Today, tens of thousands of business all over the world rely on DB2 databases to store their key corporate data assets and run their business both traditionally and over the Web.

Your decision to become an IBM Certified Solutions Expert for DB2 Universal Database is one of the most effective ways for you to prove your skills as a database expert to prospective employers. IBM DB2 Certification offers you a comprehensive program for building and enhancing your skills, as well the benefit of opening new and exciting career paths.

Your first step is preparing for the certification tests. *DB2 Fundamentals Certification For Dummies* is written in a straightforward and conversational manner to take you through the certification process step-by-step. It also outlines the different levels of certification making it simple for you to determine which is the right path for you. It helps to prepare you for the tests by providing all the information you will need and includes sample tests for you to take to increase your comfort level.

DB2 Fundamentals Certification For Dummies teaches you the fundamentals of the DB2 family and its components and functions. It takes you through the different DB2 products and packaging As well as installation and planning exercises to get you running on DB2 in no time.. This book covers the fundamentals of security; creating and accessing DB2 databases, SQL, database objects, concurrency, and more! After reading this book, you will know all that you need to know about DB2 for the exam, as well as various hints and tips to sharpen your technical edge.

The 21st century promises to be one of the fastest moving and challenging decades in computing history. As a computer professional, you will be tasked with keeping ahead of the technology demands of tomorrow's companies that are building applications, services, and portals for e-commerce, customer relationship management, B2B, B2C, supply chain management, and business intelligence. With the growing demand for skilled data management professionals, there is no better time to obtain your certification.

Wishing you much success with your studies.

Judith Escott
Worldwide Executive, Channel and Skills Development
Data Management, IBM

Introduction

So you want to take that first step on the path to becoming a DB2 certified professional and you therefore bought this book (thanks, by the way). You promised yourself, your boss, or your mother (just in case she likes DB2 as much as we do) that you will pass the DB2 Family Fundamentals exam in the next couple of months and from there branch off into either the DB2 Application Development, DB2 Administration, or DB2 Business Intelligence exams and become the database nerd that you were born to be! Well, perhaps you weren't born solely to know DB2, but after reading this book, you will definitely have an idea about the DB2 family. In your hands right now is *the* best resource available to help prepare you for the DB2 Universal Database Version 7.1 Family Fundamentals Exam 512.

We'll get you started on your first step, in case this is the first time you've ever heard of DB2. There is no DB1. Got it? The rest of the book is going to help you with what you need to know.

About This Book

This book prepares you for the DB2 Family Fundamentals Exam Test 512, the first step toward becoming a DB2 certified professional. The contents of this book introduce you to the various flavors of DB2, how to install DB2 clients and servers and get them to talk to each other without arguing, SQL, the DB2 tools, and some techy database stuff that the exam expects you to know.

Who Should Read This Book

If you want a great resource to prepare for the DB2 Family Fundamentals Exam 512, you should read this book. If you aren't interested in writing an exam on DB2, but would like to wipe that stupid look off your face when you meet with the Information Technology department, read this book. If you want to solve all the world's problems, read this book (we have to warn you that it may not work, but it's definitely a first step).

Even if you're new to DB2, you can trust that this book will introduce you to DB2 without the bombardment of condescending tones and text so thick that you need to be a math professor to sort through it.

Conventions Used in This Book

Now, we know that your first thought when we say *conventions* is of hordes of people getting together in a big hotel and chattering about something that (presumably) interests the whole slew of them. However, what we mean by conventions here is to clue you in to how we do things with the text in this book to make your life easier.

When we want you to type something, we say, "enter **this**" and put the text that we want you to type in **bold** font so that you know exactly what you have to type. For commands, filenames, directory names, URLs, and text that appears on-screen (such as the results of entering a command at a command prompt), we use what the *For Dummies* editors call `monofont` to set it apart from other text. This style makes this stuff easier for you to find.

When we show you a command (this book has a lot of SQL commands, for example) we put them in what we call *generic* form. Now, this doesn't mean that the command is cheaper than the name brand and infinitely more stale; it means that we write our commands such that you can easily identify those parts of the command you have to replace and what you have to replace them with. To do this, we use italics within angle brackets in commands to indicate that you should replace whatever the command requires for the angle brackets and the italic text within.

For example, assume that you want to set up support for the TCP/IP communication protocol each time your instance is started by using the `db2start` command. You enter the following command to do this:

```
db2set DB2COMM=TCPIP
```

In the book, because this command can take on multiple values, you'll see it as follows:

```
db2set DB2COMM=<supported_protocols>
```

This means that you need to replace <*supported_protocols*> with the name of the protocol(s) that you want DB2 to support when you start an instance. Don't worry about instances and all that jargon for now; just know that when you type in the command, you should replace the <*supported_protocols*> with the protocols that you want to support (which may be just TCP/IP or a bunch of them).

Remember: Do not type the angle brackets! They're just to clue you in that what's between them needs to be replaced — a variable, if you will. The angle brackets are not part of the command.

When we tell you something such as "press Ctrl+Alt+Del," that means we want you to press the Ctrl, Alt, and Del keys at the same time (not add them using a calculator).

If you're a Windows person, you can associate words with arrows in the middle of a menu path option. For example, where we tell you to "click the Start button and choose Programs⇨IBM DB2⇨Control Center" or something like that with funny arrows in between, we mean that you should click the Start button with your mouse pointer and then choose the Programs menu, the IBM DB2 menu, and then the Control Center item. If you're a UNIX person, then you likely hate anything graphical (or easy . . . just kidding) and you won't need to worry about a Start menu, but you can interpret these arrows the same way for options from the action menu bar or pop-up windows in the DB2 tools.

Foolish Assumptions

We've all fallen for misplaced assumptions in our lives, so we want to make sure that you understand some basic assumptions that we think you already know before you start reading this book. We have to assume a few things about you so that the content of this book can focus on the topic at hand: DB2. So, following are the assumptions that we make about you:

- If you want to use the version of DB2 that's packaged in the back of this book, we assume you have a Pentium II-class (or newer) computer running Windows NT 4.0 with Service Pack 5 or later, or Windows 2000 (see the CD Appendix for more info on hardware requirements).
- You want to prepare for the DB2 Family Fundamentals exam (you actually don't need to be doing this to read this book, but we do make this assumption when we speak to you).
- You know what a computer is and have one that can run DB2. In other words, you aren't expecting to run DB2 on a Commodore VIC-20 or TRS-80.
- You know the basics on how to use your computer and the operating system you have (we won't elaborate on this, but let's just say we've seen cases of CD-ROM drives being used as coffee holders — no joke).

How This Book is Organized

Knowing how this book is organized will help you work through the book more efficiently and enable you to jump directly to parts that interest you the most. (Did we mention that all the parts in this book are interesting?) We broke this book down into five parts, each of which we describe briefly in the following five sections.

Part I: DB2 Certification: What Do I Need to Know?

This part won't pull you through any technical details of DB2 and won't give you the information you need to know to pass the exam. So why read it? If you want to know about the whole DB2 Certification process and program, you will find that here. However, there is far more value than that in this part. Part I shows you the things that no other book on the market today can tell you about the DB2 Family Fundamentals Exam. This part shows you the breakdown of the exam, what percentage of questions come from what section so that you know where to focus your attention, what the testing software looks like so that you can feel right at home when you write the exam, and why you should care about DB2 certification. If you're planning to write the DB2 Family Fundamentals exam, make sure that you read the chapters in this part. If you aren't planning to write the DB2 Family Fundamentals exam, you can skip this part (though it would likely still do you good to read it).

Part II: Introducing DB2

After reading this part, you will know about all the different editions of DB2 and DB2-related products (which you are expected to know for the exam). You can also get some hands-on experience with DB2 in this part by first installing a DB2 server and then a DB2 client to make that server useful! We show you how to get your DB2 client to talk to your DB2 server. You also get a sneak preview at the DB2 graphical tools and see how to create the oh-so-creatively titled SAMPLE database. Finally, you can find a primer on Data Warehousing and Online Analytical Processing (OLAP).

Part III: The Geeky Stuff: Inside DB2

This part introduces you to the major objects and theory of DB2, including information on how to create and manage DB2 instances (the heart of a DB2 database) as well as how to create a database from scratch. We also describe the concept of tablespaces and how they can be used to store and retrieve data more efficiently. We show you how to create the actual tables that are going to hold your data, and we describe some other odds and ends, such as indexes, buffer pools, views, and schemas. We refer to all this stuff as the building blocks of DB2. You'll also find information on how DB2 handles security as well as database concurrency.

Part IV: Talking to DB2 with Structured Query Language

SQL, pronounced S-Q-L or "Sequel," is the language that you use to talk to databases, including DB2. The DB2 Family Fundamentals exam focuses a lot on SQL. You're expected to know SQL; in fact, if you want to pass the exam, you better know it pretty well. Fortunately for you, this part takes you through the basics of SQL and then gets you using relational online analytical processing (ROLAP) extensions.

Part V: The Part of Tens

Last but certainly not least is this *For Dummies* prerequisite. A *For Dummies* book just isn't a book without the Part of Tens! This part of the book has two short chapters chock-full of useful information or pointers to more information about DB2, including some SQL problems to work through and some pointers to showcase your new skills in a job search.

Study aids

In Chapters 4 through 13, you'll find special elements that we use to help you assess what you know and what you need to work on more. Each of these chapters begins with the exam objectives that the chapter covers. The Quick Assessment section helps you gauge what you know now. Labs are exercises that you'll encounter throughout the chapter to help you accomplish a task. The chapters end with a Prep Test, which both helps you tell whether you know the chapter content and gives you some practice for the actual exam.

Icons in This Book

Various eye-catching icons appear throughout this book, but they're not just for show. They actually help you find certain types of important info, as follows:

This icon represents something that can really help you get things done or avoid hassles. Remember these, you can share them with your friends and make it look like you knew what were you doing all along!

Hint. Hint. Hint. These icons are about the closest thing to cheating on the test that we can tell you and not feel guilty about. If you're thinking about writing the DB2 Family Fundamentals exam, pay close attention to these. We tell you things such as what to study, what the exam is picky about, what's in the book but not covered on the exam, and so on. Read them now; thank us later!

This icon draws your attention to the way things work "outside of our box," so to speak. Quite simply, you get a hint of how things are done when you come across DB2 in a business. For example, in this book, we tell you how to give yourself all sorts of authorities that pretty much let you do whatever you want with your databases. We do this because we trust you and we want to say thanks for buying our book; truthfully, it's the best way to learn. Anyway, your bosses at work are likely to be less trusting than us, and when they are, we point it out with an icon like this one.

Okay, the bomb in this icon may be a little extreme. If you don't follow what we tell you to do, your computer isn't going to blow up and you aren't going to become a suspect on the FBI's ten most-wanted list. This icon warns you about things you may not like if you don't follow the instructions in this book. Don't skip over these; they're here because *we* fell for this stuff and we want *you* to avoid them.

Part I

DB2 Certification: What Do I Need to Know?

The 5th Wave
By Rich Tennant
JERRY CRAMS FOR THE EMOTICON SECTION OF THE DB2 CERTIFICATION EXAM.
©RICHTENNANT
Oo-I know this one! It's... uh...
C'mon Jerry. Over 800 more to go.

In this part . . .

This part introduces you to the nontechnical aspects of the test. The chapters in this part take you through a trial run of the test. We show you all the screens that you'll see in this test. This walk-through will make you feel right at home when you sit down on exam day. This part also discusses the value of becoming certified in DB2 and the kind of fulfilling life you'll lead when you pass.

Chapter 1

What the Heck Is Certification and Why Should I Care?

In This Chapter

- Understanding certification and what it's worth
- Understanding the levels of certification
- Realizing the return on your investment

Certification can mean many things to many different people, so we start with a broad definition:

> ***certification*** [sert-a-fa-'kā-shun] — *n.* to declare formally or in writing, usually with authority, a declaration of some fact; a testimonial of character.

What is certification and why should you care? Well, it only happens to be the coolest thing around, the best way to prove to everyone that indeed you know what you are talking about. It's a statement of credibility, a statement of competence, and, of course, a statement of achievement!

Do you care whether people are certified? Of course you do! Many professional organizations have some sort of certification or accreditation that identify an individual's expertise. Identifiers can be in the form of a degree, diploma, designation, and others. Would you visit a dentist who wasn't a D.D.S.? The D.D.S. bit (though just three simple letters) says something about the person who has the drill in your mouth. What about that mechanic who is charging you $60 an hour to work on your car? Would you let people charge you that kind of money if they did not have a nonbiased source that could prove to you they knew what they were doing? Finally, what about the doctor with that thermometer? Well, we are sure you get where we are going with this (the importance of certification, that is).

The point here is that certifications (remember, formal written authoritative declarations of fact) are everywhere we go. In fact, as consumers, we demand them. You bought this book because we were able to demonstrate certifiable and credible skills in DB2 — validated by our certifications and our employment with IBM. So, if consumers can demand declarations of competency while transacting the marketplace, shouldn't people who interact with Information Technology professionals be able to ask the same? You bet, and that in itself is a great reason to get certified.

It is likely that you have already decided to become certified and that is why you bought this book. Nevertheless, we thought we would take a couple of pages to tell you about the benefits of certification. Check out the Acknowledgements section and that funny line — you will likely learn 20 percent more than you thought you knew about certification after reading this chapter.

This chapter discusses what certification is, what it means to you, and how it can help you. Buying this book is the first step you can take on the road to certification for the IBM data management product, DB2.

What Is Certification?

Certification is a tool to help objectively measure the performance of a professional on a given job at a defined skill level. This measurement comes from a credible neutral source, in this case IBM (though many software and hardware companies have their own certification programs).

In today's ever-changing business environment, keeping pace with complex technologies and products is essential. Most businesses are looking for complete solutions rather than tactical efforts. IBM's professional certification programs offer a business solution for skilled technical professionals seeking to demonstrate their expertise to the world.

The IBM certification program is designed to validate your skills and demonstrate your proficiency with the latest IBM technology and solutions. It provides individuals with a structured program leading to an internationally recognized qualification. The program is flexible and allows you to select your role and preparation time, and to take tests all at your own pace — not someone else's.

Because certification by a credible source (such as IBM) provides a person with credentials that are validated by a reliable source, it is beneficial for individuals who want to validate their own skills and performance levels and/or that of their employees.

For a certification program to be worthwhile, the certification tests must reflect the critical tasks required for a job, the skill levels of each task, and the frequency with which a task needs to be performed. IBM prides itself in designing comprehensive, documented processes, which ensure that IBM certification tests remain relevant to the work environment of potential certification candidates. Because we wrote the exams, we can tell you that these exams are no cakewalk. You have to work hard for these, but that makes you that much prouder when you achieve your goal.

Who's Getting Certified?

Everyone! Well, if you work with DB2, they are. More and more, employers are demanding certifiable skills. DB2 Certification is growing at an incredible rate, and IBM is focusing heavily on the skills development arena.

What Is Certification Worth?

If you work with DB2 everyday, and even if you don't, DB2 certification has its benefits. Certification provides your resume with a badge of distinction and a better chance of landing that killer job. Certification helps everyone really, from IBM, to the employer, to the very people who write the test (because everyone will see you for the IBM expert you are).

What do I get out of it?

In addition to assessing job skills and performance levels, you can expect professional certification from IBM to help you promote recognition as an IBM certified professional. Certification may accelerate your career potential by validating your professional competency and increasing your ability to provide solid, capable technical support.

This is a pretty important benefit. IBM professionals are known around the world for their outstanding technical ability and leadership in an ever-changing and competitive IT environment.

Certification will also help create a stronger presence and advantage in interviews. Whether you are interviewing for a job for DB2 or something else, achieving this level of distinction says something about you.

As a certified professional, you will receive the certification mark associated with your role for use in advertisements and business literature, such as business cards. You will also receive a certificate of completion, a lapel pin, and a wallet-size certificate. The intangibles are the reputation that you have earned for possessing inherent competency, drive, and, of course, distinction. These demonstrated characteristics assist in salary increases and corporate advancement; they can increase your self-esteem and boost your confidence.

The Professional Certification Program from IBM acknowledges an individual as a technical professional. The certification mark is for the exclusive use of the certified individual. People, companies, and consultants who are not certified are not allowed to use the IBM Certification logo. The Certification Logo is truly a badge of distinction that is licensed for use by a select group of individuals, which you are on your way to becoming a part of.

Can employers gain from having certified employees?

It isn't just you who benefits from certification, and this is a good reason to hit your boss up to pay for any testing fees that you may incur, and of course for this book! You have our permission to photocopy this page and show your boss just why he or she should back you in your quest for certification.

Certification offers employers a way to measure the effectiveness of training. If your job is DB2 related and your employer has spent resources on training you with valuable DB2 skills, this is a way to benchmark what you know. This benefits employers because it can help to reduce course redundancy and unnecessary expenses, and that makes long-range planning for employee skill acquisition easier.

Certification also helps to manage an employee's professional development. It provides a definite target to work toward, a place to start, and a place to end. Of course, indirectly it fosters employee morale and loyalty as employees feel they are acquiring skills that keep them current in an ever-changing and competitive job market (and they are). What do you get when you have skilled, loyal, and motivated employees? An increase in productivity, of course, and that helps everyone — including the bottom line.

Finally, having IBM certification as a job requirement aids as a hiring tool. It presents a way to separate the probables from the possibles and helps to identify the best employees in the candidate pool.

If anyone else benefits from certification . . . please stand up!

Well, we know that employees and employers benefit from certification, but anyone else? Sure, both business partners and consultants can benefit from IBM certification. Why? Certification provides an independent validation of technical skills and expertise. When you work with a consultant or a business partner, and they are certified by IBM, that tells you something about them (as far as their knowledge about the certified product goes). Consultants and business partners create competitive advantages and business opportunities when certified, and certification enhances the prestige of their services.

For example, our friends Susan Lawson and Richard Levich of Levich, Lawson, and Associates (www.ylassoc.com) are highly regarded IBM Gold Consultants. They are also certified professionals. We speak with customers all over who have had experiences with these consultants, and words like *amazing*, *incredible*, and *lifesavers* are always included in those conversations. Do you think it is a coincidence that they are some of the best consultants in their field, have IBM's Gold Consultant's designation, and possess DB2 certification? Are you starting to get the picture?

Levels of Certification

The IBM Professional Certification Program offers three levels of certification, each characterized by a different level of competency. The higher the certification level, the more it says about your skills in a particular area.

Not every certification track has certification roles at all levels. For example, the database certification series, the track that you are preparing to follow, is so advanced that it encompasses only Level 2 and Level 3 certification levels.

IBM Level 1 Certifications — The Certified Specialist and Certified Developer Associate

Two certifications belong to the Level 1 certification group: the IBM Certified Specialist and the IBM Certified Developer Associate.

A Certified Specialist is one who can perform key operational services, such as basic planning, configuration, installation, support, management, and maintenance, all with limited assistance. A Certified Developer Associate has working product and environment knowledge and can code to design.

This level is not applicable to the DB2 certification track, but it does apply to other IBM hardware and software products. For information, check out www.ibm.com/certify.

IBM Level 2 Certifications — The IBM Certified Solutions Expert, Certified Systems Expert, Certified Developer, and Certified Instructor

An IBM Certified Solutions expert demonstrates breadth of basic operational services skills in more than one environment, as well as depth of advanced operational services skills, such as customizing, integrating, migrating, and tuning. This is where you fit into the picture. After writing the DB2 Family Fundamentals exam, you can choose one of the database management track certifications. The database management track has three different IBM Certified Solutions Expert exams. You can attain this level of certification in database administration, business intelligence, and DB2 application development.

You may notice that the database certifications start at Level 2, so that should be an indication of their challenge and reputation in the industry. When you attain this certification, you really stand out in a crowd.

There are three other certifications that are not part of the data management track, so we won't do more than mention them in this section. The following certifications are other IBM Certification Level 2 certifications that are available for Information Technology professionals:

- IBM Certified Developer: Demonstrates the capability to plan and design an application requirement and build a prototype.
- IBM Certified Instructor: Demonstrates training skills and has been certified in a Level 1 or Level 2 track for the topic he or she wants to teach.
- IBM Certified for e-business: Demonstrates a broad working knowledge of the IBM Application Framework for e-business, and the ability to apply its methodologies, best practices, and use of open standards to sell, advise, design, and consult on e-business solutions.

IBM Level 3 Certification — Certified Advanced Technical Expert

This is the most difficult and challenging level of certification available from IBM. The Certified Advanced Technical Expert (CATE) designation is available in three areas for the database management track.

Professionals with IBM CATE certification must demonstrate multiple skills, such as expert advice and leadership in understanding and use of IBM solutions without assistance and with references. Candidates with this level of certification usually have demonstrable skills that are characterized by job experience.

To qualify for certification, you need to have a Level 2 certification and then to pass the Level 3 test.

Your Return on Investment (ROI)

A study on certification ("Return on Investment" for IBM Certification, published by IBM in July 1999) was conducted with employers who participated in the IBM Certification program. The goal was to gain feedback and impressions of employers who adopted this program, and to monitor any improved business results.

This study looked at areas such as the following:

- Revenue (Profitability)
- Efficiency (Productivity)
- Customer Satisfaction (Credibility)

The study included approximately 200 business partner participants (cross disciplines and cross platforms). These disciplines and platforms included areas such as the following:

- Selling hardware
- Selling software
- Selling e-business solutions
- Designing and implementing solutions
- Providing technical support
- Developing applications

The study overwhelmingly found that investment in certification yielded a positive return on investment, as one would expect. After all, we know the benefits of certification. Both employees and employers benefit from certification and therefore we should assume that business would as well. Complete details of this study are available at: `www.ibm.com/education/certify/program/roistudy.phtml`.

Categorically, the study found that the majority of respondents indicated that certification has a positive effect on sales volumes, profitability, and ability to close a sale. Questions asked in this category included, "Does certification increase your ability to close a sale?" and "Does it help to increase sales volume?" Sixty-four percent of respondents answered yes to the first question, and 59 percent answered yes to the second question. Participants felt that certification positively affected the bottom line. Better people, better skills, motivated individuals, and loyalty synergize to make a better business.

The correlation between productivity and certification was also examined in the Return on Investment certification study. Again, the majority of respondents indicated that certification reduces the time it takes to perform various tasks and increases efficiency. Sixty-four percent of respondents felt that after employees had become certified, they could work with the certified software faster than non-certified employees. The study also found that 62 percent of those surveyed agreed that certified professionals take less time to resolve a problem with the certified software than those without certification.

Finally, the study found that most respondents agreed that certification has a positive effect on customer satisfaction. In today's Customer Relationship Management (CRM) -focused landscape, one of the key components to survival is addressing customer vulnerability issues and resolving complaints in a time sensitive and satisfactory fashion. Sixty-percent of respondents agreed that certification increased a company's customer satisfaction *and* the number of customer referrals.

So what do these results mean? It means that IBM's certification is a highly regarded program that identifies talented employees who can drive business value through their day-to-day work. Don't you wish that all people that you dealt with in your day-to-day lives were certified?

Chapter 2

How to Get Certified and What's Available

In This Chapter

- Getting acquainted with the IBM certification program
- Registering for the test

The IBM Professional Certification Program is recognized worldwide and offers a range of certification options for DB2 Professionals in Database Administration, Application Development, and Business Intelligence (and soon Content Management). Two distinctions for which you can strive are IBM Certified Solutions Expert and the challenging IBM Certified Advanced Technical Expert (CATE). Whatever your database certification goals are, it all begins with the DB2 Family Fundamentals exam that this book is aimed at helping you prepare for. The DB2 Family Fundamentals exam serves as a launch pad to all database certifications that DB2 offers.

Figure 2-1 illustrates the path that you take to earn your certifications.

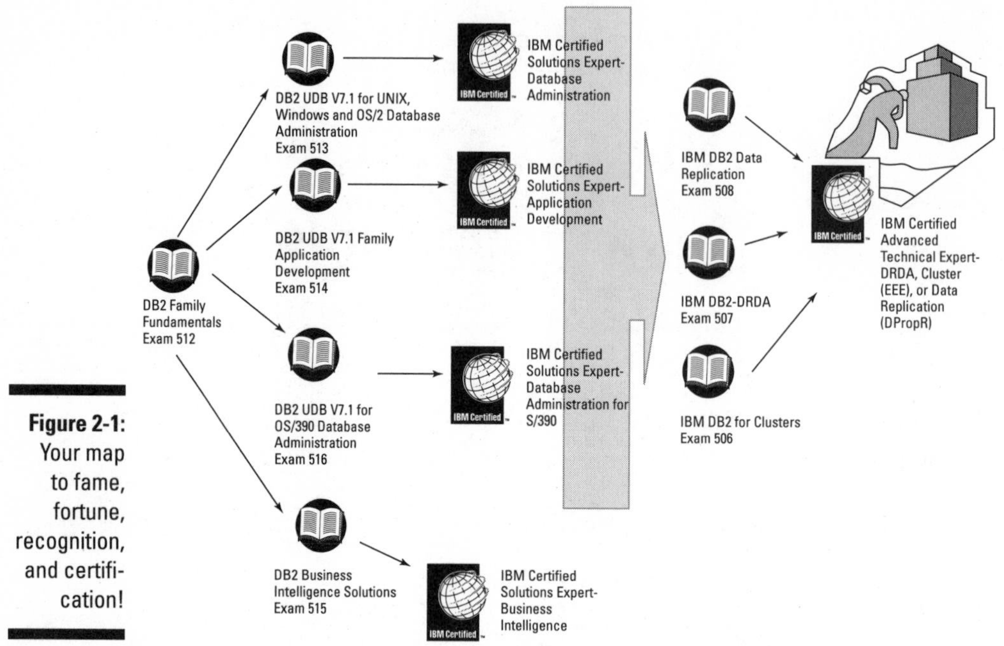

Figure 2-1: Your map to fame, fortune, recognition, and certification!

Beginning with the Fundamental Challenge: Exam 512

No matter what database certification path you want to follow, you should start here: the DB2 Family Fundamentals exam 512. This exam has been around since DB2 Version 5 and has continued to evolve right along with DB2. We recommend that, whatever certification path you want to follow, you start with DB2 Version 7.1 Family Fundamentals exam 512; preparing and writing this exam will make sure that you are up-to-date with DB2 technology. After all, if you want to become an expert, you should be an expert in what's out today, not what was out three years ago!

This exam, as its name suggests, expects you to understand the fundamentals of the DB2 family of products and features. Fundamentals include such topics as DB2 products and packaging, SQL, database objects, security, and so on. This exam is supposed to be platform independent, so you will not see questions that are for Windows NT only, nor will you get some UNIX command that you have to decipher (that would be an exam in itself).

When you successfully pass this exam, you are eligible to write the IBM Certified Solutions Expert exams and become certified. When you pass the DB2 Family Fundamentals exam, you do not get a certificate, but you will be mailed your score sheet (this takes about four weeks). You want this because it includes your results for each section of the exam. If you do need to write the test again (which you won't if you read this book), you can use this to focus your studying on weak areas.

Becoming an IBM Certified Solutions Expert

There are four types of IBM Certified Solutions Experts for DB2. To obtain any of these certifications, you need to pass two exams: the DB2 Family Fundamentals exam plus one of the following:

- Exam 513: DB2 Database Administration for UNIX, Windows, and OS/2
- Exam 516: DB2 Database Administration for OS/390
- Exam 514: DB2 Family Application Development
- Exam 515: DB2 Business Intelligence

Maybe you already know which certification you will be pursuing (or maybe your boss hasn't made up his or her mind yet). At any rate, to help you decide, a description of the content associated with each of these certifications follows. No matter what certification you want to pursue, you have to write the DB2 Family Fundamentals exam! When you successfully pass any of the IBM Certified Solutions Expert exams, you receive a certificate (it looks like a diploma) that you can frame, a certificate card for your wallet, a fancy pin, and the right to put the IBM Certification Logo (shown in Figure 2-2) on your business cards so that all the world can know you are truly a professional.

Figure 2-2: The IBM Certification Logo — a well-deserved distinction.

You can learn more about any of the DB2 Certification exams for all IBM hardware and software products at `www.ibm.com/certify`.

Exam 513 — DB2 Database Administration for UNIX, Linux, Windows, and OS/2

To pass Exam 513, you need skills that allow you to perform intermediate to advanced tasks required in the day-to-day administration of DB2 instances and databases on UNIX, OS/2, Linux, and Windows systems. If you want to write this exam, you should not be frightened by DB2 jargon, such as backup, roll forward, dbm cfg, binding, load, import, and so on.

In order to write this exam you must have passed a DB2 Family Fundamentals exam. If you passed the DB2 Version 6 Family Fundamentals exam, you don't have to take the DB2 Version 7.1 Family Fundamentals exam; you can just go ahead and write Exam 513. We recommend that you take the DB2 Version 7 Family Fundamentals exam anyway because Version 7.1 introduces many new features that you need to know about to pass the Database Administration exam.

Exam 516 — DB2 Database Administration for OS/390

Exam 516 is largely the same as exam 513, but the focus is on DB2 for OS/390. In many regards, DB2 is DB2 on all the platforms. However, DB2 on the OS/390 has some distinct features that can affect decisions an administrator makes and you are expected to know them for the test. If you are looking to be known as a mainframe nerd instead of a distributed one, this test is for you. (Perhaps you may even want to be known as both, and that is fine, too — although you will have to write both exam 513 and 516).

Exam 514 — DB2 Application Development

To pass this exam, you should know that JDBC isn't a college, and ODBC, ADO, COM+, CLI should all make sense to you as well. You will also need to know about basic and intermediate SQL, the jargon of application development, such as binding and prepping, isolation levels, basic database objects and data types (schema, naming conventions), as well as transaction concepts (commit scope, states).

If you are ready for this exam, you have built your own DB2 applications that contain static and dynamic SQL. If you don't know what those are, you are a long way from this test, but you can get there!

Like all Certified Solutions Expert designations, you need to pass the DB2 Family Fundamentals exam before being granted this dubious honor.

Exam 515 — DB2 Business Intelligence

Having this certification means that you are knowledgeable about IBM Business Intelligence solutions and the fundamental concepts of DB2. A person who writes and passes this test is also capable of performing the intermediate and advanced skills required to design, develop, and support Business Intelligence applications.

This certification is for experts who have to understand the value of Business Intelligence opportunities, identify their required business and technical requirements, plan the architecture for, and manage Business Intelligence solutions. The Business Intelligence exam is software-based and is not platform specific.

Because this exam is more of a nontechnical exam, you can prepare for it without access to DB2. After you have read this book, you will be well on your way to understanding the issues the Business Intelligence exam covers because we cover a lot of this stuff in this book. Again, you need to have passed a DB2 Family Fundamentals exam to write this test.

Because this exam is more qualitative than technical, passing this exam does not qualify you to write any of the DB2 Certified Advanced Technical Expert exams. Nonetheless, people with this designation definitely should be listened to when talking about Business Intelligence-related issues.

Becoming an IBM Certified Advanced Technical Expert (CATE)

IBM Certified Advanced Technical Experts (CATEs) are experts in their fields. The IBM CATE tests are intense and require thorough technical knowledge and understanding about the certified topic. IBM CATEs demonstrate multiple skills because they have a strong administrative and fundamental understanding about DB2 and can provide advice and leadership in the understanding and use of IBM solutions. They likely also have demonstrable skill or experience on the job.

To be eligible to write an IBM CATE exam, you must have passed one of the IBM Solutions Expert exams (except the Business Intelligence exam, which is a nontechnical exam). You achieve IBM CATE status in a specific area when you have successfully written one of the three IBM CATE exams. Of course, it makes sense that whatever IBM CATE exam you write is the topic for which your IBM CATE designation is registered.

It used to be the case that you had to write and pass two IBM CATE exams in order to achieve IBM CATE status — so if you're dreading the work, remember that your predecessors (like us) had it tougher.

Three different fields of expertise exist whose skills are recognized by IBM CATE exams: Clusters, DRDA, and Data Replication. Likewise, three types of IBM CATEs exist. To get this certification, you need to pass one of these exams:

- Exam 506: DB2 Clusters
- Exam 507: DB2 DRDA
- Exam 508: DB2 Data Replication

Exam 506 — DB2 for Clusters

The DB2 for Clusters certification is for people who want to have their valuable skills with DB2 Enterprise - Extended Edition (DB2 EEE) recognized for the world to see. This exam tests your knowledge on all aspects of DB2 EEE, including tasks such as creating, managing, and scaling a partitioned database environment. DB2 EEE is a high-powered database system that takes transaction and analytical processing beyond the regular power of DB2 and SMP hardware. Computer enthusiasts refer to this ability as "scale out." We just call it super fast. You can find out more about this product in Chapter 4, "An Introduction to DB2 Products and Packaging."

Exam 507 — DB2 DRDA

The DB2 DRDA certification is for people who provide services using DB2 and its related products to provide heterogeneous access to DB2 enterprise data in a DRDA environment. DRDA is a communication structure invented by IBM that piggybacks on either TCP/IP or APPC (SNA). DRDA has become a standard protocol for communications. DB2 Connect uses DRDA and allows DB2 clients on UNIX, Windows, Linux, and OS/2 to connect to a DB2 database that resides on an OS/390, AS/400, or VM/VSE mainframe. In fact, when OS/390, AS/400, or VM/VSE machines want to talk to DB2 on UNIX, Windows, Linux, or OS/2 platforms, they use DRDA, too.

Whereas DB2 uses it own communication structure (called DB2RA) for communication between distributed platforms, if you want to talk to a DB2 server on a mainframe, you need to use DRDA. To find out more about DRDA and

DB2 Connect, see Chapter 4. For now, just be aware that you can become certified (DRDA certified, that is) on this technology as well.

This is a good exam to take because soon DRDA will replace DB2RA, and all DB2 communications with any DB2 family member will use DRDA.

Exam 508 — DB2 Data Replication

This certification is for people who provide services using DB2 and its related products to retrieve and replicate data from a number of different sources. Replication technology is built into DB2 on the distributed platform and is a separately priced option on other DB2 platforms. A product called Data Propagator (DPropR) provides Data Replication in a DB2 environment. Data replication has many uses, from pervasive devices that run DB2 Everyplace, to data archive functions and business intelligence, and let's not forget high availability. This exam tests your knowledge on the capture and apply process, CD and UOW tables, staging tables, and other concepts.

Registering for the Test

Now that you are all excited and prepared (after reading this book) to become certified, you need to register for it. This section details the steps involved in this process.

Locate and contact a testing center

First, you need to locate an authorized testing center (your mother can't proctor the exam for you). This isn't as difficult as it may sound. IBM authorized testing centers are located around the world. You can contact either of the following two groups to set up a certification exam:

- IBM Learning Centers
- Prometric

Writing an exam through IBM

IBM Global Services provides a global certification and assessment program through its Learning Services departments. You can use IBM Learning Centers to set an appointment to write any IBM certification test — even if it isn't a DB2 test. To set up an appointment, go to the Web site at: `www.ibm.com/services/learning/global/itprod/certify.html` or call 1-800-IBM-TEACH.

IBM offers free database certification testing at the larger database conventions such as IDUG and DB2 Tech. Registering for these exams depends on the registration process of the conference.

Writing an exam through Prometric

A company called Prometric (formerly known as Sylvan Learning Centers) also handles IBM certifications. You can visit the company's Web site at `www.2test.com/index.jsp` for more information. Prometric provides testing for all types of fields (for example, medical, science) and specializes in technology-based testing for IBM certifications. To arrange to write the exam, you need to contact the test center directly.

Writing exams in different places

Because the vendor that runs exams at conferences may not be Prometric, you may want to pick your own ID for writing tests. Generally, when you write your first test with a particular vendor, that vendor will assign you an ID. These IDs are not interchangeable because each vendor has distinct identifiers. A problem will arise if you have two IDs, especially in the case of cumulative certificates. So, for example, if you write the DB2 Family Fundamentals exam with Prometric and then write the Database Administration for UNIX, Windows, Linux, and OS/2 exam at a conference with another vendor, IBM won't know that you are eligible for the IBM Solutions Expert Certification that you so rightly deserve because only one exam shows up under each ID.

It might be a good idea to tell the testing center that you want to choose your own ID rather than be assigned one of that testing center's. You can pick any unique number — your social security number or driver's license number, for example.

If you do end up with two different ID numbers, it's easy enough to fix. You can send an e-mail to `certify@us.ibm.com`. Let the certification folks at this address know what your two ID numbers are and what you would like your ID to be. Someone at the IBM Certification Center will then combine all your results under one ID and you can use that for any subsequent exams you write.

You can also e-mail `certify@us.ibm.com` with questions about the program or to get a listing of the exams you've already taken. The certification folks can also handle address changes or questions about why you haven't received your certificate.

To locate one of Prometric's testing centers, perform the following steps:

1. **Click the Find a Test Center tab.**
2. **Click the Select the testing program drop-down box and select IBM/Tivoli.**

3. **Select the country where you want to take the test and click Next.**
4. **Follow the remaining screens to locate a testing center that can house the test you are interested in.**

Prometric also offers online registration. You'll need an online login ID and password, which you can get by following prompts from the home page at `www.2test.com/index.jsp`

Register to take the test

When you find a location that suits you, call or register online and be ready with the following information:

- Name (exactly as you want it to appear on your certification certificate)
- Identification number (social security number (or Social Insurance Number, if you live in Canada), or an ID number issued by the testing vendor)
- Phone numbers (FAX, home, work)
- Mailing address (where you want your certification welcome package sent)
- Number of test that you want to take (know the test name as well, but the number is the key identifier)
- Method of payment (credit card or check)

You can sign up to schedule a test any time up to the day before the date you want to take the test. The registrar will help you select a time and location most convenient for you. If you need to reschedule or cancel a test, you must do so at least 24 hours before your scheduled test time.

Payment and confirmation procedures vary by testing vendor. In general, if you pay by credit card, you can immediately schedule your test. If you pay by check, you need to wait until it is received and payment is confirmed. If time permits, you will be sent a letter of confirmation with instructions about the test date, time, and location. If you register within 48 hours of the test date, you will not receive a letter.

How much will this cost?

Tests are $120 in the U.S., but the cost does vary worldwide. When you are registering for an exam, you'll be asked to pay in advance and your seat will be confirmed only after payment has been received. If you need to cancel, you must give the testing center advance notice, just like going to the doctor's office (but they won't stick you with a needle) or you are still charged.

IBM is very generous with certification charges at IBM events. In fact, at almost any Data Management event (IDUG Conferences around the world, DB2 Tech Conference, and other events) you will usually find DB2 Certification representatives offering free examinations!

If you're a scholar, let us hear you holler!

IBM loves to help people who want to learn IBM technology. Through the IBM Scholar's Program, students and education institutions can get a significant discount on certification exams. You need a coupon to get the discount, and getting one has to be coordinated through your education institution (usually by a professor or instructor). Ask your professor or someone in the know at your school. If your institution currently does not have a relationship, set one up with IBM, forge new ground, and make a difference — it's a pretty simple process.

In order to register, representatives from your institution have to e-mail IBM at `db2schol@ca.ibm.com`. In the e-mail, they need to include their names, how many students need coupons, each student's name, respective student numbers, and the students' e-mail addresses. Of course, they'll need to state the name of the education institution and the mailing address as well. Our friend Les Chapman runs this program and has dedicated the better part of the last two years to increasing DB2 skills in education facilities throughout the world — and he's doing a great job. For more information on IBM's Scholars Program, check out the Web site at `www.ibm.com/software/data/highered/certdb2.htm`.

To complement the DB2 Scholar's Program, your institution can arrange special software licensing so that all students have access to IBM software. Of course, individuals can always download a free version of DB2 Personal Developer's Edition (you find out more about this product and how to get it later in this book).

What you need the day of the test

On test day, you should arrive 15 minutes prior to the scheduled test time to sign in. You should bring two forms of identification: one must have a photo and the other must have a signature. Examples include a driver's license (photo) and a credit card (signature). All the questions are multiple choice; these tests are closed book and are administered on a personal computer. Tests generally contain between 55 and 75 questions and take one to two hours to complete.

You will receive a detailed report with section analyses at the conclusion of the test. You can reregister for a test if you fail. When you pass a test, you will automatically receive credit.

After a test has been taken, your demographic data (including name, address, phone number, and so on.) and test results are sent automatically from the testing vendor to IBM for processing within five working days.

Chapter 3

Taking the Test: A Trial Run

In This Chapter

- Knowing where the exam objectives are covered in this book
- Gaining a feel for what the test is like
- Knowing the rules

Sometimes, knowing what you are in for can make all the difference in the world. Olympic athletes often fly to the city hosting the games weeks before they actually begin. Marathon runners want to walk a course before running it; speed skaters want to lap the rink before qualifying; even race cars at the Indianapolis 500 lap the track before the flag has them going crazy speeds. Why? They all want to get a better feel for their surroundings before they compete.

Here's the low-down on the DB2 UDB Family Fundamentals exam. You will have 75 minutes to write the exam. There are 55 questions and you need 55 percent, or 31 questions answered correctly, to pass. The exams are experience based, meaning that the more you use DB2 UDB, the better you'll do on the exam.

If you don't pass, you can take the test one more time in the thirty-day period following your first test date. If you don't pass the second time, you have to wait thirty days before you can write the test again. This is actually a good thing because you should probably take some time to better prepare for the exam. By the way, all your personal information is confidential and your results will not be released to anyone but you.

This chapter gives you a better feel for your surroundings before you take the DB2 Family Fundamentals exam. We show you the testing screens, discuss the type of questions you are likely to see, and tell you about the rules for taking the test. This chapter is the best nontechnical information that you can find before taking this test, and you won't find this information in any other book. Yes, you read that correctly. Exclusively the authors and the folks at Hungry Minds, Inc., bring this information to you as the best preparation aid for the DB2 Family Fundamentals exam.

Knowing the Exam Objectives

Obviously, you need to know what is on the test before you take it, although we can't provide the actual questions, of course. You should know that *anything* in this book is subject to question on the test, and that includes references to Web sites that we point you to for more information, samples we ask you to run, and tutorials we ask you to take. To be more specific, a proportional number of questions from any of the following pools can appear on your exam.

I — Installation, Planning, Products, and Packaging

This part of the exam expects you to know the difference between DB2 Relational Connect and DB2 Connect, how to install DB2 products, the tools available with the different editions and versions of DB2, and some basic concepts of the technologies that DB2-related products extend to your environment. This part of the exam accounts for 11 percent of your exam, which is about six of 55 questions.

The objectives of this section of the exam are as follows:

- Ability to Install DB2 Universal Database, DB2 Clients, and Developer's Edition
- Knowledge of and ability to use the DB2 UDB GUI Tools and CLP
- Knowledge of concepts of Data Warehouse and OLAP Issues
- Knowledge of new V7.1 tools

You can find the information that you need to prepare for this section of the exam in the following chapters:

- Chapter 4, "An Introduction to DB2 Products and Packaging"
- Chapter 5, "Installing a DB2 Server"
- Chapter 6, "Installing a DB2 Client"
- Chapter 8, "The DB2 Tools"

II — Security and Instances

Section II of the exam focuses on Security and Instances. You are expected to know how to create instances, the different types of instances (the Database

Administration Server [DAS] instance and user instances), how to give authority on database objects, and other items. Security and Instance questions make up nine percent of the exam, or about five of 55 questions.

The objectives of this section of the exam are as follows:

- Ability to describe the functionality of the Administration Server Instance (DAS)
- Ability to provide users with authority on DB2 objects

You will find the information that you need to prepare for this section of the exam in the following chapters:

- Chapter 5, "Installing a DB2 Server"
- Chapter 9, "Database Building Blocks"
- Chapter 10, "Security and DB2"

III — Creating and Accessing DB2 Databases

This section of the exam tests you on your knowledge of creating databases, table spaces, tables, and indexes, as well as how to set up DB2 clients to access remote DB2 servers. Questions on this section of the exam represent about 13 percent of your exam, which means seven of the 55 questions that you will face on exam day are from this section.

The official objectives of this section are as follows:

- Ability to create a DB2 database
- Ability to catalog a remote database or local database or DRDA
- Ability to use the DB2 GUI tools to create, access, and manipulate DB2 objects
- Ability to create and access basic DB2 objects

You can find the stuff that will help you breeze through these questions in the following chapters:

- Chapter 7, "Getting Clients and Servers Talking"
- Chapter 8, "The DB2 Tools"
- Chapter 9, "Database Building Blocks"
- Chapter 10, "Security and DB2"

IV — SQL Usage

To pass the DB2 Family Fundamentals exam, you need to know this section well. SQL questions on the exam account for 38 percent of your exam. This translates to a whopping 21 questions of the 55 you will square off against. You pretty much have to understand SQL if you hope to pass this exam. Of course, it is possible to pass without knowing SQL (because you could get 31 of the remaining 34 questions that have nothing to do with SQL), but you would have to be one sharp tack, and if you were that smart, you would take the time to study the chapters that cover this section of the test. Do yourself a favor: Don't just read and skim the chapters that address this part of the test; work the samples and experiment with the sample databases.

The exam asks SQL-related questions on the following topics:

- Ability to start/end a unit of work
- Given a DDL SQL statement, knowledge to identify results
- Given a DML SQL statement, knowledge to identify results
- Given a DCL SQL statement, knowledge to identify results
- Ability to use SQL to `SELECT` data from tables
- Ability to use SQL to `SORT` or `GROUP` data
- Ability to use SQL to `UPDATE`, `DELETE`, or `INSERT` data
- Knowledge to identify the effect of a `COMMIT` or `ROLLBACK` statement
- Knowledge to identify the scope of a `COMMIT` or `ROLLBACK` statement

You are going to learn about all the acronyms in these objectives as you work your way through the book, but for now, you should know that:

- SQL (pronounced Sequel or by saying the letters S, Q, L) means Structured Query Language
- DML stands for Data Manipulation Language
- DDL stands for Data Definition Language
- DCL is an acronym for Data Control Language

The following chapters are your key to passing the 21 or so questions relating to SQL on the exam:

- Chapter 12, "SQL Boot Camp"
- Chapter 13, "The Rest of the SQL Story"

A quick peek at the SQL Getting Started Guide, part of the DB2 library, wouldn't hurt as a final primer after reading Chapters 12 and 13.

V — Database Objects

This section delves deeper into the database objects that are covered in Section III of the test. You need to know how to create, alter, drop, and configure these objects. This section of the test may force you to look at the actual syntax of the commands in the DB2 Command Reference, so we recommend that you experiment with all the objects covered in the chapters that address this section. The questions on the exam from this section account for 18 percent, or about 10 questions representing the second largest pool of questions. The exam asks SQL-related questions on the following topics:

- Ability to demonstrate usage of DB2 data types
- Given a situation, ability to create a table
- Given a situation, knowledge to identify when referential constraints are used
- Knowledge to identify methods of data validation
- Knowledge to identify characteristics of a table, view or index
- Knowledge of concepts of extenders

To prepare yourself for any questions on the exam that may be drawn from this pool of questions, make sure that you read and complete any exercises in the following chapters:

- Chapter 4, "An Introduction to DB2 Products and Packaging"
- Chapter 9, "Database Building Blocks"
- Chapter 10, "Security and DB2"

VI — Database Concurrency

Database concurrency is that last pool of questions that can be drawn from in the DB2 Family Fundamentals exam. Questions from this section make up 11 percent of the exam, which represents six questions. The following objectives define database concurrency :

- Knowledge to identify factors that influence locking
- Ability to list the objects that locks can be obtained on
- Knowledge to identify scope of different types of DB2 locks

- Knowledge to identify factors affecting amount of locks that are used
- Knowledge to identify factors affecting the type of locks obtained
- Given a situation, knowledge to identify the isolation levels that should be used

Chapter 11, "Database Concurrency," can help prepare you for this part of the exam.

Familiarizing Yourself with What the Test Looks Like

This section shows you what the testing software looks like for the DB2 Family Fundamentals exam, helping you to become accustomed to the various screens, operations, and functions of the test.

When you arrive at the testing center, the test administrator will input your information into the computer, give you a pencil, and some scrap paper, and sit you down at a desk with a computer. When you sit down to start your test, the computer in front of you should look like Figure 3-1.

The first thing you should do is make sure that you are about to start writing the right test; if not, get a hold of the person who took you to your seat and bring it to his or her attention immediately. You should be writing DB2 UDB Version 7.1 Family Fundamentals Exam, number 512.

Next, ensure that your name is spelled correctly in Figure 3-1. This may or may not be a big problem for you, depending on your name. For example, Paul runs into this problem everywhere he goes, and he always feels sorry for those people fumbling around the keyboard trying to type in all ten letters of "Zikopoulos." Jennifer on the other hand wants to be called Jennifer; don't call her Jenn or Jenny. This is something that she would check before writing this type of exam. Your name as it appears on the screen shown in Figure 3-1 may not be a big deal to you right now, but that is how your name will appear in the IBM Certification database, how all correspondence will be addressed to you, and even how your name will appear on a certificate when you achieve your coveted certification. Make sure that it is the way you want it.

Figure 3-1 also tells you how many questions are on the exam and how many you need to get right. It is good to know this, and one of the techniques called "Tally the Rally" that you can read about in Chapter 14, "Ten Things That Will Help you Pass the Exam," relies on it. Because you need to get 55 percent correct on the exam to pass, you have to answer 30.25 questions correctly. We don't quite understand that one either . . . In any case, you should be aiming to get all of them right, but 31 will do it.

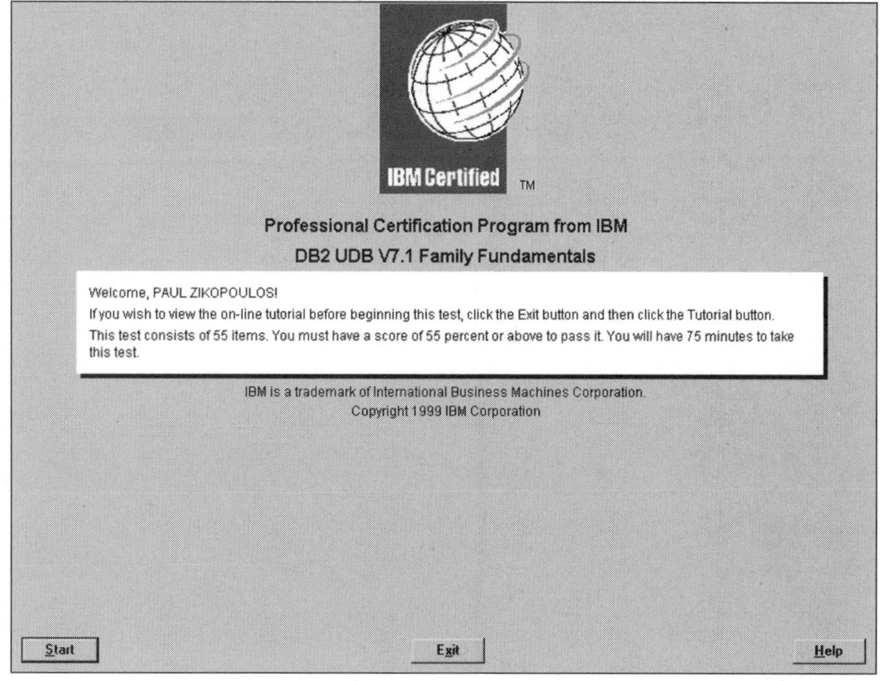

IBM Certified TM
Professional Certification Program from IBM
DB2 UDB V7.1 Family Fundamentals
Welcome, PAUL ZIKOPOULOS!
If you wish to view the on-line tutorial before beginning this test, click the Exit button and then click the Tutorial button.
This test consists of 55 items. You must have a score of 55 percent or above to pass it. You will have 75 minutes to take this test.
IBM is a trademark of International Business Machines Corporation.
Copyright 1999 IBM Corporation
Start
Exit
Help

Figure 3-1: What you see when sitting down to take the test.

Finally, this window lets you know how much time you have to write the exam, 75 minutes in case you are wondering. You need to be aware of the time restriction, but there is more than a fair amount of the allotted time to write the test. A clock is part of the testing screens, so you don't have to worry about bringing a watch or looking for a clock in the room.

When you are ready to start the test, click Start. This is when time will start to count down, you're just minutes away from having the distinction of passing this test! If for some reason you are overcome with fear (and you shouldn't be if you read this book), click Exit. It won't help you with a question that you can't answer, but you can click Help and get information on the testing software (like how to use it).

If you want to review how to use the testing software with the online help, make sure that you do this *before* clicking Start. The timer does not start until you click Start.

After you click Start, the exam begins. You will see a screen similar to Figure 3-2.

The first thing you may notice is the progress indicator in the top-left corner of Figure 3-2. This question counter tells you what question you are on and how many more you have to go. In our example, our candidate is on question 33 and therefore has 22 more questions to answer to make 55.

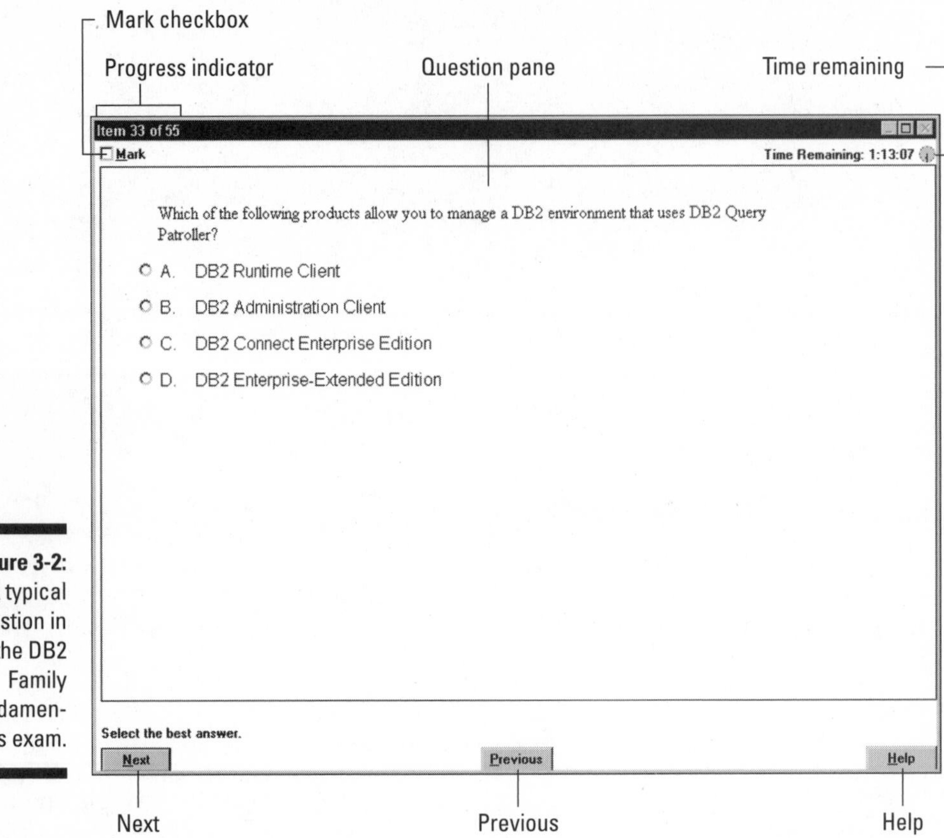

Figure 3-2: A typical question in the DB2 Family Fundamentals exam.

Below the progress indicator is the Mark check box. If you cannot answer a question and it is starting to stress you out, or perhaps you have to guess the answer, or have answered the question but are not 100 percent sure you have selected the right answer, this check box can be a real helper. If you select this check box, the question you marked will be flagged for review when you finish the test (more on that in a bit) and you can go back to it and deal with it then.

Your exam may have a Comment button. This button appears when the testing organization enables the testing software to receive comments. If you have something to note on a question, make a comment on it. This option doesn't let you discuss the issue during the test; however, for situations in which a test question's answer set could be wrong or vague, you can use this comment feedback form to bring any issues to the attention of the test administrators. This feedback process adds validity and robustness to the test and the certification program.

The right side of the screen shown in Figure 3-2 shows how much time remains for you to finish the test. This counter may make you feel as though you need to disarm it before it goes off, but it is really your friend. Don't sweat here: there is no choice of black or red wires to cut and you will likely be done with the test before time runs out.

You are not penalized for guessing on this test. *Never* leave a test question unanswered. You can mark a question to review it later, but even if you have to guess all the remaining questions because time is running out, do so.

If you need more details on the time, you can click the clock icon beside the Time Remaining field and you will get a pop-up information window like that shown in Figure 3-3.

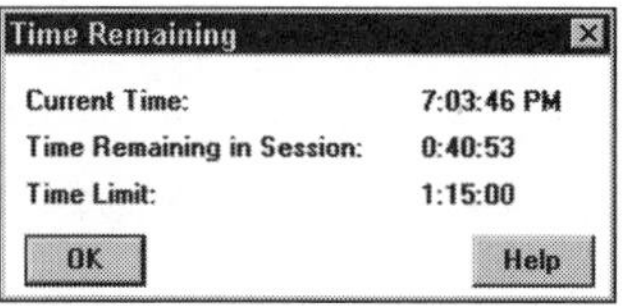

Figure 3-3: More time-based information than you could ever want to know.

The most important part of Figure 3-2 is the question pane. Here is where you see the question that you need to answer (correctly, we hope) and a list of possible answers (and any other information you need to know).

When you have answered the test question, click Next (or press Enter) and you'll be shown the next question. The Previous button can be used to move back one question and the Help button to launch the online help that you can see in the Welcome window.

Some questions require more than one answer.

Of course, if you are on Question 1 of 55, a Previous button will not show on the screen because there is no question that you previously answered. This means that the questions do not cycle. By *cycle,* we mean that when you are finished with question 55, you don't proceed to question 1 again. When you click the Previous button after answering question 55, you are finished with the test; however, you do have an option at this point to go back to any question (more on that in a bit).

When you have finished the last question, the Item Review window opens, as shown in Figure 3-4.

Item Review

55 Items — Time Remaining: 1:10:03

	1. D	23. A	45. C
	2. A	24. B	46. C
	3. C	25. B	47. D
	4. D	26. A	48. C
	5. D	27. C	49. B
	6. A	28. D	50. AD
	7. B	29. B	51. C
M	8. I	30. C	52. C
	9. I	31. B	53. B
	10. D	32. B	54. C
	11. B	33. E	55. C
	12. E	34. A	
	13. D	35. D	
	14. C	36. D	
M	15. I	37. B	
	16. D	38. C	
	17. A	39. C	
	18. B	40. D	
	19. D	41. D	
M	20. A	42. A	
	21. E	43. A	
	22. D	44. D	

M = Marked Items   I = Incomplete Items   Review Item [I]

Review Marked   Review Incomplete   End   Help

Figure 3-4: You're just about done — or are you? Here's a chance to review your answers.

In Figure 3-4, the test answers that have an *M* beside them are ones that Paul marked for review at the end of the test. You can see that Paul marked questions 8, 15, and 20. Questions 8 and 15 had some complex SQL in them and it started to make him stress, so he marked them to review after he finished answering all the other questions. He was pretty sure that he knew the answer to question 20, but he decided to look at it one last time if any time remained.

Any questions that do not have an answer are automatically marked as incomplete with an *I* in this screen, as you can see in Figure 3-4. Question 9 had no answer, but Paul didn't mark it for review. He missed that question and, without the "Incomplete" mark, this would have been one less question that he could have gotten right. Thankfully, the testing software recognizes that although we may be DB2 experts, we are only human, so it watches out for us and flags the ones we've missed.

You can use the Review Marked and Review Incomplete buttons to review any questions that you have marked for review or did not provide an answer for.

You can review any question at any time in the Item Review window by entering the question that you want to review in the Review Item field and clicking Review Item. When you click Review Item, the questions that you marked for Review will be shown. However, if you review a question using this method, you have to go through all the questions from that point on. For example, if you wanted to review question 32, you would have to cycle through questions 32 through 55 before you would be returned to the Item Review window. This isn't the most efficient way to review questions.

When you are in the Item Review window, the clock is still ticking by. If you are just about to run out of time, make sure that you at least answer all the questions that have been marked incomplete. To review all the incomplete questions, click Review Incomplete. Clicking this button returns you to the first incomplete question in Figure 3-4. Answer the question and click Next (or Enter). When you click the Review Incomplete button, you are shown only the questions that are marked as incomplete. So in the case of Figure 3-4, you would see only Questions 8, 9, and 15 and then would be returned to the Item Review window.

When you have answered all the incomplete questions, the Item Review window will look similar to that of Figure 3-5.

When no incomplete questions remain on the exam, the Review Incomplete button is available in the Item Review window.

Now that all of the questions have answers, you can review whatever test questions you have marked for review. You can cycle through all the questions that you marked for review by clicking the Review Marked button. Just as when you reviewed the questions that were incomplete, you are shown only the questions that you marked for review. When you are finished reviewing a question, uncheck the Mark check box and click Next.

Of course, if you have marked an incomplete question for review, you might very well answer it and uncheck the Mark check box at the same time.

Item Review

55 Items — Time Remaining: 1:03:36

	1. D	23. A	45. C
	2. A	24. B	46. C
	3. C	25. B	47. D
	4. D	26. A	48. C
	5. D	27. C	49. B
	6. A	28. D	50. AD
	7. B	29. B	51. C
M	8. A	30. C	52. C
	9. B	31. B	53. B
	10. D	32. B	54. C
	11. B	33. E	55. C
	12. E	34. A	
	13. D	35. D	
	14. C	36. D	
M	15. C	37. B	
	16. D	38. C	
	17. A	39. C	
	18. B	40. D	
	19. D	41. D	
M	20. A	42. A	
	21. E	43. A	
	22. D	44. D	

M = Marked Items — Review Item

Review Marked — End — Help

Figure 3-5: No more incomplete questions, but a few left to review.

Don't click End until you're sure

If you click the End button with answers remaining that are marked for review or as incomplete, the testing software will pop up a window that asks whether this is really what you want to do. If you get a window like this:

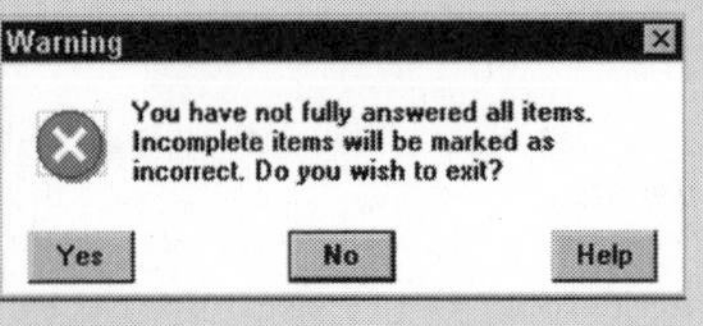

click NO because it means that questions remain for you to address. Never end a test when you see this warning message.

When all the Marked check boxes have been cleared, the Item Review window will look similar to that shown in Figure 3-6.

You can finish the exam by clicking End. When you click End, you have one last chance to review your questions. A pop-up box will confirm that you want to finish the exam. Just click OK. If you have time and you want to review some other questions, click Cancel.

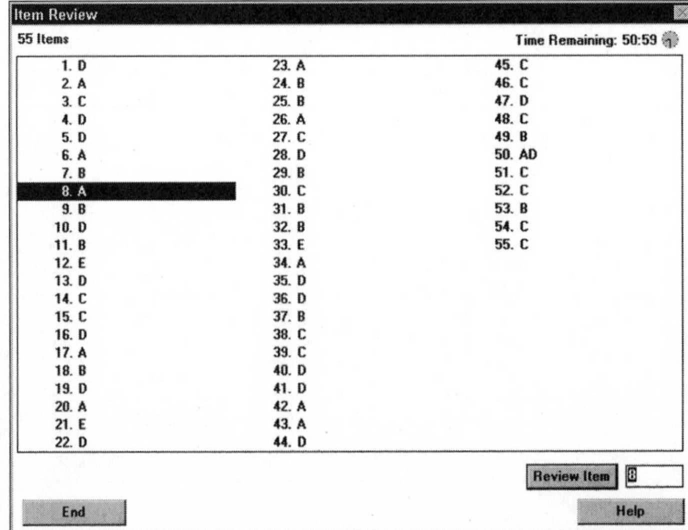

Figure 3-6: No more items to review; you are just a click away from passing the exam.

After you have confirmed that indeed you want to finish the test, the testing software computes your score and, if you passed, a window similar to Figure 3-7 will appear:

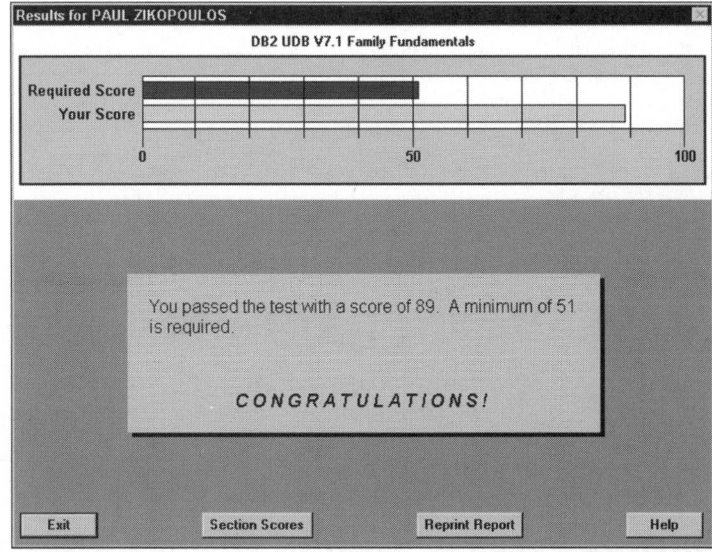

Figure 3-7: (Drum roll, please . . .) And your score is. . . .

A screen like Figure 3-7 will show you the needed score and your score in a horizontal percent bar chart. You can see in Figure 3-7 that Paul scored 89 percent. Whether you passed the exam or not, don't click Exit yet. We recommend that you click the Sections Score button to see how you fared in each of the objectives outlined in the "Knowing the Exam Objectives" section in this chapter.

When you click the Section Scores button, a window similar to Figure 3-8 opens.

Section Scores for PAUL ZIKOPOULOS

DB2 UDB V7.1 Family Fundamentals

Section Title	0 100	Score
Section 1 Installation and Planning		83
Section 2 Security/Instances		80
Section 3 Creating and Accessing		100
Section 4 SQL Usage		95
Section 5 Database Objects		70
Section 6 Database Concurrency		100

OK Help

Figure 3-8: Use the Section Scores feature to see how you fared in each section of the exam.

As you can see in Figure 3-8, you can get a better feel for how you performed on the test. If you did not pass the exam, this is your opportunity to know what section you may need to focus on for the next time you write the exam. If you passed, you may want to make note of the sections where you could use a little review anyway.

You should expect to miss some of the questions; some questions are indeed tricky and the wording can be confusing. As you can see in Figure 3-8, Paul may need to review some of the Database Objects information.

When you are finished reviewing your section scores, click OK and then Exit to leave the exam.

Knowing the Kinds of Questions to Expect

Though the questions span six separate categories, you will see two basic types: multiple-choice "single answer" and multiple-choice "pick more than one answer."

Multiple-choice, single-answer questions

For the basic multiple-choice question, you will be given a list of four or five choices and you need to choose *one* of the best answers available. Some of the answers may be completely wrong and some may have a hint of a trick to them.

There are variations of this type of question that you should be aware of. Sometimes you will just be asked to choose the best answer; this is the most basic type of multiple-choice question. The best answer means one answer. Figure 3-2 in the previous section gives a good example of this question (the answer is B, by the way).

One word of caution here: A question isn't always what it appears to be. Read questions carefully, even twice to be sure.

Another variation of the multiple-choice single-answer type of question is to be asked to view an exhibit. You are likely to encounter this situation with SQL questions. You will be given an SQL statement and a table. (This type of question will typically ask you for the results of the SQL query.) The question's exhibit will be displayed in a separate pop-up box that you can see by clicking Exhibit. The exhibit may even be large enough that it will have a vertical and horizontal scroll bar. When a lot of information appears on a testing window, you may need to click the More button to see the rest of it. Questions that extend beyond a single page on the screen can get tricky because you have to toggle or scroll between the information and the answer set.

INSTANT ANSWER

The last time the authors of this book wrote the DB2 Family Fundamentals exam, we didn't come across any questions that had exhibits. Your experience may be different, so just make sure that you know what an exhibit on the exam is.

Yet another variation of a multiple-choice single-answer question is to have negative questions. Figure 3-9 shows an example of a question with a negative slant.

In this case, you need to find the one that doesn't belong. Sometimes the question will highlight the negative word, such as *not* in italics, but it's not always made obvious. Again, we urge you to read the question carefully. (If you answered (A) in Figure 3-9, you're right!)

INSTANT ANSWER

Whenever you see radio buttons beside an answer set, this is your clue that you need to select one and only one answer. The testing software will let you select only one answer when you have to answer a question with a radio button answer set. Nevertheless, you should still read each question carefully to ensure that you haven't missed any tricky wording in it.

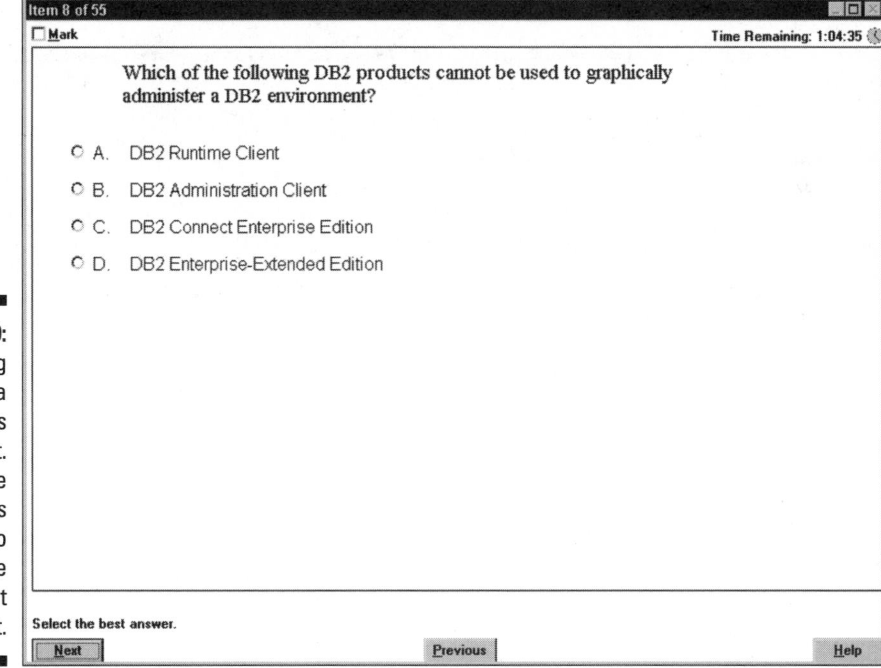
Item 8 of 55
Mark
Time Remaining: 1:04:35
Which of the following DB2 products cannot be used to graphically administer a DB2 environment?
A. DB2 Runtime Client
B. DB2 Administration Client
C. DB2 Connect Enterprise Edition
D. DB2 Enterprise-Extended Edition
Select the best answer.
Next
Previous
Help

Figure 3-9: The wording of a question is important. Some questions ask you to find the answer that isn't correct.

Multiple-choice, multiple-answer questions

Some questions on the exam require you to select more than one answer. A question will alert you to this by saying something like "Pick the best answers" or "What two products allow you to. . . ." Figure 3-10 shows an example of a multiple-choice, multiple-answer type of question.

The bottom left of Figure 3-10 contains a statement that says *Select all correct answers*. Sometimes a test question like this will tell you how many you have to choose. For example, it may say something like, "Which of the two following products can be used to. . . ." Here, you need to select two answers, obviously. Other times, as in Figure 3-10, you are not told how many you need to select; these are a little trickier.

The moment you see check boxes rather than radio buttons beside an answer set, you should be thinking in terms of more than one possible answer. The testing software will allow you to select more than one answer when check boxes appear on-screen.

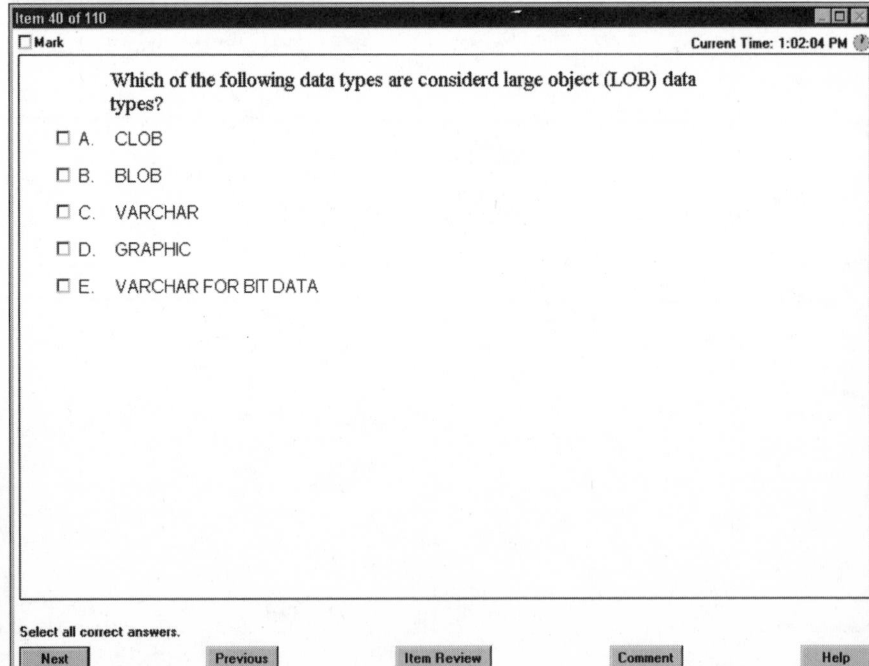

Figure 3-10: Sometimes you need to pick more than one correct answer.

We have written a lot of tests and have never seen a question with a check box answer set for which only one answer was correct. Of course, no one gets a chance to see what questions they got right or wrong after writing the exam, but you can bet your money that if there is a check box by the answer set, you have to find two or more of the right answers — not just one as with a radio button. Typically, when you see check boxes, you are required to find two answers.

Knowing the Rules

You should know the rules of the test before taking it so that you not only know what to expect but also what you can and cannot do. For the most part, this stuff should all be common sense to you, but we review them just in case.

Of course you know a lot of this stuff by now, but for the record:

- The test is composed of 55 questions and you need to get 55 percent correct to pass.

  The test is timed and you have 75 minutes to complete it. The moment you click the Start button, time begins. When you finish answering all the test questions, you are given the opportunity to review your answers. This phase is still considered part of the test because you can go back and answer questions that you either overlooked or marked for review. This means that you are still on the clock. When the clock runs out, your test scores are automatically calculated. You are not penalized for any questions that you get wrong, so guessing as a last resort — instead of leaving anything blank — is a good idea.
- When you guess, eliminate the answers that are obviously wrong; then, from the remaining answers, choose the one that seems to have the best chance of being right. If it's a single-answer question and one answer looks obviously wrong while the rest seem to sound right, reread the question — is it worded in the negative?
- When you sit in front of the computer, you are allowed to have only the items given to you by the exam proctor. These items will be a pencil and scrap paper.
- You are not allowed to talk to anyone during the exam. If you have a question, raise your hand and the exam proctor will come and help you. *Do not* leave your seat. (This is our polite way of telling you to visit the restroom before you sit down to start the exam.)
- When you leave the exam, you must return the scrap paper and any notes that you made on the exam. You are not allowed to leave the examination room with any materials.

Part II

Introducing DB2

"Hold your horses! It takes time to build a database for someone with as many parts as you have."

In this part . . .

This part's lot in life is to show you how to install a DB2 server and client and get the two talking (it's not too hard, though DB2 clients can be kind of shy when they first meet). The chapters in this part also get you intimate with the DB2 graphical tools (relax, you don't have to prepare for this date) that are used to manage your DB2 server. Finally, we reserve a chapter to showcase the DB2 Data Warehousing and Online Analytical Processing (OLAP) capabilities, which you need to know for the test.

Chapter 4

An Introduction to DB2 Products and Packaging

Exam Objectives

- Understand the DB2 products and packaging
- Knowledge of concepts of data warehouse and OLAP issues
- Knowledge of concepts of extenders

Many DB2 and DB2-related products are used to run companies these days. With the different editions, add-ons, associated, and even unrelated products that all coexist in an enterprise, you can sometimes get lost in a maze of products and their FFBs (functions, features, benefits). You can use this chapter as your map through the different DB2 products that you're likely to hear about at meetings around the world.

Quick Assessment

Becoming familiar with DB2 Products

1 If you wanted to run DB2 on your cellular phone, you would use _________.

2 You can use the ______________ with a DB2 database to store and create XML documents from the database.

3 ___________ can be used to control and manage files that are not stored in DB2 but are controlled by it.

4 ________________ allows you to partition pieces of a table across different physical machines.

Understanding DB2 in general

5 RAS stands for ____________, ____________, and _________.

6 DB2 for the mainframe refers to _____, and DB2 for host systems generally refers to ________ and __________.

7 Distributed versions of DB2 run on the following operating systems: ________, ___________, ___________, and _________.

8 You can use _____ to query data in nontraditional data, such as video clips, graphics, or text objects stored in your database.

Answers

1. *DB2 Everyplace (DB2e)*. See "The DB2 Products and Packaging."
2. *DB2 XML Extender*. See "The DB2 extenders."
3. *DB2 Data Links File Manager*. See "DB2 Data Links File Manager."
4. *DB2 Enterprise — Extended Edition*. See "DB2 Editions."
5. *Reliability, Availability, and Serviceability*. See "DB2 for OS/390."
6. *DB2 for AS/400, DB2 for OS/390, DB2 for VM/VSE*. See "The DB2 Products and Packaging."
7. *OS/2, Windows 32-bit platforms (Windows 9x, Me, NT, and 2000), Linux, UNIX (AIX, HP-UX, Solaris, Numa-Q)*. See "DB2 Editions."
8. *SQL. See "DB2 in General."*

DB2 in General

For the DB2 Family Fundamentals exam, you're expected to understand the different products and add-on features that belong to the DB2 product family.

For customers transforming their businesses to e-businesses, DB2 helps them leverage their information by delivering the performance, scalability, reliability, and availability needed for the most demanding e-commerce, CRM, BI, and ERP applications.

DB2 provides enhanced functions for all lines of business, but it's specifically tailored to the following:

- **E-commerce:** DB2 is the first and only database to combine the in-memory speed required for Internet search, complex text matching, and the scalability and availability of a relational database. E-commerce is not only about buying books over the Web; e-commerce encompasses the entire range of those practices that define business: transactions, analytics, processes, management, and so on.
- **Customer Relationship Management (CRM):** DB2 meets the wide-ranging needs of CRM applications in a single infrastructure that gives you a choice of mobile client with zero end-user administration, scalable replication, leading Internet standards exploitation, and integrated analytical features. IBM works closely with Siebel, a recognized industry leader, in this space.

  CRM is about managing customers, the entire spectrum really (from acquisition, to vulnerability assessment, to retention). Have you ever walked into a store that understood you? You know, they *knew* your needs. They knew your history with respect to their company providing you outstanding service and the type of service that makes you cry. Didn't it make you feel great when you showed up at that hotel and they upgraded you to a higher level of service because that last stay didn't go so well? That's CRM!
- **Business Intelligence:** DB2 offers a complete metadata-driven business intelligence (BI) architecture with integrated best-of-class technologies to rapidly deploy BI solutions that make a difference to the bottom line.

  BI isn't about having a smart boss. It's about using information to make better, more directed, and faster decisions that ultimately lead to higher profits. What do you think the average male who is 31 buys with a box of diapers when he visits the local grocery store on his way home from work on Thursday night? Look in Chapter 6, "Installing a DB2 Server" for the answer — it might surprise you.
- **Enterprise Resource Planning (ERP) and Supply Chain Management (SCM):** DB2 gives you leading performance and scalability from workstations through to mainframe platforms. IBM works with vendors such as i2, Ariba, PeopleSoft, and SAP in these areas.

Requirements for databases have gone through different phases over the years. At one time, databases had to be on what was known as ACID: *A*tomicity; *C*onsistency; *I*solation, and *D*urability.

- **Atomicity:** The concept of atomicity refers to an all-or-nothing type of transaction management. A transaction (or multiple transactions) is contained in a unit of work. If a transaction gets interrupted while it is processing, then it gets rolled back instead of being completed. If you've ever been to a bank machine, withdrawn money from an ATM, and then failed to receive the money, you've experienced one way that the atomicity of databases is beneficial. Because the transaction didn't complete successfully, all the transactions contained within the unit of work (taking the money out of your account before trying to give it to you) were rolled back. As a result of the rollback, your bank account wasn't debited the amount you tried to withdraw.
- **Consistency:** Consistency refers to the state of a database. Being consistent means, "Is there anything going on that hasn't completed?" For example, assume that you had a database crash and needed to recover your database (which you can do in DB2, up to any point before the system went down). You do this by recovering the database and rolling forward the logs. During that recovery time, the database is in a Roll-Forward pending state in which no access is allowed because it is not in a consistent state.
- **Isolation:** Isolation refers to the fact that transactions and such are handled on their own, independent of system resources and other things that are going on inside and outside the database. DB2 has isolation. For example, in a Windows environment, DB2 uses threads and is referred to as thread-safe.
- **Durable:** A durable transaction is one that persists, meaning, for example, that if you withdraw $40 from your bank account, your bank balance goes down by $40 and stays at this new amount until the next transaction.

Times have changed. You know how customer service was a bonus in the past and now it's a given? Well, if you're a database and you don't meet the ACID test, companies won't depend on you. Nowadays, databases need to be:

- **Available — always:** In today's environment, the only thing you can predict is that something unpredictable will happen. You never know what's coming next; you have to be ready for anything and everything! Business chaos? Use it, define it, thrive on it, and own it. If you can accomplish this, your business will never lose. DB2 is built for reliability and availability, so it's up when you are open for business and, on the Internet, that means all the time.
- **Scalable — without limits:** DB2 gives you the foundation for your business to manage the explosive growth of the Internet. DB2 supports millions of users and terabytes of data in leading e-business applications

worldwide. No one delivers database power to companies with terabytes of information like IBM.

- **Accessible — across the enterprise:** DB2 empowers your mobile workers by putting enterprise information in the palms of their hands. From occasionally connected users, to thin clients, to data access over the Web, you can access data that's managed by DB2.
- **Leveragable:** DB2 helps you extract, consolidate, integrate, summarize, analyze, and share information across your enterprise to identify new insights and opportunities.
- **Enabled for the Web:** Built for the Web, DB2 supports all the key Internet standards — WebSphere, XML, and built-in Java support — that make it easy for you to deploy e-business applications.
- **Easy to develop applications for:** DB2 delivers the tools, including Java and Web tools, that you need to rapidly deploy applications on the Internet or anywhere — everything based on an open application framework that's totally non-proprietary. This means portability and leveragability of skills from external sources.

The DB2 Products and Packaging

Now it's time to meet the DB2 products and add-ons that you need to be familiar with for the exam.

DB2 Editions

Different editions of DB2 are available that are tailored for different needs of customers. An amazing benefit of DB2 code across the *distributed* versions of DB2 (distributed in the DB2 sense of the word means the Linux, OS/2, Windows, and UNIX operating systems) is that they all share 90 percent of the code base. The 10 percent that remains is unique to each distributed platform and is used to leverage the benefits of the native operating system. For example, the copy of DB2 on the CD-ROM in the back of this book uses threads to boost performance in the Windows environment. Also, specific DB2 code enables you to take advantage of the Windows security implementation, the operating system services, and the Windows performance monitor.

DB2 on the distributed platforms runs on different types of servers. IBM makes a server for each platform that DB2 runs on. For example, you might be running DB2 for Windows on a NetFinity server. If you want to run DB2 for AIX, you need a UNIX server. However, just when everyone figured out all the hardware that IBM offers to complement software products, IBM went ahead and changed their names. Agh! NetFinity servers used for Intel-based operating systems, such as Linux and Windows, are now called xSeries servers (Numa-Q falls into this series as well). The UNIX servers are now called pSeries servers.

DB2 on the System/390, AS/400, and VM/VSE systems, also referred to as DB2 on the mainframe, have different code bases from the distributed DB2 code base. The common code base is really beneficial for distributed DB2 users because it means that applications and skills that are developed for your edition and platform of DB2 easily can be used across disparate DB2 systems. Having editions of DB2 on the distributed platforms is really about packaging, and you'll find out more about the functions, features, and benefits that are associated with each edition in this section. Furthermore, many of the DB2 skills that you acquire on the distributed version of DB2 can be leveraged on the mainframe platforms. Figure 4-1 shows the spectrum of DB2 servers across the DB2 product family. You can also run Linux on a System/390, and this environment supports the same DB2 and DB2 Connect products that run on Linux on Intel processors.

Picky people distinguish a host system as System/390 and a mainframe as AS/400. Because you have better things to do, use the terms interchangeably.

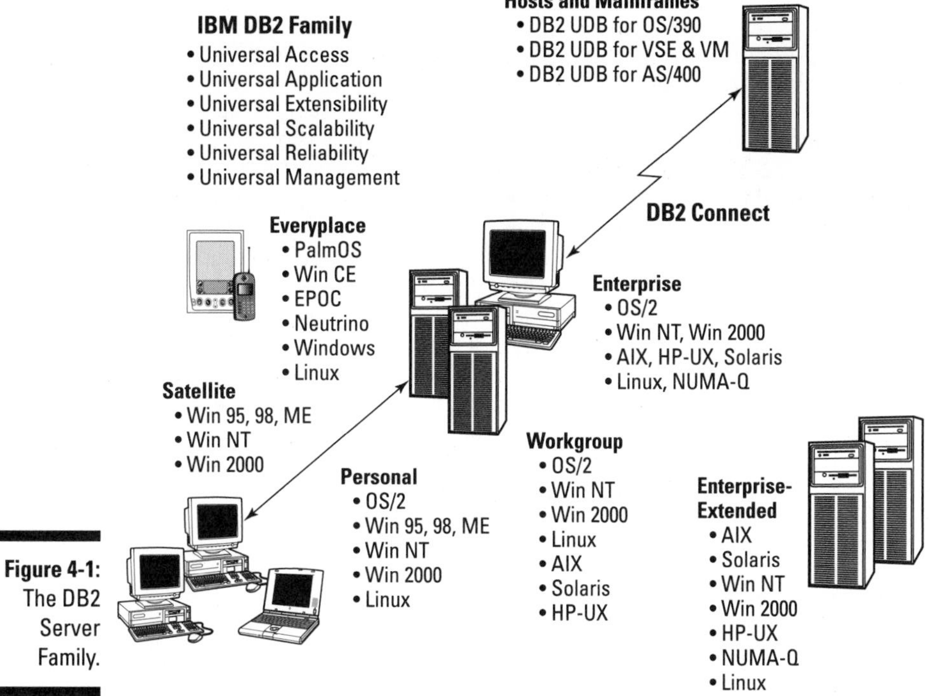

Figure 4-1: The DB2 Server Family.

One of DB2's greatest design features is its incredible potential for scalability on any platform, allowing your database and number of users to grow at the same rate as your throughput — no matter the rate. As your data storage requirements grow and more users are added to the system, you can continue to manage the database with the same tools and commands, but still increase your throughput and speed up the queries.

Whether you're running DB2 on mobile devices (for example, a Palm Pilot), a small laptop, a desktop PC, on a large server or a cluster of servers, DB2 is able to handle growth in data and take advantage of extra processing power. If you're using a PC with multiple processors, your transactions can use all the processors in the computer to perform the work at the same time! You can also move your data to a cluster of machines that are networked together, again letting DB2 divide your transactions and run them simultaneously to make it faster.

On the distributed side, DB2 server builds on each edition with respect to functionality and features. In this section, we start from the most basic DB2 servers on the distributed side and build functions and features up the chain to the most powerful editions of DB2 that you can buy. You can find more information about any of these DB2 editions at `www.ibm.com/software/data/db2/`.

DB2 Personal Edition

DB2 Personal Edition (DB2 PE) is a single-user version of the full DB2 product. It contains an object-relational database engine, BI support through the OLAP Starter Kit and Data Warehouse Center (more on those later in this chapter), multimedia support through the TAIV DB2 Extenders (that's coming later, too), replication support, federated support to access other databases in a single transaction, and a development environment with the DB2 Application Development Client (again, more on this later).

The main distinction between DB2 PE and the other editions of DB2 is that a DB2 Personal Edition server cannot accept requests for data from DB2 clients. DB2 client software is code that's installed on a workstation so that it can talk to a DB2 server over a network. Usually, you will find a copy of DB2 PE on someone's desk whose job it is to program applications. Make no mistake about it: The database engine with DB2 PE is the same engine that you find in any distributed edition of DB2.

You can find copies for DB2 PE on Windows, OS/2, and Linux-based workstations. Licensing for DB2 PE is controlled by the number of installations that exist in your enterprise. In other words, if you have five copies of DB2 PE installed, you have to pay for five licenses. No concurrent user model pricing exists because this product doesn't support DB2 clients; however, you should be aware that DB2 PE can act as a DB2 client and talk to other DB2 servers or DB2 Connect gateways.

DB2 Workgroup Edition

DB2 Workgroup Edition (DB2 WE) is where a DB2 server starts to become a true server. DB2 WE is (see Figure 4–2) designed for smaller companies that need data management capabilities but aren't planning to do the type of transactions or calculations that only the most powerful computers can handle. DB2 WE contains all the features of DB2 PE, as well as the following:

- The ability for remote clients to access data and perform administration on a DB2 WE server
- Web access through Net.Data
- IBM WebSphere Application Server

DB2 WE is licensed by counting the number of users (concurrent or named) and the number of processors (limited to 4-way Windows or OS/2 based SMP boxes and 2-way UNIX-based SMP boxes) that are used on the DB2 WE server workstation. Processor licensing has become a standard for pricing software as the advent of the Internet has made it nearly impossible to count the number of users that are connecting to a system. This is the version of DB2 that is provided on the CD-ROM with this book.

A packaging option of DB2 WE called DB2 WE Unlimited Edition allows you to run up to 8-way SMP boxes on Windows or OS/2 machines and 4-way SMP boxes in UNIX-based machines. You don't have to count the number of users for this edition of Workgroup. This edition of DB2 has the same functions and features of DB2 WE.

DB2 WE Unlimited Edition is available for Windows, OS/2, Linux, and UNIX.

DB2 Enterprise Edition

When you get into this edition of a DB2 server, you start to play with the big boys. DB2 Enterprise Edition (DB2 EE) is the most popular edition of DB2 and is used by thousands of companies to run their mission-critical transaction systems. DB2 EE is licensed only by the number of processors on your server workstation, with no licensing limits on the number of concurrent connections in your environment. DB2 EE also comes with a single-user license of DB2 Connect (you can purchase more user licenses if you want). DB2 Connect is used to access DRDA-compliant DB2 databases, such as DB2 on S/390 (check out the section called "DB2 Connect," later in this chapter, for more information). This edition of DB2 is available for Windows, OS/2, Linux, Linux/390, and UNIX.

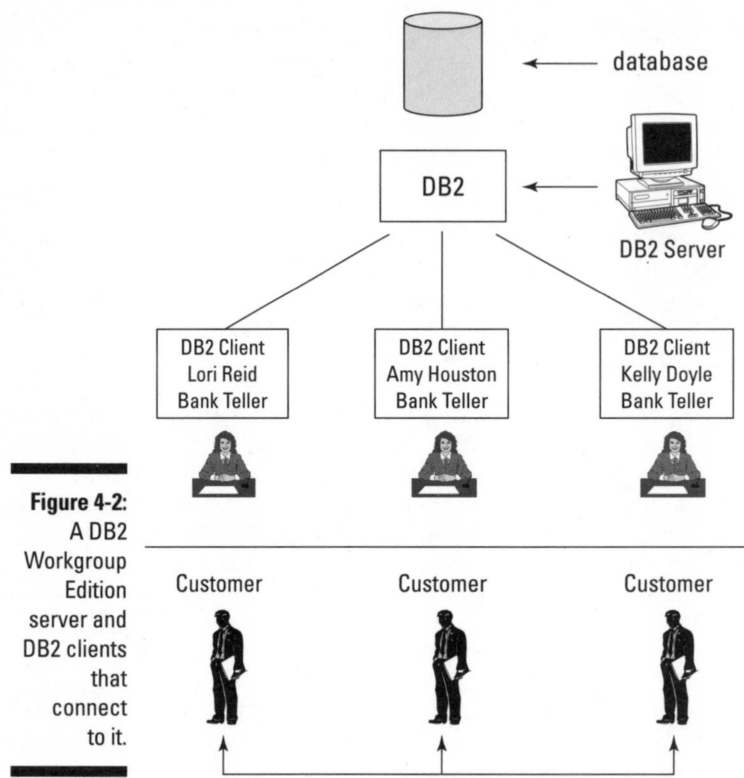

Figure 4-2: A DB2 Workgroup Edition server and DB2 clients that connect to it.

DB2 Enterprise — Extended Edition

Don't let the clunky name fool you. DB2 Enterprise — Extended Edition (DB2 EEE) is designed for the largest databases; it is the Cadillac of distributed DB2. DB2 EEE is ideal for scaling very large databases for data warehousing, data mining, and large-scale OLTP applications. DB2 EEE contains all the functionality of the Enterprise Edition, plus support for clusters of servers (also referred to as database partitions). Figure 4-3 illustrates partitioning data.

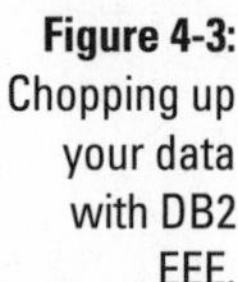

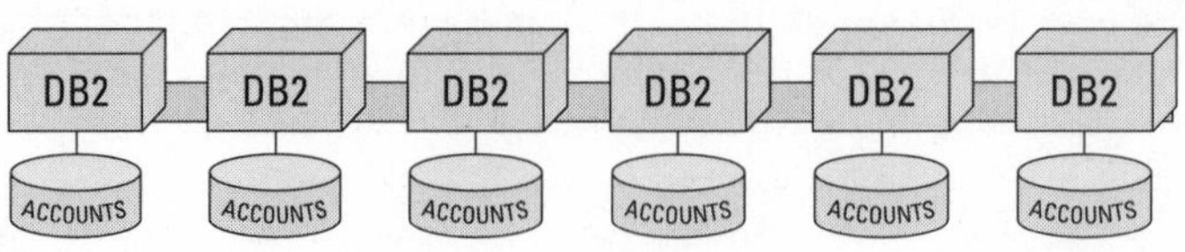

Figure 4-3: Chopping up your data with DB2 EEE.

Partitioning data allows you to take a database and its tables and chop them up along independent DB2 servers. To the end user and application developer, the database still looks like one database and one table; however, in this configuration, you have multiple copies of DB2 working on the data. For example, if you had 100,000 rows to scan in a database table and had fives copies of DB2 working on that scan, you would expect the scan to be done five times faster than with one copy of DB2. This edition of DB2 is available for Windows, Linux, and UNIX.

Now you can take advantage of SMP machines, such as in DB2 WE and DB2 EE (called intrapartition parallelism), and add the power to partition data (interpartition parallelism). As a result, you get something like Figure 4-4.

DB2 clients

DB2 clients allow you to access DB2 databases through a runtime environment (either directly or through a DB2 Connect gateway). You also can develop applications and manage DB2 systems. Three types of DB2 clients exist: DB2 Administration clients, DB2 Application Development clients, and DB2 Runtime clients.

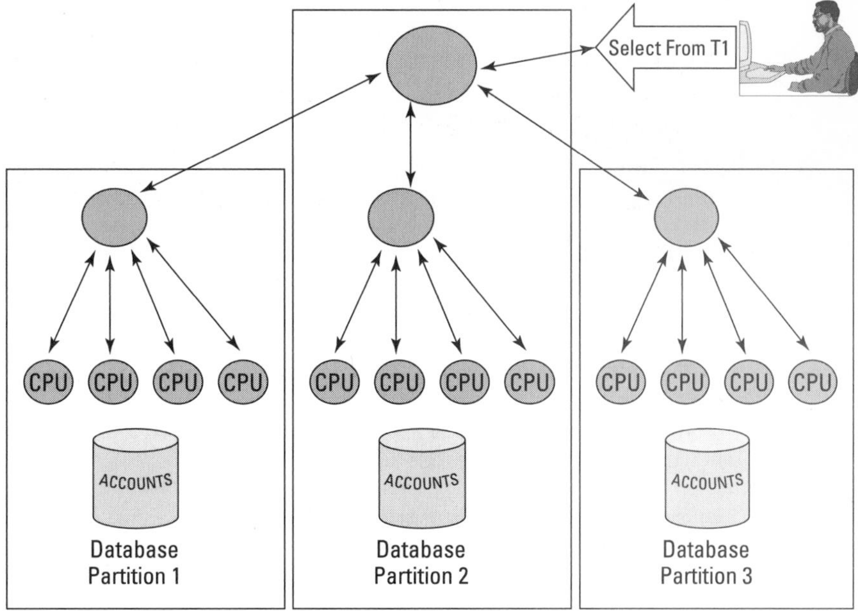

Figure 4-4: A DB2 EEE system.

All applications must access a database through a DB2 client. A Java applet can access a remote database through a Java-enabled browser. DB2 Version 7.1 clients are supported on the following platforms: OS/2; UNIX (AIX, HP-UX, Linux, NUMA-Q, SGI IRIX, and the Solaris Operating Environment); Windows 9x; Windows Me; Windows NT; and Windows 2000. See Chapter 6, "Installing a DB2 Client," for more information concerning DB2 clients.

DB2 Runtime client

A DB2 Runtime client provides basic connectivity; that is, the ability for workstations from a variety of platforms to access DB2 databases. If you need to establish connectivity to a remote DB2 server or DB2 Connect Gateway (which help you access DB2 on a mainframe or host system, such as DB2 for S/390), you have to at minimum start here; of course, you can use any client for this.

DB2 Application Development client

The DB2 Application Development client (DB2 AD client) was known as the DB2 Software Development Kit (DB2 SDK) in previous versions of DB2. DB2 AD clients provide the tools and environment you need to develop applications that access any DB2 servers. You can build and run DB2 applications with a DB2 AD client.

The applicable DB2 AD client can be found on the server product CD-ROM. The DB2 AD client for all platforms can be found on the set of DB2 Application Development Client CD-ROMs. You can find out about the tools that are provided to help you with application development in Chapter 8, "The DB2 Tools."

DB2 Administration client

A DB2 Administration client provides the ability for workstations from a variety of platforms to access and administer DB2 databases through the Control Center. A DB2 Administration client has all the features of a DB2 Runtime client and also includes all the DB2 Administration tools, documentation, and support for Thin-clients. A DB2 Thin-client is a special type of client that loads the DB2 client code from a remote location. You can find more on this in Chapter 7.

A DB2 Administration client also includes the client components for DB2 Query Patroller, a sophisticated query management and workload distribution tool used to control the flow of ad-hoc queries to a data warehouse. (To use Query Patroller, you must have a Query Patroller server installed.)

The QueryEnabler tool, used to capture queries for DB2 Query Patroller, is part of each DB2 client. A DB2 Administration Client has other DB2 Query Patroller tools that allow you to monitor, track, and manage your queries.

A DB2 Administration client is part of any default DB2 server installation.

Even though a DB2 Administration client is part of any default DB2 server installation because a DB2 server has all of a DB2 Administration client's components, people still refer to a DB2 server as having a DB2 Administration client installed. So when you perform a DB2 server installation, people will talk as though you performed a separate DB2 Administration client installation as well. Of course you didn't, but understand that this is how people (and the test) talk about this product.

DB2 Satellite Edition

DB2 Satellite Edition (DB2 SE) is meant for mobile database users, sometimes referred to as *occasionally connected clients (OCC)*. DB2 SE enables OCCs to connect to a database, download the most current version of whatever information they need from the database, disconnect, and go. This is kind of the same concept of DB2 Everyplace. However, these DB2 "satellites" are based on DB2 PE. Therefore, because they aren't limited to the restricted size of hand-held devices, you can store a lot more information and leverage more database features for your applications.

Another feature of this product edition is that it offers a central location for keeping track of all satellite activity and managing the environment. You can track things such as who's connecting from where, what information people are gathering and taking with them, when they last connected, and other information. This way, if you're administrating DB2 SE users, you can quickly gather information and statistics about the information that is being downloaded from the main database to the mobile users.

DB2 SE ultimately allows you to

- Keep deployment costs low when rolling out to a large user community
- Eliminate the need for extra synchronization software because replication and host interoperability software is included
- Keep your remote workers up-to-date with the latest application version
- Easily determine problems with a central repository of satellite activity

DB2 Developer's Editions

Two special editions of DB2 are available for people who develop DB2 applications: DB2 Personal Developer's Edition and DB2 Universal Developer's Edition.

DB2 Personal Developer's Edition

DB2 Personal Developer's Edition (DB2 PDE) provides all the tools for one software developer to develop desktop business tools and applications for DB2. This package includes all the supported DB2 PE products in addition to:

- The functionality of DB2 Connect Personal Edition
- VisualAge for Java, Entry Edition
- WebSphere Application Server and WebSphere Studio
- DB2 Extenders
- DB2 OLAP Starter Kit and Data Warehouse Center
- DB2 Clients

To encourage people to get to know DB2 and develop applications for it, IBM offers a free downloadable version of this product at `www.ibm.com/software/data/db2/udb/downloads.html`. The database and gateways can be used for development purposes only; you cannot take the copy of DB2 PE that comes with DB2 PDE and run your business with it.

DB2 Universal Developer's Edition

DB2 Universal Developer's Edition (DB2 UDE) provides all the tools required for software developers to develop applications that run on DB2, for any supported platforms. This package includes all the CD-ROMs for all platforms of DB2 EE, DB2 WE, and DB2 PE, in addition to:

- The functionality of DB2 Connect Enterprise Edition and Personal Edition
- VisualAge for Java for OS/2 and Windows Professional Edition
- WebSphere Application Server Standard Edition and WebSphere Studio
- DB2 Extenders
- DB2 OLAP Starter Kit and Data Warehouse Center
- DB2 Clients
- DB2 Satellite Edition
- QMF
- Net.Data

You must have a license for each copy of DB2 UDE that is installed. Database servers and gateways can be set up for development purposes only. You must acquire one license for each developer.

DB2 Everyplace

Mobile computing has become a key component of competitiveness in today's information-driven economy. Today, with different applications for people on the road, data and applications need to be everyplace (no pun intended) that a worker travels. Having information in the hands of workers when they need it, as opposed to only in their office, makes them more competitive and enables them to make better, faster, and more informed decisions.

Laptops have long been standard equipment for business travelers. Now, handheld devices (also called PDAs, or Personal Digital Assistants), some of which connect through wireless networks, are springing up everyplace. Perhaps the most popular PDA is a Palm Pilot, but lots of others are out there, including HP-UX's Jordana, Compaq's Aero, Ericsson's R380 cellular phone. These powerful mobile tools are limited if used in isolation. According to Sherwood Research, by 2005, 60 percent of Internet transactions in North America will occur from these type of devices, *not* your laptop or desktop computer! In fact, Europe is already well ahead of the game when it comes to Internet device penetration beyond the desktop or laptop computer.

A laptop or PDA by itself doesn't do an employee much good if the corporate database changes in the middle of a business trip. To maintain their competitive edge, mobile professionals need seamless access to current enterprise data, no matter where they may be. To accomplish this, you need powerful tools designed to connect mobile devices directly to your enterprise data.

Think about all those jobs in which employees aren't tied to desks, or work activities that take people to the scene. What about a nurse that specializes in home health care; an incredible growing industry with the shift in age demographics as Baby Boomers get older. Instead of taking charts and papers everyplace she goes, needing to enter information into a computer when she gets home, she could enter the values on a Palm Pilot at each patient's home and 'sync' up with the enterprise server at the end of the day. The server could then be updated with the most current patient information (for the doctor on call) and could even handle business logic from there.

For example, the enterprise database could receive patient records and perhaps notes on a patient that indicate that the patient's prescription is about to run out. The database manager could fire a trigger (you'll read about these later) to automatically order a refill. Neat huh?

What about an insurance adjuster on scene after a natural disaster? A policewoman on the beat? You could pretty much come up with countless scenarios that would be helped by mobile data. DB2e is about extending data from the 'glass house' (this is geek talk for your office) to the field.

Figure 4-5 illustrates a typical DB2e setup in a business environment.

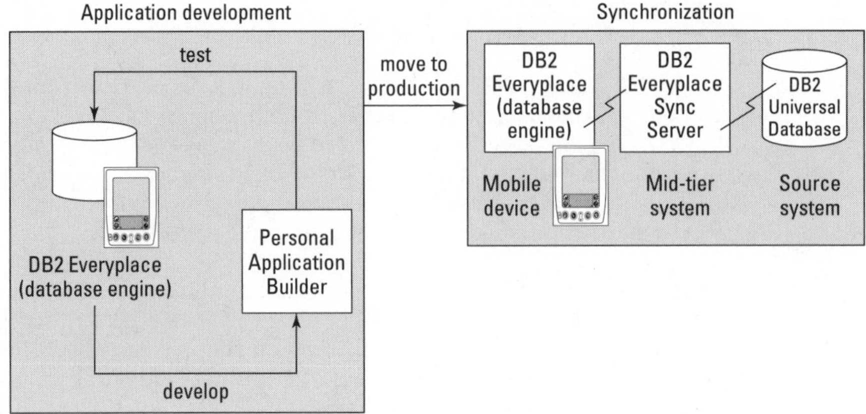

Figure 4-5: DB2e in the workplace.

In Figure 4-5, you can see that there are two sides to the DB2e environment. One side focuses on application development. This area is where the applications that the workforce will run on its PDAs get developed. DB2e allows you to develop applications in C, C++, and Java with standard off-the-shelf development products. DB2e even comes with a tool called the Personal Application Builder (PAB) that allows you to easily create applications by using a point-and-click methodology, as shown in Figure 4-6.

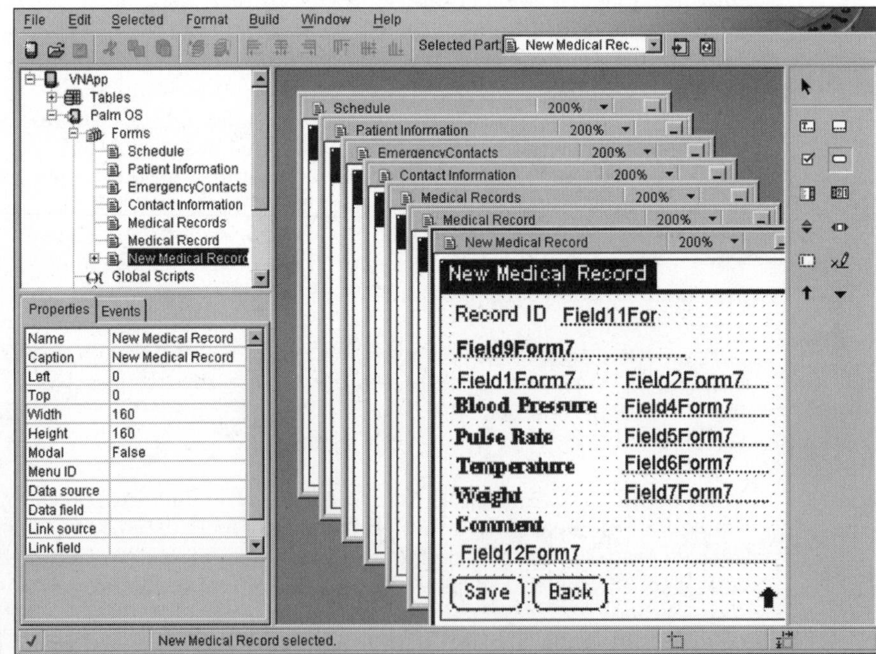

Figure 4-6: The Personal Application Builder.

On the right side of Figure 4-5, you see how DB2e works in a typical business scenario. Remember those visiting nurses? Well they have the mobile devices. When they are ready to synchronize their information with the office, they connect wirelessly or through a telephone line to the Synchronization Server, which helps to ensure that data on the mobile device gets synchronized with data on the DB2 server. The whole synchronization process, which is SyncML compliant (a markup language being developed for synchronization), is transparent to the end user, letting him or her focus on work rather than the technical issues of using the product.

DB2e runs on Palm OS, Windows CE, Pocket PC, Symbian EPOC, QNX Neutrino, Linux, AIX, Solaris, and Windows-based operating systems. The synchronization engines run on Windows NT/2000, AIX, Solaris, and Linux.

You can find out more about DB2e at `www.ibm.com/software/data/db2/everyplace/` and you can even download a trial copy.

The DB2 extenders

The DB2 extenders can take your database applications beyond traditional numeric and character data to images, XML, videos, voice, spatial objects, complex documents, and beyond. Using extenders, you can bring all these types of data into a database and work with them using SQL, the language used to talk to relational databases. Imagine selecting a subset of wallpaper based on color or patterns you're looking to find. That's extender technology.

This section outlines most of the DB2 extenders and shows you what they're used for to help businesses better manage their data but still leverage the existing skills and knowledge of SQL to work with those objects. You can find out more about all the DB2 Extenders at `www.ibm.com/sofware/data/db2/extenders`.

You aren't required on the exam to know how to use each extender, or how they work per se; however, you are expected to understand what each one is used for. We suggest you check out the Extenders Web site to familiarize yourself with all the DB2 Extenders, but you need to be knowledgeable about only the ones we cover in this section.

DB2 XML Extender

XML stands for e*X*tensible *M*arkup *L*anguage (go to `www.xml.org` to find out more about XML). XML is an emerging standard for data-interchange for the next generation of business to business e-commerce solutions. You are no doubt familiar with HTML, the language of the Web. The problem with HTML is that it tells Web browsers only how to present information; it can't describe what the data is or means. XML functions as a way to describe data with a markup language, independent of output. With XML, you can display the output of your document to any device. An example is wireless phones that can now surf the Web.

Cellular phones that can surf the Web use a markup language called Wireless Markup Language (WML), which is part of the Wireless Application Protocol (WAP) specification. Now, if `www.yahoo.com` wants to offer services to both Web users and cellular phone users, they can write two different pages that do the same thing but offer different interfaces (because what you can display on your computer's monitor is greater than on a tiny cellular phone's screen). A better solution might be to write the information in XML and let a transformation engine alter the XML source to HTML or WML, depending on the client requesting the information.

But XML adds even more power when used as a data interchange format. Emerging standards in vertical industries are creating markup languages for data interchange within industry. For example, the pharmacy industry may articulate the PML (Prescription Markup Language) as a standard way to define a prescription for a patient. PML may contain tags that note the name of the drug, dosage, side effects, portions, cautions, history, and so on. Applications built on this framework would not need to be changed in order to interpret data. You can see how XML is going to change the way we exchange information.

The DB2 XML Extender provides new data types that enables you to store XML documents in the DB2 database and adds functions that help you work with these XML documents while in a database. This makes sense, doesn't it? We know by now that databases are for managing information. XML is a language for information. DB2 should store XML data, right?

In DB2, you can store entire documents (or store them as external files managed by the database) in XML. This method is known is *XML Columns*. You can also decompose an XML document into relational tables and then recompose that information to XML on the way out of the database. Basically, this means that your DB2 database can strip out the XML and just take the data, or take the data and create an XML document. This method is known as *XML Collections*.

DB2 programmers call the process of creating an XML document from data *composition* and the process of removing data from XML *decomposition*. Decomposition is also referred to as *shredding*.

Figure 4-7 illustrates the DB2 XML Extender in a DB2 environment.

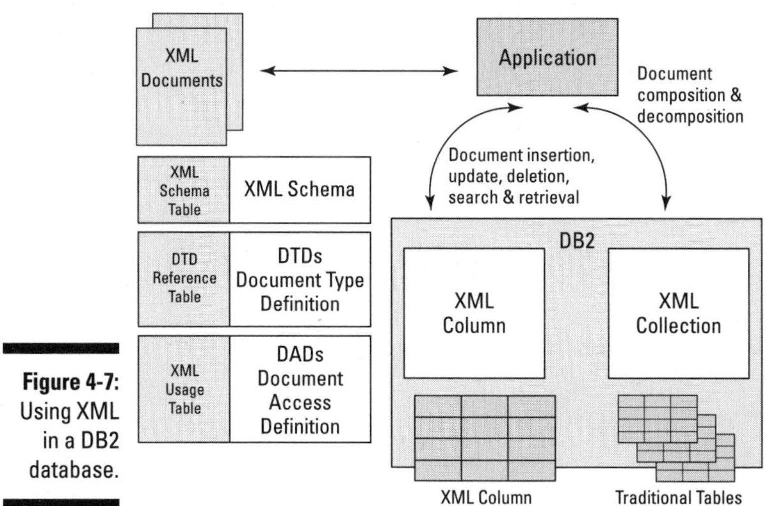

Figure 4-7: Using XML in a DB2 database.

DB2 Spatial Extender

Time and space will become the cornerstones of 21st-century data warehouses. Time series and OLAP tools allow you to exploit the time dimension, but the spatial dimension has typically been reserved for those with geographical backgrounds. The next frontier of data management and business intelligence is adding a space dimension to your data. This dimension can be added with the DB2 Spatial Extender while using the database to manage the data.

Quite simply, the DB2 Spatial Extender enables spatial data access and analysis. Spatial data (also called location data and geographic data) consists of values that denote the location objects and areas with respect to one another. Spatial objects include those that comprise the earth's surface (for example, rivers, forests, hills) and the cultural environment (cities, office buildings, houses).

Almost every query has a spatial component in it — queries that are based on distance, proximity, addresses, driving time, area/shapes, and others. In fact, it is estimated that almost 80 percent of current information has embedded geographic (or spatial) characteristics already associated with it. You likely don't have to look too hard to find an example of this. A typical data warehouse that contains all types of information likely has a spatial component to it; we just haven't thought of it in that way before. To most users, for example, an address is an example of just plain old data. However, an address can become more than an address. An address can become a point on a map — it has spatial meaning.

So now that we can mix all this spatial and business data together with the DB2 Spatial Extender, what do we have? Something like Figure 4-8.

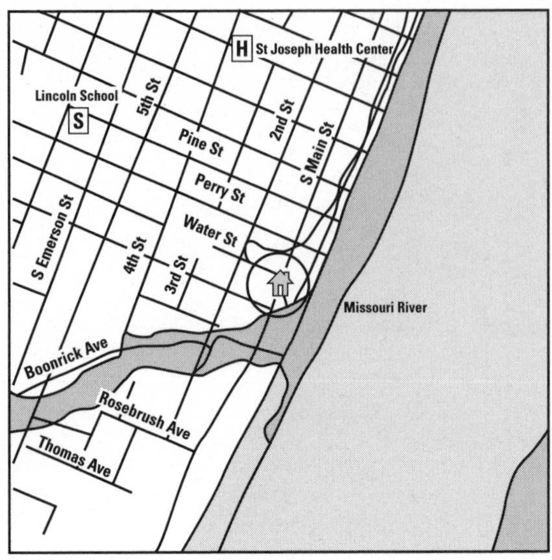

Figure 4-8: Using the spatial component of your data.

The DB2 Spatial Extender allows you to gather spatial data and attach non-spatial business data attributes to it. With the DB2 Spatial Extender, your business data and spatial data are now integrated, making the task of creating a Geographical Information System (GIS) as straightforward as any other information system — but now they're married to the relational technology that your IT department is accustomed to and trusts. Of course, you also have the benefit of using the SQL you know and love to work with this data. Now you can compose queries such as:

- What is the closest retail outlet for all of the customers who have spent >$3K during 1997 within the Chicago area?
- What customers with a home insurance policy living within 1,000 yards of a creek *do not* have a flood insurance option on their policy?

The DB2 Spatial Extender even has a Geocoder in it so that you can create points on a map on the fly with your business data! Spatial data could be a book in itself, so check out the DB2 Extenders Web site listed previously for more information.

DB2 Net.Search Extender

This extender helps businesses that need fast performance when searching for information in a database. You're likely to see this used in Internet applications, where search performance on large indexes and scalability of concurrent queries is needed. Though we aren't allowed to mention its name, a famous online book e-tailer tried this technology, and the results are illustrated in Figure 4-9.

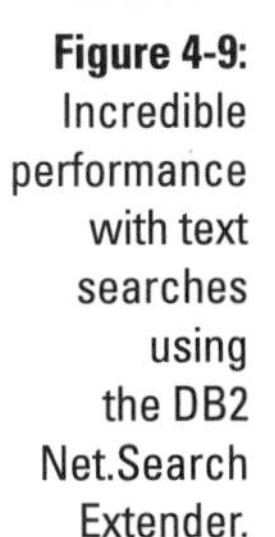

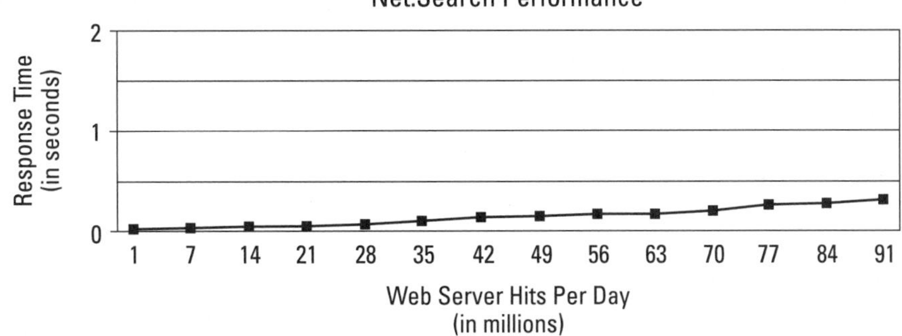

Figure 4-9: Incredible performance with text searches using the DB2 Net.Search Extender.

As you can see in Figure 4-9, this is some incredible technology. The DB2 Net.Search Extender works on stored procedures (you can find out about these in the pages to come) that help to add the power of fast full-text retrieval to Net.Data, Java, or DB2 applications. This technology is really seamless when it comes to text data that is managed by DB2. The end user has no idea it's there, but users sure are happy that it is because they're getting the information they want, fast! The DB2 Net.Search Extender is designed to rapidly search and index data without locking database tables.

DB2 TAIV Extenders

TAIV stands for Text, Audio, Image, and Video. Usually, DB2 programmers refer to this group of extenders as TAIV because they come packaged together. These extenders allow you to extend the relational database to use nontraditional forms of data, such as text, songs, pictures, and movies. Yes, you can actually store this stuff in DB2!

You can take advantage of all the DB2 TAIV Extenders in a query. For example, an advertising agency can use the DB2 Image Extender to store print ads in a DB2 database, the DB2 Video Extender to store its commercials, and the DB2 Audio Extender to store radio advertisements. Employees would be able to use a single SQL query to retrieve printed, video, and audio ads. They could even use the DB2 Text Extender to find words within the ads.

Here is a sample of an 'extended' SQL query:

```
db2 select ad_no, comments, thumbnail, script, ad from
           paulz.ads where client = 'Cash Coverters' and
           owner = 'Chris Neilson' and contains
           (AD_script_handle, 'SYNONYM OF 'money') = 1 order
           by adno asc
```

Your application would likely format all this data for you and launch it with its respected media devices. It could very well look something like Figure 4-10.

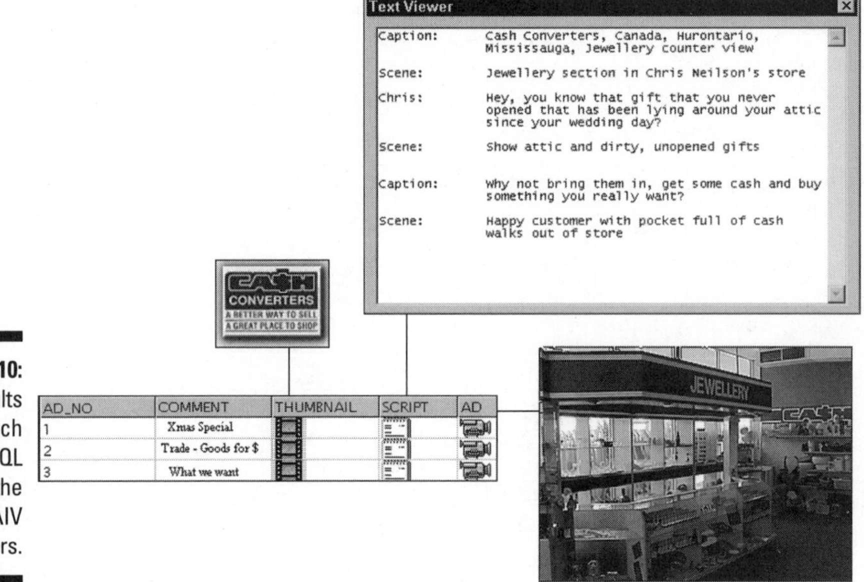

Figure 4-10: The results of a search using SQL and the TAIV Extenders.

DB2 Text Extender

The DB2 Text Extender gives you a powerful way to search for and extract key information in documents stored not only in DB2 but also in files that are stored outside the control of DB2. This product can search thousands of documents. The DB2 Text Extender is similar to the DB2 Net.Search Extender, but what the DB2 Net.Search Extender gains in performance and speed, it gives up in search functions. Applications can use Text Extender technology to search through text looking for fuzzy matches (such as Rom* for *Roman*, *Romanowski,* and so on), specific words (such as *Internet*), and other standard search functions. The DB2 Text Extender gives up some speed because index and data aren't stored in memory, but takes on more powerful search techniques. For example, you can search on a word that sounds like another word, or search variations of a word. You can even build your own Thesaurus- or Dictionary-based searches. You can see in Figure 4-10, shown previously, that we looked for any ads that were for Chris Neilson's Cash Converters store that had the word, or a synonym to the word, money in it.

DB2 Audio Extender

This extender allows you to store audio files in your DB2 database and work with them by using SQL. When was the last time your business data literally talked to you? This extender enables you to take data beyond the realm of numbers and text, and truly incorporate data that doesn't fit the traditional relational model. Going back to the Cash Converters shop shown in Figure 4-10, assume that an advertising agency was hired to create and market those ads. An account manager at that advertising agency could use one SQL query to get that ad as well as associated business data. Your data may tell that an advertisement didn't penetrate a target market as it should have, but now you can hear why, too! The DB2 Audio Extender supports WAVE and MIDI sound types.

DB2 Image Extender

That thumbnail image shown in Figure 4-10 is a great example of the image extender. But this extender isn't just about storing pictures in a database. Imagine that you're looking for an ad with a particular color, or pattern. How could you find that in a database if that database didn't understand images? The DB2 Image Extender enables you to do just that. You can see the usefulness of this extender in various business-to-business (B2B) Internet applications. You can go to an online Web site looking for a particular artist with specific colors. The DB2 Image Extender supports popular image file types such as GIF, JPEG, BMP, and TIFF.

DB2 Video Extender

The DB2 Video Extender enables you to store video clips in your database and access them with an SQL statement.

DB2 Data Links File Manager

DB2 Data Links is an interesting DB2 add-on product that definitely changes the way large objects (video, large text documents, images) are managed by DB2. This technology represents the next generation of enterprise content management. Data Links allows for the management of files that reside outside the database as though they're logically within the database.

A certain amount of overheard is associated with materializing and dematerializing large object data (this is geek talk for storing and retrieving large binary files in your database). To get video and audio files in and out of the database, the database engine has to do some work. DB2 Data Links allows you to store and manage these files outside the database by taking control of the file system. DB2 Data Links takes control of the file system and lets you control all management aspects (such as access, backup, recovery) that relate to these files, without the performance cost associated with materialization. DB2 Data Links can control DSF, NTFS, and JDF file systems. This leads to simplified administration issues, which in turn lowers the total cost of ownership (TCO) by providing a single, coordinated point of control for file and database data. Figure 4-11 shows a typical DB2 Data Links environment.

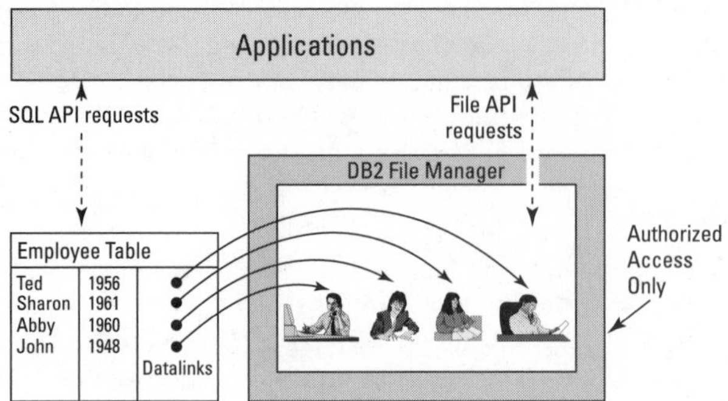

Figure 4-11: Using DB2 Data Links empowers DB2 to manage files that are stored outside of the database tables.

Figure 4-11 shows that DB2 has taken control of some images that reside outside the database. To access those images, users have to issue a request to the database. The database will issue an access token that will allow a user to access the object in question. A person in Human Resources could work with an employee's picture in the EMPLOYEE table by first waiting for the database engine to materialize the image. Then the HR person could get an access token and work with the image off the disk.

DB2 Data Links can also help when you have a large number of files that you want to keep track of with DB2 but haven't got time to commit to the materialization and dematerialization overhead that we talk about earlier and their associated management issues. Consider the thousands of engineering drawings required for a university campus. Each file could stay on the file system where it was created, but DB2 Data Links could be used to record which subdirectory each file was in and manage its recoverability. Data Links would also prevent you from erasing or accessing the file (unless you've proven to DB2 that you're authorized and have been granted the magic access token). You can find more information about DB2 Data Links at `www.almaden.ibm.com/cs/datalinks`.

DB2 OLAP Starter Kit and DB2 OLAP Server

DB2 has a very strong OnLine Analytical Processing (OLAP) offering that allows you to easily define multidimensional applications, link and populate those applications with warehouse data, and share the applications among a workgroup. When you add one of the DB2 OLAP products to your DB2 installation, you suddenly increase the power of your DB2 server to store and manage both relational and multidimensional databases.

OLAP allows users to ask questions intuitively because the OLAP data is presented in business dimensions. OLAP can perform analyses such as "Display the profit of my highest and lowest performing products last quarter in my domestic sales regions." You can use DB2's OLAP offering to deliver analytic applications that give your business a competitive edge. You can find out more about OLAP throughout this book; for now, we present it from a packaging perspective.

Relational OLAP has been extended in the latest version of DB2 and includes new SQL functions for moving aggregates, such as moving average and moving sum, that you can now leverage for analytical queries. They comply with the proposed OLAP Addendum to SQL-99.

Two offerings in the DB2 family provide OLAP services: DB2 OLAP Starter Kit and DB2 OLAP Server. Both packages come with an easy-to-use interface to build and manage OLAP applications and allow you to create, use, and analyze both relational and multidimensional databases. DB2's OLAP implementation is based on the Hyperion Essbase analytic engine.

DB2 OLAP Starter Kit

With every server copy of DB2 (except DB2 Satellite Edition), you get a copy of the DB2 OLAP Starter Kit. The installation of the DB2 OLAP Starter Kit is integrated into any DB2 server install. We include a copy of this software on one of the CD-ROMs that comes with this book, so you can install it by following the instructions in Chapter 5, "Installing a DB2 Server."

You can use the DB2 OLAP Starter Kit, a scaled-down version of the full-function DB2 OLAP Server product, to perform multidimensional analysis on your data.

The DB2 OLAP Starter Kit gives you DB2's OLAP power for up to three concurrent users. If you need to extend to power to multiple clients and add restricted OLAP functionality with this version, then you can purchase DB2 OLAP Server.

DB2 OLAP Server

With the many applications, tools, and solutions providers who support DB2 OLAP Server, you can create your own applications or have turnkey solutions built for you. DB2 OLAP Server is for enterprises that have recognized the benefits of implementing OLAP. All the model design, data manipulation, calculation, and analysis functions of the Hyperion Essbase server are available in DB2 OLAP Server.

DB2 OLAP Server allows you to take the OLAP features of the DB2 OLAP Starter Kit and build upon them to create an OLAP-based decision-support system. For more information about DB2 OLAP Server, check out `www.ibm.com/software/data/db2/db2olap/`.

DB2 Data Warehouse Center and DB2 Warehouse Manager

Data warehousing is the foundation for business intelligence and customer relationship management, so it is important to do it right. This means accurately translating your business user needs into data models and then building an easily accessible data warehouse that continually draws on diverse applications and data sources, finding a way to maintain that data warehouse in an ad hoc environment that is ever-changing. DB2 has tools that provide a graphical environment to help you create and manage data warehouses or data marts — all from the DB2 Control Center.

Most people just refer to the DB2 Control Center as the Control Center. Throughout this book, you may or may not see the DB2 prefix in front of the words "Control Center." Rest assured that if you see the term Control Center in this book, we are talking about the DB2 Control Center and not the Control Center as in NASA's headquarters.

Two offerings in the DB2 family provide data warehousing services: DB2 Data Warehouse Center and DB2 Warehouse Manager. Both packages come with an easy-to-use interface to build and manage data warehouses. We cover Data Warehousing in Chapter 8, "The DB2 Tools."

DB2 Data Warehouse Center

The power of Visual Warehouse (an old DB2 product used to create data warehouses) and the simplicity of the DB2 Control Center have been merged to provide a single new user interface for business intelligence customers. You can use the Data Warehouse Center to register and access data sources, define data extraction and transformation steps, populate data warehouses, automate and monitor warehouse management processes, and manage and interchange metadata. The DB2 Data Warehouse Center is integrated with a DB2 server installation.

You will often hear the activities involved in data warehousing referred to as ETL — Extract, Transform, and Load. *Extract* is associated with the extraction of data for input into the database warehouse; for example, for the operational side of your business. *Transform* refers to massaging (also called cleansing) data so that it is clean and usable in the data warehouse. For example, you may have told your bank that you live at 126 Rory Rd. whereas your car insurance company lists you at 126 Rory Road and your boat insurance at 126 Rory. Transform software worth its weight in gold will recognize that you have one street address and clean this type of dirty data. *Load* refers to moving that extracted and cleansed data into the data warehouse using DB2 loading utilities.

The DB2 Data Warehouse Center is available for Windows NT and Windows 2000 versions of DB2 and is limited to one worker agent that can perform requests on behalf of the administrators. An example of the DB2 Data Warehouse Center is shown in Figure 4-12.

Sometimes people get confused between the Data Warehouse Center and its more feature-enriched friend the Warehouse Manager. Think of the *C* in Data Warehouse Center as meaning *cheap* because it's free. The *M* in Warehouse Manager can mean *money* because it costs you money above what you pay for DB2 to have it. Now you'll always know the pricing difference between the two.

DB2 Warehouse Manager

DB2 Warehouse Manager is a separate product that enhances the scalability, manageability, and accessibility of your data warehouse. Remember the M? This means you have to pay for it because it doesn't come for free with DB2. DB2 Warehouse Manager adds to the Data Warehouse Center with support for DB2 server platforms, more worker agents for great scalability, query flow control tools, a query tool, and a meta data manager.

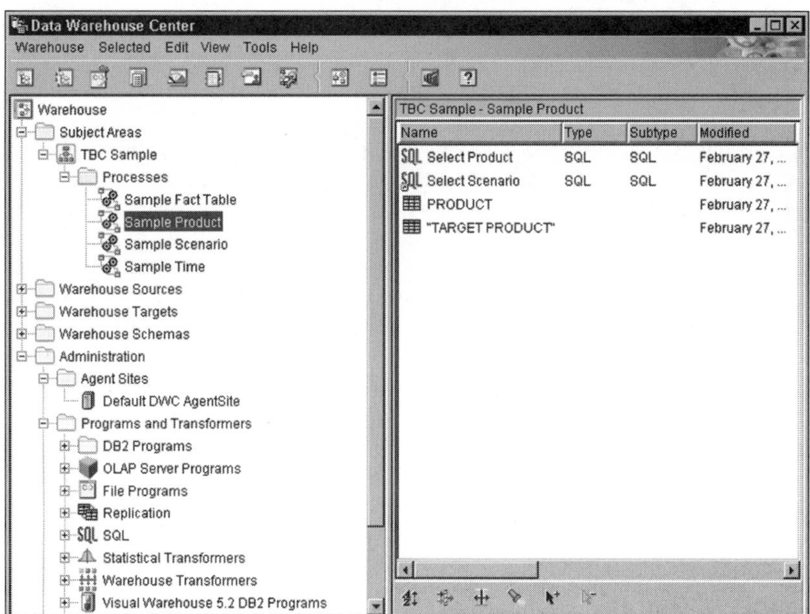

Figure 4-12: The Data Warehouse Center.

The main features of the DB2 Warehouse Manager are as follows:

- Better data scalability of the Data Warehouse Center with point-to-point data movement options for distributed systems
- Faster deployment via common, pre-built warehouse and statistical transformations
- Better user scalability by providing governing functions to manage query workloads
- Better manageability of the warehouse via resource and usage tracking
- Better end-user access by providing an information catalog to help end users find, understand, and access relevant information
- Enterprise reporting to develop and deliver reports to unlimited clients

DB2 Warehouse Manager is composed of three other products in addition to the Data Warehouse Center: DB2 Query Patroller, the Information Catalog Manager, and QMF for Windows. You can find more information about DB2 Warehouse Manager at `www.ibm.com/software/data/db2/warehouse/`.

DB2 Query Patroller

Today, database management personnel are facing increasing challenges. Although they want to deliver information to end users as quickly as possible, they're finding that it takes an enormous amount of resources to be responsive to the growing number of users demanding information. DB2 Query Patroller is now provided as an integral component of DB2 Warehouse Manager. It gives you extensive query governing for workload management and can intercept all queries that hit a database.

The steady increase of end users performing queries against corporate databases presents a huge challenge for database administrators. As the number of users performing their own queries increases, the response time of the system may decline because of increased contention. Large-scale data warehouses that provide breakthrough business value pose a challenge: How can a company's data warehouse continue to provide quick response time across large amounts of data to an ever-increasing number of end-users tapping the power of ad hoc query tools on their desktops?

Did you know that poorly written queries could take hours if not days to complete? Now imagine someone writing one of these "runaway" queries and waiting for a response. After about five hours, the user thinks that his system has crashed, so he resubmits the same query. Now the data warehouse has two of the queries from hell to contend with. Combine this problem with hundreds if not thousands of users submitting all sorts of queries at the same time and you can see the need for software to manage queries in a decision-support environment. Administrators need a way to limit the amount of resources ad-hoc queries consume.

With DB2 Query Patroller, you can set limits at a user, group, or query level. For example, if a query was deemed too "expensive" (too resource consuming), that query could be rejected or put into a Held state. You can assign priorities to different users or groups, so your boss may have more resources than you have when she submits a query. DB2 Query Patroller can even notify you via e-mail as to the status of your query. This product can do much, and you can find out more about DB2 Query Patroller at `www.ibm.com/software/data/pubs/papers/index.html#qpv7`. DB2 Query Patroller can be used with DB2 EE or DB2 EEE-based systems; an example is shown in Figure 4-13.

Information Catalog Manager

The Information Catalog Manager (ICM), previously provided with Visual Warehouse, is now an integral component of DB2 Warehouse Manager. It helps end users find, understand, and access available information by

- Populating the catalog through metadata interchange with the Data Warehouse Center and other analytical and reporting tools
- Allowing users to directly register shared information objects
- Providing navigation or searching across the objects to find relevant information
- Displaying the metadata about the object
- Launching the tools used to render the information for the end user

The ICM used to be called DataGuide.

This is an important tool in a Data Warehouse because it helps users navigate data. After all, you can have the most expensive, most powerful, biggest data warehouse known to humankind, but if it isn't enabled for users, it isn't going to be used.

Query Management Facility

Query Management Facility (QMF) is a tightly integrated, powerful, and reliable query and reporting tool set for IBM's DB2 relational database management system. It provides an environment that is easy for a novice to use but powerful enough for an application programmer. In fact, it allows novice users to build such powerful queries, it is a good thing that DB2 Query Patroller comes in this box, in case your users get a little carried away! QMF used to be a mainframe-only thing — my how times have changed; this isn't what your grandparents used, that's for sure.

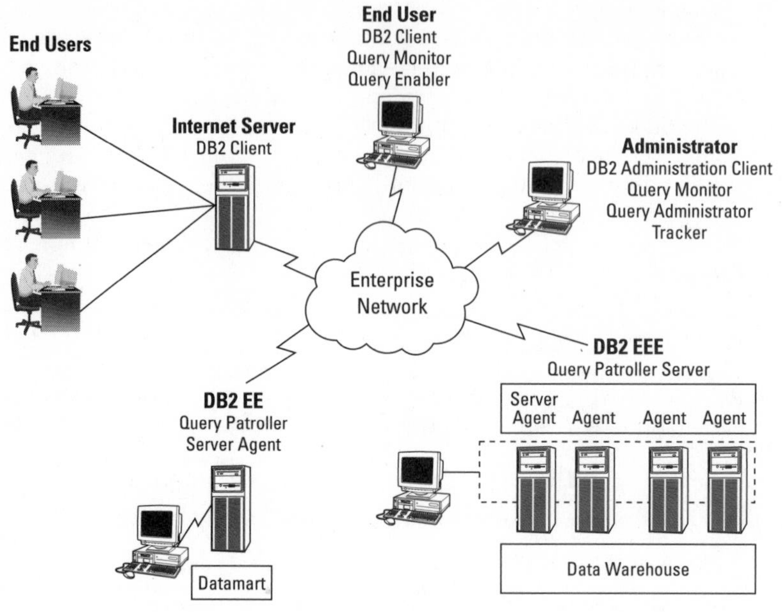

Figure 4-13: DB2 Query Patroller.

Query Management Facility (QMF) for Windows is included with DB2 Warehouse Manager to provide a multipurpose query tool for business reporting, data sharing, server resource protection, robust application development, and native connectivity to all the DB2 workstation platforms. It allows users to

- Build queries and reports easily via its quick start interface
- Use the new Java-based query capability to launch queries from their favorite browser
- Easily integrate query results with desktop tools, such as spreadsheets and personal databases
- Rapidly build data access and update applications
- Fully exploit DB2 performance, SQL syntax, and advanced database performance techniques, such as static SQL

Figure 4-14 shows a query screen from QMF for Windows.

You can find more information about QMF at `www.rocketsoftware.com/qmf/`.

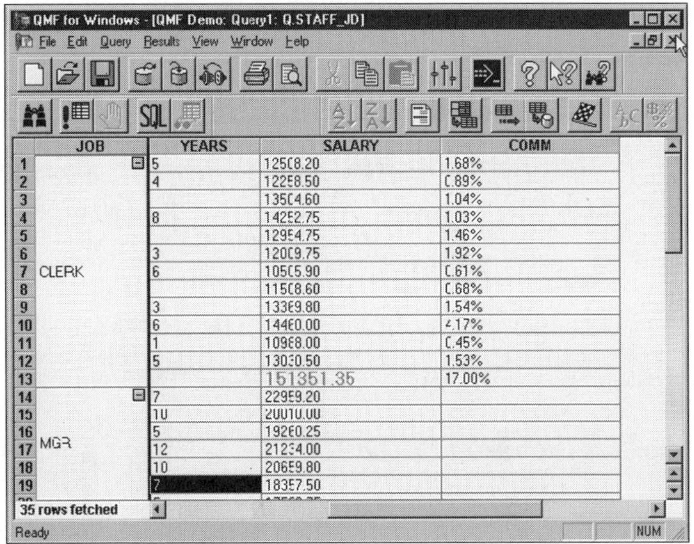

Figure 4-14: QMF for Windows.

DB2 Connect

A great deal of the data in many large organizations is managed by DB2 for AS/400, DB2 for MVS/ESA, DB2 for OS/390, or DB2 for VSE & VM. Applications that run on any of the supported DB2 distributed platforms can work with this data transparently, as if a local database server managed it.

In addition to DB2 applications, you can use a wide range of off-the-shelf or custom-developed database applications with DB2 Connect and its associated tools. For example, you can use DB2 Connect products with the following:

- Spreadsheets, such as Lotus 1-2-3 and Microsoft Excel, to analyze real-time data without having the cost and complexity of data extract and import procedures
- Decision-support tools, such as BusinessObjects, Brio and Impromptu, and Crystal Reports, to provide real-time information
- Database products, such as Lotus Approach and Microsoft Access
- Development tools, such as PowerSoft PowerBuilder, Microsoft Visual Basic, and Borland Delphi, to create client/server solutions

DB2 Connect provides connectivity to mainframe and midrange databases from Windows, OS/2, and UNIX-based platforms. You can connect to DB2 databases on OS/400, VSE, VM, MVS, and OS/390. You can find out more about DB2 at `www.ibm.com/software/data/db2/db2connect/`.

Three editions of DB2 Connect are available: Personal Edition, Enterprise Edition, and Unlimited Edition.

DB2 Connect Personal Edition

DB2 Connect Personal Edition (DB2 Connect PE) provides a direct connection from one Windows, OS/2, or Linux operating system to mainframe and midrange databases. It is designed for a two-tier environment, in which each client connects directly to the host. DB2 Connect Personal Edition doesn't accept inbound client requests for data.

DB2 Connect PE is similar to DB2 PE in that it represents a single user environment. Typically, application developers would use this to code applications that run against a DB2 mainframe database.

DB2 Connect Enterprise Edition

DB2 Connect Enterprise Edition (DB2 EE) is installed on a server and its job is to provide access for DB2 clients on a LAN to connect to a mainframe and midrange databases that reside on S/390, AS/400, and VM/VSE IBM operating systems. It is designed for a three-tier environment, in which clients connect to a host through a gateway server. DB2 Connect EE is often referred to as a DB2 Connect Gateway because it allows a path for DB2 client to access DB2 databases on mainframe systems.

An example of DB2 Connect EE and DB2 Connect PE is shown in Figure 4-15.

You can use a DB2 Administration client to manage a DB2 for OS/390 database by using DB2 Connect and the Control Center.

DB2 Connect Unlimited Edition

DB2 Connect Unlimited Edition (DB2 Connect UE) provides an unlimited number of both DB2 Connect Personal Edition and DB2 Connect Enterprise Edition licenses. In essence, this edition of DB2 Connect is simply a pricing option. You get to install as many DB2 Connect PE and DB2 Connect EE servers as you want, for one price. This price is based on the size of the OS/390 system that is being accessed. The size of a DB2 for OS/390 system is measured by a count called *MSU*.

An MSU entitlement must be obtained for each MSU on the DB2 host system. When this option is used, the customer need not count users of the DB2 Connect product. DB2 Connect UE is available only for gateways that need connection to OS/390 systems. This edition is available for any supported DB2 Connect EE and DB2 Connect PE workstation, as well as Linux/390.

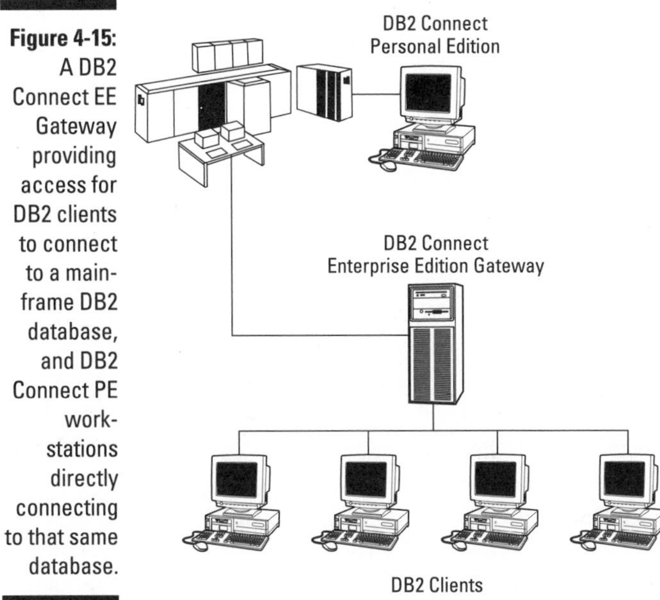

Figure 4-15: A DB2 Connect EE Gateway providing access for DB2 clients to connect to a mainframe DB2 database, and DB2 Connect PE workstations directly connecting to that same database.

Net.Data

Net.Data is a full-featured and easy-to-learn scripting language that allows you to create powerful Web applications that work with DB2. Net.Data can access data from the most prevalent databases in the industry: DB2, Oracle, DRDA-enabled data sources, ODBC data sources, as well as flat file and Web registry data. With Net.Data and DB2, you can have XML flow between your Web applications and DB2 with ease.

Net.Data gives users a high-performance macro interpreter and Web application. This allows you to satisfy clients' needs for quick server response, serving dynamic pages nearly as fast as static pages — sometimes faster! Net.Data also provides Web server interfaces (APIs), FastCGI, and allows the reuse of database connections to get your Web applications to perform even better.

The Net.Data macro language is rich, containing standard conditional logic, math, string, conversion functions, and much more. A wide variety of language environments are provided for you to use your existing applications in Java, REXX, Perl, or C++. Net.Data also provides an interface for you to create your own language environment.

This book doesn't cover Net.Data outside this section. If you want to find out more about Net.Data, check out `www.ibm.com/software/data/net.data/`.

DB2 Intelligent Miner

Another DB2 product that you can buy is called DB2 Intelligent Miner. DB2 Intelligent Miner comes in two flavors: DB2 Intelligent Miner for Text and DB2 Intelligent Miner for Data. The products allow you to gain new business insights. They help you harvest valuable business intelligence from your enterprise data, including high-volume transaction data generated by point-of-sale, ATM, credit card, call center, or e-commerce activities. With the DB2 Intelligent Miner products, you're better equipped to make insightful decisions, whether the problem is how to develop more precisely targeted marketing campaigns, reduce customer attrition, or increase e-commerce revenues.

DB2 Intelligent Miner for Text

Intelligent Miner for Text turns unstructured information into business knowledge for organizations of any size, from small businesses to global corporations. This knowledge-discovery toolkit includes components for building advanced text-mining and text-search applications.

Intelligent Miner for Text offers system integrators, solution providers, and application developers a wide range of text-analysis tools, full-text retrieval components, and Web-access tools to enrich their business-intelligence and knowledge management solutions. With Intelligent Miner, you can unlock the business information that is "trapped" in e-mail, insurance claims, news feeds, and Lotus Notes, and you can analyze patent portfolios, customer complaint letters, and even competitors' Web pages.

An example of this technology would be to have DB2 Intelligent Miner for Text analyze customer complaint e-mails that have been received to find a recurring problem with widgets that are produced in Vancouver and resold through a distribution channel in the U.S.

You can find more information about this product at `www.ibm.com/software/data/iminer/fortext/index.html`.

DB2 Intelligent Miner for Data

DB2 Intelligent Miner for Data does the same thing that DB2 Intelligent Miner for Text does for text-based documents, but for raw data. Central to this product are data-mining algorithms, developed in IBM research laboratories and proven in customer installations worldwide. Applicable to a wide range of business problems, these algorithms can be employed to facilitate decision-making in business areas, such as campaign planning, customer relationship management, process reengineering, product planning and fulfillment, and fraud detection.

These algorithms include the following:

- Creation of classification and prediction models
- Discovery of associations and sequential patterns in large databases
- Automatic segmentation of databases into groups of related records
- Discovery of similar patterns of behavior within special time sequences

Multiple techniques are often used in combination to address a specific business problem.

So how does this get used? Credit card companies do this kind of stuff all the time. Have you ever used a credit card to make a local phone call, followed by a long distance call? After making the calls, you go somewhere to purchase something and get a "Declined — call for authorization" message when you try to use your credit card to make a purchase. This is more likely to happen if you made those phone calls and then took a plane to another region and bought something. Aside from the embarrassment, what the heck is happening here? Credit companies put a lot of resources into fraud detection. One of the algorithms notes that if someone starts making phone calls and then purchases, there is a fair chance the card has been stolen; most people don't use credit cards to make local phone calls. Credit card companies may also analyze your market basket (jargon for what you buy), and if you buy something outside of that basket that is expensive, that may trigger a decline of your card as well.

For more information on Intelligent Miner for Data, check out `www.ibm.com/software/data/iminer/fordata/`.

DB2 for AS/400

A version of DB2 exists on the AS/400 servers. AS/400 servers run an operating system called OS/400. Some people will call this product DB2 for AS/400 and others will call it DB2 for OS/400. Quite the debate among DB2 scholars because we call DB2 for Windows using the operating system, but not AS/400? Oh, we digress.

The same powerful DB2 engine that you know can be run on an AS/400 server. The coolest thing about DB2 on this platform is that the relational database manager is fully integrated on your AS/400. Yes, the software comes with the hardware. Believe us, this integration thing is cool. It means DB2 runs at the machine layer, bypassing all sorts of layers. Because DB2 for AS/400 is integrated in OS/400, DB2 for AS/400 is very easy to use and manage.

IBM has renamed the AS/400 server to iSeries, so you may hear DB2 for the iSeries.

As an interface to DB2 for AS/400, the DB2 Query Manager and SQL Development Kit for AS/400 add an interactive query and report writing interface, as well as precompilers and tools to assist in writing SQL application programs in high-level programming languages. You can find out more about DB2 for the iSeries at: `www.ibm.com/servers/eserver/iseries/db2/`.

You don't need to know anything but what's written here for the exam. If you want to make yourself a better person, learn more about DB2 for the iSeries. If you're looking to just get on with the certification process, read this section and move on.

DB2 for OS/390

Remember those people long ago that said the mainframe was dead? Well, they were wrong. Let's face it, folks, if you're looking for RAS (reliability, availability, and scalability), you can't beat this thing (though its price may knock your boss off his feet). OS/390 has been around forever, and as you would suspect, so has its friend DB2. When you need ultimate database power, you would be hard pressed to beat a System/390 server with DB2 and OS/390 on it. Now advancements in technology (both hardware and software) on the distributed side are closing the gap, but industry analysts generally recognize the System/390 as the most powerful and secure computing environment you can buy (if you don't have to contend with price, then you may need to make some tradeoffs).

The hardware that the OS/390 operating system runs on is called System/390. DB2 runs on the OS/390 operating system, which runs on a System/390 machine. System/390 is often referred to as S/390. S/390 machines run other operating systems such as VM/VSE (which, by the way, DB2 runs on as well), but the most famous operating system on an S/390 machine is OS/390 (formerly known on MVS).

IBM has renamed the OS/390 operating system to z/OS and the System/390 hardware to zSeries.

If the company you work for has a System/390 host machine "in house," chances are you're running DB2. In fact, DB2 for OS/390 has more than one million user licenses and about 90+ percent database marketshare on this platform. To make things even better, you can use the Control Center that comes with a distributed DB2 server on the distributed platform and a DB2 client to graphically manage your DB2 for OS/390 databases (though you need DB2 Connect for this, don't forget, so that you can access the database). It would not be uncommon to see both versions of DB2 (distributed and host) in an IT shop. DB2 on this platform also comes with built-in DRDA AR (application requester) functionality so that it can act as a DB2 client to a distributed DB2 server, both of which have built in DRDA AS (application server) functionality.

DB2 EE and DB2 EEE have DRDA AS technology built in to the database code. If you need to connect to another database using DRDA, you must have DRDA AR function. DB2 Connect provides DRDA AR function to DB2 on the distributed platforms. So, if a mainframe or host database wanted to connect to a distributed version of DB2, you don't need to do anything else.

We can't possibly do this offering any justice with a brief description. To find out more, check out the Web site at `www.ibm.com/software/data/db2/os390/`.

IBM has renamed the System/390 server to zSeries.

DB2 for VM/VSE

This version of DB2 is a replacement for SQL/DS, IBM's database solution before relational technology hit the scene. Whenever we roam the halls of our lab and hear people say, "Back in the SQL/DS days," we know that they've been around for a long time. This version runs on the System/390 mainframes as well; in this case, however, the operating system is different.

Because this version of DB2 isn't covered on the exam, you're charged only with the responsibility of knowing that it exists, another example of DB2 scaling from the smallest to the largest systems. You can find out more about DB2 for VM/VSE at `www.ibm.com/software/data/db2/vse-vm/`.

DB2 DataJoiner

Get the feeling that you are drowning in a world of data, and what's more, that this data is managed on different platforms, and by different database management systems? Much of the Fortune 500 is feeling the same way.

One of the best current solutions is to apply multidatabase server technology, which provides a single database image to all the data no matter where it physically resides. It does so by adding a layer of software between your applications and your servers. DB2 DataJoiner, IBM's multidatabase server, allows databases to remain autonomous while bringing location transparency to your organization.

Many companies don't just use one operating system and one database. With autonomy of lines of business, mergers, and acquisitions, it would not be uncommon to see two competitors' databases in the same IT shop! How do you handle this? Perhaps migrate off the one database platform and use only one brand's database server. Aside from making the people who have skills in the database that's getting dumped angry, cost, skills, and legacy applications are just some of the implications you must consider. The notion of one platform and one database, referred to as *homogenous,* doesn't exist in the real world — though we wish it did. More accurately, companies have a variety of platforms and database systems in their framework, and these situations are referred to as *heterogeneous* or *disparate* environments.

With DB2 DataJoiner, you can view all your data — IBM, multi-vendor, relational, non-relational, local, remote, and now geographic data — as if it were local data. With a single SQL statement, you can access and join tables located across multiple data sources without needing to know the source location! What's more, DB2 can even optimize your SQL statements.

What does all this mean? Imagine an Oracle database that exists on your network that is used for OLTP but the Data Warehouse is managed by DB2. In a single SQL statement, you could work with tables that reside on both the Oracle and DB2 databases. What's more, you don't need to know anything about how Oracle implements SQL, you can write to DB2's SQL API and DB2 DataJoiner will take care of the rest — mapping of columns, data types, optimization, and so on. Amazing! Computer nerds would call this *location transparency* in your enterprise; we'll just call it *Cool.*

DB2 DataJoiner provides native support for popular relational data sources (such as the DB2 Family, Informix, Microsoft SQL Server, Oracle, Sybase SQL Server, Teradata, and others). If you need to access non-relational data sources, you would use a product called Classic Connect (we don't talk about this product in this book).

How does DB2 DataJoiner work? Well, we are not going to get into it here, but essentially everything in the global catalog is assigned a nickname. These nicknames make all the backend shuffling and sorting to get to the disparate databases transparent to users and your applications. It's like forwarding your phone number. People call your old number but, unbeknownst to them, it rings at your new place.

DB2 DataJoiner is based on DB2 Version 2.1.2. Consequently, this product is being phased out. To bring the code base up to speed, all the read and write functions for the DB2 Family in DB2 DataJoiner are being ported into a component of DB2 called *Federated* (you see this in Chapter 5, "Installing a DB2 Server"). If you want read and write access to non-DB2 databases, you'll find this functionality in a product called DB2 Relational Connect (see the next description).

In DB2 Version 7.1, the Federated component only allows read access to the DB2 Family of database servers. Point releases via FixPaks may add to this functionality.

If you want more information on DB2 DataJoiner, check out `www.ibm.com/software/data/datajoiner/`.

DB2 Relational Connect

The DB2 Relational Connect implementation in Version 7.1 represents the first phase of the functionality migration project from DB2 Data Joiner (based on DB2 Version 2.1.2) to DB2 Relational Connect (based on DB2 Version 7.1). DB2 Relational Connect at this point supports *read* only access to Oracle databases, Sybase databases, and Microsoft SQL Server. As the porting effort continues, you will see all the supported data sources available in DB2 DataJoiner available in DB2 Relational Connect in both read and write mode. The Federated component of DB2 will offer read and write mode to the DB2 Family of database servers.

Prep Test

1. **A client application on OS/390 must access a DB2 server on UNIX, Windows, or OS/2. At a minimum, which of the following is required to be the DB2 server machine?**

   A ❍ DB2 Connect Enterprise Edition
   B ❍ DB2 Universal Database Enterprise Edition
   C ❍ DB2 Connect and DB2 Universal Database Workgroup Edition
   D ❍ DB2 Connect and DB2 Universal Database Enterprise Edition

2. **Which of the following products is required to be installed in order to build an application on AIX which will access a DB2 UDB for OS/390 database?**

   A ❍ DB2 Connect Personal Edition
   B ❍ DB2 Personal Developer's Edition
   C ❍ DB2 Universal Developer's Edition
   D ❍ DB2 Universal Database Workgroup Edition

3. **Which of the following processes is *not* performed by DB2 Warehouse Manager?**

   A ❍ Query
   B ❍ Loading
   C ❍ Extraction
   D ❍ Transformation

4. **Which of the following DB2 products allows reference to Oracle and DB2 databases in a single query?**

   A ❍ DB2 Query Patroller
   B ❍ DB2 Warehouse Manager
   C ❍ DB2 Relational Connect
   D ❍ DB2 Connect Enterprise Edition

5. **Which of the following products can be used to store image data in a DB2 database?**

   A ❍ Net.Data
   B ❍ Net Search
   C ❍ DB2 Audio, Video, Image (AIV) Extenders
   D ❍ DB2 XML Extenders
   E ❍ DB2 Text Extenders

Answers

1 **B.** DB2 Connect is needed to go from a distributed version of DB2 to DB2 on a host or mainframe. DB2 has the functionality built in to service data requests from DB2 on host or mainframe machines. *See "DB2 Editions."*

2 **C.** DB2 Connect Personal Edition is a product that would provide the needed functionality, but it isn't available on AIX. DB2 Connect Personal Edition ships with DB2 Universal Personal Developer's Edition, but that isn't going to run on AIX. DB2 Connect ships with DB2 Universal Developer's Edition. *Review "DB2 Editions."*

3 **A.** ETL stands for Extract, Transformation, and Load. These are functions provide by DB2 Warehouse Manager. *See "DB2 Warehouse Manager."*

4 **C.** DB2 Relational Connect allows you to query DB2 and Oracle databases in the same unit of work. *See "DB2 Relational Connect."*

5 **C.** The TAIV (Text, Audio, Image, and Video) Extenders allow you to work with non-traditional types of data. *See "The DB2 extenders."*

Chapter 5

Installing a DB2 Server

Exam Objectives

- Ability to Install DB2 Universal Database, DB2 Clients & Developers Edition
- Knowledge of concepts of Data Warehouse and OLAP issues
- Ability to describe the functionality of the Administration Server Instance (DAS)

This chapter introduces you to the DB2 server, the software that handles all of the exciting things that DB2 can do for you. In this chapter, you find what you need to know to install a DB2 server, and some useful information about some of the components that come with a DB2 server.

Quick Assessment

Understanding DB2 servers

1 A DB2 Workgroup Edition Version 7 server can run on the following Windows platforms: _____ and ____________.

2 DB2 for _____ and DB2 for ____ will run on an IBM System/390 host.

Installing DB2 servers

3 In order to install a copy of DB2 for Windows on a Windows NT or Windows 2000 machine, the user account you use to perform the installation must have at least what level of authority?

Using Business Intelligence

4 DB2's OLAP solution is based on what leading vendor's OLAP software?

Understanding DB2 acronyms

5 OLTP stands for ___________________.

6 OLAP stands for ______________________.

7 The Database Administration Server is often referred to as the ______ and is used by the ______ to help _______ your database environment.

Answers

1 *Windows NT, Windows 2000*. See the introduction at the start of this chapter.

2 *OS/390, VM/VSE.* See the introduction at the start of this chapter.

3 *Local Administrator authority on the local machine*. See "User account".

4 *Hyperion Essbase solution*. See "Getting to know MR. OLAP".

5 *Online Transaction Processing*. See "Getting to know MR. OLAP".

6 *Online Analytical Processing.* See "Getting to know MR. OLAP".

7 *DAS, DB2 tools, manage*. See "Doing it with the DAS."

DB2 can run on all sorts of different operating systems. You can find DB2 on IBM's mainframes (for example, System/390 or AS/400) and the ever-popular Windows operating systems, as well as UNIX environments. You can even find a version of DB2 for Personal Digital Assistants (PDAs), such as a Palm Pilot, and on a cellular phone as well! This version of DB2 is called *DB2 Everyplace,* but is sometimes just referred to as *DB2e*.

You aren't expected to know anything about DB2 Everyplace on the DB2 Fundamentals exam.

When people refer to DB2 on the *distributed* platforms, they're talking about DB2 for OS/2, Windows, or UNIX. If you hear someone refer to DB2 on the *mainframe* or *host,* the reference likely means DB2 for OS/390 (formerly called DB2 for MVS), DB2 for VM/VSE, or DB2 for AS/400. Finally, when someone talks about a *pervasive* version of DB2, that person is referring to DB2e or DB2 Satellite Edition. For more information about the different DB2 products that are available, see Chapter 4, "An Introduction to DB2 Products and Packaging."

When you see the word UNIX in this chapter, assume that we're talking about Linux here as well. Most of the world usually equates the two. However, some really technical people who talk about UNIX may not equate the two. Technically, they're right for reasons outside the scope of this book. Just keep this in the back of your mind.

This chapter shows you how to install DB2 on a computer running Windows NT or Windows 2000 (from now on, we refer to these platforms simply as Windows). The DB2 Fundamentals Exam is supposed to be platform independent between the offerings of DB2 on the mainframe, OS/2, UNIX, and Windows. Keeping with this notion, you don't need to spend precious prep hours on stuff that won't be on the exam! Because a copy of DB2 for Windows is included in the back of this book, we provide detailed instructions on how to install DB2 on Windows (this way, you can be sure that you're able to complete the exercises in this book).

In this chapter, the term *DB2 for Windows* refers to any Windows 32-bit operating system that a DB2 server runs on. A DB2 server can be installed on a computer running Windows NT or Windows 2000. A particular version of DB2 can even be installed on Windows 95, 98, or Me. This version of DB2 is called DB2 Personal Edition. DB2 Personal Edition can't support DB2 clients and comes with a couple of other minor limitations, but deep inside, it's DB2. Again, if you need to know more about the different versions of DB2 that are available, see Chapter 4.

If you are starting to panic because you thought an S/390 was a type of Mercedes and you wouldn't know a mainframe if it came up and said, "Hello," don't worry! First, mainframes never come up and say hello. Second, the DB2 Fundamentals exam doesn't require you to know anything with respect to how to install DB2 on the different operating systems that it runs on. You are, however, expected to understand the different components and concepts that are presented to you during an installation, so pay attention to the "Installing a DB2 Server on a Windows NT or Windows 2000-Based Workstation" section to properly prepare for your exam.

After you learn how to install a DB2 server, we show you how to create the sample DB2 databases and help you with taking your first steps with DB2. Do yourself a favor and make sure that you follow all our recommendations throughout this chapter; we rely on this extensively throughout the book and in the exercises.

Knowing What You Need to Install a DB2 Server

The term *DB2 server* refers to the software on your computer that allows you to create and control your databases, and also allows DB2 clients to connect to your computer and retrieve data from it. If you don't have a DB2 server, databases *cannot* exist on your computer (unless you have installed Personal Edition). Of course, you can use a DB2 client to connect to a DB2 server and retrieve data from the server. Figure 5-1 shows a DB2 server. For information on DB2 Clients, see Chapter 4.

When people refer to a DB2 server, they sometimes include DB2 Personal Edition, which can cause confusion because a DB2 Personal Edition server cannot service DB2 clients. When talking about database servers, people don't always mean in the sense of client/server environments as most tech heads know them. They mean the database server that manages data.

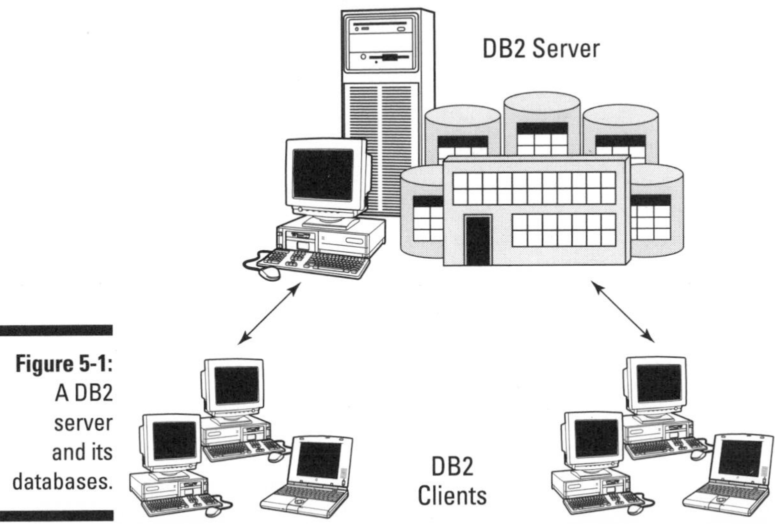

Figure 5-1: A DB2 server and its databases.

This section introduces you to all the requirements that you should be aware of before attempting to install DB2 on Windows. Because a copy of DB2 for Windows is included in the back of this book, all the examples relate to the Windows 2000 environment. If you are installing DB2 on an OS/2 or UNIX-based computer, you still need to address the same requirements for DB2, but the way you go about this is different. Check out the Quick Beginnings Guide that comes with your copy of DB2 for more information if you are installing DB2 on OS/2 or a UNIX-based platform.

If you don't have a copy of the Quick Beginnings Guide on hand, you can view a copy online at `www.ibm.com/cgi-bin/db2www/data/db2/udb/winos2unix/support/v7pubs.d2w/`.

To install the DB2 server that we provide on the CD-ROM in the back of the book, you need an IBM-compatible PC with an Intel-compatible processor. You also need hard drive space on your computer, some memory (random access memory, or RAM), and a processor with a certain amount of power (which is measured in MHz).

If you want to get a DB2 client to talk to a DB2 server, which you need to know for the exam, you're also going to need some communication software (for example TCP/IP) installed and configured on your system. Table 5-1 shows the suggested configuration for installing a DB2 for Windows server to use with the preparation for your exam. The following sections also briefly discuss each requirement for the Windows environment. A detailed list of prerequisites is available from the DB2 Launchpad, which you will see in just a bit.

Table 5-1 Suggested Hardware Requirements for a DB2 Server

Requirement	*Suggested Values*
CPU	Pentium-II class or higher
Free Hard Drive Space*	500MB
Memory (RAM)	128MB
Operating System**	Windows NT version 4.0 with Service Pack 5 or higher (or Windows 2000)
Communication Software	TCP/IP, NetBIOS, Named Pipes, IPX/SPX, or APPC

**The physical disk requirements are based on the NTFS file system and not the FAT file system. If you're using a FAT file system, you should expect these values to be considerably higher.*

***If you're installing DB2 Version 7.1 on a Windows NT–based workstation, it must be Windows NT Version 4.0 with Service Pack 5 or higher.*

CPU

The CPU (central processing unit) is the heart of your computer, and its speed can make a big difference in how smoothly DB2 runs on your workstation. You should have at least 233 MHz of clock speed with your processor, but we suggest more. Make sure that your processor is Intel compatible (meaning that Intel-compatible processors such as AMD's Athlon or Transmeta's Crusoe are okay, too, but that you can't get the copy of DB2 in the back of this book to run on a DEC processor).

Free Hard Drive Space

You can't install a DB2 server if you don't have the hard drive space for it. Sounds reasonable enough, doesn't it? The amount of hard disk space that DB2 takes on your computer is referred to as its *footprint*. You need to have enough hard disk space available to accommodate the size of the DB2 server's footprint (and any data you want to store in DB2).

The footprint for a DB2 server can sometimes be a tough thing to pinpoint with all the components and installation options that you have. Thankfully, the DB2 installation program helps you determine whether you have enough disk space to handle DB2.

On a Windows 2000 workstation, you can check the amount of free space on a drive as follows:

1. **Double-click the My Computer icon on your desktop.**
2. **Right-click the icon representing the hard drive that you want to see the free space for and then select Properties.**

   A Properties window similar to Figure 5-2 opens, informing you of the selected drive's free space.

On some versions of Windows, the free space available on the selected drive will be shown after it is selected in the left pane of the My Computer folder. If this is the case, you don't need to right-click on the selected drive and select the Properties option.

When you're a certified pro with DB2, you can definitely prune the size of the DB2 footprint. Because you're in learning mode here, however, we strongly recommend that you have at least 500MB of free space available on the drive where you want to install your DB2 server. That amount of space ensures that you can install all the tutorials and sample files that will help you prepare for exam day.

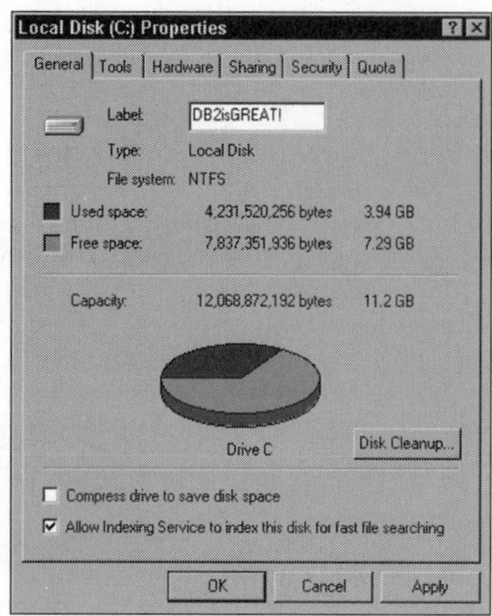

Figure 5-2: A pie chart showing the amount of available space on a selected computer's hard drive.

Memory (RAM)

You need memory to run a computer and unfortunately yours alone is not going to cut it! All applications use your computer's memory to reduce the amount of Input/Output (called I/O by those who thrive on jargon) on your machine's devices. Computer nerds refer to this type of memory as RAM, and if you're really stuffy, you'll call it Random Access Memory.

Windows-based workstations also use paging space to boost the amount of memory on a workstation. *Paging space* is actually a file that the computer uses to store and retrieve memory information. The combination of RAM and paging space is called *virtual memory.* DB2 takes advantage of virtual memory by using the swapping mechanism for the operating system on which it's running. The amount of memory you require to run a DB2 server depends on the number of DB2 clients that you're planning to have concurrently connected to the DB2 server, and whether you plan to run the DB2 tools. We recommend that you have at least 32MB of RAM if you're planning to support up to five DB2 clients simultaneously. For each group of five more DB2 clients that connect to the DB2 server at the same time, add another 4MB of RAM. So, for example, if 25 DB2 clients are going to connect to your DB2 server simultaneously, you need at least 48MB of RAM. If you're planning to use the DB2 management tools to manage your DB2 environment, which you will do while you prepare for your exam, you should add another 32MB of RAM.

To use the exercises in this book and prepare for the big exam, you should have at least 64MB of RAM, but we strongly suggest that you make this a minimum of 128MB.

To check the amount of RAM on a Windows workstation, right-click the My Computer icon and select Properties from the pop-up menu. The System Properties dialog box appears, as shown in Figure 5-3 (the General tab should be the default, but if it isn't, simply click the tab to select it).

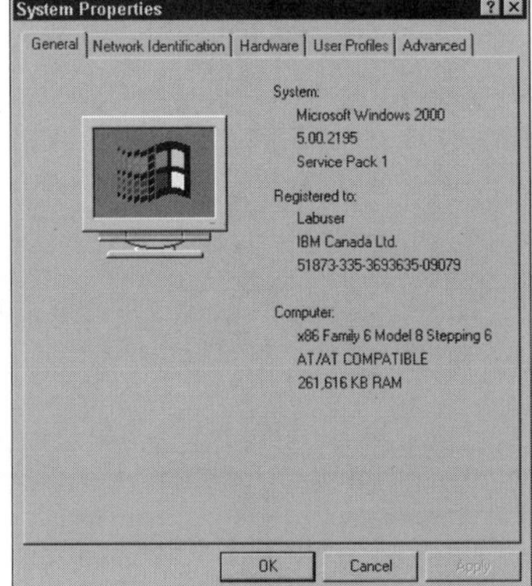

Figure 5-3: The System Properties window shows how much RAM is on your machine.

As you can see in Figure 5-3, one of the authors has a very passable 261MB of RAM on his computer. Unlike the space requirement, however, if you don't have enough memory, you can still run and install a DB2 server. However, if you use a DB2 server without enough memory, it'll likely seem painfully slow and you may ultimately receive some sort of "Out of memory" error. If you get an error like this, or if you're able to completely cook a box of Kraft dinner before a function in the Control Center completes, you've got memory problems.

Operating system

To install a DB2 server using the CD in the back of the book, your computer needs to be running at least Microsoft Windows NT Version 4.0 with Service Pack 5 (SP5) or later or Windows 2000.

If you are running Windows NT and you need to ensure which Service Pack is installed on your computer (you don't need a service pack for Windows 2000), check out the blue window that you see when your Windows NT–based workstation boots up. If you have SP5 or higher, you're fine. Otherwise, you need to upgrade to a supported Service Pack. To get a Service Pack, visit the Microsoft Windows Web site at `www.microsoft.com/ntserver/default.asp`.

Communication software (or protocols)

The computer on which you install a DB2 server should be on a network and have a functional communication protocol running. In fact, when you use any of the supplied DB2 installation programs for DB2 on any distributed platforms, it automatically configures your DB2 instances for communications. Take it from people who used to have to configure the server instances for communications manually. DB2 supports the following protocols: TCP/IP, NetBIOS/NetBEUI, IPX/SPX, Named Pipes, and APPC. Depending on the platform on which you install DB2, or the platform where the DB2 client resides that you want to connect to the DB2 server, you may or may not have support for all these protocols. We suggest that you install your DB2 server and complete the exercises in this book on a workstation that has TCP/IP running. TCP/IP is pretty much the universal protocol of choice these days; it is easy to use and likely on your computer. Do you connect to the Internet? If so, then you have TCP/IP.

The term *protocol* is just fancy computer talk for a language that computers use to talk to each other. If one computer speaks only TCP/IP and another computer speaks only APPC, then those two computers cannot talk to each other. To find out whether you have a supported protocol, ask your main computer guru (one hint: about 95 percent of the computers today run TCP/IP). If you need to find out what platforms of DB2 support what protocols, refer to the *DB2 and DB2 Connect Installation and Configuration Supplement,* which is available after you install your DB2 server or at the Web site noted earlier in this chapter.

So that you don't have any problems with the examples in this book, make sure that your computers (the ones you will use for the DB2 server and the DB2 client) can talk to each other using TCP/IP. You can quickly verify that the computer that will become the DB2 server and the computer that will become the DB2 client can talk to each other using TCP/IP by entering the **ping <*hostname*>** command, where <*hostname*> is the name of the computer that you're trying to talk to.

If you don't know the hostname for your computer, enter the hostname command. Doing so returns the hostname of your computer, which is usually the same as your computer name.

So, if you entered the hostname command on the machine that will become the DB2 client and found out that its hostname is cr689923-a, then you would enter **ping cr668934-a** on the DB2 server machine. You would follow the same steps on the DB2 client (when you determine the hostname of the DB2 server) to make sure that they can talk to each other using TCP/IP.

Figure 5-4 shows the successful results of determining a computer's hostname and pinging the remote computer on the network using TCP/IP. Try this with the two computers you have selected to become the DB2 server and DB2 client in Lab 5-1.

```
Command Prompt
Microsoft Windows 2000 [Version 5.00.2195]
(C) Copyright 1985-2000 Microsoft Corp.

C:\>ping cr689923-a

Pinging cr689923-a [192.168.255.0] with 32 bytes of data:

Reply from 192.168.255.0: bytes=32 time<10ms TTL=128
Reply from 192.168.255.0: bytes=32 time<10ms TTL=128
Reply from 192.168.255.0: bytes=32 time<10ms TTL=128
Reply from 192.168.255.0: bytes=32 time<10ms TTL=128

Ping statistics for 192.168.255.0:
    Packets: Sent = 4, Received = 4, Lost = 0 (0% loss),
Approximate round trip times in milli-seconds:
    Minimum = 0ms, Maximum =  0ms, Average =  0ms

C:\>hostname
cr689923-a

C:\>_
```

Figure 5-4: The cr689923-a machine responding to a ping command.

Lab 5-1 Ensuring that future DB2 server and DB2 client can communicate using TCP/IP

1. **On the computer that will become the DB2 server, enter** ping *<hostname>*, **where *<hostname>* is the TCP/IP hostname of the computer that will become the DB2 client.**

2. **On the machine that will become the DB2 client, enter** ping *<hostname>*, **where *<hostname>* is the TCP/IP hostname of the computer that will become the DB2 server.**

User account

You need a user account to perform the installation. A *user account* is the Windows term for the combination of a username and password, which you most likely use every day when you get to work and log on to your computer.

The user account that you use to install a DB2 server must

- Belong to the local *Administrators* group
- Not exceed 28 characters in length
- Have the following advanced user rights:
    - Act as part of the operating system
    - Increase quotas
    - Create a token object
    - Replace a process-level token

You may need to talk to your administrator to get these system rights and permissions, or to create a new user account. Usually, Administrator authority isn't given out to just anyone, so you may have to pull some teeth at work to get it. Just promise whoever is in charge that you won't do anything bad, such as install a copy of Oracle!

If you want more information on assigning rights and privileges to user accounts in Windows, refer to your operating system's online help.

Installing a DB2 Server on a Windows NT or Windows 2000–Based Workstation

You're ready to install a DB2 server on your Windows computer. You can use the copy of DB2 that's on the CD-ROM at the back of this book. This CD-ROM offers a version of DB2 called DB2 Workgroup Edition Version 7 that expires (stops working) after 60 days unless you buy it. This is called a Try-and-Buy version. The 60-day time period should be more than enough time for you to prepare for your DB2 Fundamentals Certification exam.

If you need more time than 60 days to prepare for the exam, you can uninstall and reinstall your trial version of DB2. We show you how to uninstall a DB2 product at the end of this chapter.

To install DB2 on your Windows NT or Windows 2000 workstation, follow the steps in Lab 5-2 (be sure to install of the DB2 components, as outlined in these steps):

Lab 5-2 Installing a DB2 Workgroup Edition for Windows Server

1. **Log on to your computer with a user account that meets the requirements for performing a DB2 installation.**

   For information on user accounts, see the "User account" section earlier in this chapter.

2. **Shut down any programs that are currently running.**

   You should never install any software on your computer when other programs are running; at least that is what the folks at Microsoft always tell us, so we're telling you the same thing.

3. **Insert the CD-ROM from the back of the book into the CD-ROM drive.**

   The auto-run feature automatically starts the DB2 installation program. The DB2 installation program is called *setup.exe* on the CD-ROM. People refer to the *DB2 Installation* or *setup* program when talking about the software that installs DB2 on a workstation. The setup program determines your computer's system language.

If the setup program fails to start, you can manually start it from a Windows command prompt by switching to the CD-ROM drive and entering the ***x*:\setup** command, where *x* represents the letter for your CD-ROM drive.

4. **Click the Install option in the DB2 Launchpad to start installing a DB2 server.**

   When you start the DB2 setup program, the DB2 Launchpad opens, as shown in Figure 5-5. This is new for DB2 Version 7.1 server installations. The DB2 Launchpad offers you many features, aside from just starting the DB2 installation program.

   You can view the minimum requirements for a DB2 server installation by clicking Installation Prerequisites. (Keep in mind that the prerequisites are for using a DB2 server, not for using a DB2 server to prepare for the DB2 Fundamentals exam with the exercises in this book. Stick at least to what we recommend in this book.)

   Clicking Release Notes opens an HTML page that contains all the last-minute information that didn't quite make it into the manuals before they were printed.

   The Quick Tour gives you an interactive presentation that introduces the features, benefits, and capabilities of DB2 Version 7.1 (we suggest you take it, but wait until after the installation in the "Taking your first steps with DB2" section in this chapter) and, of course, clicking Exit closes the installation program.

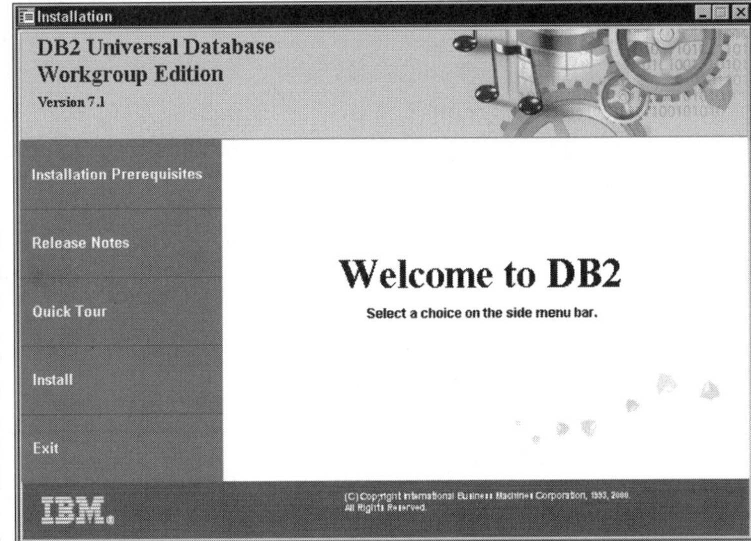

Figure 5-5: The DB2 Launchpad, your gateway to DB2 and a bunch of useful information.

5. **Select the DB2 product that you want to install from the Select Products window and click Next.**

   For this example, ensure that only the DB2 Workgroup Edition check box is selected as shown in Figure 5-6.

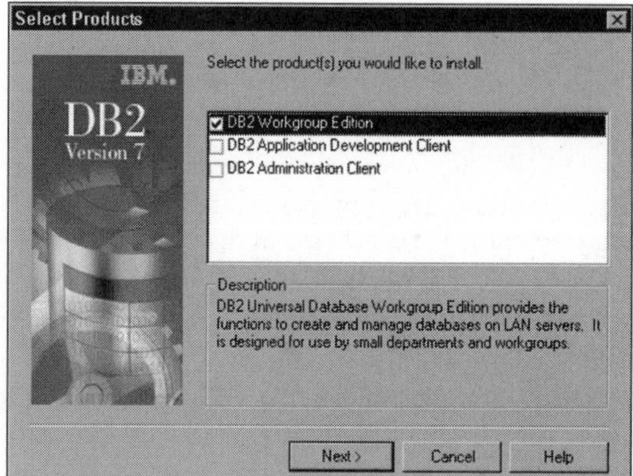

Figure 5-6: Selecting the products you want to install.

To highlight a product and read its description, click the product name instead of the check box. If you do so, a check mark does not appear beside the product name. If you want to select a product, make sure that it has a check mark in its associated check box.

Each DB2 server CD-ROM comes with a copy of a DB2 server (in this case, DB2 Workgroup Edition), a DB2 Administration Client, and a DB2 Application Development Client. For more information on DB2 clients, see Chapter 6, "Installing a DB2 Client."

6. **From the Select Installation Type window, select the radio button that corresponds to the type of installation that you want to perform, as shown in Figure 5-7, and click Next.**

   To get a better feel for the entire installation, select the Custom radio button and click Next.

   When you install a DB2 server on a Windows machine, you have to choose the type of installation that you want to perform. You can select any of the following installation types:

   - **Typical:** The fastest way to get a complete DB2 product installed. All the typical components and default settings are installed on your computer, and the setup program takes care of most of the decisions. Unless you're an expert or need a Compact installation, always install a DB2 server by using a Typical installation.

In this chapter, we show you a Custom DB2 server installation so that we can take you through all the DB2 installation windows that you could possibly see when performing a DB2 installation on a Windows workstation. If you chose a Typical installation, you may not see all the windows in the DB2 installation process. That isn't a big deal; just read this section and you should be fine for the exam.

- **Custom:** Allows you to select specific components and details of a DB2 server installation, giving you complete control over which components get installed on your workstation and which ones don't. You also get the choice to change some of the default settings that are used for an installation. Usually, experienced people with DB2 use this installation method because they know that they have no need for a specific component and don't want to hog hard drive space with components that are not used, or perhaps they need a component that is not part of a Typical installation.
- **Compact:** This option is for people who don't have the space on their workstation for a hefty DB2 server installation and just want to get the bare essentials. This option won't install the DB2 documentation or graphical tools, including but not limited to the Control Center, the Command Center, First Steps, or the Client Configuration Assistant. If you're in a position in which you can install only a Compact version of DB2, then you may want to consider buying a bigger hard drive! Selecting this option will not give you the tools that you need to prepare for your DB2 exam.

To prepare for the DB2 Fundamentals Exam, you *must* select a Typical or Custom installation.

If you choose to perform a Compact installation of DB2, you won't be able to follow most of the exercises and examples in this book.

Beside each installation type is a rough approximation of the hard drive space required to install the selected DB2 server.

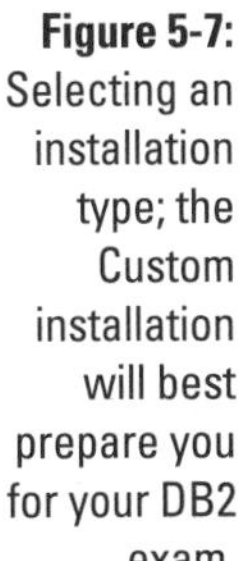

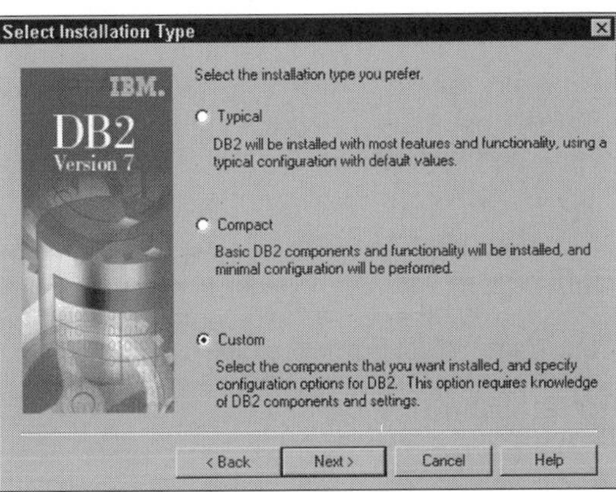

Figure 5-7: Selecting an installation type; the Custom installation will best prepare you for your DB2 exam.

7. **From the Select Components window, select or deselect any DB2 server components and subcomponents that you want or do not want to install.**

   For our example, ensure that all the DB2 components and subcomponents are selected for installation, as shown in Figure 5-8. (Notice that we don't ask you to click Next when you've finished selecting all the DB2 components and subcomponents? You didn't? Good!)

   The instructions in this book assume that every component and subcomponent is selected for installation.

   If you selected a Typical or Compact installation, you would not have the option to select components for your DB2 server installation. In a Typical installation, all the DB2 components that are typically used would be selected by default. If you selected a Compact installation, only the minimum components that are needed to run DB2 would be installed (and there aren't many). In either case, if you wanted to add a component to a Typical or Compact DB2 server installation, you would need to run the DB2 installation program again and select a Custom installation.

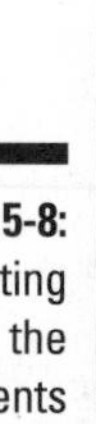

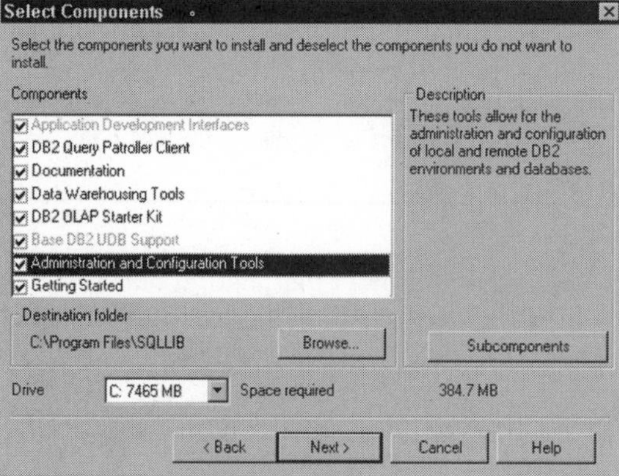

Figure 5-8: Selecting the components you want in a Custom installation.

In the Select Components window shown in Figure 5-8, you can see a brief description of any component by highlighting it and reading its associated description in the Description box on the right side of the window.

If you're the type of person who needs to know it all (and you should be if you are preparing for this exam), read and make notes on the description for each component in Figure 5-8. We recommend that you commit to memory the different components that are used (and yes, you are asked questions on the exam about them) in a DB2 environment.

If all you want to do is highlight a component, don't click the check box — click a component's name instead. To select or deselect a component, click in the actual check box. To ensure that a component is selected for installation, make sure that a check mark appears in the component's associated check box.

As you can see in Figure 5-8, one of the components we selected is Administration Configuration Tools. Did you notice when you selected this component (and some others) that the Subcomponents button in the Description box suddenly became active?

No, it wasn't your mind playing tricks on you when you went through the different component descriptions! Some components have subcomponents and some do not. If you click the Subcomponents button, you can see the subcomponents for a selected component, as shown in the example in Figure 5-9.

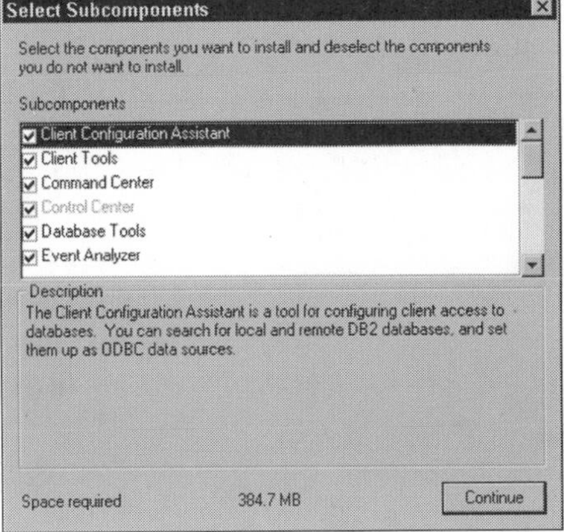

Figure 5-9: Selecting the subcomponents of the Administration and Configuration Tools component.

After you select the subcomponents for a component, click Continue. You can then move on to other components and repeat the whole sordid process. Perhaps you can now see why people choose a Typical install. When you have a big enough hard drive, it's worth the few megabytes of hard drive space to not have to haggle with all these components (unless, of course, you need them).

We suggest that you also ensure that you select all the subcomponents for each component that will be installed. Because you are preparing to be Fundamentally certified (DB2, that is) we want you to select every component and subcomponent. Doing so requires that you select each component and go through all the subcomponents for each component and manually select it, so you may as well read all the subcomponent descriptions as well. Trust us, you will thank us later when you receive a passing grade.

8. **Select the location where you want to install your DB2 server in the same window that you used to select the DB2 server components in Figure 5-8; then click Next.**

   You can click the Browse button to select a target drive and directory. The default installation directory is *x*:\Program Files\SQLLIB, where *x:* is the drive on which you installed your Windows operating system.

   Clicking the Drive drop-down box shows the space available on each of the hard drives on your system. You can compare this to the Space Required field to ensure that you have enough hard disk space to install the DB2 server. The information here may help you select a more suitable directory in the Destination Folder box.

   If you clicked Next after selecting the components for your DB2 installation, you can click Back to return to the Select Components window and select an appropriate installation directory.

9. **In the Configure DB2 Services window, select and configure the protocols and startup options that you want to use in your DB2 environment from the screen shown in Figure 5-10 and click Next.**

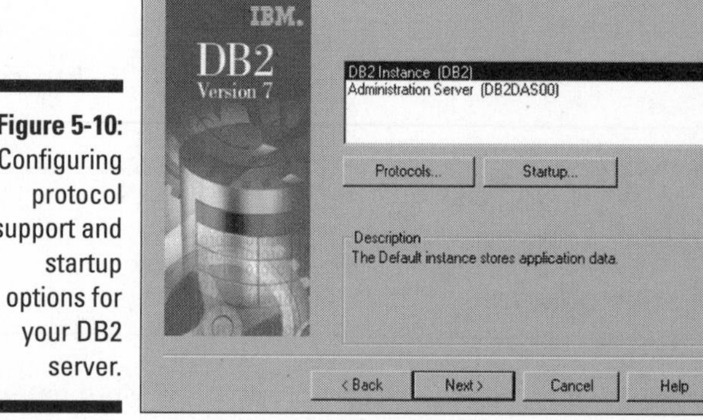

Figure 5-10: Configuring protocol support and startup options for your DB2 server.

   By default, the DB2 installation program will create two instances for your environment. One is called DB2, which will act as the default instance for your environment. The other is called DB2DAS00 (or DB2AS in the UNIX world), which is exclusively used by the Administration Server for management purposes (more on that in a bit). If you need to know more about instances, check out Chapter 9, "Database Building Blocks." You should know that you don't need to know anything about instances at this point, what you need to know is coming later in this book.

   Wondering what a Database Administration Server is? First, it is important to know that this is often referred to as the Administration Server or DAS for short. It is a special instance that is used by the DB2 management tools to manage local and remote DB2 server systems. It is really the brains behind the Control Center and helps the Client Configuration Assistant find and locate databases on your network. You do need to understand what the Administration Server is and what it is used for in order to pass the exam, so be sure to read the "Doing it with the DAS" section in this chapter.

The DB2 installation program will automatically detect and configure your DB2 server for any communication protocols that are detected on your system. Click Next and go to Step 10; all the default settings are fine.

Remember, we assume in this book that you're installing a copy of DB2 that we gave you, and on a workstation that has TCP/IP running on it.

In the Configure DB2 Services dialog box (shown in Figure 5-10), you can set up protocol support for the two instances that the DB2 installation program creates.

Setting up communications for any instance is the same, so we show you how to do it for the default DB2 instance.

To manually select which protocols you want the setup program to configure for your DB2 server, follow Steps 1 through 5 here (and then you pick back up at Step 10 in this lab):

1. **Select the instance that you want to configure.**
2. **Click the Protocols button.**

   The Customize the DB2 Instance dialog box appears, as shown in Figure 5-11.

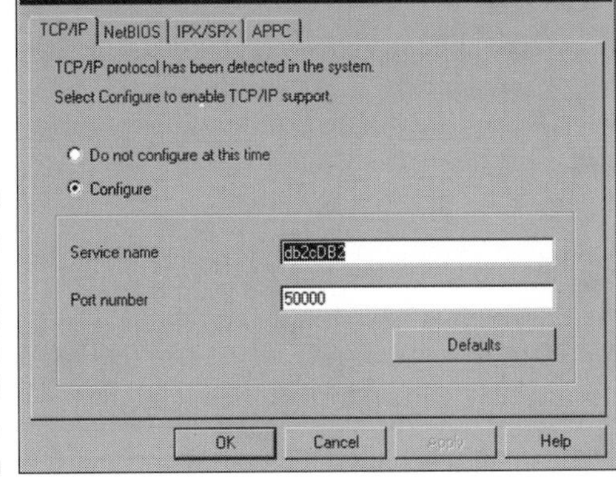

Figure 5-11: Customizing communications support for a DB2 instance.

3. **Select the tab that corresponds to the protocol that you want to configure or disable for your DB2 server.**

4. **Change or add any specific parameters for the protocol that you want to configure; each protocol will have its own specific parameters.**

   Each protocol has a separate tab, as you can see in Figure 5-11. If the DB2 installation program detects that a supported protocol exists on your system, the program generates default values for the protocol's parameters and automatically selects the Configure option for each detected protocol. We suggest that you take whatever defaults the DB2 installation program generates for you.

   In Figure 5-11, you can see that the DB2 installation program has detected TCP/IP on your the computer and generated some default values for it. The values that the setup program provides are fine.

   If TCP/IP isn't detected on your system, check the other tabs to see whether any other protocols have been detected. Found one? Okay, continue on, but you may not be able to follow the instructions in the rest of this book because we assume that TCP/IP is running on your workstation.

   If the Do Not Configure at This Time radio button is selected for a protocol, this means that the protocol was not detected as being functional on your system. You can still enter values for this protocol if you plan to add it at a later time; however, make note of these values because your instances will be configured to use them. We suggest that you just read the instructions in this step and do nothing with the installation defaults that are provided for you.

   If you enter your own value in one of the protocol-specific fields, you can restore the generated default values by clicking Defaults.

5. **Click OK when you've customized each of the protocols that you want supported in your DB2 environment.**

   If you are configuring protocol support for the Administration Server instance (DB2DAS00 in our example), you cannot change the Port Number for TCP/IP or the Socket Number for IPX/SPX. Each of these numbers is registered to work with DB2 and DB2 alone.

   Because instances are configured as services in the Windows environment, they can be automatically started each time you start your computer. This is the default, and we suggest you leave it this way. To set the startup for any instance, select the instance and click the Startup button shown in Figure 5-10.

   You cannot select the startup option for the Administration Server instance in the DB2 installation program. However, you can change the startup option after the installation completes.

10. **In the Define a Local Control Warehouse Database window, specify a user account that will be associated with the Control database in Figure 5-12 below and click Next.**

Because we selected to install all components (which includes the Data Warehouse Manager component), a sample data warehousing environment will be created and the Control database will manage it.

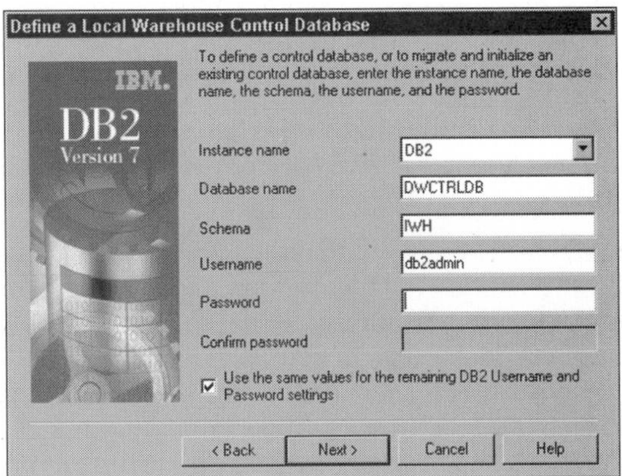

Figure 5-12: Identifying a user account that will be used for the Control database and optionally the other DB2 services setup during a DB2 server installation.

To make the installation as simple as possible, select the Use the Same Values for the Remaining DB2 Username and Password Settings check box shown at the bottom of Figure 5-12. If you don't select this check box, you have to enter the same (or a different) user account for each of the special services that DB2 sets up during the installation. The instructions in this book assume that you select this check box.

By default, the setup program will create a user account using the username `db2admin` and the password that you specify. If you do not specify a password, it will default to `db2admin` — same as the username. You can accept this default user account, create your own user account by modifying the default values, or provide your own. We recommend that you KISS it (keep it simple, stupid) and just come up with your own password.

If the Confirm Password field is not active in Figure 5-12, that means that this user account already exists and you must enter the appropriate password in the Password field.

As already noted, the default username is `db2admin` and the default password is `db2admin`. You can accept these defaults, but we recommend that you don't. We cannot tell you how many machines we've come across where we used the default `db2admin` username and `db2admin` password and logged on to somebody else's machine (it's a favorite trick when we visit customer sites). Did we ever do anything bad to those computers? Of course not; we just left scary reminders for the next user who logs on to see. If you accept the default for the password field, you're creating a definite security exposure.

You can specify a username that already exists on your system, but if you do, you have to specify the correct password. Also, the existing username that you specify must have the same rights and privileges as the user account you're using to install DB2. See the "User account" section earlier in this chapter for more information.

For the exam, it isn't so important to know the user accounts, but you need to understand the services that they are associated with. Assuming that you select the check box shown in Figure 5-12, the `db2admin` user account will be associated with the following:

Default Instance: The default instance for a DB2 installation is called DB2. You can learn what you need to know about instances in Chapter 9. The user account associated with the instance is said to have System Administrative (SYSADM) authority on the instance. By default, after an installation, any user account that belongs to the Administrators group in the Windows world will have SYSADM authority on the default DB2 instance (this means both the user account used to perform the installation and the `db2admin` user account). For more information on DB2 security, check out Chapter 10, "Security and DB2."

Administration Server Instance: This instance is called DB2DAS00 in a Windows environment. DB2-ites refer to the Administration Server as the DAS (as in the Database Administration Server). You can read more about the DAS in the "Doing it with the DAS" section later in this chapter. Because the DAS is really an instance, we cover it in greater detail in Chapter 9.

OLAP Services: If you think OLAP is a government agency, check out the "Getting to know MR. OLAP" section later in this chapter; also see Chapter 4, "An Introduction to DB2 Products and Packaging," to prepare yourself for the exam.

Control Warehouse Database: A data warehouse isn't a place where you can store data for the long term . . . wait a minute, that's exactly what it is! Check out Chapter 4 for more information.

11. **In the Define OLAP Catalog Databases window that appears as shown in Figure 5-13, just click Next.**

Not an exam thing, but it will help in a tutorial we ask you to take to prepare for the exam. In other words, don't touch anything and don't worry about it, but do click Next!

12. **Finally, you're ready to begin the installation: Scroll through the Current Settings box in the Start Copying Files window (shown in Figure 5-14) to see all the DB2 server options and components that will be installed on your machine; then click Next.**

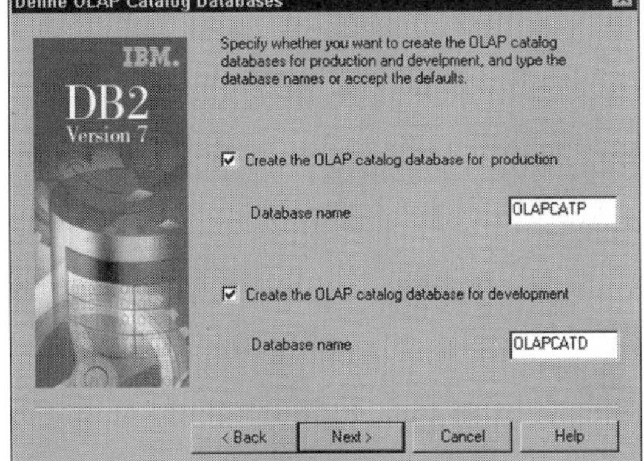

Figure 5-13: The Define OLAP Catalog Databases window.

Figure 5-14: A chance to review your selections and start the installation.

If you're not satisfied, you can click Back to return to any previous installation windows and make changes.

When the installation and configuration of DB2 completes, the Install OLAP Starter Kit windows appears, as shown in Figure 5-16 — but don't jump there just yet; we still have some stuff we want you to know about

13. **Insert the DB2 OLAP Starter Kit CD from the back of your book and select the Install the OLAP Starter Kit radio button and click Continue.**

    When the DB2 installation program has finished installing DB2, it will configure your system with a default environment (this is a good thing because it saves you time and hassles). Depending on your system, this auto-magic configuration can take some time. During the configuration, you see a pop-up window like the one shown in Figure 5-15.

    When the initial DB2 installation and configuration finishes, you're asked whether you want to install the OLAP Starter Kit, as shown in Figure 5-16. (Check out the "Getting to know MR. OLAP" section at the end of this chapter.)

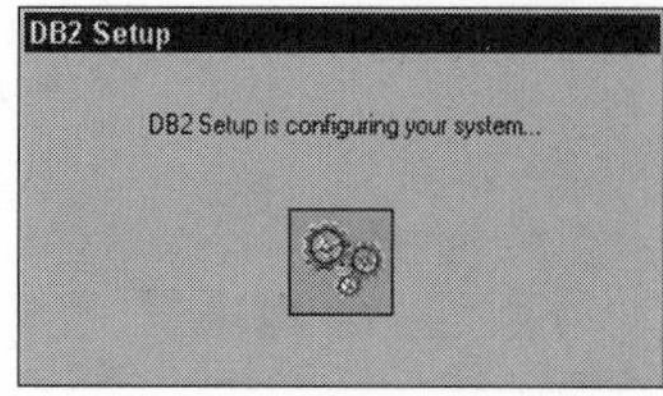

Figure 5-15: The DB2 gears hard at work for you!

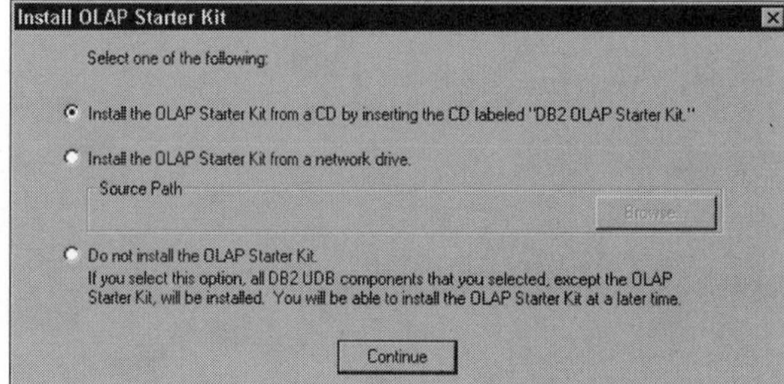

Figure 5-16: Installing the OLAP Starter Kit.

The OLAP Starter Kit is located on a separate CD-ROM from the DB2 server CD-ROM that you are using to install your DB2 server. The OLAP Starter Kit CD-ROM is also located in the back of your book.

To familiarize yourself with everything you need to know for the DB2 Fundamentals exam, you should make sure that you install the OLAP Starter Kit.

After you click Continue, you will see some more of those gears shown in Figure 5-15 while the DB2 installation program continues to configure your system.

If you've mounted the CD-ROMs in the back of this book on network drives, select the Install the OLAP Start Kit from a network drive radio button in Figure 5-16, select the appropriate drive, and click Continue.

14. **When the installation and configuration are finished, you must restart your machine before you can use your DB2 server; select the Yes, I want to restart my computer now radio button shown in Figure 5-17 and click Finish.**

The setup program gives you the option to restart your machine when the installation is finished or at a later time. If you choose to restart your machine at a later time, you cannot use your DB2 server now.

Make sure that you reboot when the setup program asks you to (after the installation is finished, that is). The drama picks up in the next section, where you *finally* get to start using DB2!

In some cases, you may not be forced to reboot your system after a DB2 server installation. If this is the case, the DB2 installation program will just prompt you to click Finish. If this is the case with your DB2 installation, you don't have to reboot your computer before you can begin using DB2.

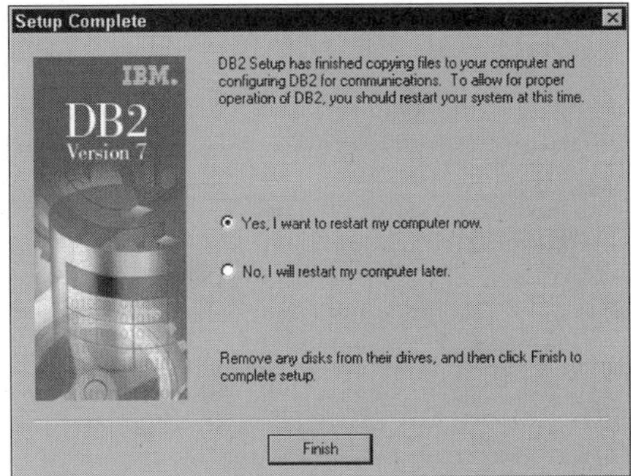

Figure 5-17: Make sure that you restart your computer by selecting the Yes, I Want to Restart My Computer Now radio button.

When the installation is complete, the DB2 server is added to the Start menu, as shown in Figure 5-18. See all the options in the IBM DB2 folder? You should recognize most of the options in the IBM DB2 folder; we discuss them in Chapter 4. By the time you're finished reading this book, you will be able to talk about them at great length and use them to amaze your friends.

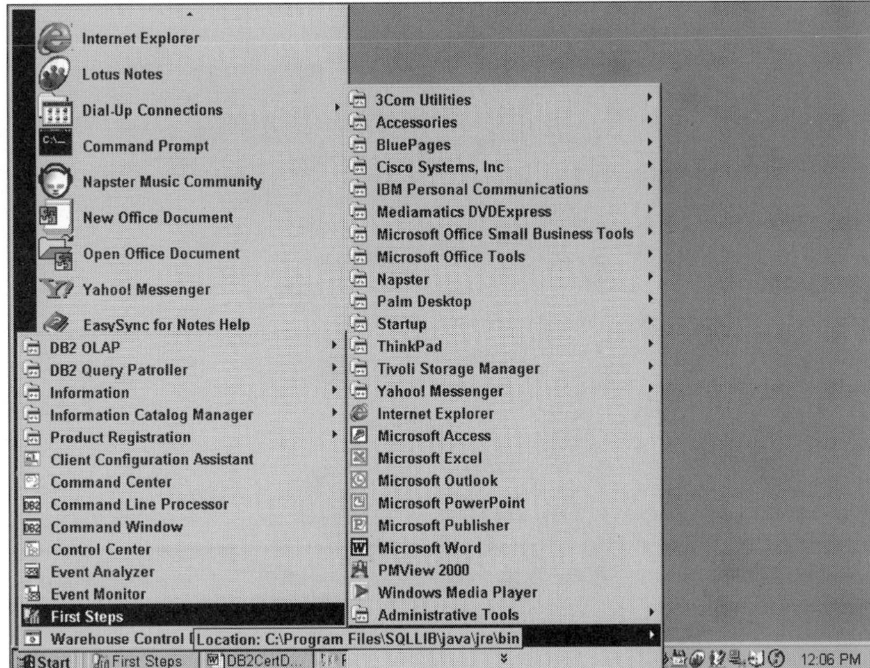

Figure 5-18: DB2 is now in the Start menu, but make sure that you reboot before starting to use it!

Taking your first steps with DB2

So you've finished installing your DB2 server and you've rebooted. Ten minutes later (ah, the beauty of Windows) your operating system starts up.

Log on to your system after the reboot with the same user account that you used to perform the installation (this is going to make things easier). After you log on to your workstation, the DB2 First Steps dialog box appears, as shown in Figure 5-19.

We ask you to log on to your system after the installation with the same user account that you used to perform the installation because we know this user account will have SYSADM authority on the default DB2 instance. By default, after a DB2 installation, any user belonging to the Administrators group in the Windows security system will have SYSADM authority on the default DB2 instance. SYSADM authority is the highest authority that anyone can have in DB2-land. For more information on authorities and security, see Chapter 10.

First Steps is a tool designed to help get you going on DB2. It allows you to create sample databases to help you get to know DB2 better, work with these sample databases by starting the Control Center, take a tutorial on Business Intelligence (relax, there is no pop-quiz afterwards), view DB2's documentation library, and take a Quick Tour of all the enhancements in this version of DB2.

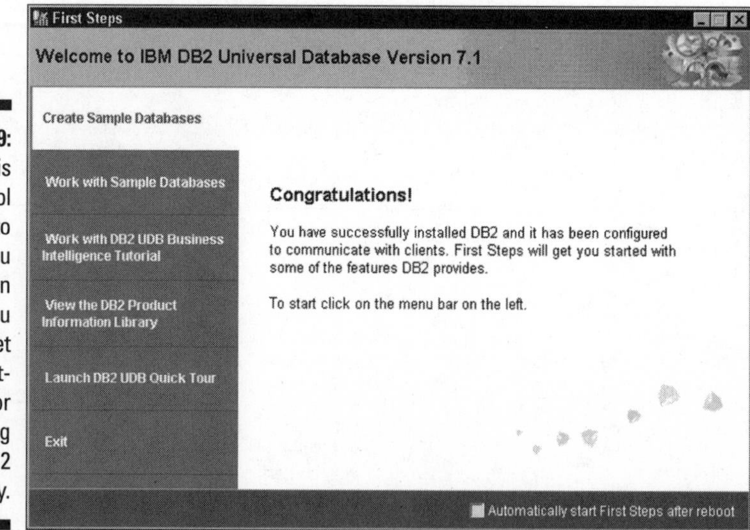

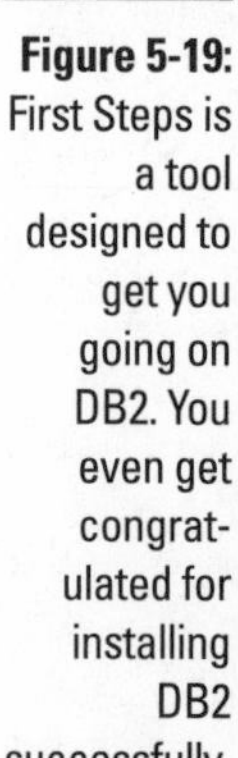
Figure 5-19: First Steps is a tool designed to get you going on DB2. You even get congratulated for installing DB2 successfully.

If First Steps doesn't start or you got scared when the dialog box appeared after you rebooted and shut it down, you can restart it by clicking the Start button and choosing Programs⇨IBM DB2⇨First Steps. First Steps won't open if you performed a Compact or Custom installation and deselected it because it won't be there!

First Steps gives you five options, which we describe in detail in the following sections. To view more details on these options, place the mouse pointer over a button and just let it sit there. The button's Hover Help appears, giving you more details on what action each button performs. The five options available in First Steps are the following:

- **Create Sample Databases:** Gives you the option to create up to three sample databases (one for general DB2 learning, one for Data Warehousing, and one for OLAP analysis) that can be used to experiment with DB2.
- **Work with Sample Databases:** Launches the Control Center, which is the main DB2 graphical management tool. You use the Control Center throughout this book to perform all sorts of management tasks on your DB2 server. You can read more about the Control Center in Chapter 8, "The DB2 Tools."
- **Work with DB2 UDB Business Intelligence Tutorial:** Starts an HTML-based tutorial that introduces you to all the Business Intelligence (BI) features of DB2. DB2 comes with a Data Warehousing tool called the Data Warehouse Center and an OLAP (Online Analytical Processing) tool called the OLAP Starter Kit. A brief discussion about OLAP appears at the end of this chapter, but also check out Chapter 4.
- **View the DB2 Product Information Library:** Launches the Information Center, which contains tips, tricks, Web links, samples, and links to the DB2 documentation, including a task-level help feature.
- **Launch DB2 UDB Quick Tour:** Launches the DB2 Universal Database Quick Tour, an interactive presentation that introduces you to the functions, features, and benefits associated with DB2 Version 7.1. This is the same tour that you had the option to launch in the DB2 Launchpad in Figure 5-5.

It's likely that we don't need to say it, but if you click Exit, you close the First Steps tool. So, in reality, First Steps has six options, but who's counting?

Creating the sample databases

The First Steps tools gives you the option to create up to three sample databases that will help you in your quest for certification. To create the sample database, perform the steps in Lab 5-3.

Lab 5-3 Create the sample databases

1. **Click Create Sample Databases (refer to Figure 5-19). The Create Sample Databases wizard will open, as shown in Figure 5-20.**
2. **Select all three check boxes to create all three sample databases. Each of these sample databases is required to complete all of the exercises in this book.**

If you're looking to pass the exam the first time around, create these databases. Working with them will help you more than you know. Trust us now; thank us later!

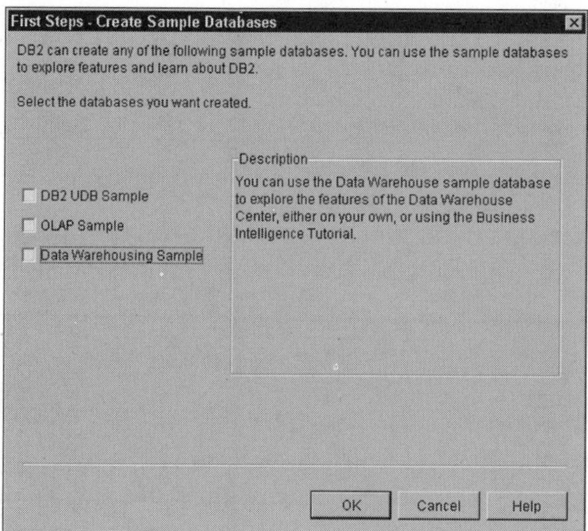
First Steps - Create Sample Databases
DB2 can create any of the following sample databases. You can use the sample databases to explore features and learn about DB2.
Select the databases you want created.
DB2 UDB Sample
OLAP Sample
Data Warehousing Sample
Description
You can use the Data Warehouse sample database to explore the features of the Data Warehouse Center, either on your own, or using the Business Intelligence Tutorial.
OK
Cancel
Help

Figure 5-20: Your First Steps — The Create Sample Databases option is used to create the three different sample databases provided in DB2 that will help you achieve DB2 Fundamentals Certification status.

The sample database that you will use the most in this book is called SAMPLE. All three of the sample databases will be created in the default DB2 instance that was created during the installation. If for some reason you need to know everything you possibly could about the sample databases, check out the DB2 SQL Reference (you can find it in the Information Center; see the "Viewing the documentation" section later in this chapter for more information).

If you didn't install First Steps, you can still create the SAMPLE database by entering **db2sampl** at a Windows command prompt. Entering the **dwcsmp** command creates the Data Warehousing sample database; **olapsmp** creates the OLAP sample database.

When you select the Data Warehousing Sample check box, the Data Warehouse Center Userid and Password dialog box prompts you for a user account, as shown in Figure 5-21. Enter the same user account that you used to install DB2 and are currently logged on to the system with. After you select all the sample databases for creation, click OK.

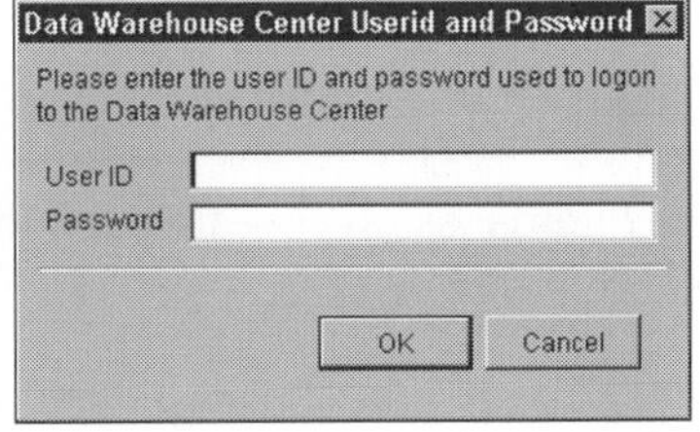

Figure 5-21: The Data Warehouse Center User ID and Password box is used to log on to the Data Warehouse Center to create the sample Data Ware-housing database.

If you get an error entering a user account in the screen shown in Figure 5-21, make sure that you enter the same user account that you used to install DB2 (you should also currently be logged on to the system with this user account). Of course, in the real world, you don't have to do this. This simplifies security right now, but you find out all about security in Chapter 10.

It can take some time for all three of the sample databases to be created. During the creation of these databases, a progress window, like that shown in Figure 5-22, will appear to let you know how things are going.

While the DB2 sample databases are being created, feel free to go about other tasks that you have to get done. When all three sample databases have been created, the OK button will become highlighted and you can then press it to return to First Steps. No message shows up to tell you that DB2 has completed creating the sample databases, though. The only way you can tell that DB2 has finished creating the sample databases is to note that the OK button has become active and that the Elapsed Time field is no longer changing. The time it takes to create all three sample databases depends on your system, but in the end, you should expect it to take about twelve minutes.

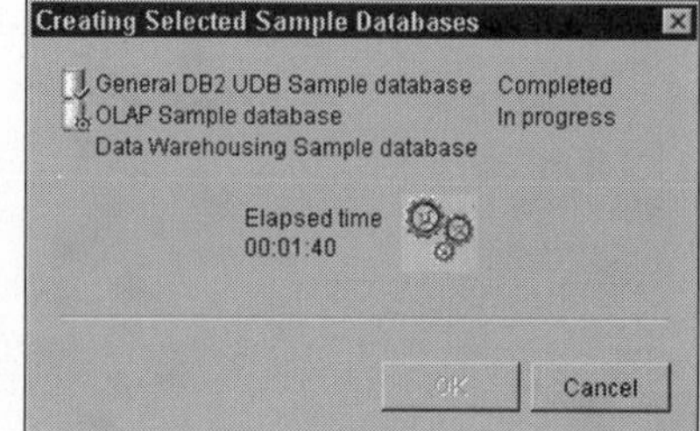

Figure 5-22: Looks like the sample database creation process is coming along just fine!

After you've created all three sample databases, the Create Sample Databases option is no longer selectable from First Steps

Creating a database with real data isn't nearly this easy, especially three of them! First Steps actually calls different script files that create the databases and imports data into them. Later chapters in this book show you how to do this; in the meantime, you can take advantage of the sample databases so that you can work with the rest of this book and not risk damaging your own data, or worse yet, someone else's!

Working with the sample databases

You can use the Control Center to work with your databases and the objects within them. The Control Center is the central management console for your entire DB2 environment. You can even use it to administer remote DB2 systems, and even DB2 on OS/390! You use the Control Center throughout this book to perform all sorts of management tasks on your DB2 server. You can learn more about the Control Center in Chapter 8.

Lab 5-4 Starting the Control Center

1. **Click the Work with Sample Databases button shown previously in Figure 5-19.**

   First Steps launches the Control Center, as shown in Figure 5-23.

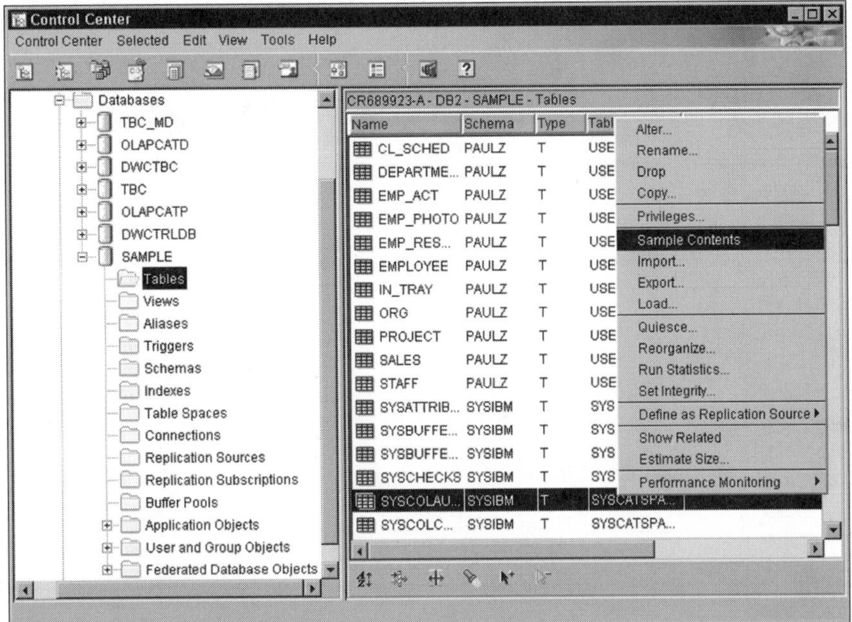

Figure 5-23: The DB2 Control Center.

You can also start the Control Center by clicking the Start button and choosing Programs⇨IBM DB2⇨Control Center, or entering **db2cc** at a Windows command prompt.

To administer any database by using the Control Center, either locally or remotely, you must have a DB2 Administration Server (DAS) running. Worried? Don't be: The DB2 installation program took care of that for you! The DAS is configured to start automatically each time you start your system.

To verify that the DAS is on your system, click Start and select Settings⇨Control Panel. In the Control Panel, double-click the Administrative Tools icon and then double-click the Services icon in the Administration Tools folder. Figure 5-24 shows the DB2DAS00 instance and that it is registered to start automatically each time the system in started. In the Windows environment, instances are registered as DB2 services. Did you see the DB2 instance in Figure 5-24? It is denoted by the "DB2 –" prefix, so it shows up as DB2 – DB2 in the Services folder.

You can use the Control Center to work with any instance or database, local or remote, as long as it has been cataloged on your system. In upcoming chapters, we show you how to use the Control Center to graphically administer your local and remote DB2 servers (even from a remote DB2 client). This is a far easier method than administering your environment by using commands entered in a DB2 command window.

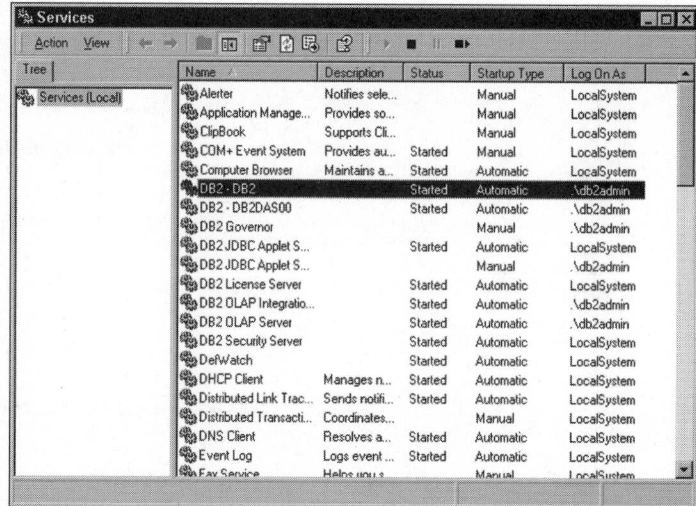

Figure 5-24: The Services folder shows a whole bunch of DB2 services that are registered with the Windows operating system. Some of these services are your DB2 instances. Do you see them?

If the Control Center doesn't start and asks you for a valid user account, ask yourself whether you're logged on to your system with the same user account that you used to install the DB2 server. If you aren't, that's the problem. You can read more about the user account that you need to run the Control Center in Chapter 8.

Working with the DB2 Business Intelligence Tutorial

Want to be a wizard with Business Intelligence? Then this tutorial is for you! To start the tutorial, click the Work with DB2 UDB Business Intelligence Tutorial, as shown in Figure 5-19.

Although you don't need to take this tutorial to prepare for the DB2 Fundamentals Exam, we *strongly* suggest you take it. It helps you understand OLAP and Data Warehousing so that you know those topics cold for the exam. The Business Intelligence tutorial uses the OLAP and Data Warehousing sample databases that we hope you created in the "Create the Sample Databases" section (if you didn't create them, go back and create them now). The tutorial takes you through the whole process of building and using a Data Warehouse. After taking this tutorial, you'll know fancy acronyms and terms such as ETL (Extract, Trasform, and Load), OLAP (Online Analytical Processing), and Multidimensional analysis!

This tutorial really does provide an end-to-end guide for typical Business Intelligence tasks. It has two main sections. The first section focusses on Data Warehousing. The lessons in this section teach you how to use the DB2 Control Center and the Data Warehouse Center to create a Data Warhouse, move and transform source data, and write this data to a target database. Completing this section should take you about 2 hours.

The second section deals with Multidimensional data analysis. The lessons in this section teach you how to use the OLAP Starter Kit to perform relational or multidimensional analysis on data using Online Analytical Processing (OLAP) techniques. Completing this section should take you about an hour. The "MR. OLAP" section at the end of this chapter will give you some more information on OLAP.

Viewing the DB2 documentation

First Steps also gives you a tour of the DB2 documentation — including books, tasks, notebooks, and so on — via the DB2 Information Center. The Information Center (see Figure 5-25) is a central starting point for all the DB2 documentation and is a very useful reference point for discovering more about DB2, performing tasks, and finding more detailed examples of the things you can do with DB2. To start the Information Center, simply click the View the DB2 Product Information Library button in the First Steps dialog box. Read more about the DB2 Information Center in Chapter 8.

You can also start the Information Center by clicking the Start button and choosing Programs⇨IBM DB2⇨Information⇨Information Center or by entering **db2ic** at a Windows command prompt.

The Information Center is shown in Figure 5-25. Take some time to experiment and browse through all of the features of the Information Center. Select different tabs and see all the links to valuable DB2 information.

Taking a Quick DB2 Tour

Click the Launch DB2 UDB Quick Tour field (shown previously in Figure 5-19) to launch a tour that quickly takes you through all the features of DB2. The DB2 Quick Tour is shown in Figure 5-26.

You should definitely go through this tour to prepare for your exam. The tour covers DB2 enhancements and functionality in exam-favorite areas, such as Business Intelligence, e-business, data management, and a host of other things. The tour takes a while to go through but isn't a snoozer. When you finish, you should feel more comfortable with the features that we discuss in this book. The DB2 Quick Tour is a great primer for the exam!

Take the Quick Tour because it'll show you all kinds of things that are referred to in the exam. Not only will you know the answer to many questions, you'll be able to amaze friends with your knowledge of DB2 Version 7.1.

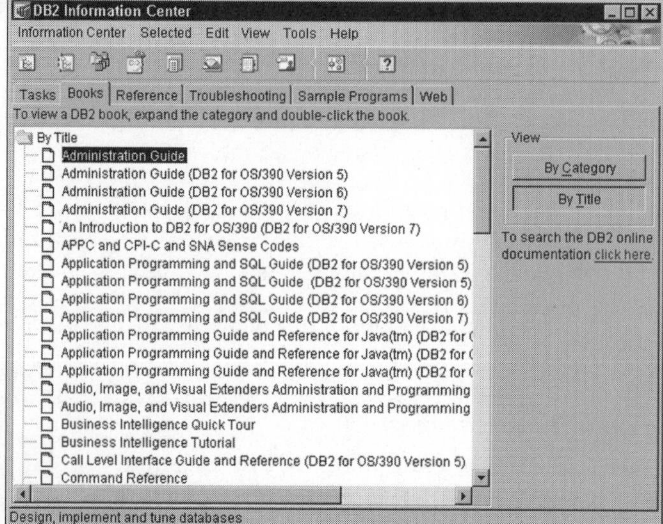

Figure 5-25: The DB2 Information Center.

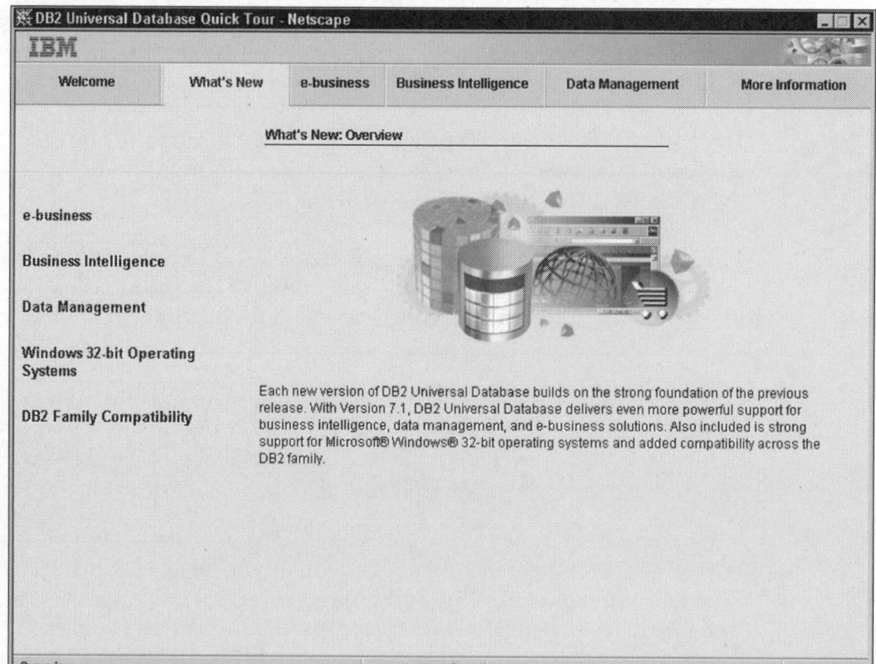

Figure 5-26: A recommended read — The DB2 Quick Tour.

Although we've said it three or four times in this chapter, we'll say it again: Many answers to the exam questions lie in the DB2 Quick Tour and the Data Warehousing Tutorial — take them!

Doing it with the DAS

The DAS (which stands for *database administration server,* though usually it is referred to as DAS or just Administration Server) is a special administration control point for a DB2 server that runs under the covers. In fact, when you get right down to it, it's an instance. The name of the instance is *DB2DAS00* in the Windows world, and in a UNIX-based DB2 environment, it is called *DB2AS* (by default, though, you can call it anything you want in the UNIX world).

The DAS assists the DB2 tools in performing administration tasks on local *and* remote DB2 servers. You *must* have a running DAS if you want remote databases to be able to tell the Client Configuration Assistant that they exist or are using the Control Center to manage a DB2 environment. So, if you don't have a DAS (or one running for that matter), a DB2 client isn't able to administer a remote DB2 server using the Control Center. In fact, if the DAS didn't exist, you wouldn't even be able to manage your own DB2 server. Needless to say, if you want to enjoy all the time the DB2 tools save you, make sure that you have the DAS (which we will create for you during the installation). If you need more information on how to work with the DAS, see Chapter 9.

The DAS assists the Control Center and Client Configuration Assistant when working on the following administration tasks:

- Enabling remote administration of DB2 servers using the Control Center.
- Providing the facilities for job management, including the ability to schedule the execution of both DB2 and operating system command scripts. These command scripts are user defined. The Control Center is used to define the schedule of jobs, view the results of completed jobs, and perform other administrative tasks against jobs located either remotely or locally against the DAS.
- Providing a means for discovering information about the configuration of DB2 instances, databases, and other DB2 Administration Servers in conjunction with the DB2 Discovery utility. This information is used by the Client Configuration Assistant and the Control Center to simplify and automate the configuration of client connections to DB2 databases. You can find out more about the discovery process in Chapter 7 "Getting Clients and Servers Talking."

You can have only one DAS per physical machine, and it is so powerful that one is all you need! If you're running DB2 Enterprise — Extended Edition, which is a physically partitioned version of DB2, you would have a DAS for each node in your environment, but that is out of the scope of this discussion and for the DB2 Family Fundamentals exam.

Because the DAS is so obviously important, it is created and set to start each time you start your computer by the DB2 installation program. In the Windows world, because it is an instance, the DB2 installation program sets the DAS up as a service and the startup is set to *automatic*.

Remember from Step 10 of the installation instructions that you set up a user account with the username `db2admin`; that is the user account associated with the DAS.

The DAS is also used to perform remote tasks on a DB2 for OS/390 host system on behalf of a DB2 request from the Control Center or the Client Configuration Assistant on a distributed platform.

Because the DAS is so important and it can do so much, the user account associated with it needs to have System Administrative (SYSADM) authority on the DB2 system. When the DB2 installation program created the `db2admin` user account for you, it gave it SYSADM authority by default. If you ever need to drop and recreate the DAS, make sure that the user account you specify for the DAS has SYSADM authority.

Some of the tasks that you ask the DAS to perform on your behalf may require specific authority to run. The DAS runs under the identifier of a specific user. The privileges granted to that user are restricted to only those commands associated with the tasks or operations to be carried out by the administrator. Generally, the tasks or operations required include:

- Query the operating system configuration information
- Query the operating system for user and group information
- Act against other DB2 instances to start or stop them
- Execute scheduled jobs
- Collect information for Connectivity and Protocol Configuration

Although the DAS has SYSADM authority so that it can perform any task that it is asked to do, you have the authority to request an action before it will perform it on your behalf.

Getting to know MR. OLAP

In case you don't know, OLAP stands for Online Analytical Processing. The two types that you hear about most are *Multidimensional* OLAP and

Relational OLAP. You will be happy to know that DB2 does them both, and very well we may add; hence the name MR. OLAP (get it . . . Multidimensional and Relational). The ability to store both multidimensional databases (they are stored in things called cubes) and relational databases makes DB2's OLAP solution one that companies can win with. To make things more appealing, IBM has partnered with Hyperion and integrated the Hyperion Essbasse OLAP engine in the OLAP Starter Kit. Hyperion is considered to be the industry leader in OLAP tools, and together they make for a winning combination!

The DB2 OLAP Starter Kit comes with every version of DB2 that you buy and gives you the tools you need to get started with the analysis of both relational and multidimensional databases. Each copy of DB2 allows up to three users to perform OLAP operations, build cubes, and so on. If you need to support more than three users, then you should buy DB2 OLAP Server.

Tools that employ OLAP technology, such as the DB2 OLAP Starter Kit, empower users to ask intuitive and complex ad hoc questions. For example, "What is the profitability for the third quarter across the southeast region for my focus products?" Such a question requires multiple perspectives on source data, such as time, regions, and products. Each of these perspectives is called a dimension.

Business analysts refer to ad hoc questions as those that are out of the blue and not pre-transcripted. They're used to answer "off-the-cuff" questions.

The DB2 OLAP Starter Kit enables you to organize your data into multiple dimensions for analysis. OLAP answers questions that you pose to the database engine and are eventually used for business decisions.

The data that you are used to working with in a database is relational data. Relational data can be considered two-dimensional because each piece of data, which you can also call a fact, correlates to one row and one column, each of which can be considered a dimension. You know all about two-dimensional analysis. Simply call up a spreadsheet in Excel or Lotus 1-2-3 and you'll see a dimension on the left side and another on the top of your spreadsheet. One problem with this type of analysis (which most decision makers use) is that businesses don't operate in just two dimensions.

The dimensions in a multidimensional database are higher-level perspectives of the data that represent the core components of your business plan, such as Accounts, Time, Products, and Markets. In an OLAP application, these dimensions tend not to change over time. Figure 5-27 illustrates the differences between relational and multidimensional analysis.

Each dimension has individual components called members. For example, the quarters of the year can be members of the Time dimension, and individual products can be members of the Products dimension. You can have hierarchies of members in dimensions, such as months within the quarters of the

Time dimension. Using the OLAP Starter Kit, you can "drill down" through members. For example, you may want to look at sales by year and then by month, days, and hours. This is what is referred to as drill down.

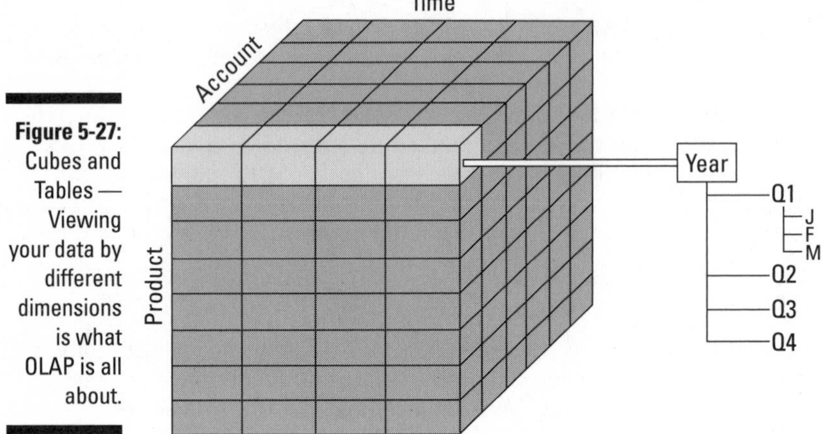

Figure 5-27: Cubes and Tables — Viewing your data by different dimensions is what OLAP is all about.

Here is a real good example of online analytical processing that helps discover relationships. Some folks at a large supermarket in the United States profiled a typical male, who is married with kids and between 30 and 35 years old; let's call him Chris. The folks at the supermarket wanted to know how to sell more products to Chris. First, they implemented a redemption program (such as AirMiles) so that they could "purchase" his transaction information from him.

Perhaps you never realized it, but every time you swipe one of those points collector cards, that company is purchasing your information. Such things as what you bought, when you bought it, how many you bought, whether it was on sale, and what time you bought it are tracked (a little scary, eh?). That trip you took last year — you did know it wasn't really "free," didn't you? Well, you know now!

Anyway, with all this data on Chris Neilson (and each and every customer for that matter), they decided to profile Chris (who represents males, 30 to 35, with kids). They noticed that Chris bought beer every Thursday night between 5:00 pm and 6:30 pm, presumably on his way home from work. This makes beer part of his market basket, which is just jargon for what he buys. Using OLAP techniques, those tech-heads in the supermarket's Information Technology department figured out that Chris also buys diapers in the same transaction. The end result? Move the diapers and the beer to opposite ends of the grocery store and try to sell Chris some chips (or any other goods for that matter) as he walks across the store to get each item.

An extension to OLAP is Data Mining. In OLAP, you ask questions and confirm hypotheses or examine trends. Data Mining reveals relationships, or correlations, that you didn't know existed before. For example, in that same supermarket, no one knew that those expensive small vegetables were bought with stinky cheese! I mean, who would know that? The result, put one on sale, but never both (and plug your noses if you work in the Produce department).

OLAP is distinct from OLTP. OLTP stands for Online Transaction Processing. As its name alludes to, OLTP deals with transactions. Ever bought a book over the Web, booked that great vacation, or updated a profile on the Web? Those are all transactions. DB2 does OLTP very well, too.

Cleaning House — How to Remove a DB2 Server

If for some reason you need to remove a DB2 server that you have installed, you have to do this through the Add/Remove utility provided with your operating system.

You need to have a DB2 server installed to perform the exercises and follow the examples in this book. We strongly recommend that you keep your DB2 server installation while you prepare for your exam. Just read this section — don't perform the steps.

To remove a DB2 server that you've installed, follow these steps:

1. **Click Start and choose Settings⇨Control Panel.**

   The Control Panel opens.

2. **Double-click the Add/Remove Programs icon in the Control Panel.**

   The Add/Remove Programs utility starts.

3. **Select the IBM DB2 entry in the Currently installed programs box, as shown in Figure 5-28, and click the Change/Remove button.**

4. **A confirmation pop-up window appears, asking you to confirm that you really want to remove the DB2 software from your workstation; click Yes.**

5. **If any DB2 processes are running, the DB2 uninstall program will ask whether you want to shut them down. Select Yes, and the rest, as they say, is history.**

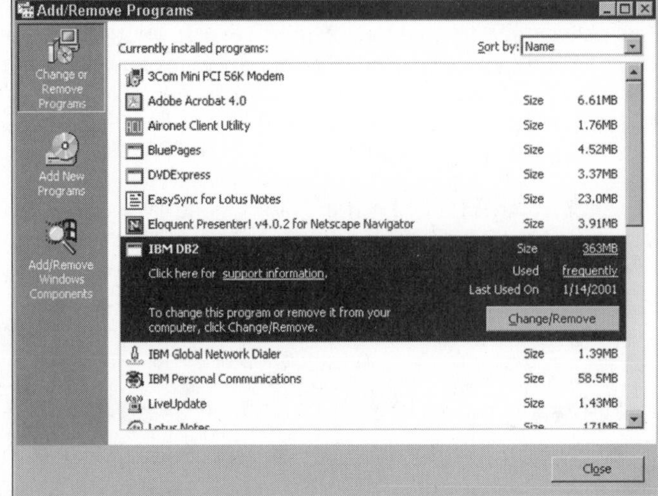

Figure 5-28: A sad farewell: Removing a DB2 server.

Final clean up

After a DB2 server is removed from your system, some various folders are left on your system that you should be aware of. When the uninstall completes, if you want to completely remove anything that is DB2-related from your system, make sure that you remove the following folders:

- **The DB2LOG folder, located on the drive where your Windows operating system is installed.** This folder is where any DB2 installation-related messages are stored.
- **The DB2 folder.** This folder is for the DB2 instance. This folder still exists after you remove DB2 because you can keep instances and databases after you remove DB2. If you are removing DB2 and plan to reinstall it on this machine, and you don't want to keep this information, remove this folder. In fact, when you reinstall DB2, you aren't able to create the SAMPLE database if you leave this folder on your computer.

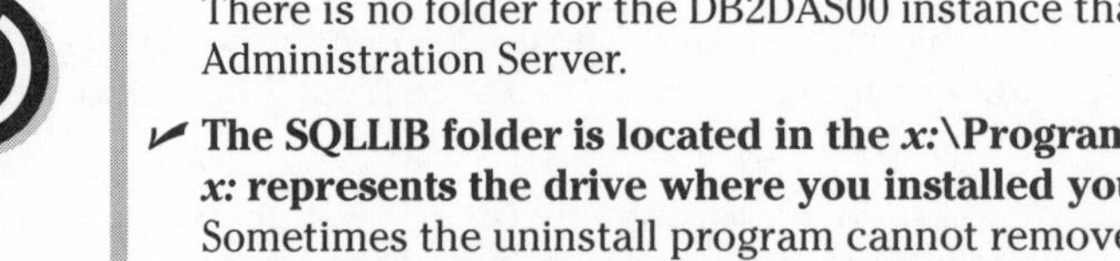

There is no folder for the DB2DAS00 instance that is used by the Administration Server.

- **The SQLLIB folder is located in the *x:*\Program Files directory, where *x:* represents the drive where you installed your copy of DB2.** Sometimes the uninstall program cannot remove this folder because it is in use by another application or some of the files are locked. If you still cannot remove this folder after a DB2 uninstall and a manual delete, reboot your computer and remove it then.

You may also want to remove the user account that you defined for the Control Center Server and the DAS. Most likely, you used the default `db2admin` user account and asked for it to be used for all user accounts that the DB2 installation program required. It isn't a big deal if you don't remove this user account; just understand that if you perform a future DB2 installation on this workstation, it will default to the `db2admin` user account and you'll have to use the password that already exists for this user account.

If you didn't use the default `db2admin` user account that was provided to you by the DB2 installation program, you don't have to worry about using the same user account in a subsequent DB2 installation.

Prep Test

1 **Which of the following types of OLAP analysis are supported by DB2 with the OLAP Starter Kit? (Pick two.)**

A ❑ Relational
B ❑ Object Oriented
C ❑ Multidimensional
D ❑ Hierarchal

2 **The Administration Server is sometimes referred to as the______?**

A ❍ A/S
B ❍ DAS
C ❍ CC
D ❍ DRDA AS

3 **Which of the following tasks will the DAS not help the Control Center with?**

A ❍ Enabling the remote administration of DB2 servers
B ❍ Providing the facilities for job management, including the ability to schedule the execution of both DB2 and operating system command scripts
C ❍ Providing the "brains" behind the wizards that help you complete common administrative tasks more quickly and with less complexity
D ❍ Providing a means for discovering information about the configuration of DB2 instances, databases, and other DB2 Administration Servers in conjunction with the DB2 Discovery utility

4 **Which of the following is an example of OLTP?**

A ❍ Finding out the relationship between the number of cases of beer sold and the day of the week at a local supermarket
B ❍ Booking an airline ticket over the Web
C ❍ Administering a local database using the Control Center
D ❍ Discovering unknown relationships between business entities via SQL

5 **In a default DB2 for Windows installation, which user account is associated with the Administration Server instance?**

A ❍ DAS
B ❍ DB2ADMIN
C ❍ DASADMIN
D ❍ IWM

6 How many Administration Server instances can you create on a DB2 Workgroup Edition server?

A ❍ As many as you want. DB2 servers can manage multiple user and management instances.

B ❍ You can have only one Administration Server instance per database server.

C ❍ It depends on the number of user instances on the DB2 Server. Each instance can have one Administration Server. So, if you created two instances, you could create two Administration Servers.

D ❍ None. You can only have an Administration Server on your machine if you install a DB2 Administration Client.

Answers

1. **A and C.** The DB2 OLAP features support both multidimensional and relational OLAP analysis. *See "Getting to know MR. OLAP."*
2. **B.** The DAS stands for Database Administration Server, though many call this feature the Administration Server as well. You can use these terms interchangeably. *Review "Installing a DB2 Server on a Windows NT or Windows 2000–Based Workstation."*
3. **C.** The DAS is used to work with database objects and schedule tasks and jobs. *See "Doing it with the DAS."*
4. **B.** Booking an airline ticket over the Web is a transaction. OLTP is transaction processing. In contrast, OLAP is about analysis and discovery techniques. *See "Getting to know MR. OLAP."*
5. **B.** The db2admin user account is the default user ID associated with the Administration Server in a DB2 for Windows installation. *See "Installing a DB2 Server on a Windows NT or Windows 2000–Based Workstation."*
6. **B.** Each server can only have one Administration Server on it. Only DB2 server can have Administration Servers. *See "Doing it with the DAS."*

Chapter 6

Installing a DB2 Client

Exam Objective

- Ability to Install DB2 Universal Database, DB2 Clients & Developers Edition

This chapter introduces you to the various DB2 clients, the software that allows you to have remote workstations talk and retrieve data (or even manage it or the DB2 server for that matter) from your DB2 server. DB2 clients come in three flavors, and the DB2 Fundamentals Exam expects you to know how to install all three of them. Don't worry, when you know one, you pretty much know them all! The main difference between the different DB2 clients is what each is primarily used for.

In this chapter, you'll find what you need to know to install a DB2 client, and some useful information on some of the components that come with a DB2 client.

The exam objectives note that you have to know how to install DB2 Universal Database Developer's Edition as well as a DB2 client. DB2 Developer's Edition products come in two flavors: DB2 Universal Developer's Edition and DB2 Personal Developer's Edition. DB2 Developer's Edition products are really a package that contains all sorts of software, and not an actual program in itself. Each Developer's Edition product comes with all sorts of DB2 server editions (such as Personal, Workgroup, Enterprise, and Enterprise – Extended), associated DB2 products (such as Net.Data, WebSphere Application Server), and non-DB2 related products (such as Visual Age for Java and Lotus Approach). The DB2 Developer's Edition products are meant to allow developers to create and test applications that will run on DB2, without paying the same licensing costs that a firm would pay to have DB2 run its business. Because the exam is mainly DB2 platform independent, you're only expected to know the concepts of installing a DB2 server and a DB2 client. In other words, reading this chapter along with Chapter 5, "Installing a DB2 Server," will more than prepare you for your exam. For more information on the DB2 Developer's Edition products, refer to Chapter 4, "An Introduction to DB2 Products and Packaging."

In order to encourage development on DB2 applications, you can download a free copy of DB2 Personal Developer's Edition at `www.ibm.com/software/data/db2/udb/downloads.html`.

Quick Assessment

DB2 Client Functionality

1 A DB2 Client allows applications to________________.

2 The Database Administration Server (DAS), which is used in conjunction with the DB2 tools to manage local and remote databases, is installed on a DB2 _____ and has to be running to use the Control Center.

DB2 Clients

3 The three types of DB2 clients are the __________________.

4 DB2 Version 7.1 clients run on the following platforms: ________________________.

5 If you want to use a DB2 client to manage a DB2 server on your network, you need to install a DB2 ________ Client.

Installing DB2 Clients

6 For the most part, to install a DB2 client, you need to have _______ authority. However, if you want to perform a single-user install, you can install a DB2 client on your machine with ____________.

DB2 Tools

7 The _____ is a graphical tool that helps you catalog databases so that the client knows the remote database names and how to get information or manage them.

8 The ____________ is a Java-based tool that can be used to build, test, and deploy stored procedures.

Answers

1. *Connect to a DB2 server to retrieve data or manage the remote system.* See "Ladies and Gentleman: A DB2 Client."

2. *server.* See "Installing a DB2 Client on a Windows NT or Windows 2000–Based Workstation."

3. *DB2 Runtime client, DB2 Administration client, and the DB2 Application Development client.* See "The DB2 Client Family."

4. *Linux, OS/2, UNIX* (specifically: AIX, HP-UX, NUMA-Q, SGI IRIX, and Solaris), *Windows 9x, Windows Me, Windows NT, or Windows 2000.* See "Ladies and Gentlemen: A DB2 Client."

5. *Administration.* See "The DB2 Administration Client."

6. *Local Administrator authority, any user account other than the Guest group.* See "User account."

7. *Client Configuration Assistant (CCA).* See "Taking your second steps with DB2."

8. *Stored Procedure Builder (SPB).* See "The DB2 Application Development Client."

Ladies and Gentlemen: A DB2 Client

A DB2 client is a piece of DB2 software that runs on a computer other than your DB2 server. The DB2 client software enables a computer to connect to a DB2 server. More technically speaking, a DB2 client provides a runtime environment that enables client applications to access one or more remote DB2 databases. All applications must access a database through a DB2 client. Without a DB2 client, you cannot talk to a DB2 server. However, DB2 servers can always talk to other DB2 servers because each DB2 server comes with a bundled DB2 client (more on that later).

DB2 Version 7.1 clients are available on: Linux, OS/2, UNIX (specifically: AIX, HP-UX, NUMA-Q, SGI IRIX, and Solaris), Windows 9x, Windows Me, Windows NT, or Windows 2000. DB2 clients have no licensing restrictions attached to them because licensing for DB2 products is controlled at the server. Because there are no licensing restrictions, you can download any DB2 client from the Web at `www.ibm.com/cgi-bin/db2www/data/db2/udb/winos2unix/support/index.d2w/report`.

In this chapter, the term *Windows* refers to any Windows 32-bit operating system. A DB2 client can be installed on a computer running Windows 95, Windows 98, Windows Me, Windows NT, or Windows 2000 (get the feeling that there are too may versions of Windows hanging around?).

A perfect example of a DB2 client is shown in Figure 6-1. This figure shows a typical bank where bank tellers use their computers to process transactions for customers. Three tellers (Lori Reid, Amy Houston, and Kelly Doyle) are waiting on customers. Each teller is going about her day-to-day business tasks. The tellers likely don't know what DB2 is, let alone that they have a DB2 client on their workstation.

The DB2 client (really it's the runtime environment) takes data and instructions from the application that each teller is using and conveys them to the DB2 server. Remember that a DB2 server can talk to another DB2 server. The DB2 server in the branch office actually talks to a DB2 server that's in the central office for the bank. That central office could be in a different building, on a different street, or even a different country! DB2 servers talk to other DB2 servers (and themselves) using the DB2 client code that is built into every DB2 server.

DB2 clients are also used with gateways. You may recall the discussion from Chapter 4 about DB2 Connect. DB2 Connect is actually a gateway that DB2 clients can use to talk to a DB2 server that's on a DB2 for OS/390, DB2 for MVS, DB2 for VM/VSE, or DB2 for the AS/400 platform.

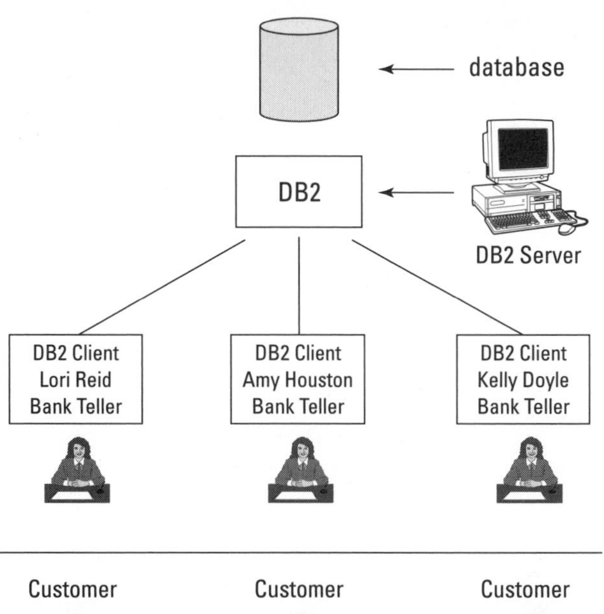

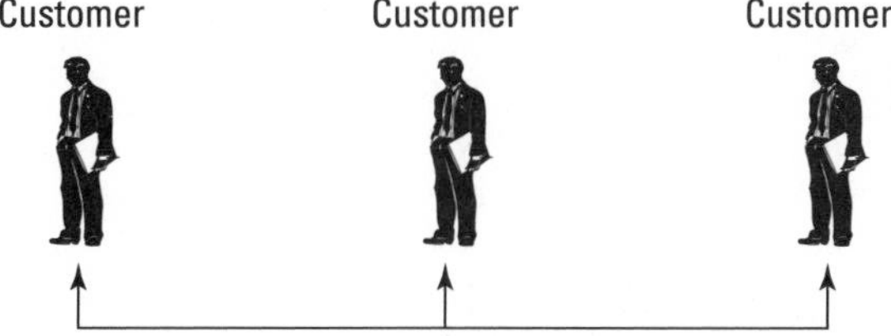

Figure 6-1: DB2 clients interacting with a DB2 server.

Make sure that you're up to speed on all the DB2 and DB2-related products that IBM offers for database environments. You're expected to know them for the test.

Figure 6-2 shows a DB2 client that's accessing DB2 data that resides on a DB2 for OS/390 system through a DB2 Connect gateway.

In Figure 6-2, the DB2 client connects to the DB2 Connect gateway that takes the request up to the DB2 for OS/390 machine. This is referred to as a three-tiered environment. Most of the world's data today is managed by DB2 for OS/390 systems, and the use of DB2 clients and DB2 Connect gateways gives users the opportunity to exploit and use that data with industry standard tools that are available in distributed environments.

Why is most of the world's data managed by DB2 for OS/390 servers? Despite the expense of maintaining and running a mainframe computer, if you are looking for a powerhouse of a computer that pretty much never crashes, you are not going to be running Windows. System/390 servers have a solid reputation for reliability, availability, and serviceability (RAS, if you want the coffee table jargon, stands for Reliability, Availability, and Serviceability).

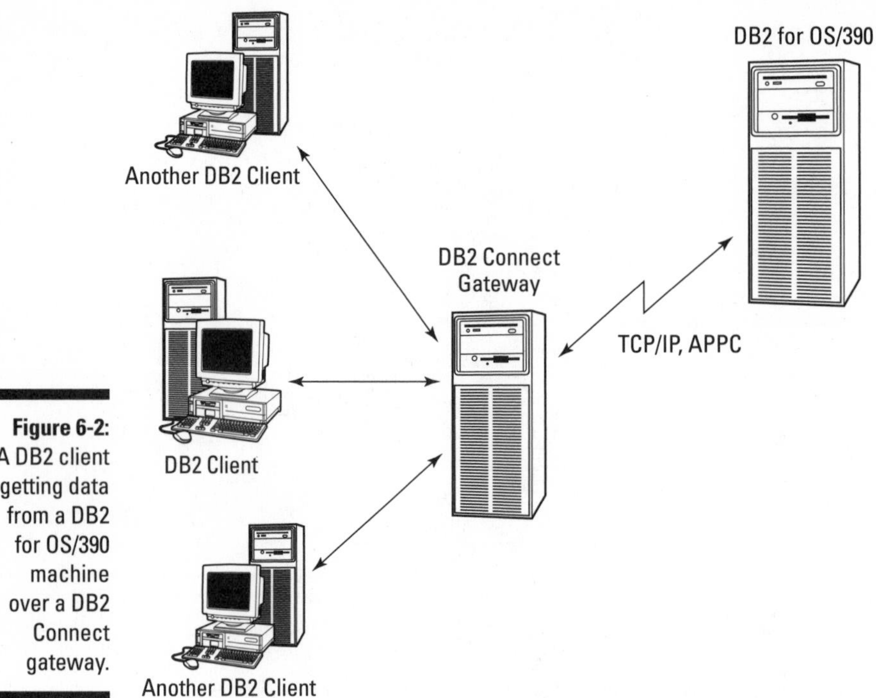

Figure 6-2: A DB2 client getting data from a DB2 for OS/390 machine over a DB2 Connect gateway.

The scenario illustrated in Figure 6-2 might be employed so that users could use spreadsheets, such as Lotus 1-2-3 and Microsoft Excel, to analyze real-time data without having the cost and complexity of data extract and import procedures. Also, analysts could use decision support tools, such as BusinessObjects, Brio, Impromptu, and Crystal Reports, to provide real-time information without moving information from a legacy DB2 for OS/390 system.

The world is moving away from a traditional business paradigm to an e-business one, and that entails a move from client/server (also referred to as distributed environments) like those shown in Figure 6-1 and Figure 6-2, toward Web-based business models. DB2 was the first Java-enabled database on the market and empowers users with standard Web-enabled database access methodologies.

Java Database Connectivity (JDBC) and Embedded SQL for Java (SQLJ) are provided with DB2 to allow you to create applications that access data in DB2 databases from the Web. The DB2 JDBC Applet server and the DB2 client must reside on the same machine as the Web server, as shown in Figure 6-3.

JDBC and SQLJ applications can be run from any systems that have a DB2 client installed; a Web browser and a Web server are not required.

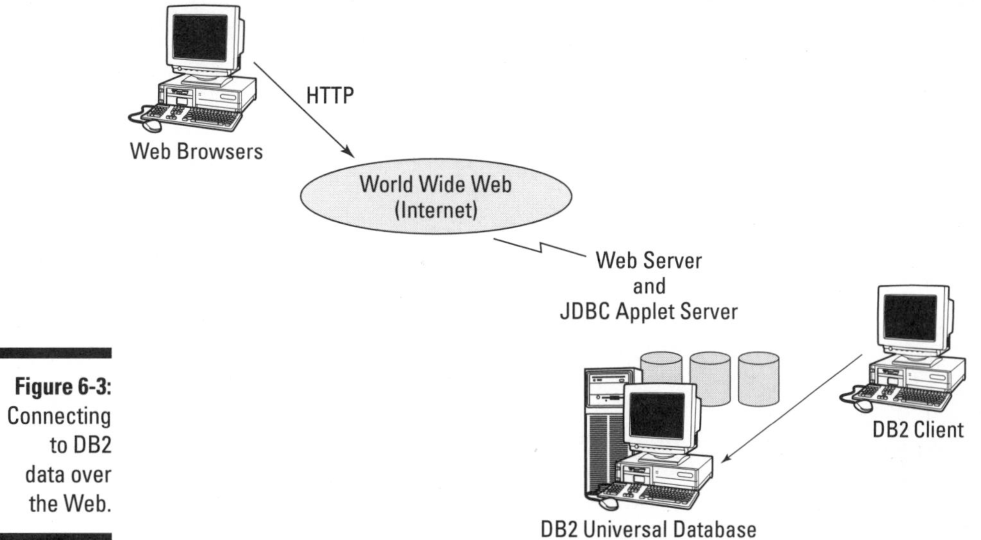

Figure 6-3: Connecting to DB2 data over the Web.

In Figure 6-3, the DB2 JDBC Applet server calls the DB2 client to connect to local, remote, and mainframe-based DB2 databases. When the applet requests a connection to a DB2 database, the JDBC client opens a TCP/IP connection to the DB2 JDBC Applet on the machine where the Web server is running. Figure 6-3 illustrates a two-tier model. A three-tier model separates the Application Server and the DB2 client, as shown in Figure 6-4.

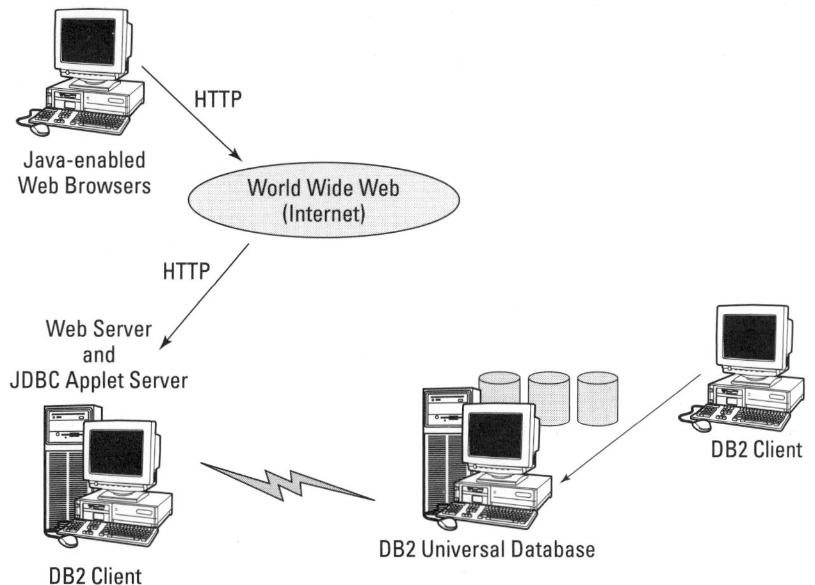

Figure 6-4: A three-tier Web access model.

As you can see by the previous discussion, DB2 data can pretty much be accessed from anywhere, at anytime.

The DB2 Client Family

You may have already noticed that there isn't just one DB2 client; in fact, there are three different types of DB2 clients that you can install. Each client is used by different people who have different requirements and responsibilities with their DB2 environment. With the exception of some components and the amount of disk space each DB2 client takes, the installation process is the same for all DB2 clients.

The three different DB2 clients that you can install are the following: DB2 Runtime client, DB2 Administration client, and the DB2 Application Development client. (To be honest, there is a fourth one called a DB2 Thin-client, and you will learn about that one as well.)

Okay, let's look at where we are today by looking in the past. At one time, DB2 shipped a single client software package called the DB2 Client Application Enabler (DB2 CAE), which included everything you needed to access or manage a database. But later, IBM took a closer look at how clients were being used and realized that in many instances, the DB2 CAE was taking up more footprint than necessary. (If you read the word *footprint* and looked at your feet, see the "Free Hard Drive Space" section later in this chapter.) As a result, IBM introduced two new clients in Version 6 that still exist today: DB2 Runtime clients and DB2 Administration clients. Although the DB2 Administration client is roughly equivalent to the old DB2 CAE and provides you both with a management and runtime environment, the DB2 Runtime client is stripped down to minimize memory and footprint and maximize performance by providing only the runtime library required for applications to access DB2 servers.

With the new packaging, DB2 Administration clients retain the management abilities of the old DB2 CAE and are installed only on those workstations that need it. It was a good move. DB2 administrators typically install many DB2 Runtime clients and only a few DB2 Administration clients. The DB2 Administration clients are reserved for guys with four-inch thick glasses, or users who need access to the documentation, whereas the DB2 runtime clients are for the rest of us who couldn't care less.

There used to be another DB2 product called the Software Developer's Kit (SDK). The SDK was used by programmers to create applications for DB2. The SDK came with application developments tools, sample programs, and header files — pretty much everything you need to build applications for DB2. Because the SDK also came with the runtime environment that DB2 clients use to connect to DB2 servers, IBM renamed it in Version 7.1 to the DB2 Application Development client.

There is a DB2 client that is suited for all kinds of users. DB2 clients kind of have a hierarchical form to them in the sense that a DB2 client that sits higher on the mountain (shown in Figure 6-5) includes all of the components of the one below it. DB2 clients that sit beside each other share some functions (such as the Control Center) but have distinct ones as well (such as the Stored Procedure Builder).

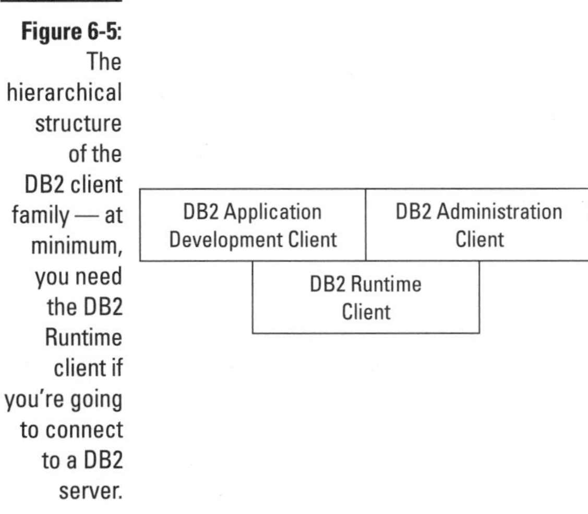

Figure 6-5: The hierarchical structure of the DB2 client family — at minimum, you need the DB2 Runtime client if you're going to connect to a DB2 server.

The DB2 Runtime Client

A DB2 Runtime client provides the ability for workstations from a variety of platforms to access DB2 Universal Database servers and DB2 Connect gateways — nothing else! This is the bare minimum if you want your computer to talk to other DB2 servers. The runtime environment is really what the DB2 Runtime client adds to your computer. Those bank tellers in Figure 6-1 are all using DB2 Runtime clients.

When you install a DB2 Runtime client, you install not only the code that allows you to run applications that connect to a DB2 server but also a few other tools. These other tools (the Command Center, the Client Configuration Assistant, and the QueryPatroller tools) allow you to enter DB2 and SQL commands and connect DB2 clients to DB2 servers. We discuss these tools at length in Chapter 8, "The DB2 Tools."

So what do you know about a DB2 Runtime client? DB2 Runtime clients don't include any management tools that you can use to administer your DB2 environment; they don't include documentation, either. No frills; just runtime code. Installing a DB2 Runtime client enables you to access data on remote databases, unless you want to manage DB2 the old-fashioned way by using commands.

If you want a DB2 Runtime client (which you don't need to complete the exercises in this book), you can get a copy from the DB2 Runtime Client CD-ROM pack, which is included in the box when you purchase a DB2 server or from the Web site mentioned earlier in this chapter: `www.ibm.com/cgi-bin/db2www/data/db2/udb/winos2unix/support/index.d2w/report`.

The DB2 Administration Client

A DB2 Administration client contains all the features of a DB2 Runtime client, but also includes the DB2 management tools necessary to manage your DB2 environment and some other add-ons when using DB2 in a more complex environment. Because it comes with more components, a DB2 Administration client has a larger footprint than a DB2 Runtime client.

For example, a DB2 Administration client comes with the Control Center and all of its bundled tools, such as the Command Center, the Performance Monitor, and so on (check out Chapter 8 for more information). A DB2 Administration client also allows you to install such things as documentation, a code server support for DB2 Thin-clients, and other miscellaneous tools.

For the most part, you don't need to install a DB2 Administration client on a DB2 server because a DB2 server already has a DB2 Administration client as part of its installation (unless you deselected it during the installation process).

Despite the fact that there is no such thing as a DB2 Administration client component in a DB2 server, most DB2 professionals feel that a DB2 Administration client is installed on a DB2 server because that server comes with the DB2 management tools and the runtime environment needed to access remote DB2 servers. So, when someone says, "I have a DB2 Administration client on my DB2 server," you know that he or she didn't actually install a DB2 Administration client — it was part of the DB2 server installation. This is a common misperception; just make things easier on everyone and go along with it. (Of course, nothing would stop you from installing a DB2 client on a DB2 server — it's just redundant to do so.)

A copy of a DB2 Administration client that corresponds to a DB2 server platform is available on every DB2 server CD-ROM. Of course, you don't have to have a DB2 Administration client on the same platform as a DB2 server; you could have a DB2 Administration client on a Windows 2000 machine that remotely manages a DB2 for NUMA-Q server.

Because no DB2 Administration client is available for the NUMA-Q operating system, a DB2 for NUMA-Q server is usually managed by a DB2 Administration client on a Windows-based platform. In fact, most UNIX-based DB2 installations are managed by Windows-based DB2 Administration clients.

If you want a DB2 Administration client other than the one that is provided on the DB2 server CD-ROM (which you don't need to complete the exercises in this book), you can get a copy from the DB2 Administration Client CD-ROM pack, which is included in the box when you purchase a DB2 server. You can also download any DB2 client from the Web site mentioned earlier in this chapter. The DB2 Administration Client CD-ROM pack contains all the CDs for DB2 Administration clients on any supported platform.

Those bank tellers in Figure 6-1 are likely using DB2 Runtime clients. Figure 6-5 builds on the business scenario that was illustrated in Figure 6-1 by adding another user whose machine has a DB2 Administration client installed. Notice the new user, Mike Godfrey, shown in Figure 6-6. This guy is responsible for keeping DB2 running in the branch office. He has a DB2 Administration client, which allows him to remotely manage that DB2 server in the office (of course, he could manage any DB2 server on his network, not just the ones in the office).

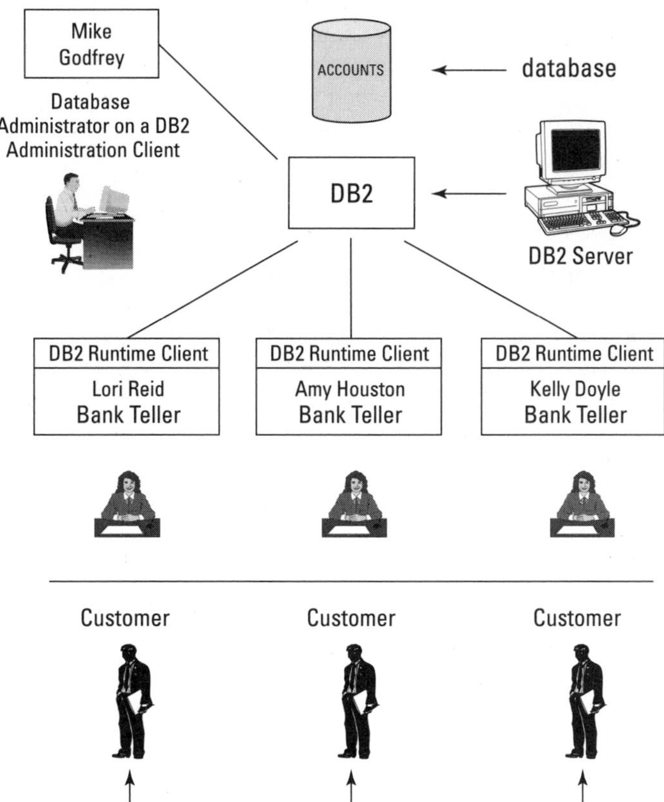

Figure 6-6: Here's Mike remotely managing the DB2 server.

Because Mike has different needs and responsibilities than the tellers Lori, Kelly, or Amy, he needs a different DB2 client: a DB2 Administration client.

The weight watcher's solution: A DB2 Thin-client

A DB2 Thin-client is a special type of client that you can install by using the Thin Client Code Server component that comes only with the DB2 Administration client. When you install a DB2 client, you take up a certain amount of footprint on your computer's hard drive. Different DB2 clients take up different amounts of space on your hard drive. Client code, or any applications for that matter, where code is installed on a workstation, are usually referred to as *Fat* clients. The term means that both the code and the processing of that code is done at the client workstation. In contrast, a *Thin* workstation is one where almost no code is actually installed on the client workstation; all the processing of the code, however, is done on the thin workstation. How does this work? The thin workstation actually loads the application code (in this case, the DB2 client software) from another machine on a network called a *code server*. After the code is loaded onto the thin workstation, the thin workstation uses its own resources (memory, CPU, and so on) to run the code.

What is the allure of thin workstations? Well, you can update the code in one spot and those updates affect everyone, so an obvious manageability benefit is associated with this type of architecture. Also, you have a drastically reduced footprint because all the DB2 clients (perhaps thousands of them) don't have to have the DB2 client code installed on them to act as a DB2 client. Each thin workstation needs only a minimal amount of code and configuration to establish links to a code server. Of course, as with anything in life, this type of environment has its drawbacks as well. What you gain in manageability and footprint, you may lose in performance (depending on your environment).

Don't confuse this configuration with a Citrix environment. In a Citrix environment, both the code and the processing are handled by the Citrix server. In a Thin-client environment, no processing is done at the code server in this environment. DB2 clients also run in a Citrix environment, by the way, but you don't need to know that for the exam.

A typical DB2 Thin-client environment is shown in Figure 6-7. A DB2 Administration client is installed on a machine with the Thin Client Code Server component. After some configuration, this machine will be known as a code server. A DB2 administration client is the only type of client that can act as a code server for DB2 Thin-client workstations. The DB2 Thin-client workstations access the code server to dynamically load any code required. After the code is loaded, all processing is done locally on the DB2 Thin-client workstations. Using local database configuration information, a connection is made to a target DB2 server and the data is retrieved. It is important that you understand that the DB2 code is actually run on the Thin-client workstations, although the code is loaded only from the DB2 Thin-client Code Server. No DB2 code is installed on the Thin-client workstations!

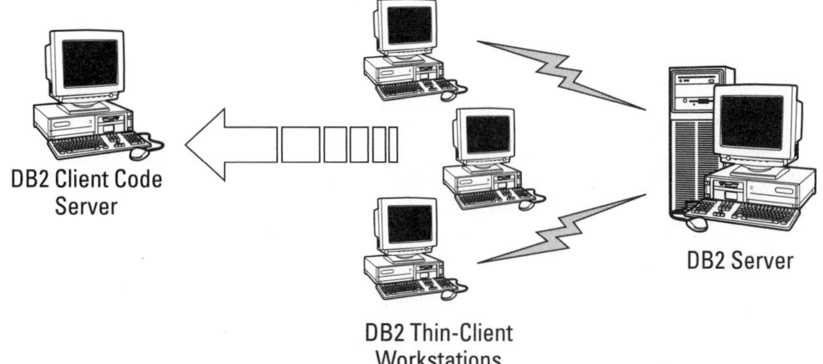

Figure 6-7: A DB2 client after losing weight.

The DB2 Application Development Client

The DB2 Application Development Client is a collection of tools for the creation of character-based, multimedia, or object-oriented database applications. It includes all the DB2 specific tools that complement your application development environment.

Let's add to Figure 6-6. In Figure 6-8, there is a group of people that are even nerdier than our DB2 administrator Mike. These guys are called *application developers* (we work with tons of people like this). These folks stay up to all hours of the evening, eating donuts and guzzling cola, to write the applications that the bank tellers use to access DB2.

In Figure 6-8, the application developers actually can access DB2 because the DB2 Application Development client builds on what is provided by a DB2 Runtime with application development tools, samples, and header files. The DB2 Application Development client even comes with the Stored Procedure Builder, a Java-based tool that can be used to build, test, and deploy stored procedures. If you want to know more about the Stored Procedure Builder, check out Chapter 8. Don't know what a stored procedure is? Check out Chapter 9, "Database Building Blocks."

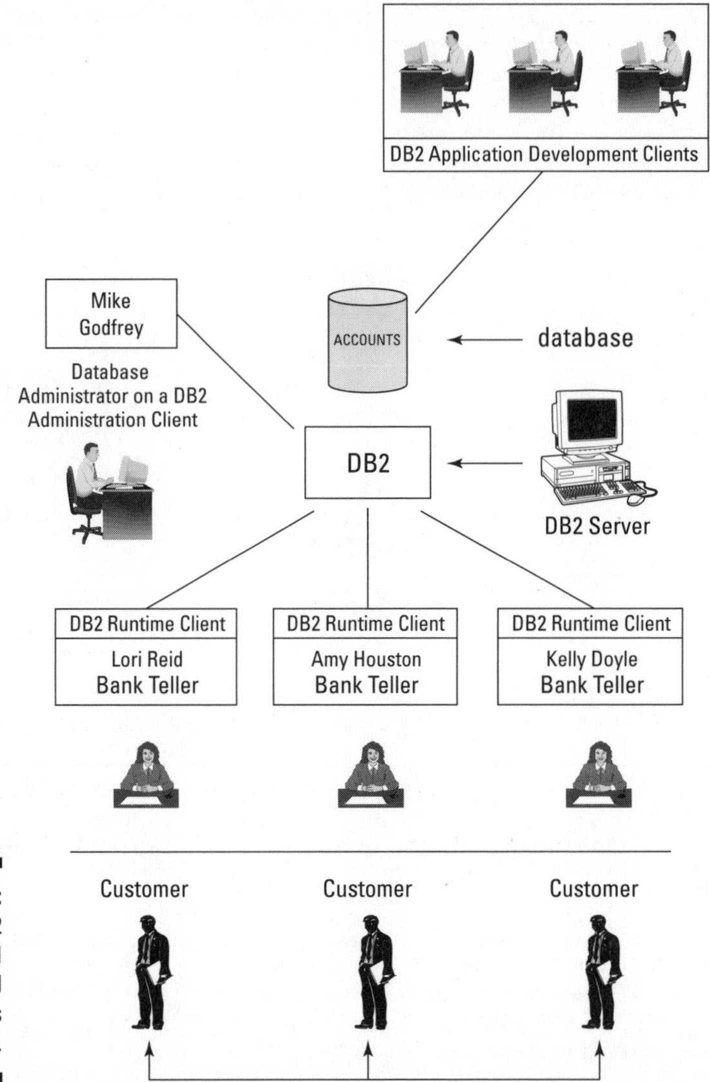

Figure 6-8: All the DB2 clients used in a typical business environment.

A DB2 Application Development client comes with the DB2 management tools as well, but it doesn't have the ability to act as a code server. As you may expect, the DB2 Application Development client takes up far more footprint than a DB2 Administration client, which takes up more footprint than a DB2 Runtime client. It's all about needs, don't you know!

If you want a DB2 Application Development client other than the one that's provided on the DB2 server CD-ROM (which you don't need to complete the exercises in this book), you can get a copy from any of the DB2 Developer's Edition products or from the Web site mentioned earlier in this chapter.

Knowing What You Need to Install a DB2 Client

This section introduces you to all the requirements that you should be aware of before attempting to install a DB2 for Windows client. Because a copy of DB2 for Windows is included in the back of this book, and because each DB2 server has an associated DB2 Administration client on the CD-ROM, the examples will relate to a DB2 Administration Client for Windows 2000 installation. If you're installing a DB2 client on an OS/2 or UNIX-based computer, you still need to address the same requirements for the DB2 client on Windows, but the way you go about this is different. Check out the *DB2 UDB and DB2 Connect Installation and Configuration Supplement* in the Information Center for information on how to install a DB2 client on OS/2 or UNIX-based systems or for requirements for any DB2 client.

The exercises in the book assume that you install the DB2 Administration client that is on the same CD-ROM as the DB2 server that you installed in Chapter 5, "Installing a DB2 Server."

To install a DB2 client, you need basically the same things as you do to install a DB2 server (we discuss this process in Chapter 5), but in different proportions or with different characteristics. See Chapter 5 for more information on the general requirements for your basic hardware setup. Table 6-1 lists the different requirements for installing a DB2 client, and the sections that follow also discuss each requirement in the Windows environment briefly.

Table 6-1 Suggested Hardware Requirements for a DB2 Client

Requirement	*Suggested Values*
CPU	Pentium-II class or higher
Free Hard Drive Space*	200MB
Memory (RAM)**	32MB
Operating System***	Windows NT version 4.0 with Service Pack 5 or higher (or Windows 2000)
Communication Software	TCP/IP, NetBIOS, Named Pipes, IPX/SPX, or APPC

**The physical disk requirements for Windows NT or Windows 2000 are based on the NTFS file system and not the FAT file system. If you're using a FAT file system, you should expect these values to be considerably higher. Also note that we assume you're installing a DB2 Administration client.*

***The amount of memory varies depending on the type of DB2 client that you are installing. Because we assume that you're installing a DB2 Administration client, we've suggested the amount of RAM required to use the DB2 management tools.*

****If you're installing a DB2 Version 7.1 client on a Windows NT–based workstation, it must be Windows NT Version 4.0 with Service Pack 5 or higher.*

To follow the exercises in this book, make sure that you have TCP/IP running on the workstation where you plan to install your DB2 client.

CPU

The CPU (central processing unit) is the heart of your computer, and its speed can make a big difference in how smoothly DB2 runs on your workstation. You should have at least 233 MHz of clock speed with your processor, but we suggest more. Make sure that your processor is Intel-compatible.

Free hard drive space

As when installing any software on a computer, your amount of available hard drive space is definitely an issue. The amount of disk space that a program consumes is known as that program's *footprint.* A typical DB2 Runtime client installation requires about 15MB of available drive space. A DB2 Administration client will cost you about 200MB, and a typical DB2 Application Development client installation will take up about 285MB of disk space. See the "Free Hard Drive Space" section in Chapter 5 for instructions to find out whether you have enough free hard drive space for a DB2 client installation.

When you get accustomed to DB2, you can definately prune the size requirements for a DB2 client. Because you are in learning mode here, we strongly recommend that you have at least 200MB of free space available on the drive where you want to install your DB2 Administration client. This will ensure that you can install all the tutorials and sample files that will surely help you prepare for exam day.

Memory (RAM)

Your system requires about 16MB of memory to run a DB2 Runtime client. If you are planning to run a DB2 Administration client or a DB2 Application Development client, you need approximately 32MB of memory. See the "Memory (RAM)" section in Chapter 5 for instructions on how to find out whether you have enough RAM on your computer for a DB2 client.

The amount of memory that you need is only a suggestion; it does not take into account other programs that may be running on your computer. Most personal computers today come with more memory than the required minimum (see Table 6-1 for the suggested requirements). If you are using your computer at the office, you may need even more memory to install a DB2 client because other applications require memory, too. The good news is that if you don't have enough memory, you can still run your DB2 client; it will run slowly, but it will run.

Operating system and communication software (or protocols)

The operating system and communication software requirements that exist for a DB2 server and a DB2 client are the same. Chances are you don't have to worry about this. For more information on how to determine whether you have the correct operating system and communication software, see Chapter 5.

You should not have to worry about the communication software requirements because in Chapter 5, we asked you to ensure that the workstations that you selected to act as a DB2 server and a DB2 client could talk to each other using TPC/IP. Remember?

If you're running Windows NT and you need to determine which Service Pack is installed on your computer (you don't need a service pack for Windows 2000), check out the blue window that you see when your Windows NT-based workstation boots up. If you have SP5 or higher, you're fine. Otherwise, you need to upgrade to a supported Service Pack. To get a Service Pack, visit the Microsoft Windows Web site at `www.microsoft.com/ntserver/default.asp`.

User account

You need a user account to perform a DB2 client installation, just as you need one for a DB2 server installation. A *user account* is the Windows term for the combination of a username and password, which you most likely use every day when you get to work and log on to your computer.

The user account that you use to install a DB2 client must

- Belong to the local *Administrators* group
- Not exceed 28 characters in length
- Have the following *advanced* user rights:
    - Act as part of the operating system
    - Increase quotas
    - Create a token object
    - Replace a process level token

You may need to talk to your administrator to get these system rights and permissions, or to create a new user account. Usually, Administrator authority isn't given out to just anyone, so you may have to pull some teeth at work to get it.

If you want more information on assigning rights and privileges to user accounts in Windows users and groups, refer to your operating system's online help.

Sometimes you just have to be selfish: A DB2 single-user installation

You can install a DB2 client without the required Administrator authority that you need to install a DB2 server. This is referred to as a single-user installation. Because this book focuses on installing DB2 as an administrator, we mention the single-user installation only briefly here. You can refer to the *DB2 UDB and DB2 Connect Installation and Configuration Supplement,* one of the DB2 books that is installed with the Information Center.

We don't recommend that you use a single-user installation unless you really know what you are doing. If you define and install your DB2 client with the same user account that you used to install the DB2 server, you won't have to worry about authentication problems when connecting to the remote DB2 server in Chapter 7, "Getting Clients and Servers Talking."

The single-user installation enables any users of a Windows-based system (except ones who belong to the Guest group) to install a DB2 client. This ability was added to DB2 because customers often complained that employees without Administrator authority on the operating system could not install a DB2 client. After all, many employees may need to access your company's database. Given that database security is usually controlled at the server, where's the harm in allowing non-administrators to install a DB2 client?

A single-user installation is for one user only. This means that other users of your system can't use the DB2 client that is installed. However, another user can install a DB2 client for his or her profile, so you may have three users on one machine installing a DB2 client as a single user. But if an administrator chose to perform an installation, it overrides and wipes out the other single-user installations and creates a global installation of the DB2 client.

Installing a DB2 Client on a Windows NT or Windows 2000–Based Workstation

You're ready to install a DB2 client on your Windows computer. You can use the copy of the DB2 Administration client that is on the CD-ROM at the back of this book.

The instructions in this section assume that you're installing the DB2 Administration Client that is available on the DB2 server CD-ROM in the back of this book.

Lab 6-1 provides the steps to install a DB2 Administration client on your Windows workstation by using the custom installation method. Ensure that you select to install all the available components and subcomponents. Use the DB2 server CD-ROM that is available in the back of your book.

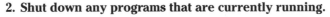

Lab 6-1 Installing a DB2 Administration client

1. **Log on to your computer with a user account that meets the requirements for performing a DB2 client installation.**

   For our example (in order to simplify any security considerations), log on to your "to-be" DB2 client workstation with the same account that you used to install your DB2 server. If this user account needs to be defined on this machine, then define it.

   For information on user accounts, see the "User account" section earlier in this chapter.

   The instructions in the remainder of this book assume that the DB2 server and client workstations can talk to each other using by TCP/IP.

2. **Shut down any programs that are currently running.**

   You should never install any software on your computer when other programs are running; at least that's what the folks at Microsoft always tell us, so we're telling you the same thing.

3. **Insert the CD-ROM from the back of the book into the CD-ROM drive.**

   The auto-run feature automatically starts the DB2 installation program. The DB2 installation program is called `setup.exe` on the CD-ROM. People refer to the DB2 Installation or setup program when talking about the software that installs DB2 on a workstation. The setup program determines your computer's system language and launches the setup program for that language.

   If the setup program fails to start, you can manually start it from a Windows command prompt by switching to the CD-ROM drive and typing the ***x*:\setup** command, where *x*: represents the letter for your CD-ROM drive.

4. **Click the Install option in the DB2 Launchpad to start installing a DB2 client.**

   When you start the DB2 installation program for a DB2 client, the DB2 Launchpad opens, as shown in Figure 6-9. This is new for DB2 Version 7.1 client installations. The DB2 Launchpad offers you many features aside from just starting the DB2 installation program.

You can view the minimum requirements for a DB2 client installation by clicking Installation Prerequisites. (Keep in mind that the prerequisites are for a DB2 client, not for using a DB2 client with the exercises in this book — stick to at least what we recommend in this book.)

Clicking Release Notes will open an HTML page that contains all the last-minute information that didn't quite make it into the manuals before they were printed.

The Quick Tour gives you an interactive presentation that introduces the features, benefits, and capabilities of DB2 Version 7.1, and clicking Exit will, of course, close the installation program.

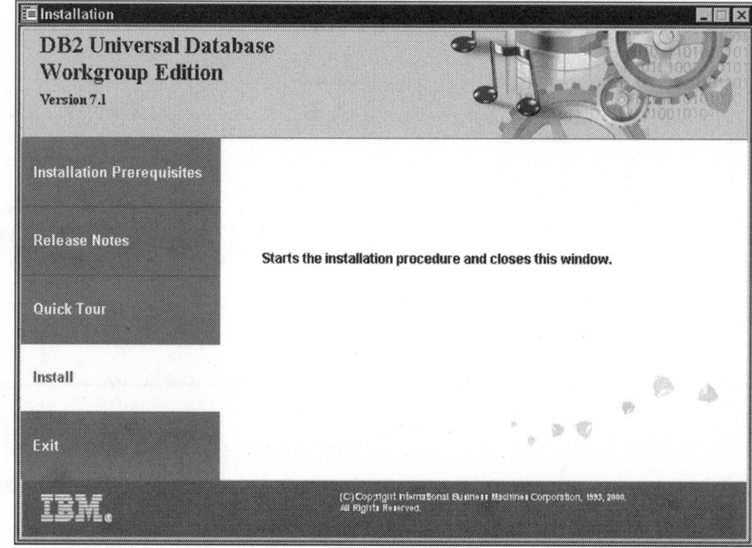

Figure 6-9: The DB2 Launchpad, your gateway to a DB2 client and a bunch of useful information.

5. **Select the DB2 product that you want to install from the Select Products window and click Next.**

   For our example, ensure that only the DB2 Administration Client check box is selected, as shown in Figure 6-10.

   To highlight a product and read its description, click the product name rather than the check box. If you do so, a check mark does not appear beside the product name. If you want to select a product, make sure that it has a check mark in its associated check box.

   Because you are using the CD-ROM in the back of this book, you are installing a DB2 Administration client from a DB2 server CD-ROM. If you were using the DB2 Administration Client Pack CD-ROM, the window shown in Figure 6-10 would not give you the option of installing a DB2 server or a DB2 Application Development client. You would see only a check box for a DB2 Administration client.

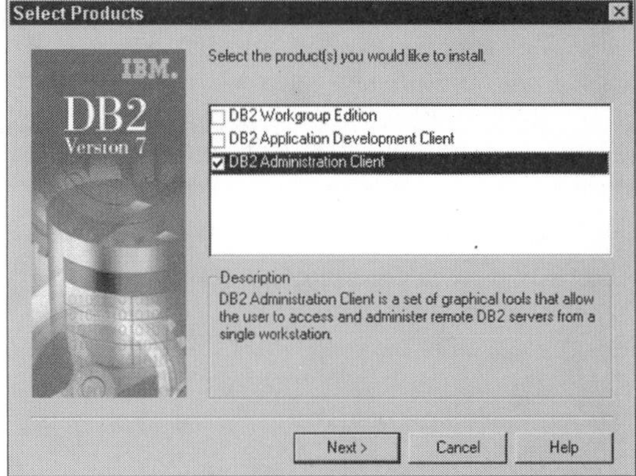

Figure 6-10: Selecting the products you want to install.

6. **From the Select Installation Type window, select the radio button that corresponds to the type of installation that you want to perform, as shown in Figure 6-11; then click Next.**

   To get a better feel for the entire installation, select the Custom radio button and click Next.

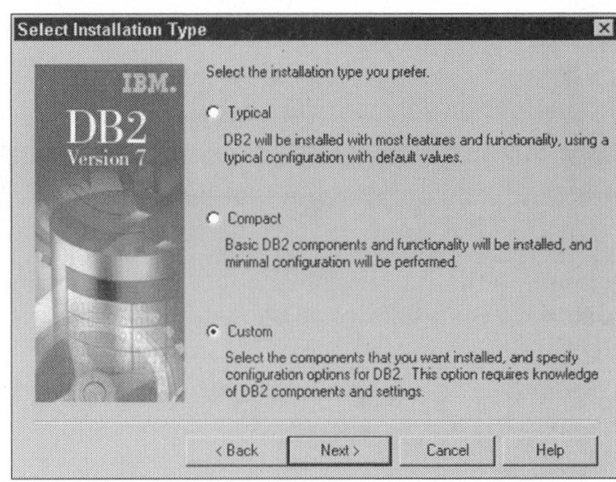

Figure 6-11: Selecting an installation type. The Custom installation will best prepare you for your DB2 exam.

When you install a DB2 client on a Windows machine, you have to choose the type of installation that you want to perform. You can select any of the following installation types:

- **Typical:** The fastest way to get a complete DB2 client installed. All the typical components, including the documentation, the runtime libraries, the Client Configuration Assistant, and the Command Center are installed on your computer with default settings.

In this chapter, we show you a Custom DB2 Administration client installation so that we can take you through all the DB2 installation windows that you could possibly see when performing a DB2 client installation on a Windows workstation. If you choose a Typical installation, you may not see all the windows in the DB2 client installation process. That isn't a big deal; just read this section and you should be fine for the exam.

- **Custom:** Allows you to select specific components and details of a DB2 client installation, giving you complete control over which components get installed on your workstation and which ones don't. You also get the choice to change some of the default settings that are used for an installation.
- **Compact:** This option is for people who just don't have the space on their workstation for a DB2 client installation and want to get only the bare essentials. This option won't install the DB2 documentation or graphical tools (for example, the Control Center or the Client Configuration Assistant). Selecting this option will not give you the tools that you need to prepare for your DB2 exam.

To properly prepare for the DB2 Fundamentals Exam, you *must* select a Typical or Custom installation.

If you choose to perform a Compact installation of a DB2 client, you won't be able to follow most of the exercises and examples in this book.

Beside each installation type is a rough approximation of the hard drive space required to install the selected DB2 client.

7. **From the Select Components window, select or deselect any DB2 client components and subcomponents that you want to or do not want to install.**

For our example, ensure that all the DB2 client components and subcomponents are selected for installation, as shown in Figure 6-12. (Don't click Next just yet.)

The instructions in this book assume that every component and subcomponent is selected for installation.

In the Select Components window shown in Figure 6-12, you can see a brief description of any component by highlighting it and reading its associated description in the Description box on the right side of the window.

Read and make notes on the description for each DB2 client component in Figure 6-12. It will help you commit to memory the different components that are used in a DB2 environment.

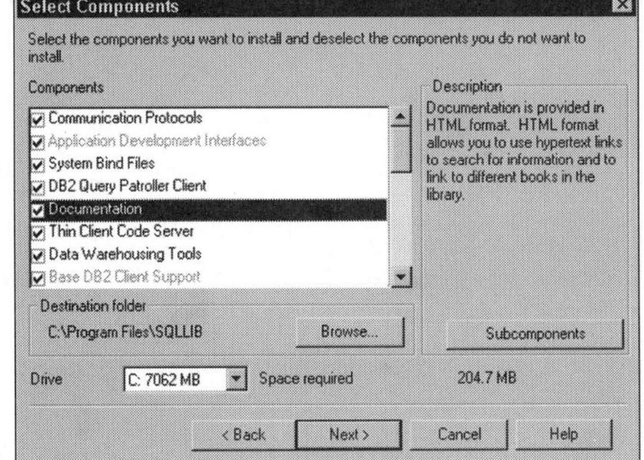

Figure 6-12: Selecting the components you want in a Custom installation.

If all you want to do is highlight a component, don't click the check box; click a component's name instead. To select or deselect a component, click in the actual check box. To ensure that a component is selected for installation, make sure that a check mark appears in the component's associated check box.

As you can see in Figure 6-12, one of the components we selected is the Documentation component. Did you notice when you selected this component (and some others) that the Subcomponents button in the Description box suddenly became active?

Just as in a DB2 server installation, some components have subcomponents and some do not. If you click the Subcomponents button, you can see the subcomponents for a selected component, as shown in the example Figure 6-13.

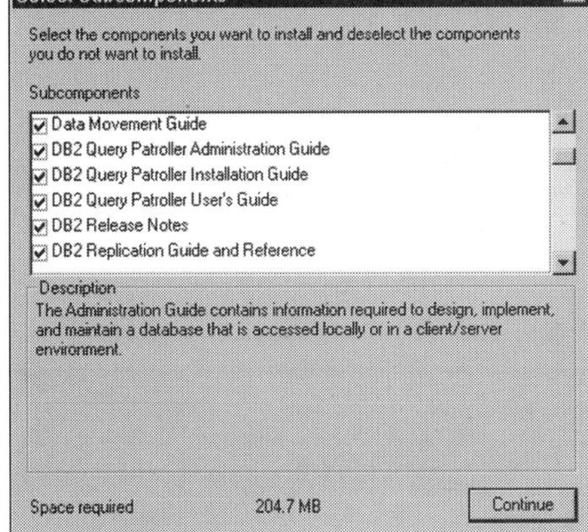

Figure 6-13: Selecting the subcomponents of the Documentation component.

After you select the subcomponents for a component, click Continue. You can then move on to other components and repeat the whole sordid process.

Again, just as with the DB2 server installation, select all the subcomponents for each component that will be installed and make sure that you read and commit to memory what each component is used for.

8. **Select the location where you want to install your DB2 client (you should be in the same window that you used to select the DB2 server component, as shown previously in Figure 6-13), and click Next.**

   You can click the Browse button to select a target drive and directory. The default installation directory is *x*:\Program Files\SQLLIB, where *x*: is the drive where you installed your Windows operating system.

   Clicking the Drive drop-down box shows the space available on each of the hard drives on your system. You can compare this to the Space Required field to ensure that you have enough hard disk space to install the DB2 client. The information here may help you select a more suitable directory in the Destination Folder box.

   If you clicked Next after selecting the components for your DB2 installation, you can click Back to return to the Select Components window and select an appropriate installation directory.

9. **In the Enter Username and Password for Control Center Server window, specify a user account that will be associated with the Control Center Server, shown in Figure 6-14, and click Next.**

   The Control Center Server is used for the management of DB2 Satellite systems; you aren't expected to know anything about this for the DB2 Family Fundamentals exam.

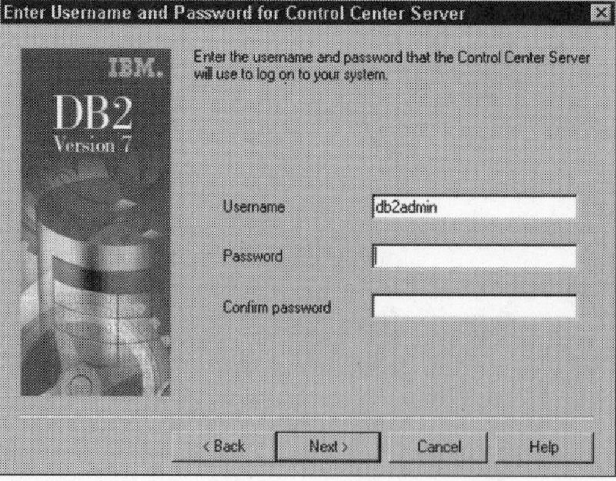

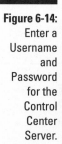

Figure 6-14: Enter a Username and Password for the Control Center Server.

By default, the setup program will create a user account using the username db2admin and the password that you specify. If you don't specify a password, it will default to db2admin — same as the username. You should be aware of the security implications and username requirements for this user account. They are the same as those for the Control Warehouse database that we discuss in Chapter 5.

If the Confirm Password field is not active in the window shown in Figure 6-14, that means that this user account already exists and you must enter the appropriate password in the Password field.

For our example, just enter a password and let the installation program create this user account for you. You *must* realize, however, that this is not the Administration Server's (DAS) user account that was created for you when you installed a DB2 server. The default user account happens to have the same username, so if it makes it easier to differentiate the two, change the default username as well. DB2 clients *do not* have a DAS on their system — only DB2 servers. When a DB2 client tries to remotely manage a DB2 server, the tools on the DB2 client use the running DAS on the DB2 server to perform any administrative tasks that require the DAS. For more information on the DAS, see the "Doing it with the DAS" section in Chapter 5, or refer to Chapter 9, "Database Building Blocks."

If you're using the NetBIOS (often referred to as NetBEUI in the wonderful world of Windows) protocol on your network, the Configure NetBIOS window opens, as shown in Figure 6-15. You're not likely to ever need to touch this window, and if you do need to, you know who you are. If you are not using NetBIOS, this window doesn't appear.

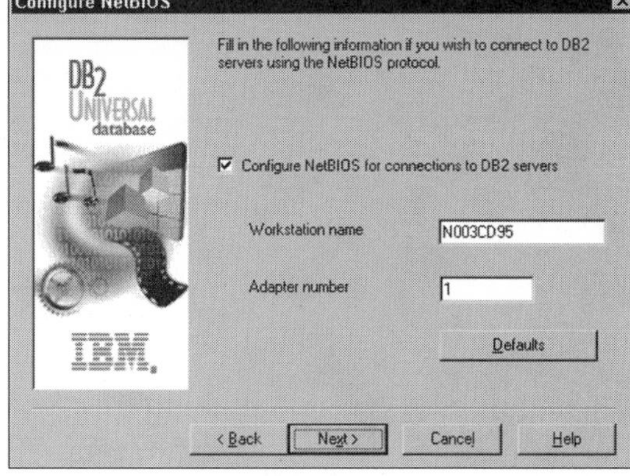

Figure 6-15: The Configure NetBIOS window.

10. **Finally, you are ready to begin the installation: Scroll through the Current Settings box in the Start Copying Files window (shown in Figure 6-16) to see all the DB2 client options and components that will be installed on your machine; then click Next.**

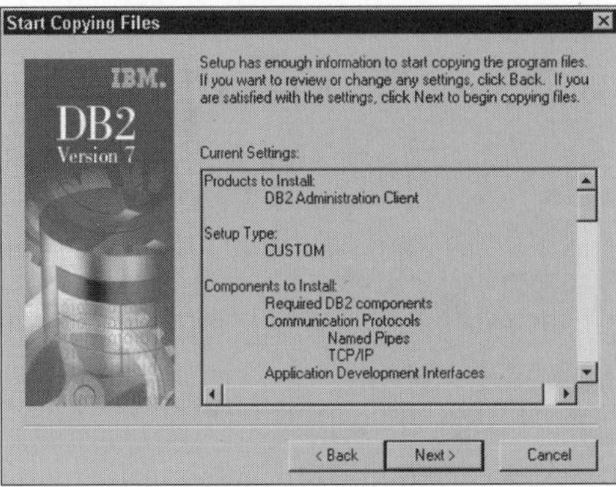

Figure 6-16: A chance to review your selections and start the installation: excitement personified!

If you're not satisfied, you can click Back to return to any previous installation windows and make changes.

11. **When the installation and configuration are finished, simply click the Finish button (see Figure 6-17).**

    Usually, you don't need to restart your workstation as you had to when you installed a DB2 server; if this is the case, just click Finish.

    TIP: If you are prompted to reboot your workstation, you must do so before you can use the DB2 client software.

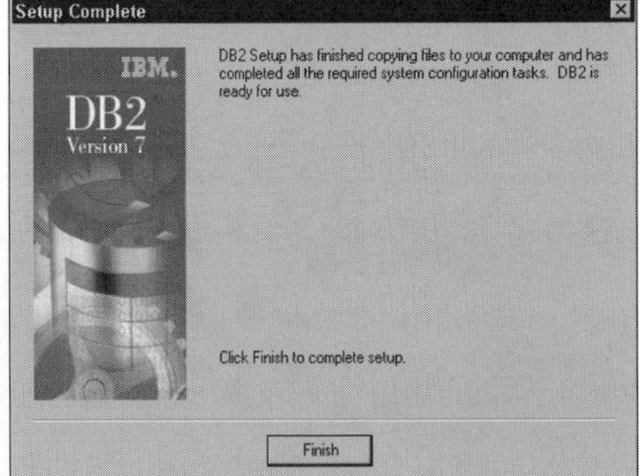

Figure 6-17: One more thing and you're done! Click Finish.

You've finished installing a DB2 client. The DB2 client is placed in your Start menu, as shown in Figure 6-18. You should recognize most of the options in the IBM DB2 folder because we discuss them in Chapter 4.

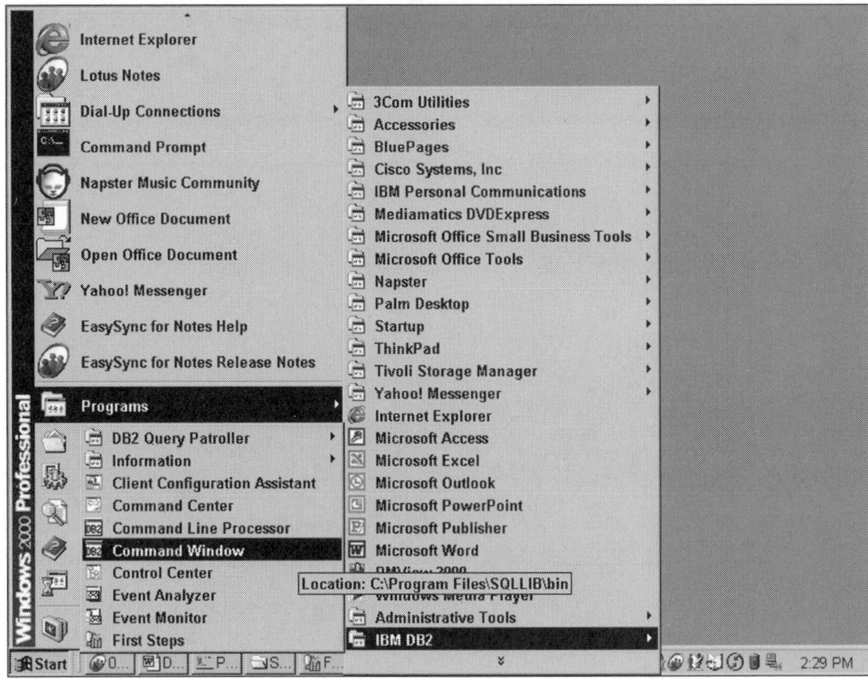

Figure 6-18: The IBM DB2 folder in the Start menu after a DB2 client installation.

Taking your second steps with DB2

So you have finished installing a DB2 client, and you likely didn't have to reboot. (When it comes to Windows, that means no 10-minute chat with your buddy on the phone.)

If you were prompted to reboot your system after installing your DB2 client, log on to your system with the same user account that you used to perform the DB2 client installation (which, by the way, you chose to be the same user account that you used to install the DB2 server). After you log on, your familiar friend DB2 First Steps starts again, as shown in Figure 6-19.

In Version 7.1, the First Steps tool was extended to a DB2 client as well. The version of First Steps on a DB2 client is designed to help get you going on the DB2 client side of the fence. It allows you to catalog the sample databases, work with these sample databases by starting the Control Center, and view the DB2 documentation library.

If First Steps doesn't start (of course, this time you didn't get scared and didn't shut it down because you've seen it before), you can start it by clicking the Start button and choosing Programs⇨IBM DB2⇨First Steps. First Steps won't open if you performed a Compact installation or a Custom installation and deselected it because it won't be there!

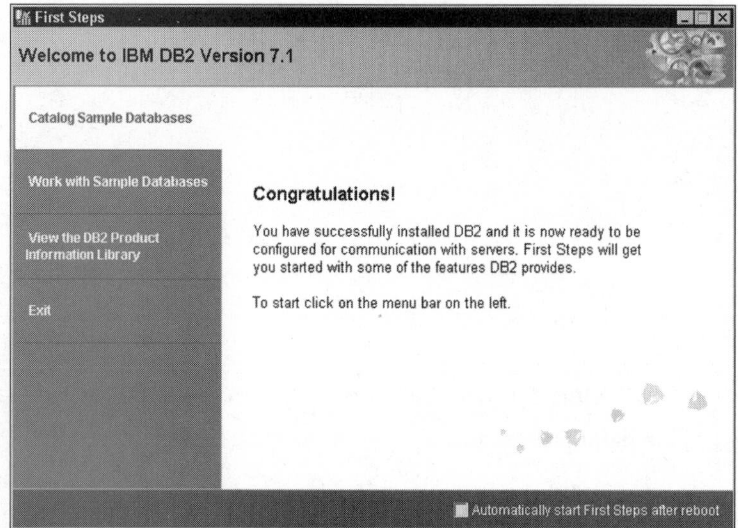

Figure 6-19: First Steps on a DB2 client.

First Steps on a client gives you four options, which we describe in detail in the following sections. To view more details on these options, place the mouse pointer over a button and just let it sit there. The button's Hover Help displays, giving you more details on what action each button performs. The four options available in First Steps are the following:

- Catalog Sample Databases
- Work with Sample Databases
- View the DB2 Product Information Library
- Exit

Cataloging the sample databases

The First Steps tools gives you the option to catalog the sample databases that you created on your DB2 server. In fact, this option really just launches the CCA (Client Configuration Assistant) and allows you to catalog any remote DB2 databases.

Of course, we say "remote" because we assume that a DB2 client is the only software that is installed on this workstation. There could never be a DB2 database here because you need a DB2 server for that. If you had a DB2 server installed, you would not need to catalog the local database because when you create a database, it's automatically cataloged on your system for you by DB2.

In order for a DB2 client to access a DB2 database, the DB2 client needs to know some information about that database, such as its name, address, and so on. Think of it like calling someone at work. If you wanted to call Pamela Burnside at work, you would need to know her office's phone number and her name (obviously). Well, the same way you need information to call Pamela Burnside, you need to let DB2 know the same kind of things so that it can correctly contact the requested DB2 database. This process is called cataloging the database.

Essentially, the DB2 catalog directories contain contact information for a database such as:

- The database name (in the phone call example, the person's name is Pamela Burnside)
- The database alias name (in the phone call example, let's call her Pamela to make it easier)
- The location of the database on the network (in our example, the phone number)

You can read all about how to get DB2 clients and DB2 servers talking in Chapter 7, "Getting Clients and Servers Talking."

You can have a DB2 server and DB2 client installed on the same machine, via two separate installation processes, but that would be redundant because every DB2 server comes with all the components of a DB2 client.

You can introduce a DB2 client to a DB2 sever using the CCA, which is a graphical tool that makes this process really easy (see Chapter 8 for more information) or using the command line processor (CLP). The CLP is the way your grandfather used to catalog databases, and also the way you catalog databases from UNIX and Linux-based clients — truly old-fashioned, painful, and slow. In order to ensure that clients and servers can talk, you have to make sure that you have a DB2 client installed on the client machine, ensure that they can talk with a supported protocol, and catalog the databases. The CCA can really help with the last part of this process.

When you select the Catalog Sample Databases option, shown in Figure 6-19, the CCA launches, as shown in Figure 6-20. Just dismiss the window by clicking Cancel and then Close. You can read all about this tool and the wonders that it performs in the Chapter 7; at this point, we just want to make sure that it works.

You can start the CCA without First Steps by clicking Start and choosing Programs⇨IBM DB2⇨Client Configuration Assistant, or by entering **db2cca** at a Windows command prompt.

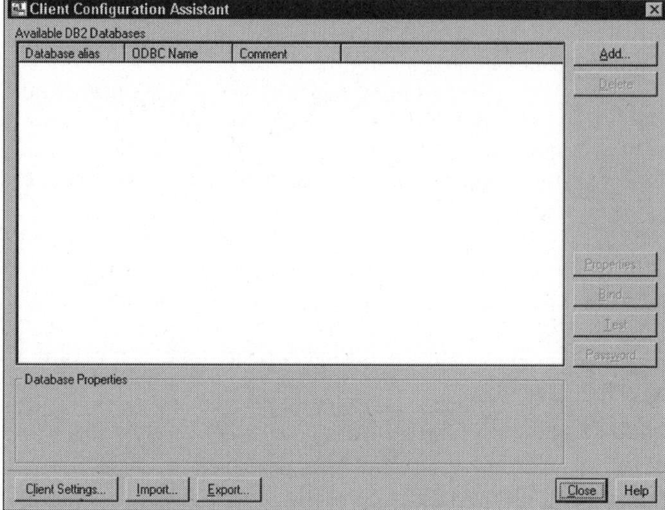

Figure 6-20: The Client Configuration Assistant (CCA) – makes cataloging remote databases, and some other tasks, we might add, as easy as 1-2-3.

Lab 6-2 Starting the Client Configuration Assistant

1. **From the Start menu, start the Client Configuration Assistant.**
2. **Ensure that it opens correctly.**
3. **Shut it down.**

Working with the sample databases

When you click the Work with Sample Databases button in Figure 6-19, First Steps will launch the Control Center just as it did with the DB2 server's version of First Steps. Launch the Control Center to ensure that it works on your client workstation, and then just shut it down. If you forget what it looks like, see the "Taking Your First Steps with DB2" section in Chapter 5.

If the Control Center doesn't start and asks you for a valid user account, ask yourself whether you logged on with the same user account that you used to install the DB2 client software — like the book says! If not, that's the problem. You can find out more about the user account that you need to run the Control Center in Chapter 8.

Viewing the DB2 Documentation

First Steps also gives you a tour of the DB2 documentation, including books, tasks, notebooks, and so on, via the DB2 Information Center. This is the same Information Center that you looked at when you installed the DB2 Server in Chapter 5. If you need a reminder, refer to the "Taking Your First Steps with DB2" section in Chapter 5 or just launch it.

You can also start the Information Center by clicking the Start button and choosing Programs➪IBM DB2➪Information➪Information Center or typing **db2ic** at a Windows command prompt.

Exiting First Steps

Just click the Exit option shown previously in Figure 6-19.

Cleaning House — How to Remove a DB2 Client

If, for some reason, you need to remove a DB2 client that you've installed, you have to do this through the Add/Remove utility provided with your Windows Operating System.

To remove a DB2 client that you've installed, follow these steps:

1. **Click Start and choose Settings➪Control Panel.**

   The Control Panel opens.

2. **Double-click the Add/Remove Programs icon in the Control Panel.**

   The Add/Remove Programs utility starts. This is the same utility that you would use if you were uninstalling a DB2 server, so refer to "Cleaning House — How to Remove a DB2 Server" in Chapter 5 if you need more detailed information.

3. **Select the IBM DB2 entry in the Currently installed programs box and click the Change/Remove button.**

4. **A confirmation pop-up window appears, asking you to confirm that you really want to remove the DB2 software from your workstation.**

   Click Yes.

   Clicking Yes removes the DB2 client software from your workstation and you won't be able to work through the exercises and examples in this book.

5. **If any DB2 processes are running, the DB2 uninstall program will ask whether you want to shut them down.**

   Select Yes and wave good-bye to your DB2 client.

Unlike a DB2 server uninstall, there isn't much left when you remove a DB2 client from your workstation. When the uninstall completes, remove the DB2LOG folder, located on the drive where your Windows operating system is installed.

You may also want to remove the user account that you defined for the Control Center Server. Most likely, you used the default `db2admin` user account. It is no problem if you don't remove this user account; just understand that if you perform a future DB2 installation on this workstation, it will default to the `db2admin` user account and you will have to use the password that already exists for this user.

If you didn't use the default `db2admin` user account that was provided to you by the installation program, you don't have to worry about using the same user account in a subsequent DB2 installation.

Prep Test

1 **Which of the following DB2 clients provide access runtime code to remote DB2 databases?**

A ❍ Thin-clients.
B ❍ Application Development clients.
C ❍ Administration clients.
D ❍ Runtime clients.
E ❍ All DB2 clients provide access to remote DB2 databases.

2 **If you were concerned with the amount of footprint available on a workstation, which two of the following DB2 clients would you likely choose?**

A ❑ Thin-client
B ❑ Application Development client
C ❑ Administration client
D ❑ Runtime client

3 **To enable a DB2 client to communicate with a remote DB2 server, all of the following tasks need to be performed except:**

A ❍ Ensure that the DB2 client and the DB2 server can communicate without DB2 using a communication protocol
B ❍ Catalog the remote database using the CCA or the command line processor
C ❍ Install a DB2 Client
D ❍ Set up the RAS (Remote Access Service) on your Windows workstation

4 **If you wanted to access local databases on a DB2 server, which of the following products would you have to install?**

A ❍ DB2 Runtime client.
B ❍ No additional DB2 products are needed as a DB2 server has the DB2 client run-time libraries as part of its installation.
C ❍ DB2 Client Configuration Assistant.
D ❍ DB2 Administration Client.

Answers

1 **E.** A DB2 client contains the necessary software to connect to a DB2 server. Different clients provide other features that allow you to build applications, manage an environment, and so forth. *Refer to "Ladies and Gentleman: A DB2 Client."*

2 **A** and **D.** Both of these clients provide minimal components and thereby take minimal space on your hard drive. *See "The weight watcher's solution: A DB2-Thin client" and "The DB2 Runtime client."*

3 **D.** You do not need to setup RAS to configure a DB2 client to communicate to a DB2 server. *See " Taking your second steps with DB2."*

4 **B.** A DB2 server has a built-in DB2 client to talk to other DB2 servers and itself! *See "Ladies and Gentleman: A DB2 Client."*

Chapter 7

Getting Clients and Servers Talking

Exam Objectives

- Ability to catalog a remote database or local database or DRDA

Many times throughout the day, we go through the process of getting the right information together to communicate with someone else, whether a colleague, friend, or family member. Worth mentioning as well is the infamous group of people we'd really rather not communicate with at all! This chapter focuses on the processes that should be followed to get remote DB2 Clients communicating to DB2 UDB databases and DB2 Host databases. It also goes into detail about DB2 directories and how they are used to store information about where a database can be found based on whether a local or remote client is looking for that database.

Quick Assessment

Ability to catalog a remote database or local database or DRDA

1 The _____ , _____, and the _____can be used to link a DB2 client to a DB2 server.

2 The DB2 _____ store information about where a database physically resides.

3 The two discovery methods are _____ discovery and _____ discovery.

4 The _____ command can be used to link a client to a server.

5 The three main steps in getting a client to access a remote server are _____, _____, and _____.

6 The six main client configuration methods are as follows: _____ ,_____ , _____ , _____ , _____, and _____.

7 The names of the four DB2 directories are _____, _____, _____, and _____.

8 DB2 supports the following protocols: _____, _____, _____, _____, and _____.

9 _____ provides the ability to send data to and receive data from different computers in potentially many different locations.

10 When using the `CATALOG` commands, the _____ command should be issued first, followed by the _____ command.

Answers

1. *Control Center, Client Configuration Center, Command Window.* Review "Sending and Receiving Data with DB2 Distributed Communication."

2. *directories.* Review "Understanding Database Directories."

3. *search, known.* Review "Linking the client to the server."

4. `CATALOG DATABASE`. Review "Linking the client to the server."

5. *setting up the protocol, configuring the server, configuring the client.* Review "Sending and Receiving Data with DB2 Distributed Communication."

6. *Search discovery, Known discovery, server access profiles, client access profiles, manual GUI, the* `CATALOG` *commands.* Review "Linking the client to the server."

7. *system database, local database, node, DCS.* Review "Understanding Database Directories."

8. *TCP/IP, IPX/SPX, NetBIOS, APPC, Named pipes.* Review "Sending and Receiving Data with DB2 Distributed Communication."

9. *Distributed communication.* Review "Sending and Receiving Data with DB2 Distributed Communication."

10. `CATALOG NODE`, `CATALOG DATABASE`. Review "Linking using the manual way."

Sending and Receiving Data with DB2 Distributed Communication

Distributed communication provides the ability to send data to and receive data from different computers in potentially many different locations. Distributed communication buzz words include networks, protocols, packets, IP addresses, clients, and servers.

DB2, of course, supports distributed communication. DB2 databases can be accessed by applications running on the same machine on which they reside (local clients), or by machines that reside halfway across the world (remote clients). These remote clients can run on any of the DB2 supported operating systems. In addition, DB2 supports the following protocols: TCP/IP, NetBIOS, Named Pipes, IPX/SPX, and APPC.

These protocols may not be supported on all DB2-supported operating systems.

The following three steps summarize how to get DB2 clients and servers talking. We expand Steps 2 and 3 to provide more detail on what they entail in the "Preparing the database server" and "Linking the client to the server" sections.

1. Ensure that the protocol software to be used for DB2 client/server communications is installed and configured on both the client and server machines.
2. Prepare the database server for communication for each protocol to be supported. This may include setting up the DAS instance and setting parameters related to discovery, if the Discovery method is to be used.
3. Prepare the client machine for communication for each protocol it is to be using. This involves two main steps: linking the client to the database server, followed by linking the client to a database on this server.

Preparing the database server

Luckily, most of these steps can be done automatically for you when DB2 is installed. Why then would you actually choose to do these steps yourself? Good question; here are some answers:

- You think this would be a fun way to spend your time!
- You want to configure a communication protocol that was not added as part of the install.
- You installed DB2 via the operating system rather than use the db2setup install program.

Here we use the DB2 Command Window to complete the actions necessary to prepare the database server.

Step 1: Set the DB2COMM variable for the DB2 instance

The DB2COMM variable defines which protocols can be used to communicate with this instance. The following example illustrates setting this variable to support TCP/IP and APPC communication.

```
db2set DB2COMM=tcpip,appc
```

A DB2STOP followed by a DB2START command must be issued for this variable to take effect.

Step 2: Follow protocol-specific setup instructions

Each protocol will have different instructions. We concentrate on the TCP/IP instructions to give you an idea of what this step involves for TCP/IP.

First, you need to edit the machine's services file to include the service name, port number, and protocol. The port number is used by the server to listen for incoming client requests. An example of such an entry follows:

```
db2svc  3300/tcp # DB2 connection service port
```

Next, you need to update the database manager configuration file with the DB2 instance with the service name used. In our example, that name is db2svc.

```
db2 update database manager configuration using svcename
            db2svc
```

A DB2STOP followed by a DB2START command must be issued for this change to take effect.

We explain the UPDATE DATABASE MANAGER CONFIGURATION command in more detail in Chapter 9.

You can also use the DB2 Control Center to prepare the database server for remote communications. From the instances folder, select the instance you want to configure and then select Setup Communications. Figure 7-1 shows what this Control Center window looks like.

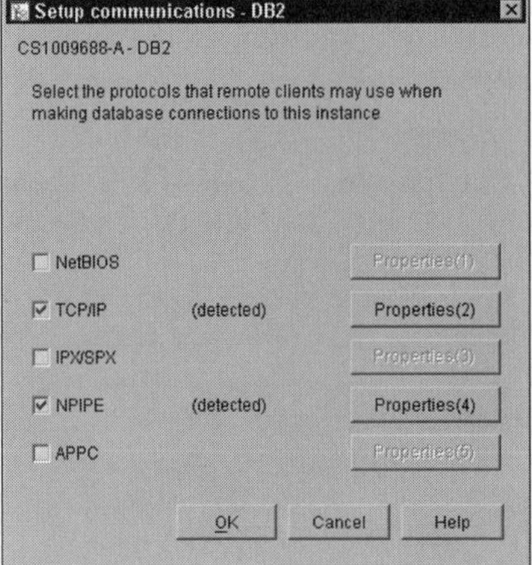

Figure 7-1: Control Center window to set up communications on the DB2 Server.

Linking the client to the server

In short, to link the client to the server, simply help the client find the server and then help it find the database on the server. This can be done using the Client Configuration Assistant (CCA), the DB2 Command Window, or the Control Center. We show you how to do this using the first two methods: the CCA and the Command window.

Using the CCA to link the client with the server

The CCA method has some really neat features to help make linking clients and servers easier.

Linking using discovery

DB2 provides a process called discovery that searches DB2 servers and their databases on a network. The major benefit of using the discovery method is that you don't have to know the location or the name of the remote database that you are configuring to connect to.

Two types of discovery exist: known discovery and search discovery. You use known discovery if you know the name of the system you are searching for and would like DB2 to find it and set everything up for you. Sounds simple enough, doesn't it? The search discovery method is even easier: DB2 will go out and search the network for all DB2 systems and databases that have made themselves known and list them for you to choose from.

Lab 7-1 shows how to issue commands from the CCA on the client machine to set up the link to a remote database using the discovery method.

Lab 7-1 Using the Client Configuration Assistant GUI tool

1. **Launch the CCA and click the Add button. Click the Search the Network radio button, as shown in Figure 7-2.**

2. **Click the Next button at the bottom of the window. Then click the [+] sign beside the Known Systems icon to list all the systems known to your client, as shown in Figure 7-3. Click the [+] sign beside the Other Systems icon to list other systems available.**

   Click the Add System button if you know the hostname of the system that you want to access as well as the protocol you'd like to use. This is considered Known Discovery. The remainder of this section focuses on the Search Discovery method.

3. **Click the [+] sign beside a system to get a list of the instances and databases that reside on this system. Select the database that you want to add, as shown in Figure 7-4. Click Next.**

   In this case, a system was chosen from the list of Other Systems. The instance name is `CORNISH01` and the database name is SAMPLE. If the system that contains the database that you want to add is not listed, click the [+] sign beside the Other Systems (Search the network) icon, as shown in Figure 7-3, to search the network for additional systems.

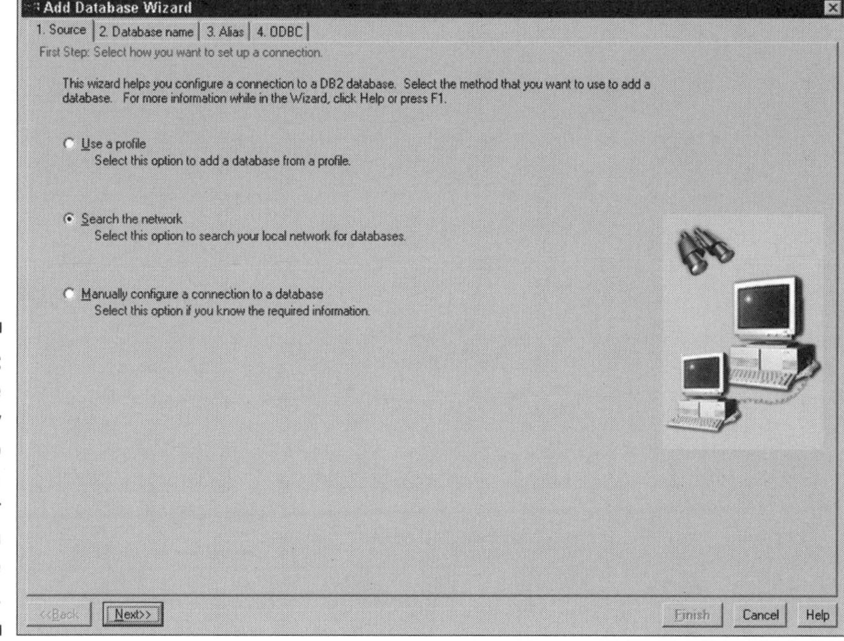

Figure 7-2: Use the discovery method to configure a client/server connection with the CCA.

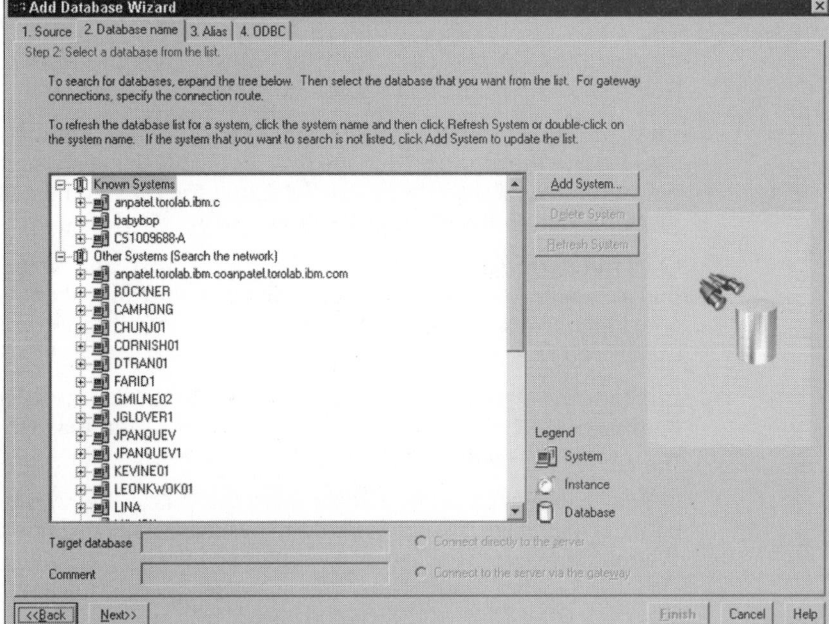

Figure 7-3: List of systems known to the DB2 client.

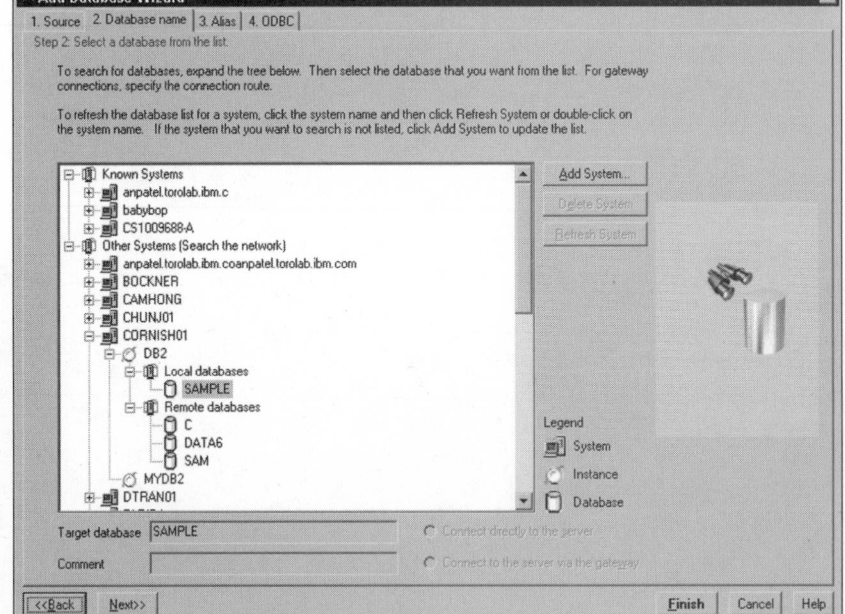

Figure 7-4: Select the instance and database that you want the client to be able to access.

4. **Type a local database alias name in the Database alias field and optionally type a comment that describes this database in the Comment field, as shown in Figure 7-5. Click Next.**

5. **You may choose to register this database as an ODBC source. ODBC must be installed, of course! Then click Finish to complete the addition of the database to this client. A window pops up, as shown in Figure 7-6, allowing you to test the connection from the client to this newly added database.**

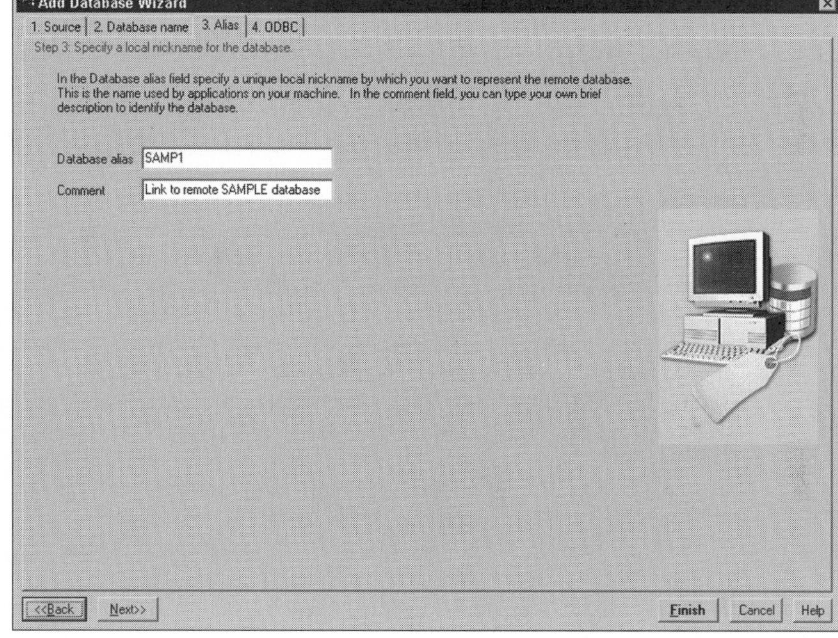

Figure 7-5: Specify the database alias that the client will use when accessing the database.

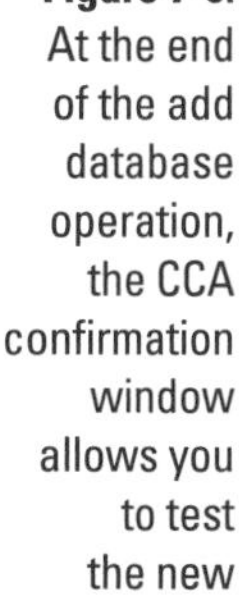

Figure 7-6: At the end of the add database operation, the CCA confirmation window allows you to test the new connection.

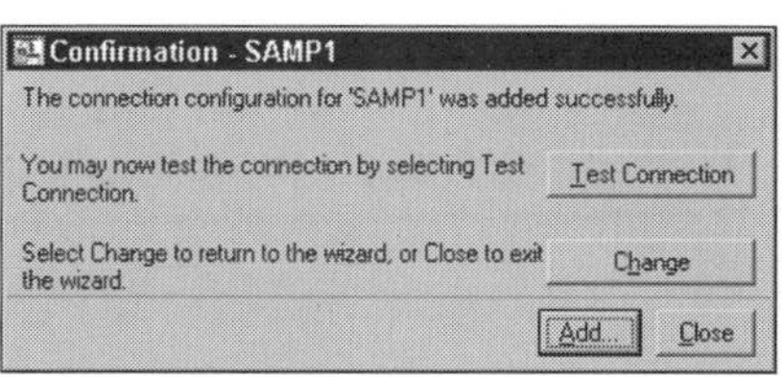

When testing the connection, a valid userid and password must be supplied.

The discovery methods can be used only to link to servers that have the DB2 Administration Server running.

The search discovery method can be used only with TCP/IP and NetBIOS. Known discovery can be used with all supported protocols with the exception of the APPC protocol.

Linking using access profiles

Just to be fair, both servers and clients can use profiles. Server profiles have all the goods on instances, databases, and protocols on the server. The client profile contains information that can be used to configure clients using the CCA import option. The information in the client and server profiles can be used to set up database connections between DB2 clients and DB2 servers. A DB2 profile is like a map to databases that are either on a DB2 server or have been cataloged on a DB2 client.

You may be wondering why anyone would use a profile. Well, you can do some nifty things with DB2 profiles! For example, server and client profiles can work together to make life easier for database administrators who have many, many clients to configure. After a server profile is created for a remote DB2 server, it can be imported into the DB2 client via the CCA. During the import, the DB2 client automatically receives the database connection information for all the databases on the DB2 server. Another attractive option is that after a DB2 client is configured for remote connections, the configuration information can be duplicated in one shot on other DB2 clients by creating a client profile and then importing it to other DB2 clients.

You can choose the access profile option of configuring clients by launching the CCA and clicking the Add button. You can then select the Use a Profile radio button (refer to Figure 7-2).

When the CCA is launched, you can see two buttons, labeled Import and Export, which you can use to import or export a profile. These buttons are shown in Figure 7-7.

Linking using the manual way

If you know the steps involved in configuring a client by using the Command Window, using the manual way via the CCA is a cinch! For this reason, we don't spend much time explaining this method. Figure 7-2 shows the radio button Manually Configure a Connection to a Database, which you can choose from the CCA window. To learn how to configure a client using the DB2 Command Window, read on. . . .

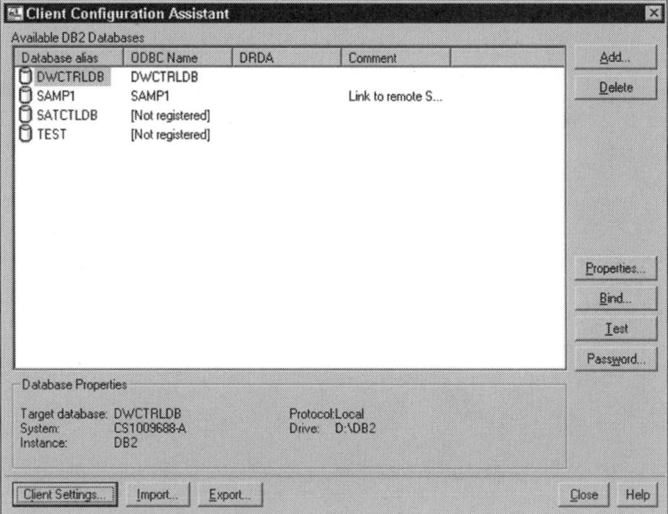

Figure 7-7: Import and export profile buttons.

Using the Command Window to link the client with the server

The `CATALOG` command is the main tool in the Command Window version of linking clients and servers. This command is used on the client to help the client find the remote server instance and then help it find the remote database within the instance.

Finding the remote instance

For this step, you need to know the protocol that you want to use, the address of the machine that the remote database resides on (remote host), and some protocol-specific setup information from the remote instance. The remote instance is hereby termed the *node*. (We discuss instances in more detail in Chapter 9.)

The basic syntax of the `CATALOG` command that carries out this step is as follows:

```
db2 catalog <protocol> node <nodename> remote <remote host>
         ... <protocol specific info>
```

We use good ol' TCP/IP again for example purposes. Near the beginning of this chapter, in the section "Preparing the database server," the following were configured in our TCP/IP example:

Service Name: db2svc

Port Number: 3300

Assume that the IP address of the remote machine containing the database that you want to access is 11.22.33.44. The hostname of the remote machine is `testmachine`. Now that you have all the required information, you can plug it into the `CATALOG` command for TCP/IP, as follows:

```
db2 catalog tcpip node <nodename> remote
            [hostname|ip_address] server
            [svcename|port_number] with "comments"
db2 catalog tcpip node mynode1 remote 11.22.33.44 server 3300
            with "This is my TCP/IP node!"
```

If you choose to specify the service name rather than the port number in the `CATALOG NODE` command, this information must be first added to the *services* file on the client. The service name and port number in the client's services file must match the values in the server's file.

If you choose to specify the hostname rather than the IP address in the `CATALOG NODE` command, the hostname and IP address of the server must be added to the *hosts* file on the client.

The `CATALOG NODE` command places an entry into the client's node directory. We discuss node directories in more detail in the "Understanding Database Directories" section later in this chapter.

Finding the remote database

Now that the client knows how to find the remote instance, we can help it to find the database it needs access to within that instance. Remember, on the client we refer to the remote instance as the *node*. To do this, the `CATALOG DATABASE` command comes into play.

The basic syntax of the `CATALOG DATABASE` command is as follows.

```
db2 catalog database <database name> as <alias name> at node
            <nodename> authentication <authentication type>
            with "comments"
```

The `AUTHENTICATION` option of the `CATALOG DATABASE` command is extremely important. Chapter 10, "Security and DB2," goes into detail about this option.

We know the node name from the `CATALOG NODE` command issued before — it is called mynode1. The database name is the database name from the server. The alias name is pretty simple — it is the "nickname" that the client will use to refer to this database. This comes in handy when a client needs to access two different databases on different remote instances that both happen to have the name, say "sample", on these instances. The alias would allow one to be referred to as "samp1" and the other as "samp2", for example.

For our example, the following command could be used to help the client find the remote database called sample within node mynode1.

```
db2 catalog database sample alias mysampl at node mynode1
          authentication server with "I can now access the
          sample database!"
```

This command will place an entry in the client's database directory. We discuss database directories in more detail in the "Understanding Database Directories" section later in this chapter.

Deciding which access method to use

With the variety of methods available to configure DB2 clients for access to remote databases, how do you choose which one to use? It's really not too difficult a decision — they all work; it's kind of just a matter of which one you are more comfortable with. However, Table 7-1 can be used as a guideline if you're one of those indecisive types!

Table 7-1 Choosing a Client Configuration Method

Configuration Method	*Real-world scenario*
Known discovery	Network is large and contains many routers and bridges; APPC is not being used.
Search discovery	Network is fairly simple and there are many clients; number of servers can change frequently; TCP/IP, NetBIOS, or both are being used.
Manually from the CCA	Advanced options are being used, especially for APPC, and a GUI is preferred.
Server Access Profile	Large number of clients to configure; these clients need access to different databases.
Client Access Profile	Large number of clients to configure; these clients need access to the same databases.
`CATALOG` commands	Configuration setup will be saved and reissued via scripts.

Understanding Database Directories

You can think of a DB2 directory as a phone book for databases. Database directories on the server store information related to where files associated with each database can be found on that server. Database directories on the client store information related to which server a remote database resides on and what name it will be referred to as on the client.

System database directory

A system database directory exists for every DB2 instance. Entries are stored in this directory implicitly when a database is created. Entries can be explicitly stored by using the `CATALOG DATABASE` command. These entries point to the physical location of each database in the instance. You can "open" the database phone book for each instance by issuing the `LIST DATABASE DIRECTORY` command. Figure 7-8 illustrates the type of information held in this directory.

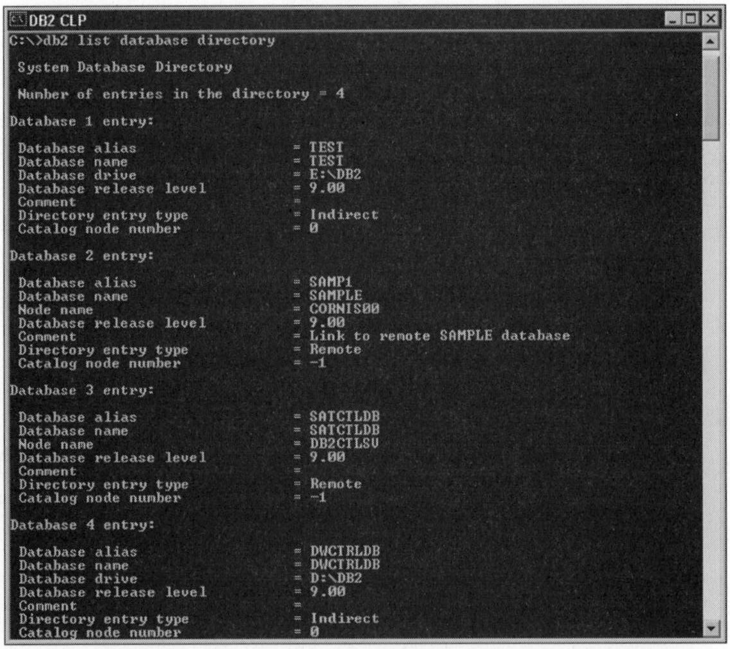

```
DB2 CLP
C:\>db2 list database directory

 System Database Directory

 Number of entries in the directory = 4

Database 1 entry:

 Database alias                       = TEST
 Database name                        = TEST
 Database drive                       = E:\DB2
 Database release level               = 9.00
 Comment                              =
 Directory entry type                 = Indirect
 Catalog node number                  = 0

Database 2 entry:

 Database alias                       = SAMP1
 Database name                        = SAMPLE
 Node name                            = CORNIS00
 Database release level               = 9.00
 Comment                              = Link to remote SAMPLE database
 Directory entry type                 = Remote
 Catalog node number                  = -1

Database 3 entry:

 Database alias                       = SATCTLDB
 Database name                        = SATCTLDB
 Node name                            = DB2CTLSV
 Database release level               = 9.00
 Comment                              =
 Directory entry type                 = Remote
 Catalog node number                  = -1

Database 4 entry:

 Database alias                       = DWCTRLDB
 Database name                        = DWCTRLDB
 Database drive                       = D:\DB2
 Database release level               = 9.00
 Comment                              =
 Directory entry type                 = Indirect
 Catalog node number                  = 0
```

Figure 7-8: System database directory for instance DB2.

Local database directory

A local database directory is on every path or drive that a database is created on. The local database directory on each path would contain all databases created on that path. The location in which the database resides is reflected in the "Database Drive" value from the system database directory. In Figure 7-8, you can see that the test database was created on drive E. You can use the command `LIST DATABASE DIRECTORY ON <PATH/DRIVE>` to view the local directory. Figure 7-9 shows the output from this command.

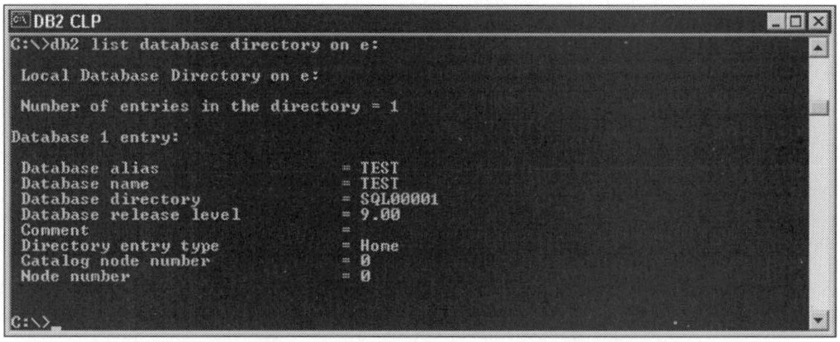

```
DB2 CLP
C:\>db2 list database directory on e:

 Local Database Directory on e:

 Number of entries in the directory = 1

Database 1 entry:

 Database alias                       = TEST
 Database name                        = TEST
 Database directory                   = SQL00001
 Database release level               = 9.00
 Comment                              =
 Directory entry type                 = Home
 Catalog node number                  = 0
 Node number                          = 0

C:\>
```

Figure 7-9: Local database directory for drive E.

Node directory

A node directory is located on machines acting as DB2 clients. This directory contains information on remote servers that contain databases that the client has access to. The DB2 client uses the communication information stored in the node directory to establish database connections or instance attachments to these servers. The command `LIST NODE DIRECTORY` lists the contents of this directory. Figure 7-10 illustrates the information stored.

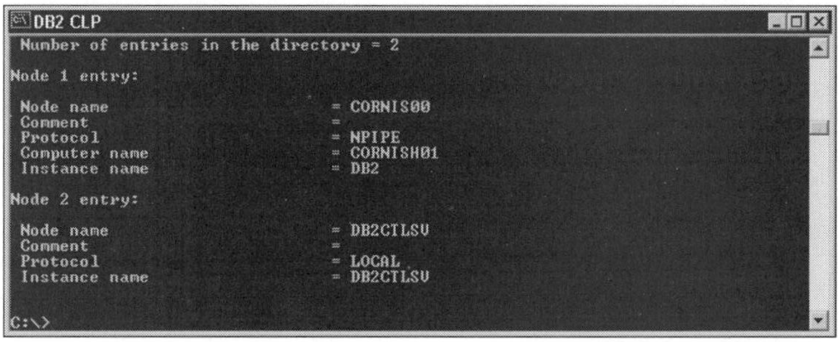

```
DB2 CLP
 Number of entries in the directory = 2

Node 1 entry:

 Node name                      = CORNIS00
 Comment                        =
 Protocol                       = NPIPE
 Computer name                  = CORNISH01
 Instance name                  = DB2

Node 2 entry:

 Node name                      = DB2CTLSV
 Comment                        =
 Protocol                       = LOCAL
 Instance name                  = DB2CTLSV

C:\>
```

Figure 7-10: Node database directory on a DB2 client machine.

DCS directory

The DCS directory, or Database Connection Service directory, resides on DB2 Connect clients and is used to store access information to DB2 Host databases. Host databases reside on host operating systems, such as OS/390 and AS/400. You can use the `LIST DCS DIRECTORY` command to list the contents of this directory.

Prep Test

1 **Which of the following protocols cannot be used with search discovery?**

A ❍ TCP/IP
B ❍ NetBIOS
C ❍ APPC
D ❍ IPX/SPX

2 **Which command should be used to link a client to an instance on a remote machine?**

A ❍ `LIST DATABASE DIRECTORY`
B ❍ `CATALOG DATABASE`
C ❍ `UPDATE DATABASE CONFIGURATION`
D ❍ `CATALOG NODE`

3 **If the following command is issued, which two of the following must have been completed first?**

```
db2 catalog tcpip node mynode remote
            hostname.loc.db2.com server 3400
```

A ❑ Port number 3400 was added to the services file on the client.
B ❑ The IP address of `hostname.loc.db2.com` was added to the hosts file on the client.
C ❑ Port number 3400 was added to the services file on the server.
D ❑ Node `mynode` was added to the node directory.

4 **Which of the following configuration methods are not available via the Client Configuration Assistant?**

A ❍ Server profiles
B ❍ Known discovery
C ❍ Catalog database
D ❍ Manual configuration

5 **Which of the following DB2 directories stores information about the physical location of the database(s) on a given DB2 instance on the server?**

A ❍ Local database directory
B ❍ System database directory
C ❍ Node directory
D ❍ DCS directory

Answers

1 **C and D.** Only TCP/IP and NetBIOS can be used with search discovery. *Review "Linking the client to the server."*

2 **D.** If TCP/IP is used, the command would read `CATALOG TCPIP NODE`. *Review "Linking using the manual way."*

3 **B and C.** The hosts file on the client must be updated because the command is using the remote hostname rather than the remote IP address. *Review "Preparing the database server" and "Linking using the manual way."*

4 **C.** The `CATALOG DATABASE` command can be issued via the DB2 Command Window or the DB2 Command Line processor. *Review "Linking using the manual way."*

5 **B.** The node and dcs directories are found on the client. *Review "Understanding Database Directories."*

Chapter 8

The DB2 Tools

Exam Objectives

- Knowledge of and ability to use the DB2 UDB GUI tools and CLP
- Knowledge of new V7.1 tools
- Ability to use the DB2 GUI tools to create, access and manipulate DB2 objects

DB2 UDB GUI tools and CLP? You have to love these acronyms! This short phrase embodies a whole assortment of goodies provided by DB2 Universal Database. The tools for administering DB2 are part of the Administration Client, a selectable component (installation option) with each of the DB2 Universal Database products. A large number of tools take advantage of really neat graphical user interfaces (GUIs) to make the job of administering your databases a snap. There is also a command-line processor (CLP) to satisfy those among you who actually prefer to interact more directly with DB2 by issuing commands from the operating system prompt, or by running command scripts that perform a number of related tasks "automatically." Whatever your preference, DB2 can satisfy it, from one extreme to the other, and everything in between.

In this chapter, we discuss these different ways of interacting with DB2. We cover the Control Center, which, as its name implies, is the main GUI tool. The Control Center gives you convenient access to many of the other GUI tools, but most important, it provides a great overview of your entire system and makes it easy to manage remote databases.

Following our discussion of the Control Center, we discuss the other DB2 GUI tools, grouped according to whether they can be accessed from the Control Center toolbar.

Quick Assessment

Using the DB2 GUI tools

1 You can use the DB2 Control Center to _____ jobs to run unattended.

2 You must catalog the _____ on the Control Center before the Satellite Administration Center can be enabled.

3 A _____ is a database that contains data that has been extracted from an operational database (for example, a sales database) and then transformed for decision making.

4 The _____ is a tool that monitors your system and that warns you about potential problems.

5 The Information Center launches a _____ to provide quick access to the DB2 product documentation.

6 Visual Explain is a graphical tool that provides a visual representation of the _____ that DB2 uses to run an SQL statement.

7 The Performance Monitor is a graphical tool that displays information from two monitoring facilities: _____ Monitor and _____ Monitor.

Using the DB2 command-line processor

8 If a DB2 command is issued from the operating system prompt (or from a DB2 Command Window on the Windows operating system), it must be prefixed by _____.

Answers

1 *schedule*. Review "The Control Center."

2 *satellite control database (SATCTLDB)*. Review "Satellite Administration Center."

3 *data warehouse*. Review "Data Warehouse Center."

4 *Alert Center*. Review "Alert Center."

5 *Web browser*. Review "Information Center."

6 *access plan*. Review "Visual Explain."

7 *Snapshot* and *Event*. Review "Performance Monitor."

8 *db2*. Review "Entering DB2 Commands."

The Control Center

You can do just about *anything* from the Control Center! In fact, you can

- Manage database objects. You can create, alter, and drop databases, table spaces, tables, views, indexes, triggers, and schemas. You can also administer or manage systems, instances, users, groups, aliases, user-defined types (UDT), user-defined functions (UDF), packages, and replication objects. All DB2 databases must be cataloged before they appear in the Control Center.
- Manage data. You can load, import, or export data, reorganize data, and collect statistics.
- Schedule jobs to run unattended.
- Back up and restore databases.
- Configure instances and databases.
- Analyze queries.
- Monitor and tune performance.
- Troubleshoot.
- Manage data replication.
- Manage database connections, such as DB2 Connect servers and subsystems.
- Manage applications.
- Change the font used for displaying menus and text throughout the Control Center.
- Launch other tools.

How can I get to this wonderful tool, you ask? That all depends on your operating system. For example, to open the Control Center window on Windows NT, click the Start button and choose Programs⇨IBM DB2⇨Control Center.

Take a look at this interface. The Control Center (shown in Figure 8-1) window has:

- A *menu bar,* which you can use to access the various Control Center functions
- A *toolbar,* from which you can launch other GUI tools
- An *objects pane* on the left side, containing all the objects that you can manage from the Control Center
- A *contents pane* on the right side, containing the objects that correspond to an object that you have selected in the objects pane

The toolbar also contains a contents pane that you can use to customize your view of the information in the contents pane; and the toolbar has hover help, which identifies each icon on the toolbar as you move the mouse pointer over it.

The top of the object hierarchy is the Systems object. To display all the local and remote DB2 objects that your system has cataloged, expand the object tree by clicking the plus signs (+) next to the objects. Figure 8-1 shows that system MELNYK contains a DB2 instance called DB2, which in turn contains two databases, SAMPLE and DWCTRLDB. When SAMPLE is highlighted, the objects associated with the SAMPLE database (its tables, views, indexes, and so on) are shown as folders in the contents pane.

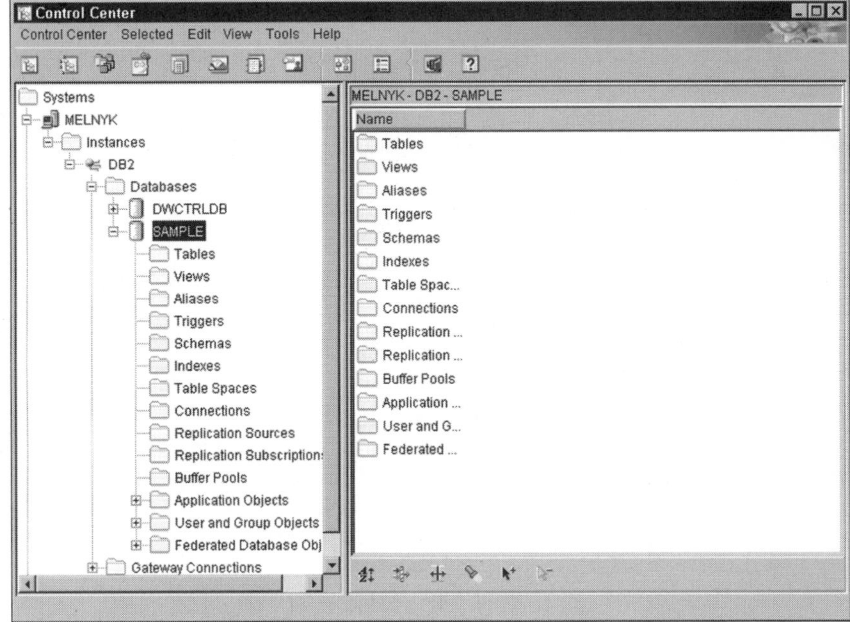

Figure 8-1: The DB2 Control Center lets you manage data and perform myriad other tasks.

To see all the actions that you can perform on an object, select the object from the objects pane or the contents pane and right-click the mouse. A pop-up menu shows all the functions that you can perform on that type of object. For example, if you select the Tables folder, you can do the following: create a new table with or without the help of a wizard; monitor the performance of tables; filter which tables appear in the contents pane; and so on. The tasks that you can perform depend on the object that you select.

Tools that can be accessed from the Control Center toolbar

By using the Control Center toolbar, you can access the following tools to help you manage and administer databases in your environment.

Control Center

We bet you're saying, "But I'm already *in* the Control Center! Why would I want another one?" With a second Control Center, you can work with two or more objects that aren't easily displayed in a single object tree or contents pane. This is really useful when you want to look at the contents of two folders at the same time.

Satellite Administration Center

The Satellite Administration Center is a set of tools that allows you to set up and administer groups of DB2 servers from a central point. Each DB2 server that belongs to a group is known as a *satellite*.

The DB2 servers in a particular group have shared characteristics. For example, they may have the same applications running on them. The DB2 servers in a group have similar database configurations and purpose. Why do this? The answer is efficiency. By grouping such DB2 servers together, you can administer them collectively rather than individually.

Information about the satellite environment is stored in a central database known as the *satellite control database*. This database records, among other things, which satellites are in the environment, the group to which each satellite belongs, and which version of an end-user application that a satellite is running. This database resides on a DB2 server known as the *DB2 control server*. You must catalog the satellite control database (SATCTLDB) on the Control Center before the Satellite Administration Center can be enabled.

To set up and maintain its database configuration, each satellite connects to the satellite control database to download the *batches* that correspond to its version of an end-user application. The satellite runs these batches locally and then reports the results back to the satellite control database. This process of downloading batches, running them, and reporting the results is known as *synchronization*. A satellite synchronizes to maintain its consistency with the other satellites that belong to its group and that are running the same version of the end-user application.

Data Warehouse Center

The Data Warehouse Center (DWC) is a set of tools that helps you to build, manage, and access DB2 data warehouses. A *data warehouse* is a database that contains informational data. *Informational data* is data that has been extracted from an operational database (for example, a sales database) and then transformed for decision-making. We say "transformed" because operational data (raw transaction data) is not usually suitable for direct use by business analysts. To be really useful, such data must be summarized in ways that are meaningful to the analyst, who can query the warehouse without creating a negative impact on the performance of the operational databases. For example, the analyst can use information about which products were sold in different regions at different times of the year to discover trends that can be exploited through focused marketing.

You can use the Data Warehouse Center to define, monitor, and maintain the processes that move and transform data for the warehouse. Following is a list of the objects that you can use to create and maintain your data warehouse:

- *Subject areas.* A subject area identifies and groups the processes that relate to a logical area of the business. For example, if you were building a warehouse of marketing and sales data, you might define a Sales subject area and a Marketing subject area. You would then add the processes that relate to sales under the Sales subject area, and add the processes that relate to marketing under the Marketing subject area.
- *Warehouse sources.* Warehouse sources identify the tables, views, or files that will provide the data for your warehouse. A source must be accessible to the warehouse.
- *Warehouse targets.* Warehouse targets are database tables or files that contain transformed data.
- *Warehouse agents.* Warehouse agents manage the flow of data between warehouse sources and warehouse targets. Warehouse agents are available on AS/400, OS/390, Windows NT, AIX, the Solaris Operating Environment, and OS/2. Agents use Open Database Connectivity (ODBC) drivers or the DB2 Call Level Interface (CLI) to communicate with different databases.
- *Processes.* A process contains a series of steps that transform and move data. A process moves source data into the warehouse, where it is transformed and summarized.
- *Steps.* A step is a single operation within a process. It can use SQL statements or call programs to transform and move data. Steps can be run on demand or be scheduled to run later. Suppose that you wanted to:

  1. Extract data from different databases.
  2. Convert the data to a single format.
  3. Write the data to a warehouse table.

  You would create a process that contains several steps, each step performing a separate task. You might need to create several steps to completely transform, format, and put the data into the warehouse table.

Here is a summary of the types of steps that are available:

- *SQL steps.* An SQL step uses an SQL `SELECT` statement to extract data from a warehouse source, and generates an `INSERT` statement to insert the data into the warehouse target.
- *Program steps.* These steps run predefined programs and utilities.
- *Transformer steps.* Transformer steps are stored procedures and user-defined functions that transform data.
- *User-defined program steps.* A user-defined program step is a business-specific transformation. Because every business has unique data transformation requirements, businesses can choose to write their own program steps or use tools provided by other vendors.

Here is a summary of data warehousing tasks:

- Identify the source data and define it as one or more warehouse sources.
- Create a database to serve as the warehouse, and define warehouse targets.
- Define subject areas for related groups of processes.
- Define process steps that specify how the source data is to be moved and transformed.
- Test the steps and schedule them to run automatically.
- If you're using DB2 Warehouse Manager, create an information catalog of the data in the warehouse. An *information catalog* is a database that contains business metadata to help you identify and locate information.

Command Center

The Command Center (see Figure 8-2) is an interactive window through which you can:

- Run SQL statements, DB2 commands, and operating system commands. You can run operating system commands in any supported operating system script language, such as REXX, by preceding them with an exclamation mark (!). The Command Center, when used in interactive mode, keeps a history of all statements and commands that have run during the current session; you can easily retrieve and modify them as you work with the database.
- See the output from one or more SQL statements or DB2 commands in a result window. You can scroll through the results and generate a report.

- Create and save command scripts to the Script Center. You can edit command scripts to create new scripts. From the Script Center, a command script can be scheduled to run as a job at whatever time or frequency you specify.
- View the access plan and the statistics associated with an SQL statement before execution.

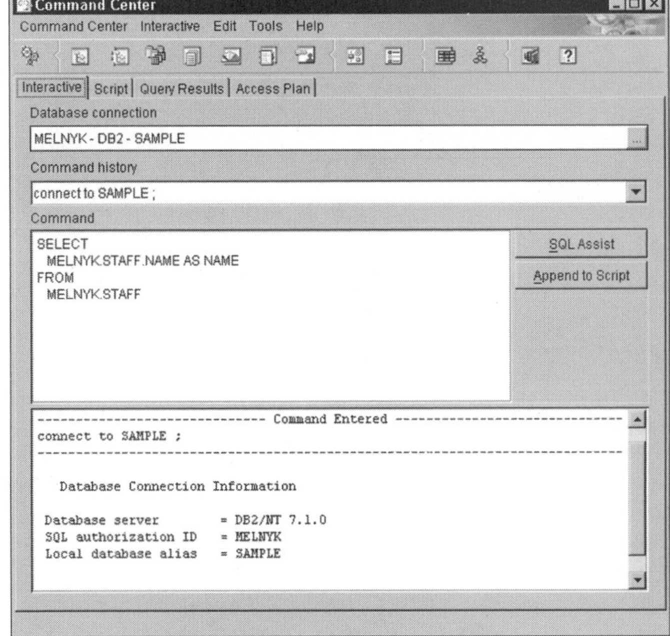

Figure 8-2: Querying the database through the Command Center.

Script Center

The Script Center (see Figure 8-3) is a tool that helps you to manage scripts containing SQL statements, DB2 commands, or operating systems commands. Did we say manage? You bet! You can create completely new scripts, or import scripts that you created earlier; you can copy scripts, edit existing scripts to create new ones, or remove scripts. Of course, you can run scripts. You can even schedule scripts to run whenever you want them to run!

If you run a script from the Script Center (instead of from a command prompt), you get the advantage of having the results logged in the Journal. In the Journal, you can see the jobs that use a particular script, or see the status of all scheduled jobs. A *job* is a Journal entry that's created whenever you schedule a script or run a script immediately (more about that later).

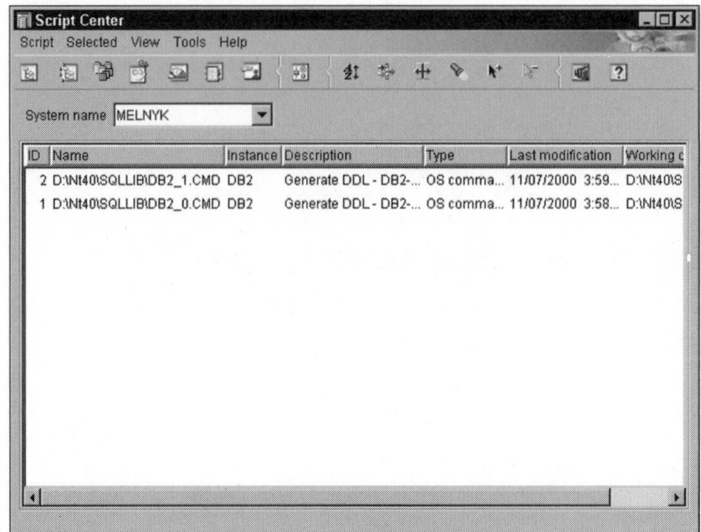

Figure 8-3: Managing scripts with the Script Center.

Alert Center

The Alert Center is a tool that monitors your system and that warns you about potential problems. You can set the Alert Center to automatically display (or alert you to) any monitored objects that have exceeded a defined threshold. You can set up thresholds for these performance variables by using the Performance Monitor (more about that later). A red icon in the display indicates an alarm; a yellow icon indicates a warning. Values for the affected performance variables are also displayed.

Journal

The Journal (Figure 8-4) is another busy DB2 tool! It records all scripts run, all DB2 messages and alerts returned, and the DB2 recovery history (details about backup, restore, and load operations) for a database. The Journal can be used to show the contents of a script, show the results of a job, or enable or disable a job. The Journal allows you to monitor pending jobs or running jobs and view job histories. You can reschedule a pending job, show the scripts that are associated with it, or run it immediately.

When a saved script is modified, all jobs that are dependent upon it inherit the new behavior.

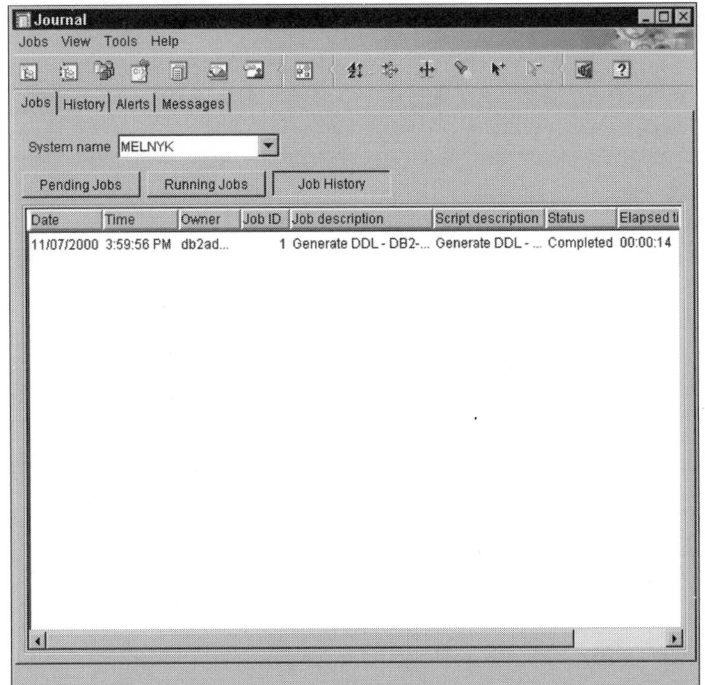

Figure 8-4: Use the Journal to track jobs.

License Center

The License Center (shown in Figure 8-5) displays the status of your DB2 license and usage information for DB2 products installed on your system. It allows you to configure your system for proper license monitoring.

The License Center allows you to:

- Add a new license.
- Upgrade a trial license to a permanent license.
- View the details of your license:
  - Product name
  - Version information
  - Expiration date
  - Registered user policy
  - Concurrent user policy
  - Number of entitled users

- Number of concurrent users
- Enforcement policy
- Number of processors (for Enterprise Edition and Enterprise – Extended Edition only)

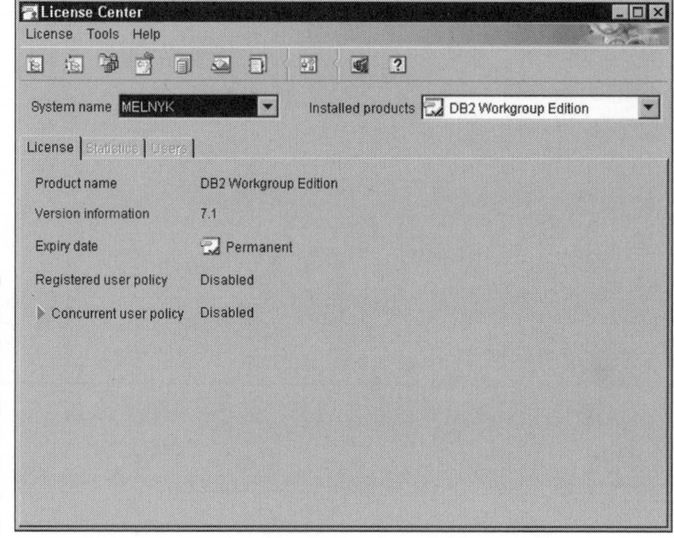

Figure 8-5: Viewing the status of your DB2 license in the License Center.

Stored Procedure Builder

DB2 Stored Procedure Builder is an easy-to-use development environment for creating, installing, and testing stored procedures that can run on the entire DB2 database family, ranging from DB2 Universal Database for a single workstation to DB2 Universal Database for OS/390. DB2 Stored Procedure Builder allows you to focus on creating your stored procedure logic rather than the details of registering, building, and installing stored procedures on a DB2 server. Using DB2 Stored Procedure Builder, you can

- Create highly portable stored procedures (in Java or the SQL procedure language).
- Build stored procedures on local or remote DB2 servers. You can develop stored procedures on one operating system and build them on other (server) operating systems.
- Modify and rebuild existing stored procedures.
- Test and debug installed stored procedures.

DB2 Stored Procedure Builder is an optional component of the DB2 Application Development Client on AIX, the Solaris Operating Environment, and Windows 32-bit operating systems.

- On Windows 32-bit operating systems, you can launch DB2 Stored Procedure Builder from the DB2 Universal Database program group, issuing the `db2spb` command from the command prompt, or from Microsoft Visual C++ 5.0 and 6.0, Microsoft Visual Basic 5.0 and 6.0, or IBM VisualAge for Java.
- On AIX or the Solaris Operating Environment, you can launch DB2 Stored Procedure Builder by entering **db2spb** at the command prompt. You can also launch DB2 Stored Procedure Builder as a separate application from the DB2 UDB program group, or you can invoke it from IBM VisualAge for Java.

You can also start DB2 Stored Procedure Builder from the Control Center for DB2 for OS/390. In this case, you can start DB2 Stored Procedure Builder as a separate process from the Control Center Tools menu, toolbar, or Stored Procedures folder.

DB2 Stored Procedure Builder uses projects to manage your work. Each project saves your connections to specific databases; when you open an existing project, you are automatically prompted to enter your user ID and password for a specific database. DB2 Stored Procedure Builder is implemented with Java, and all database connections are managed with Java Database Connectivity (JDBC). Using a JDBC driver, you can connect to any local DB2 alias or any other database for which you can specify a host, port, and database name.

Tools Settings

The Tools Settings notebook (see Figure 8-6) allows you to customize the DB2 graphical tools and some of their options. You can use this notebook to

- Set online help properties.
- Specify the server administration tools startup property.
- Obtain DB2 diagnostic information.
- Specify a command statement termination character. The statement termination character is important when you want to run multiple statements in the Command Center.
- Set replication properties.
- Set Alert Center properties.
- Invoke an action when the status of a node changes to down or unknown.
- Change the fonts for menus and text.
- Set DB2 Universal Database for OS/390 Control Center properties.

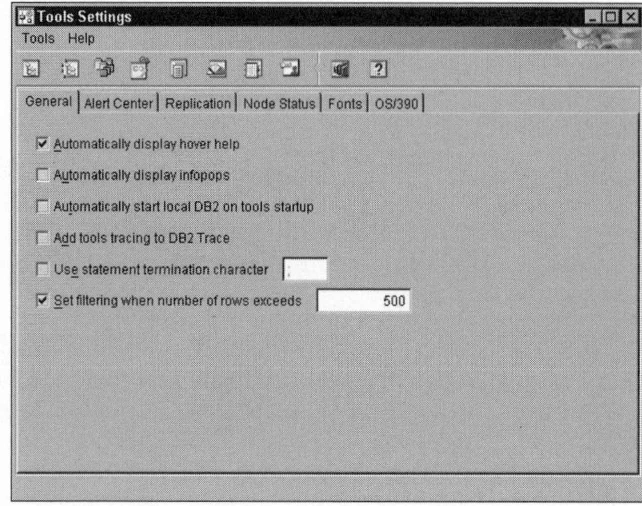

Figure 8-6: Use the Tools Settings window to customize the DB2 graphical tools and options.

Information Center

The Information Center (see Figure 8-7) provides quick access to the DB2 product documentation. It launches a Web browser to display the information you want.

Use the Information Center to find

- Task instructions. Use the Tasks page of the Information Center notebook to find instructions for a particular task. This page lists the most common tasks that you can perform using the Control Center, and other major administrative and application development tasks.
- A particular book. Use the Books page of the Information Center notebook to look up information from a particular book, or to see what books are available. To download printable versions of the books, go to the Web page of the Information Center notebook and select Download DB2 Documentation in Postscript or PDF Format.
- Reference information. Use the Reference page of the Information Center notebook to find reference information. This page gives you quick access to information contained in the *SQL Reference,* the *Command Reference,* the *Administrative API Reference,* or the *CLI Guide and Reference*.
- Troubleshooting information. Use the Troubleshooting page of the Information Center notebook to find solutions to problems encountered while using DB2 Universal Database. This page includes descriptions of error messages and associated recovery actions, and links to IBM sites on the World Wide Web where you can find up-to-date information about problems and solutions.

You can also get error message help in the DB2 Command Center, the DB2 command-line Processor, or a DB2 Command Window, by typing **? SQLnnnnn**, where SQLnnnnn is the error message number.

- Information about sample programs. Use the Sample Programs page of the Information Center notebook to view the descriptions and source of the sample programs that come with the DB2 Application Development Client. The sample programs are formatted with color and hypertext links to make them easier to understand.
- DB2 information on the World Wide Web. Use the Web page of the Information Center notebook to find information about DB2 on the World Wide Web (if you have Internet access). This information includes product fixes and documentation that you can download, as well as answers to frequently asked questions. The links may not work if your machine is behind a firewall or disconnected from the network.

If you know part of the title of an item, you can search for it by selecting Edit⇨Find. To search the entire DB2 document library, follow the hypertext link beneath the By Title push button to go to the DB2 online information search form. Some items may not be available if the corresponding online information isn't installed.

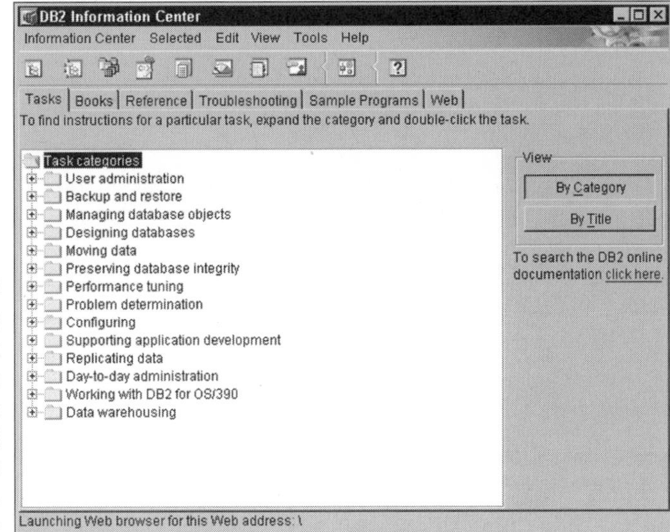

Figure 8-7: Find product information through the DB2 Information Center.

To practice some of the things that you read about in this section, do the exercises in Lab 8-1.

Lab 8-1 Exploring the Control Center

1. **On Windows NT/2000, click Start and select Programs⇨IBM DB2⇨Control Center.**

   This brings up the Control Center window.

2. **Expand the objects tree in the objects pane.**
3. **Select Databases⇨Create⇨Database Using Wizard.**

   The Create Database wizard opens.

4. **Let the wizard guide you through the process of creating a new database.**
5. **Select other objects in the tree, such as Systems or Instances, and use the Selected pull-down menu or a pop-up menu to see what actions you can perform against those objects.**
6. **Explore the Control Center interface. See what's available from the menu bar and from the contents pane toolbar.**

Other GUI tools

You can also use the following tools to help you manage and administer databases in your environment.

First Steps

First Steps is a graphical tool that helps you to get started using DB2 UDB. First Steps has a number of options; all are available by clicking on the icon next to the action. You can

- Create the sample databases. DB2 now includes the SAMPLE database, along with OLAP and Data Warehousing databases that you can use to try out the new features in the product.
- Work with the sample databases. You can, for example, list the tables and view their contents.
- Work with the DB2 UDB Business Intelligence tutorial. This tutorial provides an end-to-end guide for typical business intelligence tasks.
- View the product information library. This is helpful in finding out what DB2 UDB information is available online and how it is organized.

Get some practice using the First Steps tool by doing the exercises in Lab 8-2.

Lab 8-2 Creating the SAMPLE database

1. **On Windows NT/2000, click Start and select Programs⇨IBM DB2⇨ First Steps.**

   This brings up the First Steps main screen.

2. **Select Create Sample Databases.**

   The First Steps - Create Sample Databases window opens.

3. **Select DB2 UDB Sample and click OK.**

Client Configuration Assistant

Ah, the CCA! A wonderful tool! More like a collection of wizards that make connecting DB2 clients to local *or remote* DB2 servers, and even to DB2 Connect servers, easy. Easy in this case is really good, because these tasks can be quite tricky to do manually. The CCA can be invoked from the DB2 Desktop Folder, or from the operating system prompt (if you issue the `db2cca` command).

What does it mean to "configure DB2 clients"? The CCA keeps a list of databases to which your applications can connect; in other words, it *catalogs* nodes and databases. For all the details about cataloging nodes and databases, see Chapter 7, "Getting Servers and Clients Talking."

Using the Client Configuration Assistant, you can

- Add, modify, or delete database connection entries.
- Test your connection to a particular database.
- Update (change the value of) certain database manager configuration parameters.
- Configure CLI/ODBC settings.
- Bind DB2 utilities and other applications to a particular database.
- Import or export configuration information, making it easy for you to use the existing configuration on a machine to configure new machines.
- Change the password for the user ID that you use to connect to a particular database.

SQL Assist

SQL Assist is a graphical tool that you can use to build `SELECT`, `INSERT`, `UPDATE`, and `DELETE` statements. The tool uses a notebook to help you organize the information that you need to create an SQL statement. SQL Assist is available in the Control Center, the Stored Procedure Builder, and the Data Warehouse Center.

Create Index Wizard

Use the Create Index wizard if you want advice on which indexes to create for a given set of SQL statements. The wizard will make recommendations based on the workload that you specify. If the workload does not accurately reflect actual statements run against your database, the recommendations will not improve the performance of your database.

Wait a second! What's a workload? A *workload* consists of a number of SQL statements that are run against a database. The Create Index wizard uses the specified workload to determine which indexes to recommend and create.

You can use the Create Index wizard to

- Create a workload.
- Edit a workload.
- Add an SQL statement to a workload.
- Change an SQL statement in a workload.
- Import SQL statements.
- View workload details.
- View an SQL statement in a workload.

The Workload Details window shows you the runtime for each SQL statement in the workload, expressed in timerons. The Current column shows the run time for the statement with your current indexes. The Recommended column shows the runtime for the statement with the recommended indexes.

A *timeron* is an abstract unit of measure. It does not equate to actual elapsed time, but gives a relative estimate of the resource cost of a particular access plan. *Cost* is derived from a combination of CPU cost and input/output activity (I/O).

The cost shown for an operator node of an access plan graph is the cumulative cost from the start of access plan execution up to and including the execution of that particular operator. It does not reflect the workload on the system or the cost of returning data to the user.

Visual Explain

Visual Explain is a graphical tool that provides a visual representation of the access plan that DB2 uses to run an SQL statement. Tables, indexes, and each operation on them are represented as nodes, and the flow of data is represented by links among the nodes. The Visual Explain utility captures information about how SQL statements are compiled. The tool itself is available from the pop-up menus for various database objects in the Control Center, or from the Command Center.

Why would you want to see the access plan for an SQL query? Well, the short answer is that the access plan can help you tune your SQL queries for better performance.

More specifically, you would use Visual Explain to

- View the statistics that were used at the time of query optimization. (The *optimizer* is a component of the SQL compiler that chooses an access plan for an SQL statement. It does this by modeling the execution cost of many alternative access plans, and choosing the one with the lowest estimated cost.) You can then compare these statistics to the current catalog statistics to figure out whether rebinding the package might improve performance.
- Determine whether or not an index was used to access a table. If an index was not used, Visual Explain can help you decide which columns should be included in an index. A wizard is also available to help you decide what indexes to create (see the "Create Index Wizard" section, earlier in this chapter).
- View the effects of various tuning techniques by comparing the "before" and "after" versions of the access plan graph for a query.
- Obtain cost information about each operation in the access plan.
- Understand how two tables are *joined* (more about joins in Part IV, "Talking to DB2 with Structured Query Language").

Performance Monitor

The Performance Monitor is a graphical tool that displays information from two monitoring facilities: Snapshot Monitor and Event Monitor.

- The Snapshot Monitor captures database information at specific points in time. You determine the time interval between these points and what data will be captured. The Snapshot Monitor can help analyze performance problems, tune SQL statements, and identify exception conditions based on limits or thresholds.
- The Event Monitor is a tool that enables you to analyze resource usage by recording the state of the database at the time specific events occur. Use the Event Monitor, for example, when you need to know how long a transaction has taken to complete, or how much CPU an SQL statement has used. Entering **db2emcrt** at a command prompt creates an Event Monitor. Event Monitor records are usually stored on disk and then analyzed after the data has been captured. The Event Analyzer tool provided with DB2 can be used to analyze the captured data. An Event Analyzer is invoked by entering **db2evmon** at a command prompt. There is one *connection event record* for each database connection that has occurred, and there is one *statement event record* for each statement that has run during a particular connection. Each connection event record maps to one row in the Connections View window of the Event Analyzer,

and each statement event record maps to one row in the Statements View window of the Event Analyzer. For each connecting application, the Connections View window of the Event Analyzer shows the following items:

- Application name
- Application ID
- Execution ID
- Connect time
- Total sort time
- Lock wait time
- Deadlocks
- Total CPU time
- Disconnect time

The Performance Monitor keeps track of DB2 objects such as instances, databases, tables, table spaces, and connections. From the Control Center, you can capture snapshots from only one instance of a database manager at a time. Use the Performance Monitor to

- Analyze performance trends by creating a visual representation of database information, such as disk activity, buffer pool usage, and lock usage.
- Detect performance problems.
- Tune databases for optimum performance.
- Analyze the performance of database applications.

You can use the predefined monitors that are included with DB2, or you can create your own monitors. To see what information the Performance Monitor is collecting, click the right mouse button on the object and select Show Monitor Activity in the pop-up window.

When an object is being monitored, the color of its icon is green, yellow, or red to indicate status: green means that the monitor is running and that everything is fine; yellow is a warning that the monitor is detecting levels that are approaching thresholds that you set earlier; red is an alarm raised because some monitored variable has reached its threshold.

You can use the predefined monitors that are available with DB2, or you can create your own monitors. For each predefined monitor, a variety of performance variables can be monitored. The Performance Variable Reference Help, available from the Help menu of any Snapshot Monitor window, provides a description of all of the more than 200 performance variables. These variables are organized into categories. By default, all performance variables are monitored, but the categories can be turned on and off through the administration tools. The following categories are set to On by default:

- Instance: Agents, Connections, Sort
- Database: Lock and Deadlock, Buffer Pool and I/O, Connections, Lock and Deadlock, Sort, SQL Statement Activity
- Table: Table
- Table space: Buffer Pool and I/O
- Database Connections: Buffer Pool and I/O, Lock and Deadlock, Sort, SQL Cursors, SQL Statement Activity

The DB2 Performance Monitor contains a set of predefined monitors, which you can use as is, or which you can copy and modify (by adding or removing performance variables) to meet your requirements. You can't change the name, equation, or text description of an IBM-supplied Performance Monitor; however, you can change the threshold values and the alert actions.

The predefined monitors that are supplied with DB2 are the following:

- **Monitoring Capacity.** Use this monitor to get information on system capacity. This monitor can be checked on a regular basis to see the overall usage of your system over time.
- **Sort.** Use this monitor to ensure that your sort heap and sort heap threshold parameters are set correctly. This monitor should be run when you first start your system, during peak periods of activity, or as applications change.
- **Locking.** Use this monitor to determine how much locking is occurring in your system and whether your lock list parameters are set appropriately.
- **Cache.** Use this monitor to optimize cache usage. By monitoring these values during peak periods, you can determine whether you need to increase the size of the cache.
- **Bufferpool.** Use this monitor on small tables to determine whether they require their own buffer pools.
- **Deadlocks.** Use this monitor to determine whether your applications are getting into deadlocks.
- **Fast Communication Manager.** Use this monitor to see the percentage of memory used to transfer information between nodes.
- **Prefetchers.** Use this monitor to determine whether you have enough prefetchers defined for the system. *Prefetchers* are agents that retrieve data from disk and move it into the buffer pool before applications need the data.

- **Disk Performance.** Use this monitor to watch input and output. This monitor contains performance variables that focus on disk performance at the database and table space levels.
- **Global Memory.** Use this monitor to watch application memory use.
- **Long Running Memory.** Use this monitor to help determine why a query is taking a long time to complete.
- **Gateway Connections.** Use this monitor to watch DB2 Connect server connections.

To see a list of available monitors from the Control Center, click the right mouse button on the Systems folder and select List Monitors from the pop-up menu. The List Monitors window opens. It lists the monitors that are stored on the JDBC server to which you are currently connected. For each monitor, you see the name of the monitor, a description, the status, whether it is the default monitor, and who created the monitor. The status of the monitors indicates the status of the monitors on the local system, not the JDBC server.

Replicating data

Replication is the process of taking changes stored in the database log at the source server and applying them to the target server. You can use replication to define, synchronize, automate, and manage copy operations for data across your enterprise. You can automatically deliver the data from a host system to target sites. For example, you can copy data and applications to branch offices, retail outlets, and even sales representatives' laptops.

The two operational components in replication are *capture* and *apply*. The capture component captures changes made to data in source tables that have been defined for replication by reading the database log. The apply component reads the changed data previously captured and stored in a change data table, and applies it to the target tables.

Using the Control Center, you can do the setup required for replication by using the Define as replication source and Define subscription actions. The capture and apply replication components run outside of the DB2 administration tools.

You can perform the following actions from the Control Center:

- Define replication sources
- Define replication subscriptions
- Specify SQL to enhance data during the apply process

Query Patroller

DB2 Query Patroller is designed to help you better understand the resource costs associated with your queries. Use Query Patroller to provide query and resource management for decision support systems (DSS) that use data warehouses and other data mining intensive database structures.

What does DB2 Query Patroller do? The DB2 Query Patroller server traps queries from DB2 clients that have Query Patroller client installed, analyzes them, and then dynamically prioritizes and schedules the queries for processing. If applicable, Query Patroller can distribute its workload across different database partition servers by using a DB2 Query Patroller Agent. It can also produce detailed system utilization and database usage reports.

DB2 Query Patroller consists of the following components:

- DB2 Query Patroller Server accepts, analyzes, prioritizes, and schedules database requests. The server consists of several software components, including request server, cost analyzer, and job scheduler.
- DB2 Query Patroller Agent processes database requests. The agent consists of two software components, node manager and executor.
- The Command Line Interface enables you to monitor and control DB2 Query Patroller from a command line prompt.
- QueryAdministrator is a Java application that provides a GUI interface for administering the DB2 Query Patroller system. QueryAdministrator helps you manage DB2 Query Patroller system parameters, create or delete profiles for DB2 Query Patroller users, and manage nodes, result destinations, data sources, and job queues.
- The Tracker is a system administration GUI tool that provides reports displaying database usage history for queries that have been managed by the DB2 Query Patroller system.
- QueryEnabler places submitted queries under the management of the DB2 Query Patroller system. You can wait for the query results to return, or you can have the query results returned at a more convenient time later.
- *QueryMonitor* is a GUI tool used for monitoring and managing queries that have been submitted through the DB2 Query Patroller system. You can monitor query status, view job details, cancel jobs, submit new jobs, drop result tables, and resubmit completed jobs.

OLAP Server Starter Kit

The DB2 OLAP Server Starter Kit lets you perform multidimensional analysis on relational data using Online Analytical Processing (OLAP, pronounced "oh-lap") techniques. *Multidimensional analysis?* What on earth is that?

Well, relational data can be considered two-dimensional because each piece of data (a *fact*) is associated with the intersection of a row (first dimension) and a column (second dimension). Multidimensional analysis extends this perspective to other dimensions that represent the core components of your business plan, such as products, markets, and time. Each dimension has individual components called *members*. For example, individual products can be members of the Products dimension. You can also have member hierarchies, such as quarters and months in the Time dimension. Multidimensional analysis enables you to use your relational databases to answer complex questions such as "What is the profitability of my focus products across the southeast region during the third quarter?"

An *OLAP model* is a logical structure that describes your overall business plan. A data warehouse with a *star schema* design has multiple dimension tables and one fact table, which can be joined in different ways during analysis. A star schema represents relationships among its components in a star-like configuration, at the center of which is a fact table that contains the actual data that you want to analyze. Completing this configuration are dimension tables that "radiate" from the fact table.

You can create many metaoutlines from one or more OLAP models. An OLAP *metaoutline* describes how the multidimensional database will look to the OLAP user. Each metaoutline can look at some specific aspect of your business. You can specify what dimensions are visible to OLAP users, and set filters that determine what data is retrieved.

Use the DB2 OLAP Integration Server to create OLAP applications, which you can use in turn to analyze DB2 data through Lotus 1-2-3 or Microsoft Excel. An OLAP application contains data structured by a template that's based on the metaoutline. The DB2 OLAP Integration Server contains the following components:

- The OLAP Model interface is a tool for creating OLAP models.
- The OLAP Metaoutline interface is a tool for creating OLAP metaoutlines.
- The Administration Manager tool lets you perform simple OLAP database administration tasks, such as exporting data to the data warehouse, managing storage, creating new users, and granting them access to applications.

Common Tool Features

The following features are available in several of the DB2 GUI tools:

- Wizards
- Generate DDL

- Show SQL/Show Command
- Show Related
- Filter
- Help

Wizards

For some tasks (but not on DB2 for OS/390), you have the option of using a wizard. Wizards can be "conjured up" from the pop-up menus in the Control Center and can really help you get the job done quickly and painlessly! Use wizards when:

- Creating a database
- Creating tables
- Creating table spaces
- Creating indexes
- Backing up a database
- Restoring a database
- Tuning performance (configuration)
- Configuring multisite updates

Generate DDL

Generate DDL (Data Definition Language; see Figure 8-8) allows you to re-create and save in a script file the DDL and SQL statements and statistics for:

- Database objects
- Authorization statements
- Tablespaces, nodegroups, and buffer pools
- Database statistics

This allows you to:

- Save the DDL to create identically defined tables, databases, and indexes in another database
- Use the DDL to copy a database from a test environment to a production environment, or from one system to another
- Edit the DDL to create similar objects

Clicking the Generate DDL push button opens the Show Command window with statements generated by the db2look utility. You can click the Save Script push button to write the statements to a script file.

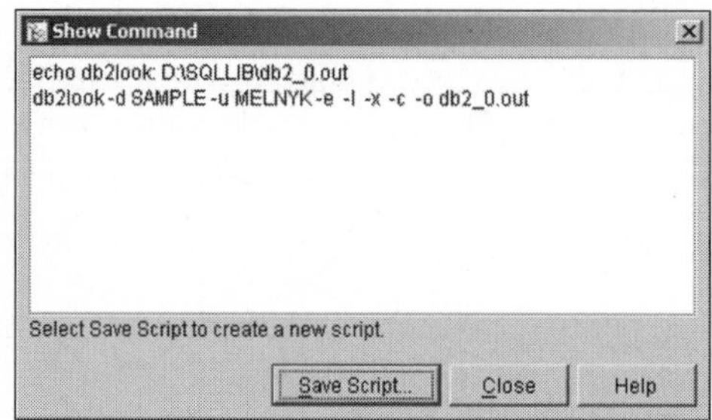

Figure 8-8: The Generate DDL window, from which you can request the data definition language for a database object, in this case, the SAMPLE database.

Show SQL/Show Command

If a tool generates SQL statements, the Show SQL push button is available on the tool interface. Similarly, a tool that generates DB2 commands has an available Show Command push button. Clicking one of these pushbuttons allows you to do the following:

- See the SQL statements or DB2 commands that the tool generates based on the choices you made in the graphical interface. This information helps you to understand how the interface is working (see Figure 8-9).
- Save the statements or commands as a script for future use. This saves you from having to retype SQL statements or DB2 commands if you want to run the same statements or commands again. After the SQL statements or DB2 commands have been saved in a script, you can schedule the script, edit the script to make changes, or create similar scripts without having to retype the statements or commands.

If you click the Create Script push button, the New Command Script window opens and you can edit the SQL statements or the DB2 commands before saving the script.

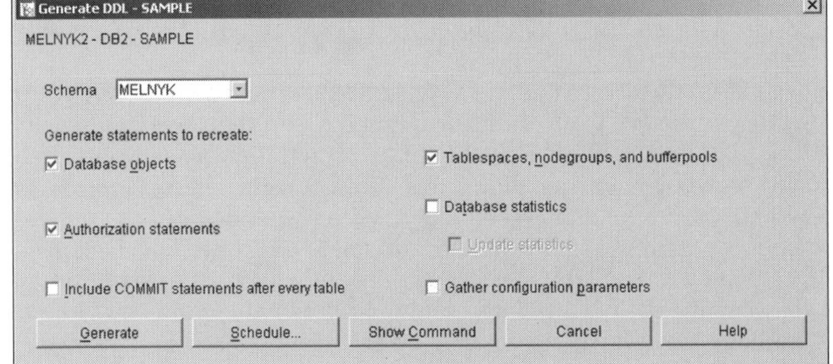

Figure 8-9: The Show Command window, displaying the `db2look` command that will generate the data definition language for creating the SAMPLE database.

Show Related

Show Related shows the immediate relationship between tables, indexes, views, aliases, triggers, table spaces, user-defined functions (UDF), and user-defined types (UDT). For example, if you select a table and choose to show related views, you see only the views that are based directly on that table.

Showing related objects helps you to

- Understand the structure of the database.
- Determine what indexes for a table already exist.
- Determine what objects are stored in a table space.
- Know what other objects are related to an object, and which may be affected by actions that you take. For example, if you want to drop a table with dependent views, this feature shows you which views will become inoperative.

You can click the right mouse button on a related object and again select Show Related from the pop-up menu. The page changes to show the objects related to this selection. You can also click the down arrow next to the selected object to display the relationships among the objects that you previously selected.

Filter

You can filter the information that is displayed in the contents pane of the Control Center, or you can filter the information that is returned by a query.

To automatically invoke the Filter notebook based on number of rows returned, select Tools from the menu bar and then select Tools Settings from the pop-up menu. The Select Filtering When Number of Rows Exceeds check box allows you to predefine a threshold of returned rows from any selection. When the threshold is reached, the Filter notebook opens so that you can limit the current retrieval based on defined criteria. This is especially useful when a table has grown unexpectedly and was previously unfiltered. Depending on your platform, and your data, you could be trying to return millions of rows when all you need are a few!

Help

Extensive help information is provided with the administration tools. A Help push button exists on all dialog boxes as well as on the menu toolbar. You can get general help or information on how to perform specific tasks. From the Help menus, you can also access an index of terms or the information provided in the product manuals.

To practice some of the things that you read about in this section, do the exercises in Lab 8-3.

Lab 8-3 Exploring some DB2 UDB GUI tools

1. **Start the Command Center. On Windows NT/2000, click Start and select Programs⇨IBM DB2⇨Command Center.**

   This brings up the Command Center window.

2. **Use the Interactive page of the Command Center to issue some DB2 commands and SQL statements. For example, to connect to the SAMPLE database, type** connect to sample; **in the Command field and click the Execute icon, which is the first icon in the toolbar near the top of the Command Center window.**

   Output resulting from statement or command execution appears in the Results field, immediately below the Command field.

3. **Use the Script page of the Command Center to create a DB2 command script that contains queries against the SAMPLE database.**

   Use the Append to Script button on the Interactive page to build your script from statements and commands that you retrieve from the Command history drop-down list.

4. **Save your script and run it. To save the script, select Script⇨Save Script As. The Save as window opens. Type the path, or use the directory list box and drive combination box to build the path on which your script will be saved. Type a brief (< 99-character) description of your script in the Script description field and click OK to save the script. To run the script, click the Execute icon near the top of the Command Center window.**

5. **Schedule your script to run later. Select Tools⇨Script Center. The Script Center opens. If your script does not appear in the list, select View⇨Refresh. Click the script entry and select Selected⇨Schedule. The Schedule window opens. Ensure that the Once radio button is selected. Change the start time to some future value; for example, one hour after the current time. Type a valid user ID and password in their respective fields and click OK to complete the scheduling operation.**

6. **Look in the Journal to find entries pertaining to your script. Select Tools⇨Journal. The Journal opens. Select your system name from the drop-down list. Your scheduled script should appear in the Pending Jobs view of the Jobs page. Click the job entry and select Jobs⇨Run Now. The Run Script window opens. Type a valid user ID and password in their respective fields and click OK to start the job. Your completed job should appear in the Job History view of the Jobs page. Click the job entry and select Jobs⇨Show Results. The Job Results window opens, showing job output resulting from the execution of your script.**

7. **Back up the SAMPLE database. On Windows NT/2000, click Start and select Programs⇨IBM DB2⇨Control Center. The Control Center opens. Expand the objects tree in the objects pane until you can see the SAMPLE database. Click the SAMPLE object in the Databases folder and select Selected⇨Backup⇨Database Using Wizard. The Backup Database Wizard opens. Let the wizard guide you through the steps required to back up the SAMPLE database.**

8. **Generate and examine the data definition language (DDL) for the SAMPLE database. Click the SAMPLE object in the Databases folder and select Selected⇨Generate DDL. The Generate DDL window opens. Click Generate to generate the data definition language for the SAMPLE database. The Run Script window opens. Type a valid user ID and password in their respective fields and click OK to start the job. Your completed job should appear in the Job History view of the Jobs page. Click the job entry and select Jobs⇨Show Results. The Job Results window opens, showing the generated DDL.**

9. **Open the Information Center and explore some of the DB2 documentation that's available from there. On Windows NT/2000, the Information Center can be launched from the Control Center toolbar, the Control Center Help menu, or by clicking Start and selecting Programs⇨IBM DB2⇨Information⇨Information Center.**

Entering DB2 Commands

The command-line processor (CLP), common to all DB2 products, is an application that you can use to run DB2 commands or SQL statements. Remember that this is only one way of invoking these commands; you might very well prefer to issue DB2 commands or SQL statements through the Command Center. Or, you may prefer to store often-used sequences of commands or statements in a file that can be run when necessary.

On Windows NT, `db2cmd` opens the DB2 Command Window and initializes the DB2 command-line environment. Issuing this command is equivalent to clicking the DB2 Command Window icon. On other platforms, DB2 commands can be issued from a normal operating system prompt.

The `db2` command starts the command-line processor. The CLP can be started in the following:

- Command mode, where each command is issued from the operating system prompt and must be prefixed by `db2`. Following execution of the command, control returns to the operating system prompt and you can enter more commands.
- Interactive mode, characterized by the `db2 => input` prompt.
- Batch mode, which uses the `-f filename` input option (more about that later!).

The shell command (!) allows operating system commands to be executed from interactive or batch mode on the Windows (but not Windows 3.1) operating system, on UNIX-based systems, and on OS/2; for example, `!dir` or `!ls`.

The command-line processor consists of two processes: a *front-end process* (the `db2` command), which acts as the user interface, and the *back-end process* (`db2bp`), which maintains a database connection. Each time that `db2` is invoked, a new front-end process is started. The back-end process is started by the first invocation of the `db2` command. The `quit` command stops the command-line processor. The `terminate` command also stops the command-line processor but removes the associated back-end process and frees any memory that is being used.

We bet you can't wait to see the syntax of the `db2` command! Well, wait no more; here it is:

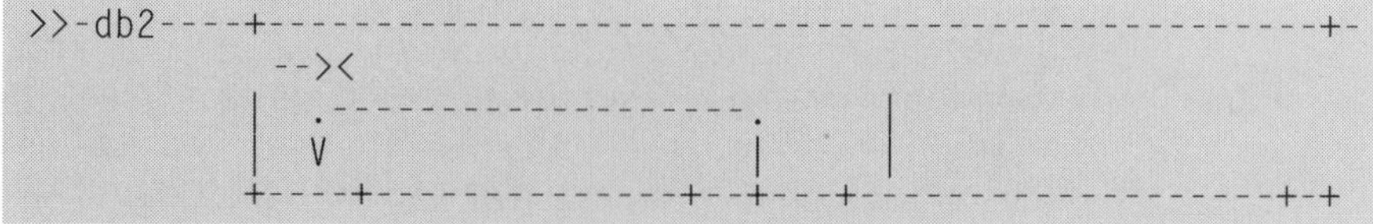

```
     |       '-option-flag--'      +-db2-command-------+ |
     |         +-sql-statement-----+ |
     |         '-?--+-----------+-' |
     |              +-phrase-----+   |
     |              +-message----+   |
     |              +-sqlstate---+   |
     |              '-class-code-'   |
     '-----comment-------------------------------------'

option-flag
     Specifies a CLP option. For a description of valid CLP
            option flags, see Table 10-1.

db2-command
     Specifies a DB2 command. For a description of all the
            DB2 commands, refer to the IBM DB2 Universal
            Database Command Reference.

sql-statement
     Specifies an SQL statement. For a description of all the
            SQL statements, refer to the IBM DB2 Universal
            Database SQL Reference.

?
     Requests general CLP help.

? phrase
     Requests the help text associated with a specific
            command or topic. If DB2 cannot find the requested
            information, it displays the general help screen.
            ? options requests a description and the current
            settings of the CLP options. ? help requests
            information about reading the online help syntax
            diagrams.

? message
     Requests help for a message specified by a valid SQLCODE
            (? sql10007n, for example).

? sqlstate
     Requests help for a message specified by a valid
            SQLSTATE.

? class-code
     Requests help for a message specified by a valid class-
            code.

-- comment
     Input that begins with the comment characters -- is
            treated as a comment by the command line
            processor.
```

A blank space must separate the question mark (?) from the variable name.

The CLP *command options* can be set by specifying one or more CLP option flags. Table 8-1 summarizes these flags. The flags are not case sensitive and can be specified in any sequence and combination. To turn an option on, prefix the corresponding option letter with a minus sign (–). To turn an option off, either prefix the option letter with a minus sign and follow the option letter with another minus sign or prefix the option letter with a plus sign (+). For example, `@msc` turns the auto-commit option on, and either `@msc@ms` or `+c` turns it off.

Table 8-1 CLP Command Options

Option Flag	*Description*	*Default Setting*
@msa	Display SQLCA data.	OFF
@msc	Automatically commit SQL statements.	ON
-e{c|s}	Display SQLCODE or SQLSTATE. These options are mutually exclusive.	OFF
-f filename	Read command input from a file instead of from standard input.	OFF
-l filename	Log commands in a history file.	OFF
-n	Remove the new line character within a single delimited token. If this option is not specified, the new line character is replaced with a space. This option must be used with the -t option.	OFF
-o	Display output data and messages to standard output.	ON
-p	Display a command-line processor prompt when in interactive mode.	ON
-r filename	Write the report generated by a command to a file.	OFF
-s	Stop execution if errors occur while executing commands in a batch file or in interactive mode.	OFF
-t	Use a semicolon (;) as the statement termination character.	OFF

Option Flag	Description	Default Setting
-tdx	Define and use x as the statement termination character.	OFF
-v	Echo command text to standard output.	OFF
-w	Display SQL statement warning messages.	ON
-z filename	Redirect all output to a file. It is similar to the -r option, but includes any messages or error codes with the output.	OFF

You can view the current settings for the CLP option flags by issuing the DB2 `list command options` command. You can change an option setting by issuing the DB2 `update command options` command.

DB2 commands or SQL statements can be entered either in uppercase or in lowercase. If a command exceeds a character limit, you can use a backslash (\)as the line continuation character. When the CLP encounters the line continuation character, it reads the next line and concatenates the two lines.

Although you're allowed to use some special characters, such as $ & * ( ) ; < > ? \ ' ", with CLP commands, if you're operating in command mode, these characters may be misinterpreted by the operating system shell. Quotation marks or an escape character is required if you want the shell to ignore such special characters.

Most operating systems allow input and output to be redirected. For example, the following statement queries the STAFF table and redirects the output to a file called staff.txt in the Data directory. Notice the quotation mark statement delimiters.

```
db2 "select * from db2admin.staff" > Data\staff.txt
```

If output redirection is not supported, you can specify a CLP option flag. For example:

```
db2 -r Data\staff.txt "select * from db2admin.staff"
```

Get some practice using the DB2 command-line processor by doing the exercises in Lab 8-4.

Lab 8-4 Using the DB2 command-line processor

1. **On Windows NT/2000, enter** db2cmd **from a command prompt to open a DB2 command window and initialize the DB2 command-line environment.**
2. **If the database manager is not already running, enter** db2start.
3. **To connect to the SAMPLE database, enter** db2 connect to sample.

   Database connection information returns.
4. **To see a list of the user tables in the SAMPLE database, enter** db2 list tables for user.
5. **To see the first three records in the EMPLOYEE table, enter** db2 select * from employee fetch first 3 rows only.
6. **To see information about the table spaces for the SAMPLE database, enter** db2 list tablespaces show detail.
7. **To identify the containers for the table space that stores user data (table space 2), enter** db2 list tablespace containers for 2.
8. **To break your connection to the SAMPLE database, enter** db2 connect reset.
9. **To use the command-line processor in interactive input mode, enter** db2.

   The db2 => command prompt appears.
10. **To see current settings for the DB2 command options, enter** list command options.
11. **To turn on the "display SQLCA" command option, enter** update command options using @msa on.

    Error message SQL0104N returns, because the correct option is `a`, not `@msa`. (We had you do this so that you could see how to get help when something goes wrong. See the next step.)
12. **To request the help text for this message, enter** ? sql0104.
13. **Enter** update command options using a on.

    Verify that the option value has changed by re-issuing **list command options**.
14. **To turn off the "display SQLCA" command option, enter** update command options using a off.

    Verify that the option value has changed by re-issuing **list command options**.
15. **To stop the command-line processor, issue** quit.

Prep Test

1 **Which of the following tools can be used to catalog a database?**

A ❍ Journal
B ❍ Alert Center
C ❍ License Center
D ❍ Client Configuration Assistant

2 **If, for a given table, the Control Center does not show the choice Generate DDL, which of the following describes the reason?**

A ❍ The table is a system object.
B ❍ The table is a summary table.
C ❍ The table is in LOAD PENDING.
D ❍ The table is a replicated table.
E ❍ The table was created by a different user.

3 **Which of the following *cannot* have an autocommit setting?**

A ❍ Embedded SQL
B ❍ The Command Center
C ❍ The command-line processor
D ❍ The DB2 Call Level Interface

Answers

1 **D.** The CCA keeps a list of databases to which your applications can connect; in other words, it catalogs nodes and databases. *Review "Client Configuration Assistant."*

2 **A.** Generate DDL allows you to recreate and save in a script file the DDL and SQL statements and statistics for database objects, authorization statements, table spaces, nodegroups, buffer pools, or database statistics. *See "Generate DDL."*

3 **A.** Embedded SQL is not a tool, so it can't have an autocommit setting. *Study "Entering DB2 Commands."*

Part III

The Geeky Stuff: Inside DB2

"I couldn't get this 'job skills' program to work on my PC, so I replaced the motherboard, upgraded the BIOS, and wrote a program that links it to my personal database. It told me I wasn't technically inclined and should pursue a career in sales."

In this part . . .

Reading the chapters in this part will really make you feel alone in the world, but relax, you're preparing for certification! In this part, we take you on an in-depth journey through DB2 and the things that make it work. You can find out about database objects and how to create and manage them, as well as how to implement a secure environment so that your peers can't get to your personal data. Finally, you find out how DB2 acts like a patient parent when it has to contend with tons of clients asking for things at the same time. Ready to exercise your head? Grab something with caffeine and pay special attention.

Chapter 9

Database Building Blocks

Exam Objectives

- Ability to create a DB2 database
- Ability to create and access basic DB2 objects
- Ability to demonstrate usage of DB2 data types
- Given a situation, ability to create a table
- Given a situation, knowledge to identify when referential constraints are used
- Knowledge to identify methods of data validation
- Knowledge to identify characteristics of a table, view, or index

This chapter gives you plenty of technical dirt that is sure to cause a slight brain ache if taken in too quickly. Here we introduce you to how DB2 organizes and stores its various parts, which together allow you to store and retrieve data. These parts include instances, databases, tablespaces, containers, tables, views and indexes, bufferpools and logfiles — just to name a few. It's important to understand how each part relates to another and how to create and configure them.

Quick Assessment

Creating and accessing basic DB2 objects

1 DB2 databases are created within a DB2 _____.

2 DB2 databases are created using the _____ command. They can be created with different _____ in order to hold the character sets of different languages.

3 The three tablespaces created by default when a database is created are called _____, _____, and _____.

4 Tables can be created using the _____ command.

Using DB2 Data Types

5 The names of the DB2 numeric data types are _____, _____, _____, _____, _____, _____ and _____.

6 The names of the three types of DB2 Large Objects are _____, _____ and _____.

Identifying methods of data validation

7 _____ further define rules that must be enforced whenever data is inserted into or deleted from the table or when rows are updated.

8 _____ defines relationships between tables and enforces rules within these relationships.

Identifying characteristics of a table, view, or index

9 Indexes are defined on one or more _____.

10 Tables physically hold the data using rows and columns. Three types of tables are _____, _____, and _____.

11 _____ are logical tables that provide alternative ways to access the data in one or more base tables.

Answers

1 *instance*. Review "Using Instances — The Database 'House.'"

2 `create database`, *codepage.* Review "Constructing Databases — The Rooms."

3 `SYSCATSPACE`, `TEMPSPACE1`, `USERSPACE1`. Review "Using Tablespaces — The Storage Areas."

4 `create table`. Review "Tackling Tables."

5 *smallint, integer, bigint, double, real, float, decimal*. Review "Defining columns with data types."

6 *BLOB, CLOB, DBCLOB.* Review "Defining columns with data types."

7 *Table constraints*. Review "Understanding Table Constraints."

8 *Referential integrity*. Review "Understanding Table Constraints."

9 *Columns*. Review "Understanding Indexes."

10 *System, user, temp*. Review "Tackling Tables."

11 *Views*. Review "Understanding Views."

Using Instances — The Database "House"

A DB2 instance is a logical environment containing DB2 code that is used to house one or more databases. A neighborhood may contain one or many houses. In a similar way, a physical machine may have one or more DB2 instances defined on it. Each instance gets its own copy of the DB2 executables and libraries. By default, these are found under a directory called SQLLIB. A DB2 instance can also be called the Database Manager. The Database Manager is started using the `db2start` command and is stopped using the `db2stop` command. To find out more about DB2 instances, read on!

Creating the instance — Building the house!

You can create a DB2 instance during or after the DB2 install process. DB2 provides various scripts for dealing with instances. The instance scripts require root authority (UNIX) or Local Administrator authority (Windows or OS/2) in order to execute.

First, though, you create a user ID that is designated as the owner of the instance on the system. This ID is known as the DB2 instance owner, or DB2 instance owner ID.

After DB2 is installed, you can create a DB2 instance by using the `db2icrt` command. The basic syntax of the `db2icrt` command is as follows.

```
db2icrt <instance_owner_ID>
```

On UNIX systems, you can also specify a user ID under which you'd like fenced User Defined Functions (UDFs) to execute. This ID can be different from the instance owner ID. When fenced User Defined Functions are created, they run in an address space that is separate from DB2's address space.

The syntax of the command in this case is as follows:

```
db2icrt -u <fenced_user_ID> <instance_owner_ID>
```

Updating the instance — Doing some renovations?

There may unfortunately come a time when you need to apply some fixes to the DB2 code installed on the machine. Or, you may require some additional DB2 features that are shipped via a fixpak or refresh install of DB2. If this happens, on UNIX only, the code that the DB2 instances are using must also be refreshed. The `db2iupdt` command is provided to do just that — refresh, renovate, and update. Again, the instance owner ID must be specified when this command is issued:

```
db2iupdt <instance_owner_ID>
```

Dropping the instance — Tearing down the house

You can drop instances by using the `db2idrop <instance_owner_ID>` command. If this command is issued, the user ID remains on the system but the SQLLIB directory is removed, which essentially removes the DB2 libraries and executables. The database files, however, aren't removed if an instance is dropped. They aren't located in the SQLLIB directory. You will find out more on this in the "Constructing Databases — The Rooms" section.

The `db2ilist` command is also provided; it lists all the instances on the machine.

DAS instance — That special house on the corner

A special instance is provided by DB2 that is called the DAS instance. DAS stands for DB2 Administration Server. It is used by DB2 clients that want to remotely administer databases on the machine that the DAS instance resides on. Because the DAS is a special instance, special commands are available to create, drop, start, and stop this instance. The DAS is usually created automatically during the install process but it can be created after the install. The DAS is assigned the name DB2DAS00 by default. In other words, DB2DAS00 is the DAS instance owner ID. Only one DAS instance can exist on any given machine. See Chapter 5 for more detailed information on the DAS instance.

You can create the DAS instance using the following commands. Note that the first command is specific to Windows and OS/2 systems and the other is specific to UNIX systems.

```
db2admin create /user:<name> /password:<password> (Windows
          and OS/2)
```

```
dasicrt <DAS_instance_owner_ID> (UNIX)
```

The DAS instance owner ID can be displayed using the following command:

```
db2admin
```

Unlike the other DB2 instances, the DAS is started and stopped using the following commands:

```
db2admin start
```

```
db2admin stop
```

Other differences between the DAS and other DB2 instances include the command to update the instance on UNIX systems and the command to drop the DAS.

The DAS way to update is with the `dasiupdt <DAS_instance_owner_ID>` command. To drop the DAS, you use the following commands (the DAS instance must be stopped before it is dropped):

```
db2admin drop
```

```
dasidrop <DAS_instance_owner_ID>
```

Configuring the instance — Setting up the house!

The general environment can vary among houses in terms of temperature, humidity, and other aspects. Each instance has configuration parameters that are used to set up just the right environment for your instance.

When an instance is created, the default parameters are contained in the Database Manager configuration file. You can view this file by issuing the following commands from the DB2 command-line processor (unless you're a speedy typist, we recommend the short form!):

```
db2 get dbm cfg
```

```
db2 get database manager configuration
```

The values set in this file apply to all databases within the instance. These values control things such as the amount of diagnostic information to log and the amount of monitoring to perform. Updating these values is very easy! For example, to increase the amount of diagnostic logging to the db2diag.log file, issue the following command:

```
db2 update dbm cfg using diaglevel 4
```

The basic syntax of the command is

```
db2 update database manager configuration using <parameter
           name> <new value>
```

Most changes made to the Database Manager Configuration File won't be effective until the instance has been restarted. To restart an instance, enter **db2stop** followed by **db2start**.

To get back to basics — meaning to reset the configuration parameters back to the defaults — enter **db2 reset dbm cfg**.

DAS instance config commands — Gotta be different!

Here again, the DAS must set itself apart from the other instances. The commands to configure the DAS are slightly different from other DB2 instances. These commands are listed here:

To view the configuration file:

```
db2 get admin cfg
```

To update the configuration file:

```
db2 update admin cfg using <parameter_name> <new_value>
```

To reset the configuration parameters back to the default values:

```
db2 reset admin cfg
```

Constructing Databases — The Rooms

Finally, we get to the heart of the matter — the database itself. Using our house analogy, within each house there can be many different rooms. For example, you might have a toy room for the kids, a reading room to get away from the kids, and an entertainment room for everyone to enjoy. Similarly, in a DB2 instance, you can have one or many databases. You may have one that stores data related to toys, one that stores data related to books, and another that stores data related to TVs and stereos. Figure 9-1 illustrates a DB2 instance containing two databases.

Often Database Administrators will create two identical databases. One will be used for production purposes and another will be used for test and development purposes.

Instance: DB2INST1
db2 create database test on e:\mydir
db2sampl e:\mydir

Test

Sample

Database directory
e:\mydir\db2inst1\
NODE0000\SQL00001

Database directory
e:\mydir\db2inst1\
NODE0000\SQL00002

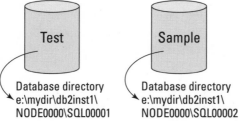

Figure 9-1: An instance containing two databases.

You can create a DB2 database by using the following command from the DB2 command-line processor:

```
db2 create database test
```

This command creates the database directory, default tablespaces, and database configuration file. The database is created under the $HOME directory of the DB2 instance owner. The database can be created on a different directory by using the `ON` clause of the `create database` command as follows. The first command is specific to Windows and OS/2 systems. The second command is specific to UNIX systems.

```
db2 create database test on e:\mydir
```

```
db2 create database test on /mydir
```

You can create the SAMPLE database provided by DB2 by using the following command. If no location is specified, the SAMPLE database will be created in the $HOME directory of the DB2 instance:

```
db2sampl <location>
```

We can't forget about the codepage!

First of all, what the heck is a codepage? A codepage (and codeset) defines the way that character data will be stored in the database and the way it will be formatted once retrieved. DB2 is indeed a universal database and is used in many different countries around the world. The phrase "many different countries" implies, of course, many different languages, which leads to many different forms of character data. The English language, for example, uses a single-byte codepage because all characters in the English language can be represented with one byte. The Japanese language, on the other hand, requires two bytes to represent its characters and therefore uses a multibyte codepage.

Only one codepage can be associated with a given database. This codepage is specified when the database is created with the `using codeset` and `territory` options of the `create database` command. If no codepage is specified, the codepage defined for the operating system is used by default. Following is an example of a `create database` command for a database using the U.S. – English codepage.

```
db2 create database test using codeset IBM-1252 territory US
```

It is important to note that an application accessing the database can have a different codepage than that of the database. When this is the case, codepage conversion must take place. This can have a negative impact on the performance of the application. For this reason, it is generally advised that the codepage of the applications match that of the database that it is accessing.

You can also create DB2 databases by using a Unicode codepage. Unicode databases can be used to hold data in many different languages. This is because this codepage uses multiple bytes for any character stored in the database.

Codepages are directly related to character or string data types. You can find more information on data types in the "Defining columns with data types" section later in this chapter.

Using database directories

In some homes, you need a map just to find your way to the bathroom! It can be equally difficult to determine where your databases are located if many are defined within the instance. Luckily, two database directories (or maps) are available to help you to locate your databases. The first is the System Database directory. This directory lists all databases created under the instance and their location. It can be viewed by issuing the following command:

```
db2 list database directory
```

The second directory is called the Local Database directory. This directory lists all databases created under the instance that reside in a certain location. For example, if you want to list all databases that reside on the e:\ drive, you would enter the following command:

```
db2 list database directory on e:
```

The database directory has the following structure:

UNIX: $DBHOME/instance/NODE0000/SQL00001

Windows and OS/2: $DBHOME\instance\NODE0000\SQL00001

If you create more than one database under the same instance, another directory will be created called SQL00002 and then SQL00003, and so on in sequence.

Configuring the Database — Decorating the rooms

You should take as much care in configuring your database as you would in decorating a room in your house. You can configure a DB2 database by altering the database parameters in the Database configuration file. These parameters affect memory usage per process, amount of memory to be allocated to perform various tasks, the logging strategy to be used, and other elements. When a database is created, default parameter values are set in this file. You can view the database configuration file by using the following commands:

```
db2 get db cfg for <dbname>
```

```
db2 get database configuration for <dbname>
```

Updating these values is also fairly simple. For example, if you want the applications running on your database to wait for only 10 seconds to acquire a lock on a database object, you can set the `LOCKTIMEOUT` parameter to `10`. We discuss locking and database concurrency in more detail in Chapter 11.

```
db2 update db cfg for <dbname> using locktimeout 10
```

```
db2 update database configuration for <dbname> using
        locktimeout 10
```

The basic syntax of this command is as follows:

```
db2 update database configuration for <dbname> using
        <parameter name> <new value>
```

Changes to the Database configuration file don't take effect until after the database has been restarted. A database can be restarted by first forcing all applications to disconnect from the database. After this, the first application to connect to the database restarts the database.

You can make a connection to the database by using the `db2 connect to <database name>` command.

Lab 9-1 gives you some practical experience creating DB2 instances and databases.

Lab 9-1 Creating an instance and a database

1. **Bring up the DB2 Command Window and create a new instance called** `myinst`.
2. **Make the** `myinst` **instance the active instance by issuing** `set db2instance=myinst`.

   Issuing **set db2instance** should return `myinst`.
3. **Create the sample database by using the** `db2sampl` **command and then create a database called** `test` **by using the** `create database` **command.**
4. **View the database manager configuration file for the** `myinst` **instance and the database directory. The directory should contain two entries:** `sample` **and** `test`.

Scrapping a database

For whatever reason, you may want to delete or remove a database altogether. With luck, the decision is well thought out before the actual removal takes place! The command to remove a database entirely is `db2 drop database <database_name>`.

Usually, backup images of databases are taken regularly. If a database was mistakenly dropped, the database files could be recovered from a DB2 database backup image — as if they had never been removed at all!

Using Tablespaces — The Storage Areas

Storage containers in a room may consist of closets, boxes, or bookcases, to name a few. To put it very simply, a tablespace is a logical space or grouping of storage containers to hold database stuff, such as tables, indexes, and LOBs (Large Objects). This logical tablespace is mapped to physical containers known as tablespace containers. Tablespace containers can consist of directories, files, or raw devices. A logical volume is an example of a raw device on UNIX systems.

Don't be too concerned about tablespaces for the DB2 Family Fundamentals Exam. Understand their purpose and the default tablespaces created. Don't worry too much about how to create them. We go into more detail here for the sake of completeness.

Tablespace types

There are two main DB2 tablespace types: SMS and DMS. The tablespace type that is chosen for a given database is important because they each have maintenance and performance implications.

SMS — System Managed Space

SMS tablespaces consist of directory containers only and are managed by the operating system. When a table or index is created, DB2 will create a file under the defined directory. This file will be used to hold all data in that table. The space in an SMS tablespace is allocated on demand. The size of an SMS tablespace can be increased by increasing the size of the underlying O/S filesystem or drive.

DMS — Database Managed Space

DMS tablespaces can consist of file containers, raw device containers, or a combination of both. DMS tablespaces are managed by the database. The space defined for them is preallocated when they're created. This size can be increased through the SQL `add container` command.

Default tablespaces

A DB2 database will always have at least three tablespaces defined: `SYSCATSPACE`, `TEMPSPACE1`, and `USERSPACE1`. These are created by default when the database is created. Unless you specify otherwise through the `create database` command, these three tablespaces are SMS tablespaces with one tablespace container each.

The definitions of the default tablespaces can be altered by using the `catalog tablespace <definition>`, `user tablespace <definition>`, and `temporary tablespace <definition>` options available with the `create database` command.

SYSCATSPACE

This tablespace holds all the system catalog tables. These are the tables that keep track of everything else in the database. The default tablespace container for `SYSCATSPACE` is the directory called SQLT0000.0 under the database directory. For example, if there is one database defined on drive e:\ under instance name `db2inst1`, the `SYSCATSPACE` tablespace container would be defined as `e:\db2inst1\NODE0000\SQL00001\SQLT0000.0`.

TEMPSPACE1

This tablespace is used for storing temporary tables and is appropriately referred to as a temporary tablespace. Temporary tables are created when needed by DB2 to perform tasks such as sorting data. The database must have at least one temporary tablespace defined. Using the same example as before, the `TEMPSPACE1` tablespace container would be defined as `e:\db2inst1\NODE0000\SQL00001\SQLT0001.0`.

USERSPACE1

This tablespace is a data tablespace. Data tablespaces are used to store data tables and indexes. Again, using the same example, the `USERSPACE1` tablespace container would be defined as `e:\db2inst1\NODE0000\SQL00001\SQLT0002.0`.

Figure 9-2 illustrates the default tablespaces in a DB2 database and the environment in which it lives. We discuss the objects that exist within tablespaces further in the "Tackling Tables" section.

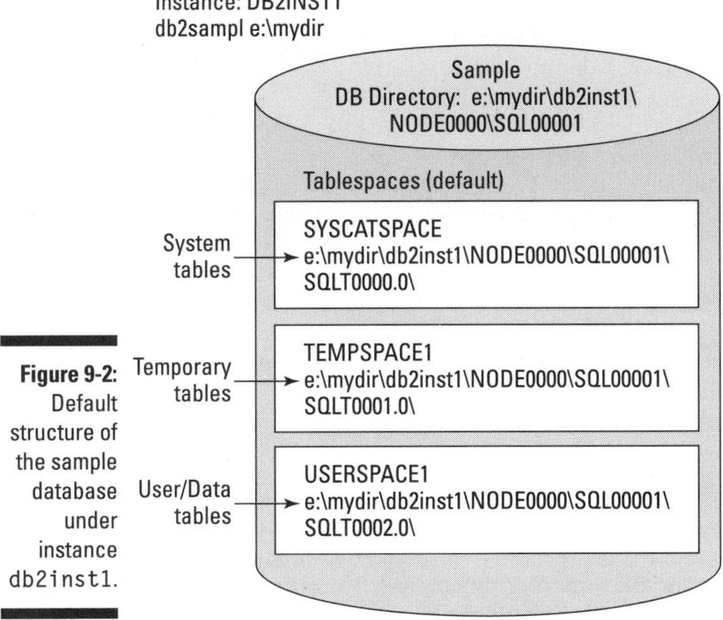

Figure 9-2: Default structure of the sample database under instance `db2inst1`.

Creating more tablespaces

You can define additional tablespaces for the database using the `create tablespace` command. Wouldn't it be great if an additional storage space in a house could be created just as easily! The following command creates a DMS tablespace with two file containers: one with 1,000 pages and the second with 2,000 pages. The default page size is 4096 bytes.

```
db2 create tablespace myDMSspace managed by database using
         (FILE 'e:\tbsp\cont1' 1000, FILE 'f:\tbsp\cont2'
         2000)
```

An SMS tablespace with two directory containers can be created just as easily! Check out the following command:

```
db2 create tablespace mySMSspace managed by system using
         ('e:\tbsp2\', 'f:\tbsp2')
```

Tablespaces can be dropped using the `db2 drop tablespace <tablespace_name>` command. You cannot drop a temporary tablespace if only one is defined in the database, nor can you drop the `SYSCATSPACE` tablespace. If two or more tablespaces are dependent on each other, they must be dropped together.

Tackling Tables

Tables really are the meat of the database. (Okay, we've lost the house analogy and have moved on to food.) They are the database objects that hold the actual data. A table consists of one or more columns and zero or more rows. The type of data that a table is destined to hold is specified when the table is created. Every table is distinguishable by a two-part name. The first part is a qualifier called the schema and the second is the table name; for example, in the name `db2inst1.mytable`, `db2inst1` is the schema name and `mytable` is the table name. You can have two tables with the same table name as long as the schema names are different. We discuss schema names in more detail later in this section.

System tables

System tables are special tables created by DB2 when the `create database` command is issued. They keep track of all the defined objects in the database including their names, statistics, sizes, and dependencies. They also keep track of which users have permissions to perform which operations. DB2 will automatically retrieve data from these tables when processing queries. DB2 may also automatically update these tables when DDL or Data Definition Language statements are issued against the database. A user cannot create or drop system tables. We discuss DDL Statements in more detail in Chapter 12.

All system tables reside in the SYSCATSPACE tablespace. System tables can have one of the following four schema names:

- SYSIBM: Read only system tables

  The SYSIBM schema tables are also considered Permanent tables. Permanent tables physically contain the table records.
- SYSCAT: Read-only views on the system tables
- SYSFUN: UDFs (User Defined Functions) provided by DB2
- SYSSTAT: Updateable views on the system tables; used for holding statistics on all other tables within the database

SYSSTAT views can be updated in several ways including running the `runstats` or `run statistics` command, which can be invoked via the CLP or the Control Center, or issuing the SQL `update` statement. It is good idea to keep the SYSSTAT views current using these commands because the optimizer consults these views when generating the best access plan for an SQL statement.

Table 9-1 summarizes some of the system tables and the information that they contain. The system tables and views, along with their creation time, can be viewed by issuing any of the following three commands:

- `db2 list tables for system`
- `db2 list tables for schema <schema_name>, where <schema_name> = SYSIBM, SYSCAT, SYSFUN, SYSSTAT`
- `db2 list tables for all`

Table 9-1 DB2 System Catalog Table and View Names

Database Object	*SYSIBM system table*	*SYSCAT system table view*	*SYSSTAT updateable view*
Tablespace	SYSTABLESPACES	TABLESPACES	
Table	SYSTABLES	TABLES	TABLES
Schema	SYSSCHEMATA	SCHEMATA	
View	SYSVIEWS	VIEWS	
Column	SYSCOLUMNS	COLUMNS	COLUMNS
Index	SYSINDEXES	INDEXES	INDEXES
Data Type	SYSDATATYPES	DATATYPES	
Check Constraint	SYSCHECKS	CHECKS	

(continued)

Table 9-1 *(continued)*

Database Object	*SYSIBM system table*	*SYSCAT system table view*	*SYSSTAT updateable view*
Referential Integrity	SYSRELS	REFERENCES	
Function	SYSFUNCTIONS	FUNCTIONS	FUNCTIONS
Bufferpool	SYSBUFFERPOOLS		BUFFERPOOLS

Temp tables — Derived and declared

Temporary Derived tables are created dynamically by DB2 when needed to process certain queries. For example, a temporary table might be created to improve the time required to sort several data records. Temporary Derived tables reside in temporary tablespaces. They are automatically dropped when the transaction requiring them has completed.

New to Version 7 is the ability to create Temporary Declared tables. This allows users to create temporary tables within their applications. These are similar to Temporary Derived tables in that they're created, used, and dropped during the execution of the application. Temporary Declared tables are created with a schema name called `SESSION`.

User tables

User tables are simply tables created by the users of the database. User tables are also a type of Permanent table. They reside in data tablespaces. We discuss these types of tables in more detail in the next section.

You can list all the user tables, system tables, and views in the database, along with their creation time, by issuing `db2 list tables for all`.

More on schemas

Tables are identified by a combination of two things: a schema name and a table name. There are several ways to define the schema for an object. There are also several ways to let DB2 know which schema you want to work with when accessing tables.

Setting the schema on creation of the table

The schema is set by default to the authorization ID in effect when the table is created and no schema name was specified in the `create table` statement. This is known as implicit schema. For example, if the `db2inst1 ID` connected to the database and then created a table called `mytable`, the full table name would be db2inst1.mytable. The desired schema can also be explicitly specified in the create table statement. A third option is to use the CURRENT SCHEMA register. In this case, the schema is set to the value of the CURRENT SCHEMA register when the create table command is issued. This special register can be set using the set current schema statement.

Determining the schema used for Dynamic SQL

DB2 allows you to explicitly include the schema in the statement itself. An example of this is db2 select * from db2inst1.mytable. In this case, db2inst1 is the desired schema name. A second option is to set the CURRENT SCHEMA register with the set current schema statement. In this case, DB2 will use the value contained in this registry to determine the schema. If neither of these options is used, DB2 will, by default, use the authorization ID in effect at the time the dynamic statement was issued.

Determining the schema used for Static SQL

As in dynamic SQL, the schema can be specified along with the table name within the SQL itself. For example, rather than use mytable as the name in the statement, it is qualified with the schema db2inst1.mytable. Otherwise, the schema used is determined at BIND time. The default schema used is the authorization ID in effect at the time the BIND command issued. The BIND command itself provides a QUALIFIER option as well that can be used to set the schema.

The authorization ID is set to the ID of the user that connected to the database.

Creating tables

Before creating a table it is important to understand what type of data will be stored in it. For example, is it to be used to store employee information, inventory, and pricing or resumes of potential hires? A table consists of an unordered set of rows and columns. Each column can represent only one data type. Fortunately, DB2 provides many data types to choose from and also allows you to create your own data types. They can be used to represent many different types of information. We go into more detail on data types in the next section. After you know what you'd like to store in the table (the data types), the tables and columns should be assigned meaningful names. For example, it might not make sense to call a column containing date values Name. Some other important decisions to make for each column include:

- Can this column contain any NULL values?
- Is there a default value that should be automatically set for the column?
- Must all data in this column be unique?
- Is the data in this column dependent on data in any other table?

After making all these decisions, you can plug the information into the `create table` command fairly easily.

We start with a simple example (we get into more depth after discussing data types in the next section). Say that you decide that you want a table to hold the names and ages of your coworkers. (This information could make someone very powerful!) You want three columns. These will be used for the last name, first name, and age of each person. If you don't know the age, you will leave it NULL for that person. After connecting to the database with `ID db2inst1`, you can issue the following command from the db2 command window:

```
db2 create table blackmail (lname varchar(25) not null,
          fname varchar(25) not null, age smallint)
```

A table called `db2inst1.blackmail` will now be created and registered in the DB2 system tables. At this time, it doesn't contain any data. The column definitions for the table can be reviewed by issuing `db2 describe table db2inst1.blackmail`.

You should familiarize yourself with all the options available with the `create table` statement. These options can be found in the SQL Reference available in the Information Center.

Modifying existing tables

You can use the `alter table` statement to alter the definition of existing tables. Some of the `alter table` options include:

- Adding one or more columns
- Adding or dropping a primary key
- Adding or dropping one or more constraints on the table
- Altering the length of a `VARCHAR` column
- Setting the `not logged initially` attribute on the table
- Modifying table attributes such as `data capture`, `pctfree`, `locksize`, and `append mode`

Defining columns with data types

The previous example of the blackmail table illustrates the use of two of DB2's built-in data types: `VARCHAR` and `SMALLINT`. In addition to the built-in data types, DB2 also allows users to define their own data types; these are appropriately known as User Defined Data types. An overview of the data types that we discuss in this section is illustrated in Figure 9-3.

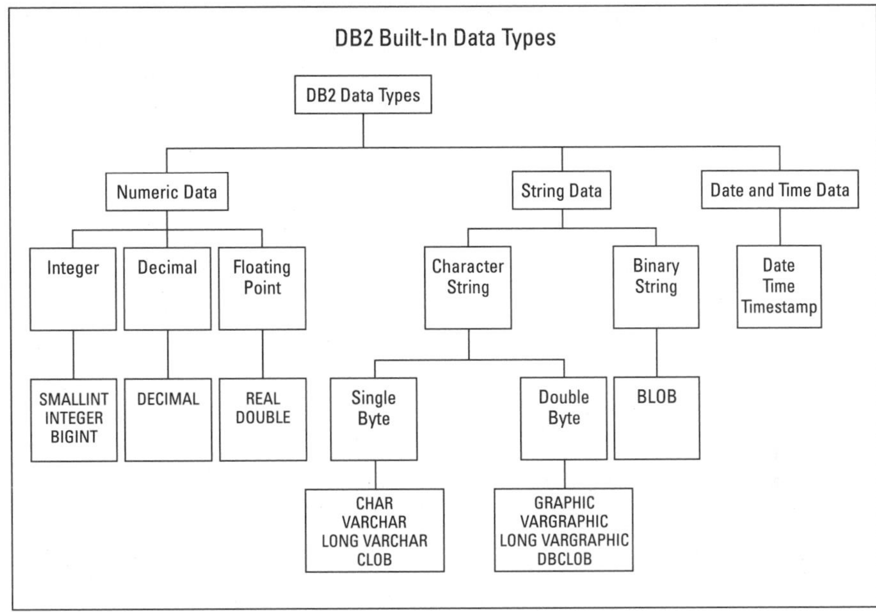

Figure 9-3: DB2 data types.

This section describes the different data types, the range of data values they can hold, and any restrictions they may have. Information on the data types within a database can be found in the `SYSCAT.DATATYPES` system table.

When choosing appropriate data types for columns, keep in mind two things: which data types can hold this type of data and which data types will use the least amount of disk space given the minimum/maximum values (the data range) to be inserted.

DB2-supplied data types

DB2 conveniently provides a variety of built-in data types that can be used to classify almost all types of data that might be stored in a database. We give you the "goods" on these data types in this section.

Numeric — For numbers of all shapes and sizes

As the name suggests, numeric data types are used to store numbers, specifically numbers that will be used for arithmetic operations. If a column is needed to store numeric data, determine the range of data you may need to insert into the column and the level of precision needed.

SMALLINT (Integer)

This numeric data type uses the least amount of storage — two bytes, to be exact! It allows only integer values to be assigned. For those of you who are a bit rusty in the math department, integers don't include values to the right of the decimal point. The range for the `SMALLINT` data type is –32,768 to 32,767, five digits to the left of the decimal. If you plan to use a column to keep track of the population of various countries, for example, you likely wouldn't want to use this data type because many countries have populations greater than 32,767.

INTEGER (Integer, obviously!)

The `INTEGER` data type is similar to the `SMALLINT` data type except that it uses four bytes of database storage, giving it a much larger data range. The range for the `INTEGER` data type is –2,147,483,648 to 2,147,483,647, 10 digits to the left of the decimal. The `INT` keyword can also be used to define an integer column.

BIGINT (Integer)

Otherwise known as Big Integer, this data type dwarfs the `INTEGER` and `SMALLINT` data types. The `BIGINT` data type uses eight bytes of database storage and allows for data ranges from –9,223,372,036,854,775,808 to 9,223,372,036,854,775,807, 10 digits to the left of the decimal.

DECIMAL/NUMERIC (Decimal)

The `DECIMAL` or `NUMERIC` data type is used to hold numbers that may require digits to the left of the decimal (precision) and digits to the right of the decimal point (scale); in other words, numbers with fractional parts. When this data type is used, the precision and scale should be specified, for example `DECIMAL(8,2)`. Otherwise, the precision and scale are set by default to (5,0). The amount of database storage used for this data type is based on the precision — P/2 + 1. A precision of (8.2) would use 5 bytes of storage; (5,0) would use 3 bytes (5/2 + 1) — truncate the fractional part. Monetary values often use this data type: the cost of a sweater or the total sales per day, for example.

This data type has several synonyms. These include `DECIMAL`, `NUMERIC`, `DEC`, and `NUM`. Use whichever one suits your fancy. For you programmer types, if your C program uses a host variable to insert data into this type of column, the host variable should be declared a `DOUBLE`.

REAL (Single precision)

The `REAL` data type holds approximations of numbers. These are the values that can potentially have an infinite number of digits to the right of the decimal. Remember the value of π in high school math? The `REAL` type uses four bytes of database storage.

DOUBLE (Double precision)

The `DOUBLE` data type is similar to the `REAL` data type except that it allows greater precision. In order to do so, it must use 8 bytes of database storage.

FLOAT (Single or double precision)

The FLOAT data type is a synonym to both the REAL and DOUBLE data types, depending on the precision set. If the precision of the FLOAT data type is set between 1 and 24, then it's identical to a REAL. If it's set between 25 and 53, then it's identical to a DOUBLE.

REAL, DOUBLE, and FLOAT values are stored in scientific notation. A REAL value of 123.45678 would be represented as 1.2345678x10^2.

Following is an example of a create table command that defines several different numeric data type columns:

```
db2 create table nums(n1 integer, n2 decimal(6,2), n3
          float(45), n4 double)
```

String — For characters, words, and phrases of all shapes and sizes

String character types are used to hold strings of one or more characters. When put together, the characters might represent a word, a sentence or a paragraph, or a newspaper article. There are a variety of string data types to choose from to allow you to choose one that is most appropriate and takes up the least amount of space.

As mentioned in the "Constructing Databases — The Rooms" section earlier in this chapter, if the codepage of an application differs from that of the database, codepage conversion will take place for character data. To avoid this costly conversion, the FOR BIT DATA clause can be used following a character string column definition. This will cause DB2 to treat the character data as binary data.

CHAR

The CHAR data type should be used for fixed length strings between 1 and 254 characters. The amount of storage allocated is dependent on the length specified. When CHAR(33) is specified, for example, space for 33 characters is allocated, even if only one character is inserted into the column. The CHAR data type is most appropriate when the number of characters in the column is fixed. A good use of the CHAR data type is for holding postal codes. If a length isn't specified with the CHAR data type, CHAR(1) is used by default. The term CHARACTER can be used as a synonym for CHAR.

VARCHAR

The VARCHAR data type can be used for character strings of varying length. VARCHAR data will use only the amount of storage required to store the data itself. The range in length of a VARCHAR column is 1 to 32,672 bytes. The maximum length for each column is specified in the form VARCHAR(integer), where *integer* is the maximum length permitted for the column. There are a couple of synonyms for this data type, including CHAR VARYING and VARYING CHARACTER. A restriction of this data type is that the column record must fit onto one database page.

DB2 Version 7 allows for page sizes of 4K, 16K, and 32K.

LONG VARCHAR

The `LONG VARCHAR` data type is also used for character strings of varying lengths. The maximum length of this data type is 32,700 bytes. It's not much larger than the `VARCHAR` data type, so why use it? In previous releases, the `VARCHAR` column had a much smaller range, so `LONG VARCHAR` was used when larger data was being inserted. The `LONG VARCHAR` was used prior to the introduction of LOB data types and the 32K `VARCHAR` data type. It has been carried over into current releases for consistency. The `LONG VARCHAR` data type is handled a bit differently internally, so it doesn't have the restriction that the `VARCHAR` data type has in that each column record doesn't have to fit onto one database page. Because it lacks this restriction, data in this column can spill onto more than one data page. This can result in potential processing delays.

At this point in the chapter, it might be a good idea to stretch your legs and take a break. This stuff can be a bit dry, but it's important to remember the details of each data type for the exam.

The LOBs (Large Objects)

LOBs, or Large Objects, are used to store very large amounts of unstructured data. There are various types of large objects, and multiple LOB columns can be defined within a single table. All the LOB data types store variable length data. A couple of examples of LOB data include sound clips and pictures from a digital camera. There are some special `create table` options associated with LOB column creation because of their sheer size. The `NOT LOGGED` option will cause DB2 to not log any operations on that LOB column to help avoid filling up the DB2 log files. This option must be specified for all LOB columns defined to be greater than 1GB in size. The `COMPACT` option is also specific to LOBs. This option instructs DB2 to avoid allocating extra disk space when the large object is being stored in the database table.

CLOB (Character Large Object)

This data type can be used to store variable length character data than is greater than 32K in size. The characters can be from a single-byte character set or multi-byte character set. The maximum size of this column is 2GB. One example of this is the text of a book. The maximum desired column length should be specified when the column is created.

DBCLOB (Double Byte CLOB)

The `DBCLOB` is similar to the `CLOB` except that it uses 2 bytes to store each character. This column is used to store large amounts of double byte character data, such as Chinese text. The maximum desired column length specified represents the maximum number of double-byte characters allowed in the column.

BLOB (Binary Large Object)

BLOB is used to store variable length binary data. The maximum size of the BLOB column is also 2GB. Some of the more common examples of BLOB data include video, sound, and pictures.

Following is an example of a create table command that defines several different strings or character data type columns.

```
db2 create table strings(s1 char, s2 varchar(33), s3 char(3),
        s4 clob(20000))
```

DATE

This data type is stored in the database as a packed string of 4 bytes. The external representation of the DATE value is dependent on the country code of the application and/or the value of the DATETIME option when the application using the column is bound to the database, using the BIND command. Table 9-2 shows the possible DATE formats.

TIME

This data type is stored internally as a packed string of 3 bytes. Again, the external representation is dependent on the country code of the application and/or the value of the DATETIME option of the BIND command. Table 9-2 shows the possible TIME formats.

Table 9-2 Valid DATE and TIME Formats

Format Name	*Abbreviation*	*Date Format*	*Time Format*
International Standards Organization	ISO	YYYY-MM-DD	HH.MM.SS
IBM USA Standard	USA	MM/DD/YYYY	HH:MM AM or PM
IBM European Standard	EUR	DD.MM.YYYY	HH.MM.SS
Japanese Industrial Standard	JIS	YYYY-MM-DD	HH:MM:SS
Site Defined	LOC	Depends on local database country code	Depends on local database country code

TIMESTAMP

This data type is stored internally as a packed string of 10 bytes. The external representation of the TIMESTAMP value is YYYY-MM-DD-HH-MM-SS-NNNNNN.

TIME, DATE, and TIMESTAMP data types look like character data types but can be used in arithmetic operations, such as addition and subtraction. They can also be used as input to functions such DAY, YEAR, and SECONDS to extract measures of time.

Special Types

The following four data types may not be as commonly used as the previously listed data types but are just as interesting and important.

GRAPHIC

The GRAPHIC data type is used for storing characters which each require 2 bytes of storage, such as Japanese characters. This data type is for fixed-length data strings with a maximum of 127 characters.

VARGRAPHIC

Same as the GRAPHIC data type except that it holds variable-length data strings with a maximum of 16,336 characters.

LONG VARGRAPHIC

Same as the VARGRAPHIC but a bit larger, the LONG VARGRAPHIC type holds a maximum of 16,350 characters. To hold even larger sets of double-byte characters, the next option is the DBCLOB, which we cover in the previous section on LOBs.

DATALINK

All the data types that we've described so far deal with data that exists within the database itself. In this respect, a DATALINK column is quite different. Within this column are values that act as "pointers" to where the data actually resides. This data might reside on the same machine or on a separate machine, which is often referred to as a "file server." If the files reside on the same machine, then the database server and file server have the same IP address. To recap, the DATALINK column doesn't contain the data but contains a logical pointer to the data itself. The database can access this data via the pointer value in the column. The DATALINK values are comprised of the following elements:

- Link Type: The only supported link type in Version 7 is URL (Uniform Resource Locator)
- Scheme: Related to the URL element and can be set to either FILE or HTTP. It is set to FILE by default. This value always appears in uppercase in the database.
- File Server Name: The complete IP address of the file server in which the data resides. This value is set by default to the IP address of the database server. This value always appears in uppercase in the database.
- File Path: The location and identity of the file on the file server. This name is case sensitive.

- Access Control Token: Not a permanent part of the DATALINK column but is used when DATALINK values are extracted from the database. This value is not required when the DATALINK value is inserted into the database.
- Comment: Descriptive information about the data referenced in this column. The comment can be up to 254 bytes.

DB2 provides special built-in scalar functions for inserting and extracting data from tables that contain DATALINK columns including DLVALUE (for inserting), DLLINKTYPE, DLURLSCHEME, DLURLSERVER, DLURLCOMPLETE, DLURLPATH, DLURLPATHONLY, and DLCOMMENT (for extracting).

User-defined data types

If the DB2 built-in data types just don't cut it for the applications that you want to develop, you can get creative by defining your very own data types within the database.

User-defined distinct type

Distinct types are user-defined data types that use previously defined data types for their internal representation. The best way to explain these is through an example. A Web site might provide video and music clips for its customers to help them make DVD, CD, or video purchase decisions. Within the database that holds the clips for this Web site, two distinct types have been created: VIDEO and AUDIO. Both of these types are based on the DB2 supplied data type, BLOB. In this case, BLOB is considered the "source" type. Owing to strong typing enforced by DB2, VIDEO, AUDIO, and BLOB are considered separate and incompatible data types — they can't be directly compared with SQL.

User-defined structured (Abstract data type)

Structured data types or abstract data types are data types that have a structure that is defined in the database. They contain a sequence of named attributes, each of which has a data type. These attributes can use base data types or they can use other structured types. Using other structured types as attributes creates nested structure types.

For example, a column defined with a structured data type might hold a structure of CHAR, INTEGER, and VIDEO data.

Structured data types are examples of object relational support found in DB2 Version 7.

User-defined reference type

Reference types are related to structured types. They are also similar to a distinct type in that a reference type is a type that shares a common representation with one of the built-in data types. This same representation is shared for all types in the type hierarchy.

Special columns

In addition to the data type of the column, you can also specify characteristics of the column that you want to be upheld whenever data is inserted into the column.

Identity columns

Values are sequentially generated and inserted into identity columns whenever a new data record is inserted. Columns defined as identity columns can be extremely useful for a variety of applications. Take an application used for inserting new students into a university's student database as an example. Each new student must be assigned a new, unique student ID. As each student's information is inserted into the database — name, number, address, and so on — the database creates a new, unique student ID via the identity column and assigns it to the student. Very handy! Here's an example of the SQL statement that would create such a table:

```
db2 create table student (studentID int generated always as
           identity, lname varchar(25), fname varchar(20),
           address varchar(45))
```

You can also specify on the create table command the identity column value to start with and the number to increment this starting value by — for example, start at 100 and increment by 10 to give 100, 110, 120, and so on.

NOT NULL, with default

There may be columns that do not have any value associated with them at the time a record is inserted into a table. The definition of the table will determine how the missing information for the column is handled. If the column is defined as `NOT NULL`, then the insert operation will fail. If the column allows `NULL` values, the column value will be set to `NULL` on insert. If the column is defined as `NOT NULL` with `DEFAULT`, the specified default value will be inserted. An example from a department store follows. If a product doesn't have a product ID assigned to it, it will be assigned `ID 12345`. If there is no department number specified, what will be inserted into the dept column? In this case, an explicit default value was not used. DB2 will choose one for you based on the data type of the column. For example, for integer data types, DB2 chooses the value `0`. So, in this case, DB2 populates the rows in the dept column with the value `0`.

To determine which default values will be chosen by DB2 for other data types (assuming you don't specify one!), review the `create table` or `alter table` command in the SQL Reference via the Information Center.

```
db2 create table inventory (productID smallint not null with
           default 12345, quantity integer, price
           decimal(4,2), dept smallint with default)
```

See Chapter 12 for details on how to insert data into tables.

Understanding Table Constraints

Table constraints further define rules that must be enforced whenever data is inserted into or deleted from the table or when rows are updated. DB2 keeps track of all the table constraints or rules in the system catalog tables. These extra rules might make creating tables seem even more complicated. However, imagine a big city without any traffic lights or stop signs — mass chaos! The same thing can happen in a database if table rules and relationships aren't clearly defined and enforced before inserting massive amounts of data into them.

In the previous section called "Special columns," we discuss how it is important to decide whether columns values can be `NULL` or whether they should be set to a default value. This section goes into more detail about the allowable column values based on some of these questions: Is there a specific range of values allowed only for the column; is a value in this column dependent on a value in a column in a separate table; do the values in this column, or set of columns, have to be unique?

Ensure that you understand the effect of an `update`, `insert`, or `delete` on a table with constraints defined on it.

"Key" concepts

The concept of a key is very important in database design. A *key* is a set of one or more columns that are used to identify certain rows in a table. A key consisting of one column is called an *atomic key*. Keys consisting of more than one column are called *composite keys*. A table can have many keys defined on it, and a column can be part of more than one key definition.

Primary keys

A table can have only one primary key defined on it. In addition, the columns comprising the primary key cannot contain any `NULL` values. The rows in the primary key, by definition, must be unique. An attempt to insert a duplicate value into a primary key will fail.

Foreign keys

A table can have more than one foreign key defined on it. When a table has a foreign key defined, it is said to be dependent on another table, called a *parent* table, in the database. Any values inserted into the foreign key of the dependent table must already exist in the parent key in the parent table. The parent key must have a unique constraint defined on it.

Check constraints

Check constraints are probably the easiest to understand. They can be defined using the `create table` or the `alter table` statement. Check constraints are also known as table check constraints, because they check the integrity of data at the table level. Check constraints make life a little easier for application programmers because they can leave some of the extra checking of data inserts/updates out of their programs, knowing that the database manager will do the checking for them.

These constraints are checked for validity whenever the table has values inserted or updated. They can define the range of data allowed for a certain column or perhaps restrict the allowable data entries for other columns. You might have a check constraint for a column holding the months of the year; something like `CHECK` (month in "January", "February," and so on), for example. You likely wouldn't want anyone to enter the word *spring* as a month of the year.

Creating tables with check constraints

Take a look at another example. You may have a salary column that should always have data values greater than 100,000. (Wouldn't that be fantastic!) If this is the case, a check constraint on the salary column can be defined to ensure that all values in this column are greater than that number. Another example would be that the value in the salary column plus the value in the bonus column is less than 200,000. The following `create table` statements would define the constraints mentioned previously on a table holding employee salary information:

```
db2 create table salary (lname varchar(25), fname
           varchar(20), salary decimal(6,2), bonus
           decimal(6,2), constraint chk_salary CHECK (salary
           > 100000))
```

The second constraint can be added later via the `alter table` command. If there are values already in the table that violate the constraint, the following `alter table` statement will fail:

```
db2 alter table salary add constraint chk_salbonus CHECK
           (salary + bonus < 200000)
```

It's possible to turn off constraint checking in order to add constraints to a table or to load a large amount of potentially noncompliant data. This is done by using the `set integrity` statement. When constraints are turned off on a table, the table is placed in check pending state. When a table is placed in check pending state, only limited access is allowed on the table.

Check constraint definitions can be found in the SYSCAT.CHECKS system table view.

Unique constraints

Unique constraints create unique keys in a table. The rows in the key contain only unique values — no duplicates! A primary key is a special example of a unique constraint on a table. There can be many more unique keys defined on the table. In addition, primary keys cannot contain any NULL values, whereas unique keys can. Of course, because no duplicates are allowed, only one NULL value would be allowed as well.

Only one unique constraint can be defined on the same set of columns. A parent key is a unique key that is referenced by a foreign key constraint.

The uniqueness of these keys is maintained by indexes. We discuss indexes in more detail later in this chapter.

Creating tables with unique constraints

Now, add a primary key to the salary table example from the "Check constraints" section in this chapter, called employeeID. Each employee ID must be unique, so it is definitely an appropriate column for a unique constraint.

```
db2 create table salary (employeeID smallint not null primary
           key, lname varchar(25), fname varchar(20), salary
           decimal(6,2), bonus decimal(6,2))
```

The unique constraint — primary key — is used in the previous example. Following is another way to create a unique key constraint on the salary table:

```
db2 create table salary (employeeID smallint not null, lname
           varchar(25), fname varchar(20), salary
           decimal(6,2), bonus decimal(6,2), constraint
           uempID UNIQUE(employeeID))
```

Referential Integrity

Referential Integrity, otherwise known as RI, can get a bit complicated. It is all about defining relationships between tables and enforcing rules within the relationships. Sounds a bit like a family reunion! Anyway, a database is said to be in a state of Referential Integrity when all the foreign key values defined in the database tables are valid. A foreign key value is considered valid when it appears as a value in the parent key or when some component of the value is NULL.

Figure 9-4 depicts a simple RI scenario between three tables. One table holds personal information for students at a university; the second table holds grades of students for each course they're enrolled in; and the third table holds information on courses offered that term.

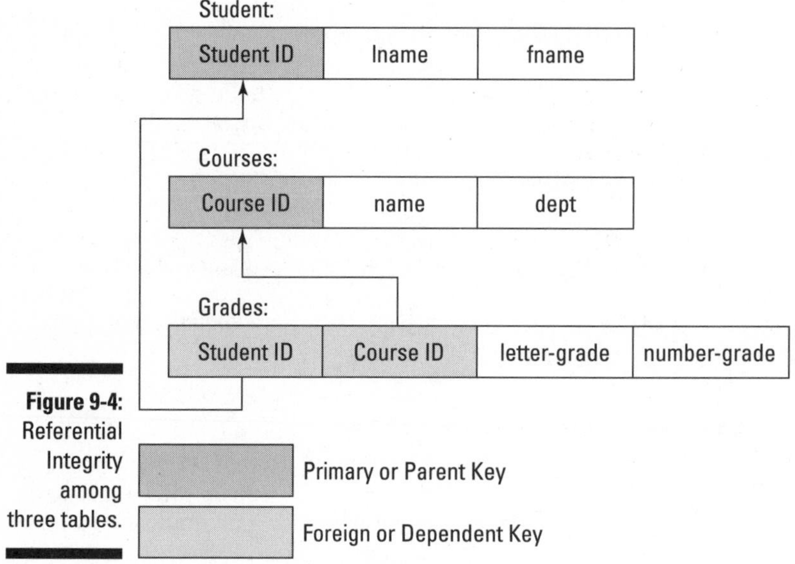

Figure 9-4: Referential Integrity among three tables.

The RI situation gets a bit tricky when parent key values in the parent table are deleted, for example. What happens to the foreign key in the grade table when a course is deleted from the course table? As you may have guessed, DB2 follows certain rules to help it decide how best to react in order to maintain the RI of the tables in these situations.

The database manager follows three sets of rules to maintain RI on a table: the insert, delete, and update rule.

Understand how these rules affect the outcome of insert, delete, and update operations on dependent and parent tables.

Insert rule

The insert rule is directly associated with the creation of the foreign key itself; it is therefore an implicit rule. It's actually quite simple: Any value inserted into the foreign key of the dependent table must already exist in the parent key of the parent table. If it doesn't, the insert will fail.

Inserts into the parent table don't cause any action to be taken on the dependent table.

Using the example in Figure 9-4, say that an attempt to insert information related to `studentID 2468` into the grade table is made. What will the result be? The dependent table is the grade table and the parent table is the student. Because `studentID 2468` does not appear in the parent table, the insert into the dependent table will fail.

Delete rules

Four delete rules can be specified when a foreign key constraint is defined on a table. Which one is chosen is really determined by what makes the most sense based on what the data represents to the users of the database.

Deletes from the dependent table do not cause any action to be taken on the parent table. This is exactly the opposite of the insert rule.

NO ACTION

This is the default delete rule. The rule ensures that after all referential constraints are applied following a delete, there is a matching value in the parent key of the parent table for every row in the foreign key of the dependent table. If this is not the case, no action will be taken and the delete will simply fail.

RESTRICT

This is almost identical to the `NO ACTION` rule except it differs slightly as to when the rule is enforced. The `RESTRICT` rule is enforced before any other rules are enforced. The `RESTRICT` rule basically prevents any row from being deleted in the parent table if any rows are found in the dependent table(s) by causing the delete command to fail. For the delete to succeed in this case, rows in the dependent table must be deleted first.

Return to Figure 9-4 for an example of these two rules. Say that you decide to delete `studentID 1000` from the student table. Perhaps this student attended the university 100 years ago and you decide that it's time to retire his student ID. Interestingly enough, you still have his grades recorded in the grade table. If the `RESTRICT` or `NO ACTION` rule is in effect, the only way to delete `studentID 1000` from the student table is to first delete all the grades related to `studentID 1000` from the grades table. After this delete is committed, `studentID 1000` can be successfully deleted from the student table.

CASCADE

Unlike the `RESTRICT` and `NO ACTION` rules, the `CASCADE` rule ensures that the database manager takes action on dependent tables when a delete is attempted on a parent table. This rule states that when a row is deleted from a parent table, all related rows in the dependent tables are automatically deleted at the same time. Talk about cleaning house!

In the previous example, the end result would be the same — all rows related to studentID 1000 would be deleted from both the student and grades tables. The difference here is that only one DELETE is issued. The database manager automatically performs any additional deletes required.

SET NULL

The SET NULL rule also causes the database manager to take action on dependent tables should a delete command be issued against a parent table. In this case, the deletion of any row in the parent table will cause the database manager to set the foreign key column(s) in the related rows of the dependent table to NULL (if there are nullable columns). The other values in the row are unaffected. If the database manager is unable to set the value to NULL — because the column was created with the NOT NULL clause, for example — then the delete will fail.

In the student example, if the SET NULL rule was in place when studentID 1000 was deleted from the student table, rows in the grades table containing studentID 1000 would be automatically updated by the database manager. The value 1000 would be set to NULL.

Update rules

There are two options when it comes to updating rows defined in a referential integrity relationship. The update rules come into effect when an update is attempted on the parent table. These are very similar to the NO ACTION and RESTRICT rules for deletion.

NO ACTION

This is the default rule. This rule states that an update on a parent key will fail if a row in a dependent table still matches the original values of the key after the update is completed.

RESTRICT

This rule is the same as the NO ACTION rule except that it is applied before (rather than after) any other rules are enforced. This timing issue can make a difference in the success or failure of the update, but we won't get into the details of how in this book.

Going back to our famous studentID 1000 example, if you attempted to update the student table by changing studentID 1000 to any other value, this would fail because studentID 1000 still exists in the grades table.

Restrictions exist on updates to foreign keys in dependent tables as well. The new value of the key must still match a value in the parent key or the update will fail.

Creating tables with RI constraints

Now that you're an expert in keys and RI and constraints and all that good stuff, we want to go over how one actually creates a table with such things through the DB2 Command Window. In a nutshell, RI constraints can be introduced by specifying a foreign key constraint in the `create table` command, or by using the `alter table` command to add a foreign key to the table after it's been created.

You may not be able to successfully add a constraint to a table by using the `alter table` command. The command may fail if the existing table data doesn't satisfy the constraint.

Because you are so familiar with the student, grades, and courses tables, you can start with those.

The `student` and `courses` tables are the parent tables; they each have three columns, with one being the primary key. The following two `create table` statements can be used to create them:

Student table:

```
db2 create table student(studentID smallint not null primary
           key, lname varchar(25), fname varchar(20))
```

Courses table:

```
db2 create table courses (courseID smallint not null primary
           key, name varchar(30), dept varchar(20))
```

Next you'll create the dependent table, which we're calling `grades`. This is where it seems to get complicated, but have no fear! Everything is explained as you go along. The `grades` table has four columns and two foreign keys defined. In this case, no delete or update rules have been explicitly defined, so the default `NO ACTION` rule will be in effect.

Grades table:

```
db2 create table grades (studentID smallint, courseID
           smallint not null, number_grade smallint,
           letter_grade char(2), constraint FKstudentID
           FOREIGN KEY(studentID) references
           STUDENT(studentID), constraint FKcourseID FOREIGN
           KEY(courseID) references COURSES(courseID))
```

We have a few things to point out with respect to how these tables have been created. The `grades` table is the dependent table in this case because it has the foreign key constraints defined. The basic syntax of the foreign key constraint is as follows:

```
CONSTRAINT <constraint_name> FOREIGN
           KEY(column(s)_in_dependent_table) REFERENCES
           parent_table_name(parent_key_column(s))
```

When defining any constraint, the user has the option to designate a name to the constraint. In this example, we have chosen the names FKstudentID and FKcourseID. If no name is specified, DB2 will assign a unique identifier to the constraint. Designating a meaningful name is beneficial, however, because DB2 will supply this name in error messages should an SQL statement attempt to violate the constraint. A meaningful name will, with luck, make the error message more meaningful.

Two parent key columns arise from the creation of the grades tables. One parent key is the studentID column in the student table and the other is the courseID column in the courses table. As stated in the definition of a foreign key in the "'Key' concepts" section, parent keys must also be unique keys, and in this case, they are! This is because the create table statements for the student and courses tables both defined their parent key columns to be primary keys. Remember, primary keys are a special kind of unique key. See the section on "Unique constraints" for a refresher on unique and primary keys.

The third thing to point out here is that the parent key column names and the foreign key column names happen to be the same in this example — studentID and courseID. This isn't always the case. In fact, the names are often different, which is perfectly acceptable. The main requirements are that the parent key is a unique key and that the data types of the parent and foreign key columns are the same.

Often, tables will be both parent tables and dependent tables at the same time.

Okay, just to make things interesting, you'll add delete rules to the dependent table definition. You have to decide how you'd like the database manager to react should an attempt be made to delete rows from either of the parent tables. Remember, you have four delete rules to choose from: NO ACTION, RESTRICT, CASCADE, and SET NULL.

Consider using the SET NULL rule on the FKcourseID constraint. This could pose a problem because the courseID column of the grades table is defined as NOT NULL. The SET NULL rule would mean that if a courseID is deleted from the courses table, the courseID column in the corresponding rows in the grades table would be set to NULL. Because the courseID column in the grades table is defined as NOT NULL, the delete would always fail.

Using the SET NULL rule for the FKstudentID constraint and the CASCADE rule for the FKcourseID constraint, here is how the grades table would have to be created. Notice that the definitions of the student and courses tables remain unaffected.

```
db2 create table grades (studentID smallint, courseID
           smallint not null, number_grade smallint,
           letter_grade char(2), constraint FKstudentID
           FOREIGN KEY(studentID) references
           STUDENT(studentID) ON DELETE set null, constraint
           FKcourseID FOREIGN KEY(courseID) references
           COURSES(courseID) ON DELETE cascade)
```

These delete rules were chosen for illustration purposes only. They may not be ideal for a real database containing student information.

Lab 9-2 gives you some experience creating tables with various constraints defined on them.

Lab 9-2 Creating tables with RI constraints

1. **Connect to the test database by entering** db2 connect to test.
2. **Create a table called** strings **that consists of three columns defined with** string **data types. Ensure that one of the columns is defined as a primary key.**
3. **List the system catalog tables and then list all the tables in the database.**

   Notice the schema name given to the strings table.
4. **Create a table called** nums **consisting of four different numeric data types.**
5. **Define a check constraint on the first column that states that the value of the column must be less than 100.**

Understanding Indexes

An index can be defined as an ordered (sorted) set of pointers to rows of data in a base table. Figure 9-5 shows a simple index on a table containing names and addresses.

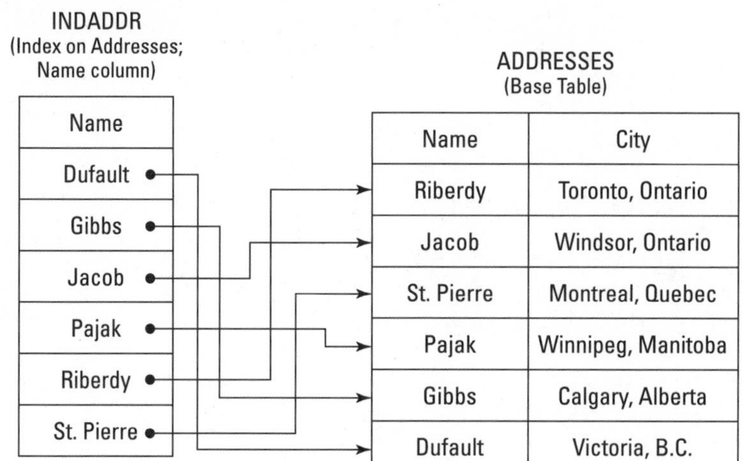

Figure 9-5: Ascending index on a base table.

Many indexes may be associated with the same base table. It's fairly easy to understand the purposes of an index in the world of databases. You can almost directly compare them to the index of a book. Just as an index in a book can provide fast access to sections of data in a book, a database index can provide fast access to data within a database table because the data sorting is already done. It's all about performance these days, and a properly defined index can significantly improve the time it takes DB2 to return data that was requested.

The second and equally important purpose of an index on a base table is to ensure the uniqueness of any unique keys defined on the base table. Tables with unique key or primary key indexes defined on them cannot have rows with identical keys. In addition, primary keys cannot contain any `NULL` values. Uniqueness is checked when a value is inserted or updated and when the `create index` statement is executed.

You can find detailed information on the indexes defined in the database in the SYSCAT.INDEXES system table view.

Types of indexes

Several different types of indexes are provided by DB2. Following are details on system-defined, user-defined, unique, clustering, and bi-directional indexes.

System-defined indexes

System-defined indexes are created automatically by the database manager and belong to the SYSIBM schema.

Many indexes are created automatically by the database manager when the `create database` command is executed. These indexes are associated with the DB2 system tables. Some of these indexes are created for performance purposes and others are created because unique keys are defined on the system tables.

The database manager will also create an index whenever a unique key is defined on any user tables within the database. So, if a primary key or unique key constraint is specified in the `create table` command, or added via the `alter table` command, an index is created to maintain the uniqueness of the key. The names of these indexes begin with the letters *SQL* and are then followed by the index creation timestamp. The `SYSIBM.SQL001231143033440` index, for example, was created on December 31, 2000.

User-defined indexes

User-defined indexes can be created with the `create index` SQL statement. You can create an index on the student table that was defined previously. Say that you plan to do a lot of queries on the last name of the students in this table. The column that holds the last names is called `lname`. An index can be created on this column by issuing the following SQL command:

```
db2 create index stlname on student(lname desc)
```

In this case, the index will be created in descending order according to last name. By default, the order is ascending.

An index can be also created on both the last name and first name of the student. This would be a very useful index because many students may share the same last name.

```
db2 create index stlfname on student(lname, fname)
```

In this case, the index will use the last name as the first sort column and the first name as the secondary sort column.

Unique indexes

We have mentioned before that unique indexes are automatically created when a primary or unique key constraint is placed on a table. You can actually think of a unique constraint and a unique index as being essentially the same thing; a unique constraint implies that a unique index is created and a unique index implies that a unique key constraint has been placed on the table. For example, say that a table is created using the following command:

```
db2 create table gifts (name varchar(25), gift_type
         varchar(10))
```

In this case, no constraints have been defined on the table. Next, you add a unique index on the name column with the following command:

```
db2 create unique index giftname on gifts(name)
```

Notice the key word `unique` in the `create index` statement. If duplicate names exist in the table when the statement is issued, the statement will fail. If not, the statement will succeed. As long as this index is in place, DB2 will ensure that no duplicate names exist in the table as a result of an `insert` or `update` command.

Clustering indexes

If a clustering index is defined on a table, the database manager will attempt to physically locate new rows adjacent to rows that would be next to each other in the index.

An example might help illustrate this better. A table called `names` is created to hold — you guessed it — names! The names `Brian` and `Ken` are already inserted. If the name `Lee-Ann` is to be inserted next, the database manager will attempt to physically locate this row next to the row containing the name `Ken`. The manager does this because `Lee-Ann` would follow `Ken` in an ascending index created over the `name` column of this table.

This clustering index could be created with the following command:

```
db2 create index inames on names(name asc) cluster
```

If you are creating a clustering index, you would normally specify the `PCT-FREE` option along with the `CLUSTER` option in the `CREATE INDEX` statement. The `PCTFREE` option specifies the percentage of free space DB2 should leave on each index page.

Bi-directional indexes

To make things even more interesting, DB2 provides bi-directional indexes. That is, one index in DB2 can act as both an ascending index and a descending index. DB2 is able to do this by internally storing the index keys (pointers) in such a way that it can follow the keys in order from left to right, or in the reverse order, from right to left.

Using the `names` table again, we'll create a bi-directional index on the name column, To do this, you use the `allow reverse scans` option of the `create index` command:

```
db2 create index binames on names(name asc) allow reverse
         scans
```

Even though the index is specified as ascending, if the data from the table was requested in descending order, DB2 would not have to sort the table data to do this. It would simply scan the bi-directional index in the reverse order.

If you need to modify an existing index, you must drop the index and then recreate it, because no `alter index` command is available. An index can be dropped using the `drop index <index name>` command.

Understanding Views

Views are logical tables that provide alternative ways to access the data in one or more base tables. Views can be used to control which parts of a table users can access — perhaps restricting most users to only a subset of the rows and/or columns of the base table. Views might also be used to combine subsets of two or more tables in order to simplify data retrieval. To the naked eye, or the "eye" of an application, a view and a table are essentially the same because views can be accessed in the same ways: through `select`, `insert`, `update`, and `delete` statements.

Creating views — The simple stuff

A view is created using a `select` statement in the `create view` statement. The column names within the view don't have to match those of the base table. Also, the data types of the view columns can be inherited from the base table or changed when the view is created. Here we deal only with columns that have inherited the data types from the corresponding base table columns.

After a view is created, its definition is kept in the DB2 system tables. You can find Information on views in the SYSCAT.VIEWS and SYSCAT.VIEWDEP system table views. The view definition is "reapplied" to the base table by the database manager whenever an application references the view. In this sense, a view is actually a temporary table. Check out Chapter 12 for more information on `select`, `insert`, and `update` statements.

Before we go over the `create view` statement, try creating a simple table called `base` containing three character columns. This will be the table that the view is based on.

```
db2 create table base (c1 char(1), c2 char(1), c3 char(1))
```

You can restrict the view to either a subset of the columns and/or of the rows of a base table.

Subset of the columns

The following example creates a view on a subset of the columns in the base table.

```
db2 create view v1 as select c1 from base
```

Notice that the `select` statement in the `create view` command specified only one column from the base table. Now, if a `select` is issued on the `view v1`, values from column `c1` in table `base` will be returned.

If highly confidential data happens to be in columns `c2` and `c3`, but common information only was in `c1` in the base table, the database administrator could revoke access to the base table from most users and then grant access to the `view v1` to all users.

Subset of the rows

The following example creates a view on all the columns in the base table but only on a subset of the rows in the base table.

```
db2 create view v2 as select * from base where c1='a'
```

In this case, the `select` statement includes all three columns from the base table but restricts the rows to only those that have the value `a` in column `c1`. Restricting a view to a subset of rows requires a predicate (`WHERE` clause) in the `select` statement when the view is created. If no rows in the base table satisfy the predicate, in this case, `c1='a'`, then a `select` statement on `v2` will not return any data. If 20 rows are in the base table but only three of them have `c1` set to `a`, then only three rows will be returned by the statement `db2 select * from v2`.

If `c1` happened to represent departments in a company, this view would contain information only for department `a`. A database administer could then restrict access of the view to only those people within department `a`.

Subset of rows and columns

The following example illustrates how a view can be created on a subset of both the rows and columns of the base table.

```
db2 create view v3 as select c1, c2 from base where c3>'b'
```

In this case, the view `v3` would contain only data from columns `c1` and `c2` of the base table. View `v3` would contain all rows from the base table that have a value greater than `b` in column `c3`.

Inserting and updating view columns — It gets trickier

Issuing an insert or update against a view can actually cause an insert or update to occur on the base table on which the view is defined. However, there are some ways to restrict when and if updates and inserts are allowed on the view.

Using WITH CHECK OPTION

If the view is not defined as read only, whether an insert or update command will succeed on a view depends on whether the with check option of the create view statement was used.

Assume that the with check option wasn't used, as was the case with views v1, v2, and v3 in our previous examples. Inserts and updates to the view would automatically cause an insert or update to the base table that the view is defined on.

The data type of the new values must of course match those of the view columns. This is true in general for any update or insert attempt, regardless of whether you're dealing with tables or views. Also, if the view contains only a subset of the base table columns, an insert attempt will fail.

We can use this view definition for view v5 as an example. The definition is as follows:

```
db2 create view v5(c1, c2, c3)  as select * from base where
          c1='a'
```

Proofreader: The single quotation marks in the parens below are going the same direction on purpose. –sc

An attempt to insert values (123, 'c', 'd') into v5 would definitely fail because column c1 is defined as a CHAR column and 123 is numeric. The following values, however, could be successfully inserted into the view: ('a', 'b', 'c'), ('b', 'e', 't'), ('c', 'a', 't'). The insert on the view would result in the base table containing these three new rows. Also, the following update command would succeed, causing column c1 in the base table to be set to z wherever c2 is set to b:

```
db2 update v5 set c1='z' where c2='b'
```

Okay, time to introduce the with check option option of the create view command. This option ensures that any predicates specified in the create view statement will be checked whenever an insert or update is attempted on the view. If the predicate is not satisfied, the attempt will fail. Note how the previous example changes by adding `with check option` to the definition of view `v5`. The predicate in this case is that `c1` must be equal to the value `a`.

```
db2 create view v5 as select * from base where c1='a' with
         check option
```

The values ('a', 'b', 'c') would still be successfully inserted into the view because `c1='a'`. The values ('b', 'e', 't') and ('c', 'a', 't'), however, would not be inserted because `c1` is not equal to `a`. These three insert attempts on the new `v5` view would result in the base table containing one new row only, with values ('a', 'b', 'c'). Also, the following update command would definitely fail because it specifies that `c1` be modified to the value `z`:

```
db2 update v5 set c1='z' where c2='b'
```

The update would succeed if it were changed to the following:

```
db2 update v5 set c1='a' where c2='b'
```

Dealing with nested views — Okay, this is really tricky stuff

Nested views are views that are created on top of views, which are created on top of views, and so on. This means that the number of predicates that must be evaluated during an insert or update attempt is potentially multiplied. The view may inherit the predicates of the views on which it depends. Determining which predicates the database manager must apply can be very tricky. Again, it all depends on whether `with check option` was specified when the views were created.

There are two forms of `with check option`. These are `with local check option` and `with cascaded check option`. If local or cascaded is not specified, cascaded is the default.

In the following sections, we start with the basic rules for inserting and updating data in nested views and then go over some examples to help illustrate these rules.

In the process of determining which predicates are inherited, you can move from Rule 1 to Rule 3 or Rule 2 to Rule 3, for example.

Rule 1: with check option NOT specified

If a view is created without `with check option` specified, its predicates are not evaluated. However, if any updateable views that it directly or indirectly depends on do include `with check option`, the predicates specified in those definitions must be evaluated.

Rule 2: with cascaded check option or with check option specified

If a view is created with these options specified, the predicates of the view are evaluated. In addition, the predicates on all updateable views on which the view depends are inherited. This is true even if the view definitions on which the view depends do not include `with check option` or if one of them includes `with local check option`. If any of the predicates is not satisfied, the update or insert will fail.

Rule 3: with local check option

If a view is created specifying `with local check option`, its predicates are evaluated. However, the view does not inherit predicates from any updateable views on which it depends.

Examples to illustrate these rules

Here, we create a base table and then some nested views to start with. In this case, `nv5` depends on `nv4`, which depends on `nv3`, and so on. We just use the `insert` statement in our examples, even though the rules apply to both `insert` and `update`.

```
db2 create table nbase(c1 smallint, c2 smallint, c3 smallint,
            c4 smallint, c5 smallint)
```

```
db2 create view nv1 as select * from nbase where c1=1
```

```
db2 create view nv2 as select * from nv1 where c2=1 with
            local check option
```

```
db2 create view nv3 as select * from nv2 where c3=1
```

```
db2 create view nv4 as select * from nv3 where c4=3 with
            cascaded check option
```

```
db2 create view nv5 as select * from nv4 where c5=1
```

Rule 1 examples

We will attempt to insert various values into the views that did not include the check option clause in their definition. These are views `nv1`, `nv3`, and `nv5`.

Inserting into nv1 is fairly simple because it does not depend on any other view definitions. It is defined directly on top of the base table. In addition, without the check option clause on this view, any value can be inserted or updated into it as long as the data types match.

Inserting into nv3 is a bit more complicated. Rule 1 states that nv3 will inherit any predicates that the views it depends on have. View nv3 depends on views nv2 and nv1. Going to nv2 first, you can see that Rule 3 must now be applied, which states only that the predicate on nv2 needs to be evaluated. This means that the following insert statement would fail because c2 is not equal to 1.

```
db2 insert into nv3 values (1,2,2,1,1)
```

This next command would succeed because the predicate for nv2 is satisfied.

```
db2 insert into nv3 values (2,1,2,1,1)
```

Inserting into view nv5 seems even more complicated, but if you keep going back to the rules, you'll find that it is a bit simpler. Starting with Rule 1 again, view nv5 first depends on nv4, which has the cascaded check option specified. This moves you on from following Rule 1 to following Rule 2. This states that you must evaluate the predicates of nv4 and also that you inherit all the predicates from the views on which nv4depends — nv3, nv2, and nv1 — even if these views do not have the check option clause specified or if they have with local check option specified. This means that the following commands will fail. In the first insert, the predicate for nv3 is not satisfied, and in the second insert, the predicate for nv1 is not satisfied.

```
db2 insert into nv5 values (1,1,2,3,2)
```

```
db2 insert into nv5 values (2,1,1,3,1)
```

Next are examples of inserts that will succeed on nv5.

```
db2 insert into nv5 values (1,1,1,3,6)
```

```
db2 insert into nv5 values (1,1,1,3,9)
```

Rule 2 examples

View nv4 is the only one defined with the cascaded check option clause. Following Rule 2, this means that you evaluate the predicate for nv4 and all the predicates on the views it depends on — nv3, nv2, and nv1. The following insert commands would fail. In the first, the nv4 predicate is not satisfied, and in the second, the nv1 predicate is not satisfied.

```
db2 insert into nv4 values (1,1,1,4,2)
```

```
db2 insert into nv4 values (2,1,1,3,6)
```

The following command would succeed because all inherited predicates are satisfied:

```
db2 insert into nv4 values (1,1,1,3,2)
```

Rule 3 examples

View nv2 was defined specifying with local check option. Following Rule 3, any insert statement that does not satisfy the predicate for nv2 would fail. No other predicates are inherited. Here is an example of a failing insert, followed by a successful insert on nv2:

```
db2 insert into nv2 values (1,2,1,3,1)
```

```
db2 insert into nv2 values (4,1,4,4,4)
```

Ensure that you understand how a view and its corresponding base table are affected when data is updated or inserted into the view, particularly when nested views are involved. The exercises in Lab 9-3 can help test your understanding of views.

Inoperative views

Views are said to be inoperative when one or more of the views or tables it depends on have been dropped since the view was created. An attempt to access an inoperative view results in an error message. Inoperative views can be dropped by issuing `db2 drop view <view name>` from the DB2 command window. If the tables it depended on are recreated, the view can then be recreated as well. Information on whether a view is inoperative can be found in the SYSCAT.VIEWS system catalog view.

Lab 9-3 Working with views

1. **Disconnect from the test database using by entering** `db2 terminate`**.**
2. **Then connect to the sample database by using the command** `db2 connect to sample`**.**
3. **Use the** `describe` **command to display the column definitions for the table called** `sales`**.**
4. **Next, create a view called** `vsales` **based on the table** `sales` **that includes all the columns in the table** `sales` **but restricts the** `sales` **column to values greater than 5.**
5. **Enter** `db2 select * from vsales`**. Ten records should appear.**

6. **Create another view called** vsales2 **based on the** vsales **view that includes all the columns in** vsales **but restricts the** sales_person **column to values greater than** Hanson**. Also specify** with check option **when creating this view.**

   Entering db2 select * from vsales2 should return seven records.

7. **Use the** db2 insert **statement to attempt to insert different sales values into the** vsales2 **view.**

   For example, the value ('01/07/2001', 'St. Pierre', 'Ontario', 7) will be successfully inserted; the value ('07/07/2001', 'Ribbs', 'Ontario, 3) would not be successfully inserted. Issue a db2 select * from <table name> statement, where <table name> = vsales2, vsales, and sales. Notice the records that were inserted into the sales table.

Other Important Objects

Bufferpools and log files are important objects within a database but are a bit different than the DB2 objects already mentioned. Bufferpools have a big impact on database performance; log files are key contributors to database recoverability.

Bufferpools — Swimming pools for database pages

Well, maybe the database pages don't actually swim in bufferpools. A DB2 bufferpool is a portion of memory that DB2 uses to cache database pages. The hope is that all pages required by DB2 for data retrieval or updates are cached in a bufferpool before they're actually needed. This avoids costly I/O operations resulting from DB2 having to get the page from disk rather than memory. Therefore, the size and number of bufferpools defined in a database can have an incredible impact on the performance of applications accessing its data.

By default, each database must have at least one bufferpool defined. When the database is created, a bufferpool called IBMDEFAULTBP is automatically created. To create additional bufferpools, the create bufferpool command is available.

A bufferpool can be accessible to all tablespaces in the database or it can be specifically assigned to a tablespace using the create tablespace or alter tablespace command. Bufferpools can also be altered (to increase/decrease size) or dropped by using the following commands:

```
db2 alter bufferpool <buffer_pool_name> size <number_pages>
db2 drop bufferpool <buffer_pool_name>
```

Bufferpools can be created using any of the supported database page sizes: 4K, 8K, 16K, and 32K. Details on the bufferpools defined for a database can be found in the SYSCAT.BUFFERPOOLS system catalog view.

Log files — Not the wooden kind

Log files are extremely important to the day-to-day operations of the database. There are a configured number of log files associated with each database. Transactions issued against the database while the database is active are recorded in the DB2 log files. This is similar to a video camera recording the events of a party where the video camera is turned on when the party starts, and then turned off when the party finishes.

DB2 uses a write-ahead logging method. What this means is that when database pages are manipulated in memory, the changes to the pages are recorded or written to a log file before those changed pages are written from memory onto disk. Should the database be stopped abruptly because of a power outage, for example, the changes in memory at the time would not be lost. They can be replayed or reapplied to the database pages by replaying or reading the log files.

Not logged initially tables

It is possible to turn logging off temporarily on a specific table. There are risks involved in doing so but the performance benefits might outweigh the risks in certain situations. To turn logging off, you use the `alter table` command with the `not logged initially` option. The transaction on this table following the `alter table` command will be applied to the table and will not be logged. After the transaction commits, logging will be turned back on for the table.

Some administrators will turn logging off on a newly created table and then insert thousands of rows into it. This can significantly lower the execution time of the insert.

Prep Test

1 **A table is needed, called** `game_results`**, to keep track of the results of a series of hockey games for our local hockey team. We need columns to keep track of the date of each game, the name of the opposing team, their goals scored, and our goals scored. Which of the following statements would create this table?**

A ❍ db2 create table game_results(game_date date, opponent varchar(25), goals_for num, goals_against num)

B ❍ db2 create table game_results(game_date datetime, opponent char(25), goals_for decimal(3,0), goals_against decimal(3,0))

C ❍ db2 create table name game_results(game_date date, opponent varchar(25), goals_for int, goals_against int)

D ❍ db2 create table game_results(game_date date, opponent varchar, goals_for int, goals_against int)

2 **Given the following table definitions and data, and the statement** `db2 alter table sales add foreign key(prodID) on delete cascade`**, how many records will be deleted when processing the statement db2 delete from product where ProductID > 3000?**

PRODUCT

Name varchar(25)	*ProductID int not null*	*Quantity int not null with default 0*
Sweater	1234	10
Jeans	5678	25
Shoes	2468	10

SALES

SalespersonID int not null	*prodID int*	*Num_sold int with default 0*
1	1234	10
2	5678	25
3	5678	10

A ❍ 1
B ❍ 2
C ❍ 3
D ❍ 4

3 **Which of the following** `create view` **statements should be specified to create a nested view that inherits the predicates of all the views on which it depends?**

A ❍ db2 create view v3 as select * from v2 where c1=2 with cascade delete
B ❍ db2 create view v3 as select * from v2 where c1=2 with check option
C ❍ db2 create view v3 as select * from v2 where c1=2
D ❍ db2 create view v3 as select * from v2 where c1=2 with local check option

4 **Given the statement** `db2 create view v1 as select * from b1 where c1=2` **and the statements** `db2 insert into v1 values (5)` **and** `db2 insert into v1 values (a)`**, how many new rows would be inserted into table b1?**

A ❍ 0
B ❍ 1
C ❍ 2
D ❍ 3

5 **How many indexes will be created by the following command?**

```
db2 create table test (c1 int not null primary key,
             c2 varchar(10) not null, c3 int not null,
             constraint ucon  unique (c3,c1),
             constraint chkcon check (c1 > 25))
```

A ❍ 0
B ❍ 1
C ❍ 2
D ❍ 5

6 **On which of the following data types is codepage conversion possible?**

A ❍ VARCHAR FOR BIT DATA
B ❍ BLOB
C ❍ CLOB
D ❍ FLOAT

7 The following data is to be stored in a DB2 table called `products`**:**

```
ProductID (less than 10000), Sales (in the thousands),
          Comment (400 characters or less),
          Chart (binary, potentially 1GB in size)
```

Which statement would create this table making the most efficient use of storage, ensuring that all constraints are enforced?

A ❍ db2 create table products (productID smallint not null primary key, sales decimal(6,2), comment varchar(400), chart blob(1 G), constraint chkcon (productID < 10000))

B ❍ db2 create table products (productID integer not null, sales real(8), comment varchar(400), chart blob(1 G), constraint ucon unique (productID), constraint chkcon (productID < 10000))

C ❍ db2 create table products (productID smallint not null primary key, sales decimal(6,2), comment long varchar(400), chart blob(1 G), constraint chkcon (productID < 10000))

D ❍ db2 create table products (productID smallint not null, sales decimal(6,2), comment varchar(400), chart blob(1 G), constraint chkcon (productID < 10000))

Answers

1 **A.** Connect to the sample database and then issue these statements yourself to determine why the other answers are incorrect. *Review "Tackling Tables."*

2 **C.** One record in the `product` table and two in the `sales` table. *Review "Understanding Table Constraints."*

3 **B.** The `with check option` clause defaults to `with cascaded check option`. *Review "Understanding Views."*

4 **B.** The predicate is not checked on insert because the `with check option` clause was not specified in the `create view` statement and `a` is not a valid integer value. *Review "Understanding Views."*

5 **C.** An index will be created for the primary key and unique key constraints. *Review "Understanding Table Constraints" and "Understanding Indexes."*

6 **C.** All other datatypes are either binary or numeric. *Review "Defining columns with data types."*

7 **A.** All other options don't use the most efficient data types. *Review "Defining columns with data types" and "Understanding Table Constraints."*

Chapter 10

Security and DB2

Exam Objectives

- Ability to provide users with authority on database objects
- Given a DCL statement, knowledge to identify results

How important is database security? Well, imagine your colleague logging onto the company HR database and getting access to your salary information! Or, what about your neighbor, with that dog that is always barking, getting access to your bank accounts and transferring money from your vacation account to his retirement account? We think you get the picture: Security is vital to a database. For this reason, every database should have a detailed security plan in place. This chapter goes over the key security features of DB2 that restrict or allow access to instances, databases, and various other database objects including tables, views, and packages. After you know what the security features are, you can see how to create a secure DB2 database. Into the "AAP" world we go: Authentication, Authorization, and Privileges!

Quick Assessment

Providing users with authority on database objects

1 Three main components of a DB2 security plan are _____, _____, and _____.

2 DB2 uses _____ to determine what types of operations users or groups of users can perform.

3 There are five main authorities in DB2 Version 7.1. These are _____, _____, _____, _____, and _____ authorities.

4 The SYS* authorities are controlled in the _____ configuration file.

5 On the database server, authentication types are controlled by the _____ parameter in the _____ configuration file. On the DB2 Connect Server (gateway) or on a DB2 client, authentication types are controlled by the _____ option in the _____ command.

6 There are three types of clients - _____, _____, and _____.

Identifying results of a DCL statement

7 Privileges can be controlled explicitly using the _____ and _____ commands.

8 The `GRANT` and `REVOKE` commands are known as _____ statements or _____ statements.

9 Database privileges are stored in the _____.

10 The five main types of privileges are _____, _____, _____, _____, and _____.

11 The _____ and _____ authorities are controlled by the `GRANT` and `REVOKE` commands.

Answers

1 *authorization, authorities, privileges.* Review chapter introduction.

2 *authorities*. Review "Gaining Authorization: Group Membership."

3 *SYSADM, SYSCTRL, SYSMAINT, DBADM, LOAD* Review "Gaining Authorization: Group Membership."

4 *database manager.* Review "Gaining Authorization: Group Membership."

5 `AUTHENTICATION`, *database manager,* `AUTHENTICATION`, `CATALOG DATABASE`. Review "Understanding Authentication — DB2's Security Guard."

6 *host, trusted, untrusted.* Review "Different types of clients."

7 `GRANT`, `REVOKE`. Review "Different ways of obtaining privileges."

8 *Data Control Language, DCL.* Review "Different ways of obtaining privileges."

9 *system catalog tables.* Review "Privileges."

10 *database, table/view, package, schema, index.* Review "Privileges."

11 `DBADM`, `LOAD`. Review "How do authorities get assigned?"

Understanding Authentication — DB2's Security Guard

Authentication is the first door a user goes through to gain access to the instance or to the database. Authentication is performed using security methods external to DB2, usually those provided by the operating system. However, DB2 also allows DCE and Kerberos security protocols to be used for DB2 authentication.

For authentication to be successful, a valid userid and password must be (implicitly or explicitly) supplied. The database manager sends the userid and password to the external security program to be validated. Picture a large security guard standing outside the gate to the instance or database, asking, "Who the heck are you and what makes you think you can enter?"

When does authentication take place?

Authentication is performed whenever an `attach` or `connect` command is issued. The `attach` command is used whenever access to an instance is required. The `connect` command is used whenever access to a database is required. Following are some examples to show how these commands might be used.

Authentication commands: Example 1:

Userid `Noreen` with password `tika` wants access to instance `db2inst1`, cataloged as `db2tcp1`. This user issues the following command:

```
db2 attach to db2tcp1 user Noreen using tika
```

If the user were already logged onto the system with userid `Noreen`, she could alternatively issue this command:

```
db2 attach to db2tcp1
```

DB2 will implicitly use the userid and password used to log onto the system if none are supplied.

The `catalog` command is discussed in detail in Chapter 7. We also discuss this command again later in this section.

Authentication commands: Example 2:

Userid `Noreen` with password `tika` wants access to database `sample`. Userid `Marie` is currently logged into the system. User Noreen issues the following command:

```
db2 connect to sample user Noreen using tika
```

Note that the userid connecting to the database and the current userid logged onto the system do not have to be the same.

Authentication commands: Example 3:

Userid `Noreen` with password `tika` wants access to database `sample` and wants to change her password to naja. To do so, she issues the following command:

```
db2 connect to sample user Noreen using tika new naja confirm
            naja
```

In this case, `Noreen` is authenticated using password `tika` by the security program first; then the password change request is handled. If this statement was successful, the command issued in Example 2 would fail if it were to be issued next.

The `NEW` and `CONFIRM` options are also available with the `attach` command.

Authentication commands: Example 4:

Userid `Noreen` has successfully logged into the system. This user wants access to database `sample`, which exists under instanceID `Noreen`. To do so, she issues the following:

```
db2 connect to sample
```

In this case, the instanceID is also the current ID that requires access to this database.

If a userid and password are not supplied but are required, DB2 will prompt for this information.

Where does authentication take place?

Let's face it: DB2 is very scalable! A DB2 environment may include hundreds of clients, gateways, servers, and host systems, all on varying platforms and all connected. So, who does the authentication when an `attach` or `connect` command is issued? Where does our huge security guard stand?

The authentication type controls which system will perform the authentication. The authentication type can be found in the database manager configuration file on the database server. It can also be specified when a remote database is cataloged on the client or DB2 Connect gateway. The authentication type, along with where the `attach` or `connect` command is issued, determines which system asks the question, "Who the heck are you and what makes you think you can enter?"

Authentication types — database server with remote clients

This section deals with a database environment similar to the one shown in Figure 10-1. A DB2 UDB database server and one or more DB2 clients require access to this server. In this case, you can find the authentication types we describe on both the server and the client.

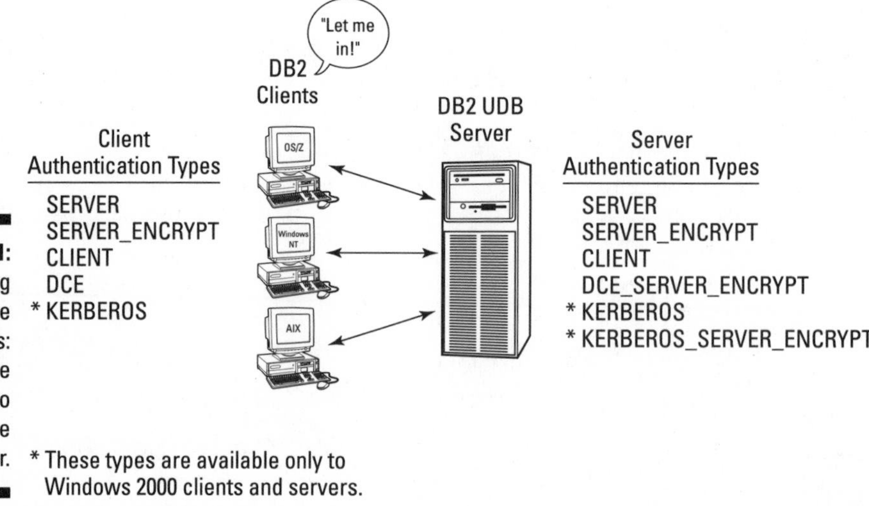

Figure 10-1: Requesting database access: Remote client to database server.

Authentication types in the DBM CFG at the DB Server

As mentioned previously, an authentication type can be specified in the catalog database command on the remote client and in the database manager configuration file on the database server. The general rule is that the authentication type specified in the database manager configuration file on the database server is the one that is used to determine where our security guard will stand. A couple of exceptions to this rule exist, of course, which we will get into more detail about shortly.

The authentication type of the database server can be altered by issuing the following command from the DB2 command window. The instance must be restarted before any changes take effect.

```
db2 update dbm cfg using AUTHENTICATION <authentication_type>
```

Altering the database manager configuration file is also discussed in Chapter 9.

The following is a list of possible authentication types that you can specify in the database manager configuration file.

SERVER

This one is quite straightforward. Authentication will be done at the database server by the operating system. A userid and password must be sent by any remote DB2 clients issuing the `connect` or `attach` commands. Local clients do not have to send a userid and password.

SERVER_ENCRYPT

This is the same as authentication `SERVER` with the exception that passwords will be encrypted at the client before they are sent to the server. After the password arrives at the server, it is decrypted and then authenticated by the operating system.

If the `connect` or `attach` command also includes a request to change the password (with the `new` and `confirm` options), the password will not be encrypted, even though this authentication type is specified.

CLIENT

This type is also pretty straightforward. When authentication is set to client, the database server has indicated that the client is to check the userid and password for validity. You can think of it as the server contracting out the security guard responsibilities to the client machine. The authentication is then performed by the client.

Some situations exist in which the client cannot perform the authentication. We discuss this further in "Different types of clients," later in this chapter. Stay tuned . . .

DCE

When you're setting up the database's security plan, you may choose DCE security software to perform the security guard work (authentication) rather than use the operating system's security features. The DCE software must be installed and set up prior to using this authentication type. If this type is specified, only DCE connections/attachments are allowed.

DCE stands for Distributing Computing Environment.

DCE_SERVER_ENCRYPT

Do not confuse this type with the SERVER_ENCRYPT authentication type. DCE_SERVER_ENCRYPT has a slightly different meaning. When this type is specified in the DBM CFG file, the actual authentication method will be one of DCE, SERVER, or SERVER_ENCRYPT. Which one is chosen depends on what the authentication type of the client is set to. See Table 10-1 for more details.

KERBEROS

Kerberos is another security software product that you can use instead of the operating system security services to perform DB2 authentication. Before you choose this authentication type, Kerberos should be installed and set up on both the client and server machines. Once chosen, Kerberos will use cryptography to create a shared secret key between the client and server, eliminating the need to send the userid and password over the network as text. Cool stuff!

KRB_SERVER_ENCRYPT

If this type is specified in the DBM CFG file, the actual authentication method used is dependent on the authentication type specified on the client. The actual authentication type used will be either KERBEROS or SERVER_ENCRYPT. See Table 10-1 for more details.

The KERBEROS and KRB_SERVER_ENCRYPT authentication types are new to DB2 Version 7.1. They are limited to clients and servers running Windows 2000.

Authentication types in the catalog statement at the client

Authentication types can be specified at the DB2 remote client using the catalog database command. To ensure that the connection attempts are successful, the authentication type at the client must match that of the server. Exceptions to this rule are if the DCE_SERVER_ENCRYPT or KRB_SERVER_ENCRYPT authentication types are specified at the server. Cataloging a database on the client without specifying an authentication type is possible. The following is an example of how you can use the catalog database command to catalog the sample database on a remote client with client authentication set to <authentication_type>:

```
db2 catalog database sample at node mysamp AUTHENTICATION
         <authentication_type>
```

The catalog database command is covered in more detail in Chapter 7.

The possible authentication types for the client are as follows. These have the same meanings as described in the server authentication list:

- SERVER
- SERVER_ENCRYPT
- CLIENT
- DCE
- KERBEROS

Mixing client and server authentication types: Who wins?

Which security guard is more powerful, the one on the client or the one on the database server? As already mentioned, the one on the server is the winner in almost all cases. When DCE_SERVER_ENCRYPT and KRB_SERVER_ENCRYPT types are specified, the security guard on the server lets the security guard on the client decide which authentication method to use. Table 10-1 shows different combinations of client and server authentication types and the resulting authentication method that is used.

In most cases, the client and server types should be the same. Take note of the last five rows of the table for the exceptions to this rule.

Table 10-1 Authentication Type Used Based on Client and DB Server Authentication Types

Client Authentication Type	*Server Authentication Type*	*Authentication Type Used*
Must be SERVER	SERVER	SERVER
Must be SERVER_ENCRYPT	SERVER_ENCRYPT	SERVER_ENCRYPT
Must be CLIENT	CLIENT	CLIENT
Must be DCE	DCE	DCE
Must be KERBEROS	KERBEROS	KERBEROS
DCE	DCE_SERVER_ENCRYPT	DCE
SERVER	DCE_SERVER_ENCRYPT	SERVER
SERVER_ENCRYPT	DCE_SERVER_ENCRYPT	SERVER_ENCRYPT
KERBEROS	KRB_SERVER_ENCRYPT	KERBEROS
Anything other than KERBEROS	KRB_SERVER_ENCRYPT	SERVER_ENCRYPT

Authentication types — DB2 Connect gateways

This section deals with a database environment similar to the one shown in Figure 10-2. In this case, the database resides on a host system, DB2 for OS/390, for example. Our DB2 UDB client can get access to the host database by going through a DB2 Connect Server, also known as a gateway. In this case, the authentication type determines whether authentication will take place on the client, on the gateway, or on the host system. We introduce new authentication types, DCS and DCS_ENCRYPT, in this section.

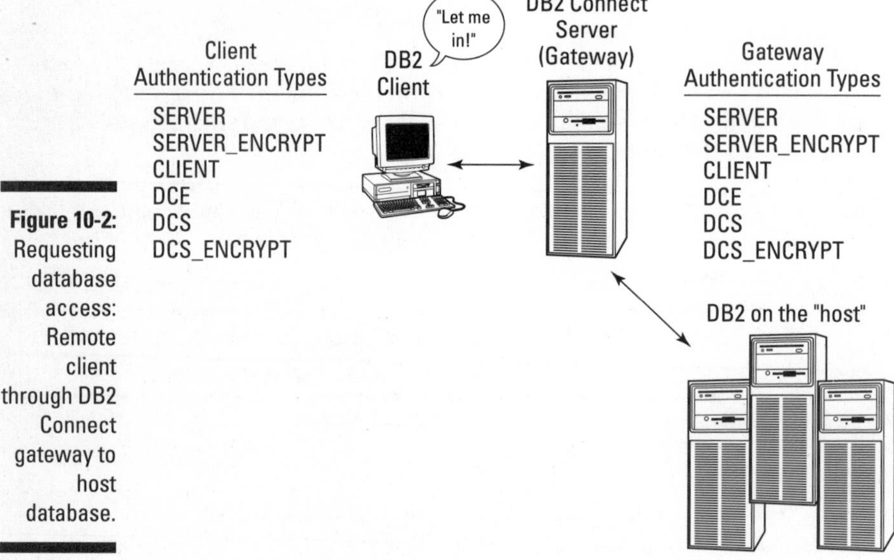

Figure 10-2: Requesting database access: Remote client through DB2 Connect gateway to host database.

Authentication types at the DB2 Connect gateway

You can set the authentication type on the DB2 Connect Server with the `catalog database` statement. For example, to set the authentication to `SERVER`, you can use the following command:

```
db2 catalog database hostdb at node nd1 AUTHENTICATION server
```

The authentication types available on the DB2 Connect gateway are the following:

- SERVER: This type indicates that authentication will take place at the DB2 Connect Server. This is the default authentication type when none is specified.
- SERVER_ENCRYPT: This type is the same as SERVER authentication except that the password sent by the client is encrypted before it is sent and then decrypted at the DB2 Connect Server.
- DCE: This type indicates that DCE security software will perform authentication on behalf of the host.

  DCE authentication is available only to DB2 for MVS Version 5.1 and above.

- CLIENT: CLIENT authentication forces authentication to take place at the DB2 client.
- DCS: DCS authentication indicates that authentication will take place at the host.
- DCS_ENCRYPT: This type forces authentication to take place on the host. However, the password is encrypted from the client to the gateway, from the gateway to the host, or both. Table 10-2 provides more details on this.

DCS stands for Database Connection Services.

Authentication types at the client

Authentication on the client is also set using the `catalog database` statement. The authentication types are as follows. They have the same meaning as the DB2 Connect Server types.

- SERVER
- SERVER_ENCRYPT
- CLIENT
- DCE
- DCS
- DCS_ENCRYPT

Mixing client and gateway authentication types — who wins?

Table 10-2 provides an overview of possible client and gateway authentication types in this DB2 environment. Pay particular attention to the how the decision to encrypt or not to encrypt depends on both the client and gateway authentication types.

Table 10-2 Authentication Type Used Based on Client and Gateway Authentication Types

Client Authentication Type	*Gateway Authentication Type*	*Client→ Gateway Encryption?*	*Gateway→ Host Encryption?*	*Where Authentication takes place*
SERVER_ ENCRYPT	SERVER	Yes	No	Gateway
DCS_ENCRYPT	DCS	Yes	No	Host
DCS	DCS_ENCRYPT	No	Yes	Host
DCS_ENCRYPT	DCS_ENCRYPT	Yes	Yes	Host

The APPC protocol automatically encrypts all passwords.

Different types of clients

You might be wondering what happens if the DB2 client is on an operating system that doesn't have any means of validating userids and passwords. Clients like this, which do not have security features as part of the operating system, are called *untrusted clients*. Untrusted clients are those running on Windows 3.*x*, Windows 95, Windows 98, Windows Millenium Edition and Macintosh.

It only makes sense, then, that clients running on operating systems that do have integrated security features are called trusted clients. *Trusted clients* are clients running on Windows NT, Windows 2000, OS/2, all the supported UNIX platforms, MVS, OS/390, VM, VSE, and AS/400. (The last five operating systems listed are also known as *host clients*.)

As humans, we tend to prefer those things that we can trust. Don't let this fool you into not appreciating untrusted clients, however! DB2 actually doesn't favor any of these client types. However, it must have a plan to control CLIENT authentication based on the fact that different types of clients may be attaching or connecting to the database on the server. The plan can be tailored for each DB2 instance using the TRUST_ALLCLNTS and TRUST_CLNTAUTH database manager configuration parameters.

These parameters are used to give the database server more control and flexibility when CLIENT authentication is the chosen authentication method. In order for a client to be able to authenticate on behalf of the server, the client must pass three "checkpoint" parameters. These are AUTHENTICATION, TRUST_ALLCLNTS, and TRUST_CLNTAUTH. Tables 10-3 and 10-4 provide summaries of where authentication will take place given different combinations of the TRUST_ALLCLNTS and TRUST_CLNTAUTH database manager configuration parameters.

The TRUST_ALLCLNTS parameter

We start with the TRUST_ALLCLNTS parameter. This parameter is used to determine whether the server really wants to allow all client types, or maybe just a subset of them, to authenticate. So, DB2 will first check the AUTHENTICATION type specified on the server or gateway. If it is set to CLIENT, it will then check this parameter to determine which of the three client types can really authenticate. Remember, the three main client types are trusted, untrusted, and host clients.

The TRUST_ALLCLNTS parameter can have the value YES, NO, or DRDAONLY. These values are described in the following sections.

YES

All three clients types will be allowed to authenticate users on behalf of the server when the server authentication type is CLIENT.

Setting this parameter to YES is not acceptable in most production database environments because it allows users on untrusted clients to connect to a database or attach to an instance without authenticating.

To set this parameter up, you can issue the following commands.

On the server:

```
db2 update dbm cfg using authentication client
db2 update dbm cfg using trust_allclnts yes
db2 update dbm cfg using trust_clntauth server
```

On the client:

```
db2 catalog database mydb at node nd1 authentication
      client
```

NO

Only trusted clients will be allowed to authenticate users on behalf of the server. This includes trusted and host clients. Untrusted clients must send a userid and password to the server; authentication will take place at the server.

To set this up, the following commands can be issued.

On the server:

```
db2 update dbm cfg using authentication client
db2 update dbm cfg using trust_allclnts no
```

On the client:

```
db2 catalog database mydb at node nd1 authentication
        client
```

DRDAONLY

In this case, only host clients are allowed to authenticate users on behalf of the server. As specified before, host clients are a subset of the trusted client group. They include clients running on the following operating systems: MVS, OS/390, VM, VSE, and AS/400. The other trusted clients and the untrusted clients will have to provide a userid and password to the server; authentication will take place at the server.

To set this up, the following commands can be issued.

On the server:

```
db2 update dbm cfg using authentication client
db2 update dbm cfg using trust_allclnts drdaonly
```

On the client:

```
db2 catalog database mydb at node nd1 authentication
        client
```

The TRUST_CLNTAUTH parameter

This parameter comes into play only after the authentication and `TRUST_ALLCLNTS` parameters have been used to determine which clients will be allowed to authenticate on behalf of the server. These clients might have thought they had the ability to authenticate on behalf of the server at this point in the game, but in reality they must pass one more check. That check is the `TRUST_CLNTAUTH` parameter. This parameter is used to determine whether the clients that passed the first two checks can still authenticate if a userid and password have been explicitly supplied to the `connect` or `attach` commands.

The `TRUST_CLNTAUTH` parameters can have either the `CLIENT` or the `SERVER` values, as described in the following two sections.

CLIENT

This is the default value for this parameter. In this case, authentication will take place on the client, whether a userid and password are supplied or not. If no userid/password is explicitly supplied, the userid and password that the user specified when logging into the machine will be assumed.

An example of how to set this follows.

On the server:

```
db2 update dbm cfg using authentication client
db2 update dbm cfg using trust_allclnts no
db2 update dbm cfg using trust_clntauth client
```

On the client:

```
db2 catalog database mydb at node ndl authentication
      client
```

SERVER

If a userid and password are supplied, these will be sent to the server. Authentication will take place on the server. If no userid/password is supplied, the userid and password that the user specified when logging into the machine will be assumed.

An example of how to set this follows.

On the server:

```
db2 update dbm cfg using authentication client
db2 update dbm cfg using trust_allclnts yes
db2 update dbm cfg using trust_clntauth server
```

On the client:

```
db2 catalog database mydb at node ndl authentication
      client
```

Tables 10-3 and 10-4 summarize different combinations of the TRUST_ALLCLNTS and TRUST_CLNTAUTH parameters as described in the sections above. Notice that the location in which the authentication takes place changes depending on whether a password is supplied by the user or not.

Table 10-3 Where Authentication Takes Place Based on Values of TRUST_ALLCLNTS and TRUST_CLNTAUTH Parameters (AUTHENTICATION=CLIENT; userid/password not supplied)

TRUST_ALLCLNT/ TRUST_CLNTAUTH Values	*Untrusted Clients*	*Trusted Clients (excluding host clients)*	*Host Clients*
YES/CLIENT	CLIENT	CLIENT	CLIENT
YES/SERVER	CLIENT	CLIENT	CLIENT
NO/CLIENT	SERVER	CLIENT	CLIENT
NO/SERVER	SERVER	CLIENT	CLIENT

(continued)

Table 10-3 *(continued)*

TRUST_ALLCLNT/ TRUST_CLNTAUTH Values	*Untrusted Clients*	*Trusted Clients (excluding host clients)*	*Host Clients*
DRDAONLY/CLIENT	SERVER	SERVER	CLIENT
DRDAONLY/SERVER	SERVER	SERVER	CLIENT

Table 10-4 Where Authentication Takes Place Based on Values of TRUST_ALLCLNTS and TRUST_CLNTAUTH Parameters (AUTHENTICATION=CLIENT; userid/password supplied)

TRUST_ALLCLNT/ TRUST_CLNTAUTH Values	*Untrusted Clients*	*Trusted Clients (excluding host clients)*	*Host Clients*
YES/CLIENT	CLIENT	CLIENT	CLIENT
YES/SERVER	SERVER	SERVER	SERVER
NO/CLIENT	SERVER	CLIENT	CLIENT
NO/SERVER	SERVER	SERVER	SERVER
DRDAONLY/CLIENT	SERVER	SERVER	CLIENT
DRDAONLY/SERVER	SERVER	SERVER	SERVER

Ensure that you understand these two tables. Again, notice the difference in where authentication takes place when a userid and password are supplied to the `connect` or `attach` commands.

Gaining Authorization: Group Membership

Okay, now that you've gotten past the authentication guards, what can you do? One way that DB2 determines what commands a certain user can issue is by assigning database authorities to various groups. If a user is a member of the group, he or she has the power to perform all actions permitted within the group. This is similar to everyday life. For example, if you happen to be a member of a team of doctors, you are permitted to prescribe medication to patients. Or, if you are a member of a symphony orchestra, you are permitted to play your musical instrument during a concert. Things would be chaotic if the musicians were allowed to prescribe medication or if the doctors were allowed to play an instrument during a concert! (Unless, of course, the doctor was also a talented musician and member of the orchestra . . . but you get the picture.)

Who has power within the DB2 instance?

Five group memberships, or authorities, are provided by DB2 Version 7.1. These are `SYSADM`, `SYSCTRL`, `SYSMAINT`, `DBADM`, and `LOAD`. Three of these authorities are assigned only to groups; the `LOAD` and `DBADM` authorities can be assigned to both users and groups. Each of these authorities has a certain amount of power to perform different tasks within the DB2 instance.

Memorize what each authority is allowed to perform on the database. Note that certain operations can be performed by more than one authority group.

SYSADM

You can think of users with `SYSADM`, or System Administration, authority as the kings and queens of the DB2 instance. They are allowed to perform all administrative and maintenance tasks within the DB2 instance. They also have complete access to all databases within the instances and all objects within the databases. They are able to read, update, write, delete, and/or alter data or objects. `SYSADM` users are omnipotent!

SYSADM authority on DB2 databases can be compared to root authority on UNIX operating systems and Administrator authority on Windows.

`SYSADM` users are the only users that can update the database manager configuration file. The database manager configuration file contains parameters that affect all databases within the DB2 instance. See Chapter 9 for more details on how to update the database manager configuration file.

SYSCTRL

Users with `SYSCTRL`, or System Control, authority are almost as powerful as `SYSADM` users. They also can perform all administrative and maintenance tasks within the instance. However, they cannot access the data within the databases unless they are explicitly granted privileges to do so.

We talk more about privileges in the next section.

SYSMAINT

SYSMAINT, or System Maintenance, users are allowed to perform all maintenance operations within the DB2 instance. They cannot access any user data within the databases. These users are a bit less powerful than the SYSCTRL users and much less powerful than the SYSADM users.

DBADM

The SYS* authorities are instance-level authorities. This means that their power extends over all databases within the instance. The DBADM, or Database Administration, authority is a database-level authority. Users with DBADM authority on a database are allowed to do all administrative and maintenance tasks only against that particular database. They are also able to access all data within the database. You can think of these users as the dukes or duchesses of the database. The kings and queens have power over the kingdom (instance), and the dukes and duchesses have power over certain regions of the kingdom (databases), while still being at the mercy of the kings and queens.

Reminder: DBADM authority can be assigned to both users and groups.

Don't worry — you won't be tested on the royal family or politics, but we're hoping that the analogy might help you remember the power and scope of each DB2 authority!

LOAD

The LOAD authority is new to Version 7.1. Again, this is a database-level authority but with a much smaller scope than DBADM authority. This authority is almost self explanatory: Users with LOAD authority on a database are permitted to run the load command against tables within that database. They are also allowed to issue the `quiesce tablespaces for table`, `runstats`, and `list tablespaces` commands.

The LOAD command is used to insert large amounts of data into a table. It is faster and uses less space in the log files than issuing many insert statements.

Depending on the type of load command being issued, users with LOAD authority may still need additional privileges assigned to them in order for the load command to be successful.

Table 10-5 lists different load command options and the additional privileges that users with LOAD authority would have to obtain to run the command.

Table 10-5 Load Commands That Can Be Issued by Users with LOAD Authority Plus Certain Table Privileges

LOAD/Autoload Command Options	*Insert privilege required on table being loaded?*	*Delete privilege required on table being loaded?*
`LOAD INSERT`	YES	NO
`LOAD REPLACE`	YES	YES
`LOAD RESTART/LOAD TERMINATE` after a `LOAD INSERT`	NO	YES
`LOAD RESTART/LOAD TERMINATE` after a `LOAD REPLACE`	YES	YES

If the `LOAD` command also includes an exception table, the authority user must also have insert privileges on the exception table.

Reminder: `LOAD` authority can be assigned to both users and groups.

Types of power

Each of the authority groups have certain tasks they are allowed to perform. Some of these tasks include administrative tasks, maintenance tasks, data access operations, and so on. The groups also have two main levels of authority: those that are instance wide and those that are database wide. This section goes into specifics on which DB2 commands would be considered administrative tasks, which would be considered maintenance tasks, and so on. Table 10-6 maps these commands to the authority groups that can perform them.

Administrative tasks

Administrative tasks include creating, altering, or dropping any DB2 object (database, tablespace, table, index, and so on) and forcing applications off the database(s).

Maintenance tasks

Maintenance tasks include backup and recovery operations (`backup`, `restore`, `rollforward`), updating database configuration files, monitoring the databases with the event or snapshot monitors, capturing trace information with the `db2trc` command, gathering table statistics with the `runstats` command, reorganizing tables with the `reorg` command, and starting and stopping the DB2 instance.

Data access operations

Data access operations include `select`, `update`, `insert`, and `delete` statements against database objects such as tables, indexes, and views — just to give you the general idea.

Table 10-6 assumes that no additional privileges were granted to members of the authority groups mentioned in this section. This table maps specific DB2 commands/operations to the groups that are permitted to perform them.

Know this table very well for the exam!

Table 10-6 DB2 Operations and the DB2 Authority Groups That Can Perform Them

Operation	*SYSADM**	*SYSCTRL*	*SYSMAINT*	*DBADM**	*LOAD*
Update database manager configuration file	Yes	No	No	No	No
Control which groups have `SYSADM`, `SYSCTRL`, and `SYSMAINT` authorities at any given time	Yes	No	No	No	No
Control which users or groups have `DBADM` authority at any given time	Yes	No	No	No	No
Create/Drop database	Yes	Yes	No	No	No
Create/Drop tablespace	Yes	Yes	No	No	No
Backup database/Restore into existing database/ Rollforward	Yes	Yes	Yes	No	No
Db2start/db2stop	Yes	Yes	Yes	No	No
Update database configuration file	Yes	Yes	Yes	No	No
Grant/revoke database privileges	Yes	No	No	Yes	No
Grant control privilege on an object	Yes	No	No	Yes	No
Create table	Yes	No	No	Yes	No
Load into tables	Yes	No	No	Yes	Yes
Runstats	Yes	Yes	Yes	Yes	Yes

**Allowed access to contents of database objects.*

How do authorities get assigned?

We mentioned that authorities are assigned to groups. We should first explain where these groups come from. How does a user become a member of a group, anyway? Well, when a userid is created within the operating system, it can be assigned to one or more groups. These groups will have already been created through the operating system.

For example, userid `marcel` might belong to groups `Administrator`, `db2grp`, and `osgrp`. If group `db2grp` is given `SYSADM` authority within a DB2 instance, userid `marcel` would then have `SYSADM` authority. So, when a group is given a certain authority within DB2, it is the operating system group name that is specified.

The SYS* authorities

As mentioned earlier in this section, the SYS* authorities can be assigned only to groups. These authorities are actually controlled in the database manager configuration file via the `SYSADM_GROUP`, `SYSCTRL_GROUP`, and `SYSMAINT_GROUP` parameters. If you think about it, this makes sense because these are instance-level authorities and the dbm cfg is an instance-level configuration file. There are no default values for these parameters.

As mentioned in the description of the `SYSADM` authority, only `SYSADM` users can update the database manager configuration file. Therefore, the only users that can specify which groups will be assigned `SYSCTRL` or `SYSMAINT` authorities are the `SYSADM` group members.

`SYSADM` authority is given to certain groups by default when the DB2 instance is created. For example, on UNIX operating systems, `SYSADM` authority is given to the primary group of the DB2 instance owner `ID`. On Windows NT operating systems, it is given to the `Administrator` group.

Using the previous example, the following command would specify that `db2grp` is to be given `SYSCTRL` authority within an instance:

```
db2 update dbm cfg using SYSCTRL_GROUP db2grp
```

Don't forget: Changes to the dbm cfg file do not take effect until after the DB2 instance is recycled (issuing `db2stop` followed by `db2start`).

Updating the database manager configuration file is also covered in Chapter 9.

This next command would specify that the `db2mnt` group is to be given `SYSMAINT` authority within an instance.

```
db2 update dbm cfg using SYSMAINT_GROUP db2mnt
```

To ensure that database security is maintained at all times, it is extremely important that userids are not placed into groups carelessly. Most companies have a very limited number of people who have the operating system authority required to create users and groups on machines running production databases. For example, if userid `disgruntled_employee` were accidentally placed in the `SYSADM` group of the database, that user would have the authority to drop databases, if he or she so pleased!

DBADM and LOAD authorities

Remember that the `DBADM` and `LOAD` authorities are different than the SYS* authorities in that they are database-level authorities (rather than instance level) and they can be assigned to users as well as groups.

The `DBADM` and `LOAD` authorities are stored in the database system catalog tables. The `SYSADM`, `SYSCTRL`, and `SYSMAINT` authorities are not; they are stored in the database manager configuration file.

The `DBADM` authority is implicitly given to the userid that issues the create database command. For example, if userid `marie` issued the following command, she would immediately have `DBADM` authority on database test:

```
db2 create database test
```

`DBADM` authority can also be explicitly granted to users or groups by any `SYSADM` user using the following `GRANT` command.

```
db2 grant dbadm on database to user <user_name>
db2 grant dbadm on database to group <group_name>
```

Of course, users or groups can also get their `DBADM` authority revoked by any `SYSADM` user using the following `REVOKE` command.

```
db2 revoke dbadm on database from user <user_name>
db2 revoke dbadm on database from group <group_name>
```

The `LOAD` authority must be granted to users or groups using the `GRANT` command. Anyone with `SYSADM` or `DBADM` authority can do this:

```
db2 grant load on database to user <user_name>
db2 grant load on database to group <group_name>
```

This authority can also be revoked using the following command:

```
db2 revoke load on database from user <user_name>
db2 revoke load on database to from group <group_name>]
```

Lab 10-1 walks you through the process of assigning authorities. ***Note:*** You will not be able to complete these exercises if you are using an operating system with no native security features (that is, if you are using what would be considered an untrusted client).

Lab 10-1 Assigning Authorities

1. **Create two users called** `test1` **and** `test2`**. Also create two groups called** `grp1` **and** `grp2`**. Associate group** `grp1` **with user** `test1` **and group** `grp2` **with user** `test2`**.**
2. **Log onto the operating system as the DB2 instance owner. Run** `db2sampl` **to create the sample database (if it isn't already created).**
3. **Update the database manager configuration file to grant** `grp1` **SYSCTRL authority and** `grp2` **SYSMAINT authority. Restart the instance using** `db2stop` **and** `db2start`**.**
4. **Connect to the sample database. Grant DBADM authority to user** `test1`**.**
5. **Issue** `db2 get authorizations` **to view the authorities held by the current userid.**

Privileges

Privileges are DB2's way of giving the "common folk" the ability to create and access objects within the database. All privileges are stored in the following database system catalog views:

- `SYSCAT.DBAUTH`: Database authorities

  The command `db2 get authorizations` will report the database authorities of the current user.
- `SYSCAT.TABAUTH`: Table and view privileges
- `SYSCAT.INDEXAUTH`: Index privileges
- `SYSCAT.SCHEMAAUTH`: Schema privileges
- `SYSCAT.PACKAGEAUTH`: Package privileges

The next sections go into more detail on the types of privileges available and how they are assigned to users and groups. Figure 10-3, shown later, provides a summary of all the privileges available in DB2 to various objects.

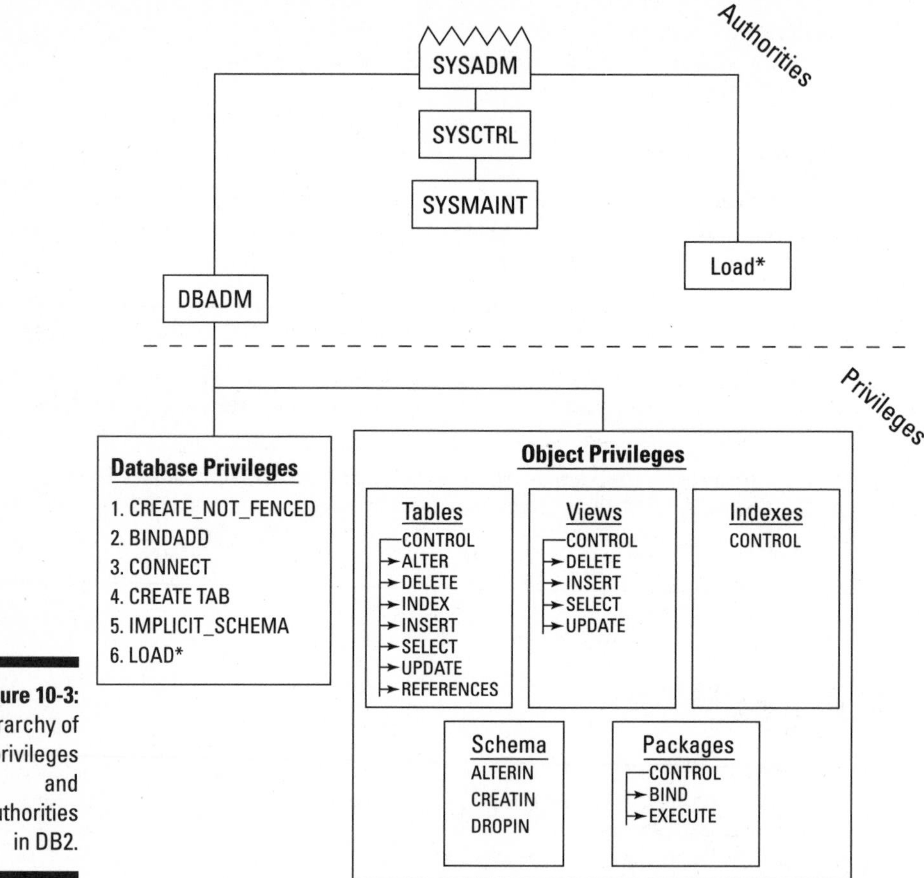

Figure 10-3: Hierarchy of privileges and authorities in DB2.

Database authorities and privileges

Database authorities determine what kind of power a user has within the database. The following is a list of the possible database authorities and privileges a user might have with a particular database:

- `DBADM`: This authority is discussed in the previous "Gaining Authorization: Group Membership" section of this chapter.
- `CREATETAB`: Users with this privilege are permitted to create tables within the database.
- `BINDADD`: Users with this privilege are permitted to create packages within the database by issuing the `BIND` command.

  DB2 packages are discussed in the "Execution Objects" section of Chapter 11.

- CONNECT: Users with this privilege can connect to the database.
- CREATE_NOT_FENCED: Users are permitted to create unfenced user defined functions.
- IMPLICIT_SCHEMA: Users can implicitly create schemas within the database.
- LOAD: Load authority is discussed in the previous "Gaining Authorization: Group Membership" section of this chapter.

Table and view privileges

Table and view privileges define what operations users are permitted to execute against specific tables or views within the database. The following is a list of possible privileges that a user might have with a particular table or view.

- CONTROL: Users with this privilege have "ownership" of the table/view. These users have full access to the object and can grant or revoke access to the object to/from other users. They can also give other users the ability to grant/revoke certain privileges.
- ALTER: Users with this privilege can alter the object and may be able to grant this privilege to other users if a user with CONTROL privilege gave them this power.
- DELETE: Users with this privilege can delete records from the object and may be able to grant this privilege to other users if a user with CONTROL privilege gave them this power.
- INDEX: Users with this privilege can create indexes on the table and may be able to grant this privilege to other users if a user with CONTROL privilege gave them this power.
- INSERT: Users with this privilege can insert records into the object and may be able to grant this privilege to other users if a user with CONTROL privilege gave them this power.

  The INSERT privilege also allows users to run the IMPORT command against a table. The IMPORT command essentially runs many inserts under the covers.
- SELECT: Users with this privilege can view the contents of the object by using the select statement. They may be able to grant this privilege to other users if a user with CONTROL privilege gave them this power.
- REFERENCE: Users with this privilege can create or drop foreign keys on the table. They may be able to grant this privilege to other users if a user with CONTROL privilege gave them this power.
- UPDATE: Users with this privilege can update values in the object using the UPDATE command. And again, they may be able to grant this privilege to other users if a user with CONTROL privilege gave them this power.

This may seem like a lot to remember, but keep in mind that, with the exception of CONTROL and REFERENCE privileges, these are pretty straightforward. In other words, SELECT privilege means that you can select data from the table; INSERT privilege means that you can insert data into the table, and so on.

Index privileges

Luckily, only one privilege can be held for a given index — less to remember! This is CONTROL privilege, which allows a user to drop the index using the DROP INDEX command.

Schema privileges

Schema privileges define what operations can be performed against objects within a particular schema. The following is a list of possible privileges that can be held. Schemas are discussed in detail in Chapter 9.

- ALTERIN: This privilege allows users to alter objects within the schema.
- CREATEIN: This privilege allows users to create objects within the schema.
- DROPIN: This privilege allows users to drop objects within the schema.

Package privileges

A package is created within a database when the BIND command is issued. For a refresher on packages, refer to Chapter 11. Package privileges determine who can create and manipulate packages within the database.

- CONTROL: Users with CONTROL privilege on a package can rebind, drop, or execute a package. They can also grant bind or execute privileges on the package to other users.
- BIND: This allows users to rebind existing packages.
- EXECUTE: This allows users to execute packages.

Figure 10-4 shows a high-level overview of the three main components in a DB2 security plan.

Different ways of obtaining privileges

There are a few different ways that users can obtain privileges on a database and the objects within it. Begging and bribing the SYSADM users for certain access privileges may work. However, in a standard business environment, this approach likely won't get you very far!

In this section, we go over some tried, tested, and true methods that you can use to grant and revoke privileges from users and/or groups. These methods fall into three main categories: explicit, implicit, and indirect.

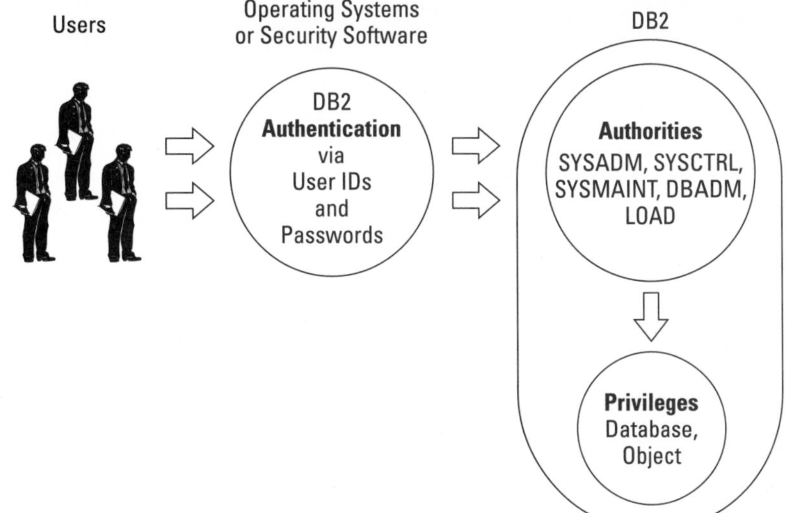

Figure 10-4: Overview of the components in a DB2 security plan.

There is a special group known to DB2 as `PUBLIC`. This group includes anyone who is using DB2. Privileges can be granted to or revoked from `PUBLIC`; this includes, for example, `db2 grant select on mytable to public`.

Explicit

The explicit method of controlling privileges involves using the `GRANT` and `REVOKE` commands. Privileges that are assigned in this way are recorded in the system catalog tables that are mentioned at the beginning of the "Privileges" section in this chapter.

The `GRANT` and `REVOKE` statements are considered Data Control Language, or DCL, statements.

`SYSADM` and `DBADM` users can grant or revoke any privilege on the database and its objects from any user and/or group. Users with `CONTROL` privilege on an object can grant or revoke any privilege on the object from users and/or groups.

The following `GRANT` and `REVOKE` commands can be used to manage the database privileges `CREATETAB`, `BINDADD`, `CONNECT`, `CREATE_NOT_FENCED`, and `IMPLICIT_SCHEMA`.

- Giving access to users and groups:

```
db2 grant <db_privilege> on database to user <user_name>
db2 grant <db_privilege> on database to group
      <group_name>
```

- Revoking access from users and groups:

```
db2 revoke <db_privilege> on database from user
       <user_name>
db2 revoke <db_privilege> on database from group
       <group_name>
```

The following GRANT and REVOKE commands can be used to manage the table and view privileges CONTROL, ALTER, DELETE, INDEX, INSERT, SELECT, REFERENCE, and UPDATE.

- Giving access to users and groups:

```
db2 grant <privilege> on <tbl/vw name> to user
       <user_name>
db2 grant <privilege> on <tbl/vw name> to group
       <group_name>
```

The GRANT command for tables and views also has a WITH GRANT OPTION option, which indicates that the user or group is also allowed to grant this privilege to other users or groups.

- Revoking access from users and groups:

```
db2 revoke <privilege> on <tbl/vw name> from user
       <user_name>
db2 revoke <privilege> on <tbl/vw name> from group
       <group_name>
```

The following GRANT and REVOKE commands can be used to manage the index privilege CONTROL:

- Giving access to users and groups:

```
db2 grant control on index <index_name> to user
       <user_name>
db2 grant control on index <index_name> to group
       <group_name>
```

- Revoking access from users and groups:

```
db2 revoke control on <index_name> from user <user_name>
db2 revoke control on <index_name> from group
       <group_name>
```

The following GRANT and REVOKE commands can be used to manage the schema privileges ALTERIN, CREATEIN, and DROPIN:

- Giving access to users and groups:

```
db2 grant <privilege> on schema <schema_name> to user
       <user_name>
db2 grant <privilege> on schema <schema_name> to group
       <group_name>
```

- Revoking access from users and groups:

```
db2 revoke <privilege> on schema <schema_name> from user
        <user_name>
db2 revoke <privilege> on schema <schema_name> from group
        <group_name>
```

The `GRANT` command for schemas also has a `WITH GRANT OPTION` option, which indicates that the user or group is also allowed to grant this privilege to other users or groups.

The following `GRANT` and `REVOKE` commands can be used to manage the package privileges `CONTROL`, `BIND`, and `EXECUTE`.

- Giving access to users and groups:

```
db2 grant <privilege> on package <package_name> to user
        <user_name>
db2 grant <privilege> on package <package_name> to group
        <group_name>
```

- Revoking access from users and groups:

```
db2 revoke <privilege> on package <package_name> from
        user <user_name>
db2 revoke <privilege> on package <package_name> from
        group <group_name>
```

You can specify multiple privileges, groups, and users within a single `GRANT` or `REVOKE` command. For example, `db2 grant connect, bindadd on database to user comet, user cupid, group elves`. You can also `GRANT` or `REVOKE` privileges from all users by using the `ALL` keyword. For example, `db2 revoke update on mytable from all`.

Implicit

Privileges can also be granted automatically by DB2 without the use of a DCL statement. For example, when a user creates a table, index, or package object, that user is implicitly granted `CONTROL` privilege over this object. This privilege is implicitly revoked from the user when the object is dropped.

When users create a view, they are given `CONTROL` privilege to the view only if they have `CONTROL` privilege over all the tables and views referenced in the view definition.

When users create a schema using the `CREATE SCHEMA` command, they are granted all three schema privileges as well as the option to grant these privileges to others.

When users create a database, those users are automatically given DBADM authority on the database. In addition, the CREATE DATABASE statement grants certain privileges automatically to a special group called PUBLIC. The privileges granted to PUBLIC in this case include IMPLICIT_SCHEMA privilege and SELECT privilege on the DB2 system catalog views.

It should be clear by now what SELECT privilege means, but what about IMPLICIT_SCHEMA? Well, what this means is that any user can create a schema by simply creating an object and specifying a schema name that does not already exist. The following example illustrates how a user might implicitly create a schema called myschema. Note that in this case, the myschema schema was not created beforehand with the CREATE SCHEMA command.

```
db2 create table myschema.tabname (col1 int)
```

It is important for database administrators to know what privileges are granted to PUBLIC implicitly. In some cases, it could be a security risk to allow users to see system table information, for example. Or, it may be too messy to allow all users to create as many schemas as they please.

Indirect

Obtaining privileges indirectly has to do specifically with packages. As mentioned in Chapter 11, a package contains one or more SQL statements in an executable form that the database manager uses to execute the statements.

Assuming that the statements contained in the package are static SQL statements that access various objects in the database, a user could run the application that is associated with this package with only EXECUTE privilege on the package. In other words, the user indirectly obtains all required object privileges for the objects referenced in the statements during package execution.

Now, if the package contains dynamic SQL statements, the user must explicitly acquire object privileges for the objects referenced in the dynamic SQL statements, or the user would not be able to execute the package.

Don't worry too much about static and dynamic SQL. Just understand that some privileges can be obtained indirectly with static SQL. Lab 10-2 gives you some practice in working with privileges.

Lab 10-2 Granting privileges

1. **Log in as user** test1. **Connect to the sample database. Enter** db2 get authorizations **to see the authorities held by** test1.
2. **Attempt to update the database manager configuration file.**

   You should receive an SQL5001N error.
3. **Grant select privilege on table ORG to user** test2.

   This should fail with an SQL0204N error.

4. **Enter** `db2 list tables for all` **to determine the schema name** `<SCHEMA>` **associated with the ORG table.**

   The schema name should be the name of the userid you used to create the sample database.

5. **After you know the schema, issue the grant statement again but specify** `<SCHEMA>.ORG` **as the table name. Then grant connect privilege on the sample database to user** `test2`**.**

6. **Log in as user** `test2`**. Connect to the sample database. Enter** `db2 get authorizations` **to display the authorizations held by** `test2`**. Attempt to drop the sample database.**

   This should fail with an SQL1092N error.

7. **Enter** `db2 select * from <SCHEMA>.ORG`**.**

8. **Enter the same** `SELECT` **statement against any other table in the database,** `<SCHEMA>.SALES`**, for example.**

   This should return an SQL0551N error.

Making Some Security Decisions

Now that you are more familiar with DB2 security, you can see how to put together a security plan for a business that we're calling OurBooks. This business is using a DB2 database to track books in inventory and all book sales. Only three employees are responsible for this database environment. Lee-Ann is the System Administrator, responsible for database security and initial database design. Ken is the Database Administrator, responsible for maintaining the database, overseeing day-to-day database operations as well as carrying out the database recovery strategy. Brian is the Application Developer, responsible for designing, testing, and debugging the applications running on the database. In addition, customers of OurBooks can buy books online through the database.

The first step is to determine the security requirements of each user based on his or her responsibilities. After this is determined, the required access has to be given to each user accordingly. For the OurBooks database design, four user IDs and four groups were created via the operating system to control database security. Table 10-7 summarizes these as well as some of the DB2 security requirements for each.

The example illustrated here is a simple one, showing very generally what types of access are required for different users. It does not give a complete view of the security requirements of a similar database environment in the real world.

Table 10-7 Users, groups, and Security Requirements for the OurBooks Database

Person using userid	*User ID*	*Group*	*Description of Database Responsibilies*	*DB2 Security Requirement*
Lee-Ann	DB2INST	DBSYS	Database security and initial database design	SYSADM authority
Ken	KEN	DBADMIN	Database maintenance, operations and backup/ recovery strategies	DBADM and SYSMAINT authorities
Brian	BRIAN	DBAPP	Designing, testing, fixing applications running on the database	Various privileges, including CONNECT, BINDADD, CREATETAB (for test tables), some schema and object privileges
Customers	CUST	DBUSER	Running applications to view and/or buy books	CONNECT on the database, | EXECUTE on the package(s),schema and object privileges if package contains dynamic SQL

Don't forget about how views and table constraints can control access to base tables! These are also important security features within a database. If you need a refresher on views and constraints, check out Chapter 9.

Now that we've defined the security requirements of each of our users and groups, we have to grant them appropriate access. Figure 10-5 illustrates some of the commands that give access to users as described in Table 10-7.

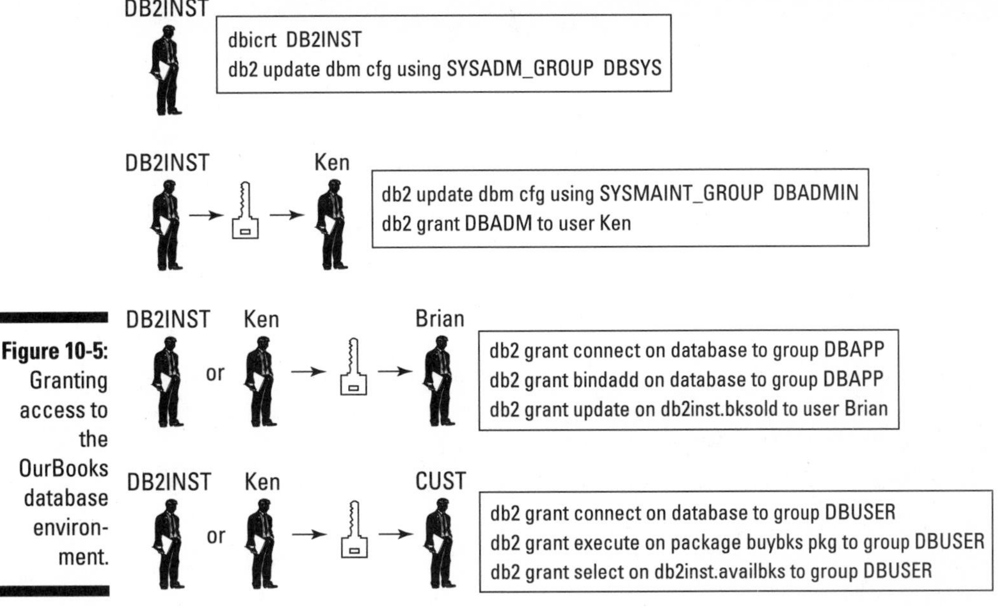

Figure 10-5: Granting access to the OurBooks database environment.

DB2 also provides a way of monitoring access to various objects with the DB2 Audit facility. This provides an audit trail of predefined database events. If someone drops an important table, for example, it would be beneficial to know who did this and exactly when. DB2 Audit provides users with this ability.

Prep Test

1 **Which of the following statements would give userid** `TEST` **the ability to create a table in the database?**

A ❍ `db2 grant CREATEIN on database to user TEST`
B ❍ `db2 grant CREATETAB to TEST`
C ❍ `db2 grant SYSADM to TEST`
D ❍ `db2 grant DBADM on database to TEST`

2 **Which of the following sets of statements would ensure that authentication between a client and server would always be performed at the server? Assume that the database name is** `SAMPLE`**.**

A ❍ `db2 update dbm cfg using authentication client; db2 catalog database sample at node mynode authentication server`
B ❍ `db2 update dbm cfg using authentication dce_server_encrypt; db2 catalog database sample at node mynode authentication server`
C ❍ `db2 update dbm cfg using authentication client; db2 update dbm cfg using trust_allclnt no; db2 update dbm cfg using trust_clntauth server`
D ❍ `db2 update dbm cfg using authentication client; db2 update dbm cfg using trust_allclnt yes; db2 update dbm cfg using trust_clntauth server`

3 **Which of the following commands cannot be issued by a userid with** `SYSMAINT` **authority?**

A ❍ `db2start`
B ❍ `db2 backup database sample`
C ❍ `db2 update database configuration for sample`
D ❍ `db2 create database mydb`

4 **Which of the following two statements would allow the user** `TEST` **to successfully create a table called** `DB2INST.MYTAB`**?**

A ❑ `db2 grant createin on schema db2inst to user test`
B ❑ `db2 grant update on mytab to user test`
C ❑ `db2 grant sysadm on database to user test`
D ❑ `db2 grant createtab on database to user test`

5 **Which of the following privileges are required in order to run the package `mypack.pkg`, which contains only static SQL statements? These statements update tables in the database.**

A ❍ `EXECUTE` on package `mypack.pkg`; `SELECT` on all tables referenced in package `mypack.pkg`

B ❍ `EXECUTE` on package `mypack.pkg`; `CONNECT` on the database

C ❍ `BIND` on package `mypack.pkg`; `CONNECT` on the database

D ❍ `EXECUTE` on package `mypack.pkg`; `UPDATE` and `SELECT` on all tables referenced in package `mypack.pkg`

6 **Which of the following are allowed to grant certain privileges to other users?**

A ❍ `SYSMAINT` users

B ❍ Users with `CREATETAB` privileges

C ❍ Users with `CONTROL` privileges

D ❍ `SYSCTRL` users

7 **Which two of the following could be used to determine what privileges have been given to user `TEST` on database `SAMPLE`?**

A ❑ Query the system catalog tables

B ❑ View the database configuration file for `SAMPLE`

C ❑ Issue the `get privileges` command

D ❑ Issue the `get authorizations` command

Answers

1 **D.** The syntax of the other options is incorrect. *Review "Gaining Authorization: Group Membership" and "Privileges."*

2 **B.** *Review "Where does authentication take place?"*

3 **D.** *Review "Who has power within the DB2 instance?"*

4 **A** and **D.** *Review "Privileges."*

5 **B.** Execute privilege on the package implicitly grants select and update on the table. *Review "Privileges."*

6 **C.** *Review "Who has power within the DB2 instance?" and "Privileges."*

7 **A** and **D.** *Review "Privileges."*

Chapter 11

Database Concurrency

Exam Objectives

- Knowledge to identify factors that influence locking
- Ability to list the objects that locks can be obtained on
- Knowledge to identify scope of different types of DB2 locks
- Knowledge to identify factors affecting amount of locks that are used
- Knowledge to identify factors affecting the type of locks obtained
- Given a situation, knowledge to identify the isolation levels that should be used

Have you ever seen what happens when two children decide they want to play with the same toy at the same time? It can get pretty messy. Add a few more children into the mix and it can become a mini-war in the toy room. Come to think about it, you've probably noticed adults participate in the same type of squabble in the grocery store!

Now, what the heck does this have to do with DB2? Well, DB2 supports multi-user, multi-transactional databases. Because of this, there may be multiple transactions trying to access the same data, at the same time. In this case, the transactions have permission to access the data but that doesn't imply they can each access it at the same time; it's all about timing, you see! Deciding on which application wins the data access battle depends on the level of concurrency set for each application. This chapter will go over how DB2 isolation levels and locks set and enforce the level of concurrency to be used within the database.

Quick Assessment

Given a situation, knowledge to identify the isolation levels that should be used

1 The level of concurrency of a given application is determined by the _____ of the application.

2 DB2 has four available isolation levels: _____, _____, _____ and _____.

3 The isolation level that allows a transaction to read uncommitted updates by another transaction is called _____.

Knowledge to identify factors that influence locking

4 Locks have three attributes: _____, _____ and _____.

5 The database manager will initiate _____ when a unit of work requires a more restrictive lock on an object on which it already has a lock held.

6 At any given time, an application can have a lock that is granted, waiting or _____.

7 _____ occurs when too many row locks are held on a particular table.

Ability to list the objects that locks can be obtained on

8 A _____ can be explicitly locked by an application using an SQL statement.

9 The _____ option on the `ALTER TABLE` statement can be used to specify the lock granularity of a table.

Knowledge to identify factors affecting the type of locks obtained

10 There are twelve lock _____, which are IN, IS, NS, S, IX, SIX, U, NX, NW, X, W, and Z.

Answers

1. *isolation level*. Review "Isolating Data with Isolation Levels."
2. *Uncommitted Read, Cursor Stability, Read Stability, Repeatable Read.* Review "Isolating Data with Isolation Levels."
3. *UR or Uncommitted Read*. Review "Isolating Data with Isolation Levels."
4. *mode, object, duration*. Review "Understanding Locks."
5. *lock conversion*. Review "What locks do for fun."
6. *deadlocked*. Review "What locks do for fun."
7. *Lock escalation*. Review "What locks do for fun."
8. *table*. Review "Explicit locks on tables."
9. *LOCKSIZE*. Review "Explicit locks on tables."
10. *modes*. Review "Understanding Locks."

Understanding Execution Objects

Execution objects refer to database objects that play very important roles in how a query is executed against other database objects, such as tables and views. These include packages and transactions.

Packages

A package is an executable form of one or more queries. It is stored in the database and used by the database manager when a request is made to run the queries contained within the package.

You can find information on packages in the SYSCAT.PACKAGES system catalog view. Packages are executed in an area of memory known as the package cache.

A package is created using the `PREP` and `BIND` commands. What is needed first is a source code program containing SQL statements. The `PREP` command is used to create a *.bnd file, which contains a modified version of the original source code. Next, the `BIND` command is used to store the executable package in the database. By default, the `PREP` command will also run the `BIND` command. A package can be rebuilt as well, by using the `REBIND` command. The important thing to know for this chapter is that associated with every package is the level of concurrency that it will use when it executes. This level of concurrency is called the *isolation level* of the package.

We discuss isolation levels, and how to set them, in more detail in the "Isolating Data with Isolation Levels" section of this chapter.

Transactions

A transaction is also known as a unit of work. A unit of work may actually contain more than one query or operation against the database objects. For example, one transaction might include querying a sales table for total sales for a salesperson that day, multiplying that value by a rate of commission, and then updating the commission record for the salesperson with the new amount.

There may also be more than one transaction to be executed within a package. The end of a transaction is marked by a successful commit or rollback of the work performed. If all statements in the transaction are executed successfully, a commit ensures that the changes made to the database pages in memory are first written to the DB2 log files and then written permanently to disk. If an error was encountered while executing a statement, or if the application decides that it doesn't want to permanently change any database pages, a rollback is performed. The rollback ensures that changes made to the database pages in memory are reversed before the page is written back to disk.

The exact time that a commit or rollback is performed varies depending on how the application source code is written. By default, a statement issued from the DB2 Command Window or Command-Line Processor (CLP) is implicitly committed if it is successful or implicitly rolled back if it fails. The CLP is a DB2-provided application.

Understanding Concurrency

The higher the concurrency, the easier it is to gain access to data that other transactions have access to. This also implies that applications will less frequently have to wait to gain access to data. The lower the concurrency, the more difficult it is for multiple transactions to access the same data. This implies that applications may have to wait to access data needed to process statements, potentially increasing the time it takes to execute the application.

So, concurrency can have a direct impact on the performance of certain applications. In summary, high concurrency can increase, and low concurrency can decrease, the performance of certain applications. So, why would you ever want to lower concurrency? Well, concurrency also determines the level of data integrity that the application requires, that's why! The following four concurrency phenomena are examples of how the integrity of data can be affected by the level of concurrency. See the "Isolation Level" section of this chapter for a discussion of which isolation level can avoid these phenomena.

Phantom reads — scary stuff?

Phantom reads actually aren't too scary. In fact, they can be quite desirable, depending on the application that is being run. Phantom reads can arise when the same query is issued more than once in an application. For example, if the first execution of a query returns five records, then the next execution of the query, within the same application, might return eight records. In this example, three additional records appeared out of nowhere!

We can put questions about this freaky phantom phenomenon to rest with an example of how these additional records might be returned. Consider an airline reservation application. Rachelle needs to book a window seat on a flight to Hawaii. The travel agent checks the available seats on Flight 123 to Hawaii and finds that two seats are still available, but these are aisle seats. Rachelle is disappointed that no window seats are available. The travel agent refreshes the screen to double-check the available seats and discovers that window seat 12A is now available on this flight. This seat is booked for Rachelle and she leaves the travel agency satisfied.

It happens that another passenger who was booked on this flight, Mary, decided to cancel her flight reservation. Her reservation was cancelled immediately after the first query was executed by Rachelle's travel agent. The concurrency of the flight reservation application allowed another travel agent to cancel Mary's seat even though Rachelle's travel agent was currently viewing the available seats.

Lost updates

The lost update phenomenon can potentially cause havoc for many applications, including our airline reservation application. Lost updates occur when one application makes a change in the database and another application is allowed to override this change shortly afterward.

Continuing with the same example as before, Rachelle has left the travel agency assuming that she now has window seat 12A on Flight 123. What she doesn't realize is that in another travel agency, Brian is also booking a seat on Flight 123. His travel agent notices that seat 12A is available in Flight 123 even though, because the query was performed, the seat has become unavailable. The travel agent proceeds to successfully reserve seat 12A for Brian, overriding the update made by Rachelle's travel agent. Needless to say, Rachelle is not very happy when she gets to the airport and realizes that her seat has been assigned to somebody else!

Fortunately, even at the highest level of concurrency, DB2 prevents the lost update problem from occurring.

Dirty reads

The more formal term for dirty read is *uncommitted read*. This phenomenon involves applications being able to see uncommitted updates made by other applications. It's as if someone were doodling on a scrap piece of paper but others see this doodling and assume that it is valid information. In some cases, it might end up being valid: A decision might be made to eventually commit the information that is being seen. However, there also is a chance that the data will not be committed, but other applications will not know this.

Going back to our previous example, say that Mary's travel agent had unassigned seat 12A for Mary but Mary wasn't sure about the decision. The travel agent decided not to commit the change until Mary is certain. In the meantime,

Rachelle's agent can see that seat 12A is now available because uncommitted reads are allowed. When she tries to book the seat for Rachelle, it fails because Mary has since decided that she will keep her seat. Her agent rolled back the initial change to free the seat. Getting uncommitted information like this can cause frustration and waste valuable time.

Nonrepeatable read

Nonrepeatable read implies that the exact same result set may not be returned if the same query is issued more than once within a transaction. This is the opposite of repeatable read. Repeatable read ensures that all qualifying rows are "locked" in such a way that the same query within a transaction will always return the exact same result set. Nonrepeatable read ensures only that any rows being updated are locked; rows that are retrieved are not locked.

In our airline reservation application, nonrepeatable read would imply that the travel agent could never be sure what data is valid each time a query on seats is executed within the same transaction. This is because other applications are able to update the seat availability data in between each query attempt. We discussed methods of avoiding these phenomena in the next section.

Isolating Data with Isolation Levels

Isolation levels define the level of concurrency for a given application. They also determine how data is isolated from other applications. In other words, it allows applications to declare, "This is my data now and you can't touch it!" The isolation levels available, in order of decreasing concurrency are as follows: uncommitted read; cursor stability; read stability; and repeatable read. Table 11-1 provides a general comparison of the four isolation levels.

Table 11-1 Comparison of Isolation Levels

	UR	*CS*	*RS*	*RR*
Allows phantom reads?	YES	YES	YES	NO
Allows non-repeatable reads?	YES	YES	NO	NO
Allows read access to uncommitted data?	YES	NO	NO	NO
Allows lost updates?	NO	NO	NO	NO

DB2 uses the definition of the isolation level to determine how it will implicitly lock rows and/or tables while the application is executing. We discuss locks in more detail in the "Lockdown" section of this chapter.

Uncommitted Read (UR)

Uncommitted read is the lowest level of isolation available in DB2 and hence, provides the highest level of concurrency. This isolation level allows an application to read uncommitted changes made by other applications. This creates a risk in that some of the data being retrieved may not be valid as it is in the process of being modified. The data is truly valid only when it's committed into the database.

Both nonrepeatable reads and phantom reads are possible with this isolation level.

The uncommitted read isolation level is most commonly used for read-only tables or for applications that are issuing only `select` statements against a table and deem it acceptable to see uncommitted changes made by other applications. In general, you would not want to use the uncommitted read isolation level for applications dealing with financial transactions.

Cursor stability (CS)

If uncommitted reads are unacceptable, the cursor stability isolation level provides the highest level of concurrency for an application. This isolation level is the default isolation level used for all applications, including the DB2 Command-Line Processor. Cursor stability ensures that any row accessed by a transaction is locked during the time that the cursor is positioned on that row. This lock isn't released until another row is fetched by the cursor, or until the transaction terminates. Furthermore, if an updateable cursor is positioned on the row, no other application will be able to update or delete the row.

Both nonrepeatable reads and phantom reads are possible with this isolation level.

Cursors are defined within applications. When a cursor is opened, a data result set is generated. Each row of the result set can then be accessed and modified (if required) by issuing the `fetch` statement.

Read stability (RS)

Read stability prevents the nonrepeatable read phenomenon. It does this by ensuring that all rows retrieved by a query within a transaction are locked. If the same query is issued again in that unit of work, the same result set will be returned, plus potential phantom rows. Read stability also ensures that uncommitted changes to rows aren't read until the change has been committed or rolled back.

Phantom reads are still possible with this isolation level.

Repeatable Read (RR)

The repeatable read isolation level provides the lowest level of concurrency for an application. It is similar to read stability except that it also ensures that no phantom reads are possible. So, using our previous example, if 10 available airline seats are returned by our airline reservation application, a second query on seat availability within the same transaction will return the exact same 10 rows.

To ensure repeatable read, DB2 must lock all rows scanned when qualifying rows are being determined for a query. If 200 rows were scanned to retrieve our 10 available seats, all 200 rows will be locked. No other application will be able to access (insert, update or delete) these rows in any way that would affect the final result set consisting of 10 rows.

Choosing an Isolation Level

An application's performance, concurrency, and data integrity requirements should be considered when choosing an isolation level. The following points can be used as guidelines in determining which isolation level is appropriate for a given application.

- UR: For applications that only query read-only tables or only issue select statements and don't care whether uncommitted data from other applications is returned; highest performance, highest concurrency, lowest data integrity
- CS: For applications requiring maximum concurrency but must only see committed data from other applications; high performance, high concurrency, low data integrity

- RS: For applications that require returned rows to remain stable for the duration of the transaction; low performance, low concurrency, high data integrity
- RR: For applications that require returned rows to remain identical for the duration of the transaction; lowest performance, lowest concurrency, highest data integrity

The meaning of *highest*, *lowest*, *high*, and *low* in the preceding statements is meant to be relative to the other isolation levels. For example, for certain applications, a CS isolation level might provide a high level of data integrity.

Setting the Isolation Level

The isolation level is set when an application package is bound to the database. A package can be bound to the database by using the `BIND` or `PRECOMPILE(PREP)` commands. Both of these commands have an `ISOLATION` option.

CLI applications define the isolation level in the `db2cli.ini` file.

By default, the DB2 CLP and DB2 Command Window use the CS isolation level. This can be changed by using the command `db2 change isolation to <new level>`. A `db2 terminate` command must be issued first for this command to be effective.

Following are four simple examples of how the isolation level can be set using the `PREP` and `BIND` commands.

Example 1:

```
db2 prep airseats.sqc isolation RS
```

The `PREP` command will automatically create a package, called `airseats`, in the database. A package is created by default by the `PREP` command unless the `BINDFILE`, `PACKAGE`, or `SYNTAX` options are specified. When the airseats application is run, it will use the read stability isolation level.

Example 2:

```
db2 bind airseats.bnd isolation RR
```

In this case, a package called `airseats` will be created in the database.

Example 3:

```
db2 bind airseats.bnd
```

Because no isolation level was specified in this BIND command, the package will use cursor stability, the default isolation level.

Example 4:

```
db2 prep airseats.sqc bindfile using airseats.bnd isolation
          RS
db2 bind airseats.bnd
```

In this case, the PREP command doesn't create a package in the database. It creates only a bind file to be used with the BIND command. Because the BIND command doesn't explicitly state an isolation level to be used, the isolation level that was used to create the bind file is used. In this case, the package is stored in the database using the RS isolation level.

If none of the applications on the database require repeatable read isolation, database administrators can remove the possibility of repeatable read by issuing `db2set DB2_RR_TO_RS =YES` from the DB2 Command Window. If this is set, the lowest level of concurrency on the database becomes read stability. This is true even if an application is explicitly bound specifying RR isolation.

When preparing for the exam, it is more important to understand what each isolation level means and how to choose them than to know how to set them. We've included the "Setting the Isolation Level" section to provide a thorough understanding.

Understanding Locks

Locks serve the same purpose in a database as they do in a house or a car. They determine who can and cannot access certain objects. Whoever has the right key at the right time will be able to gain access. In a database, the "who" is the transaction and the objects that you need to gain access to are tablespaces, tables, and rows.

Lock attributes

Every DB2 lock has three attributes, as follows:

Mode

This is also known as the state of the lock. The mode determines what access the owner of the lock is given to a resource, and the access privileges of other transactions on this locked resource.

Object

The locked object is the database object or resource that is being held by the lock owner. Objects that can be locked include tablespaces, tables, and rows. The only object that can be explicitly locked by a user is a table. The database manager will implicitly lock tablespaces, tables, and rows as needed, based on the required isolation level.

Duration

The duration of a lock represents the amount of time a lock is held on a particular object. The lock duration is determined by the required isolation level. Also, locks are automatically released if the unit of work is committed or rolled back using the `COMMIT` or `ROLLBACK` command.

The lowdown on lock modes

As mentioned previously, lock modes can apply to tablespaces, tables, and rows. There are twelve lock modes.

In addition to the lock modes mentioned in this book, other internal lock modes are used by the database manager when performing certain operations. These are not covered in the DB2 Family Fundamentals Exam.

Table 11-2 lists the lock modes, indicates which object they apply to, describes what type of access they allow, and indicates what corresponding locks will be obtained. The locks modes are listed in order of decreasing concurrency (or increasing control) on the object.

Notice that the "intent" modes are applicable only to tablespaces and tables. They do not apply to rows.

Table 11-2 Lock Modes Details

Lock Mode	*Additional Locks Obtained by Lock Owner*	*Applicable Objects*	*Allowed Access (Lock Owner)*	*Allowed Access (Concurrent Users)*
IN (Intent None)	None.	Tablespace, Table	Read access only to all rows in the table, including uncommitted data.	Read and update access to all rows in the table.
IS (Intent Share)	S or NS locks obtained on rows read.	Tablespace, Table	Read access only to all rows in the table.	Read and update access to all rows in the table.

Lock Mode	***Additional Locks Obtained by Lock Owner***	***Applicable Objects***	***Allowed Access (Lock Owner)***	***Allowed Access (Concurrent Users)***
NS (Next Key Share)	None.	Row	Read access only to the row. For CS and RS isolation levels.	Read access only to the row.
S (Share)	If an S lock is obtained on a table, no row locks are necessary.	Table, Row	Read access only to the row (row lock) or table (table lock).	Read access only to the row (row lock) or table (table lock).
IX (Intent Exclusive)	S, NS, X or U locks obtained on rows read. X locks obtained on rows updated.	Tablespace, Table	Read and update access to the rows in the table.	Read and update access to the rows in the table.
SIX (Share with Intent Exclusive)	No locks obtained on rows read. X locks obtained on rows updated.	Table	Read and update access to the rows in the table.	Read access only to the rows in the table.
U (Update)	X locks obtained on rows updated.	Table, Row	Update access to the rows in the table.	Read access only to the rows in the table.
NX (Next Key Exclusive)	None.	Row	Read access only to the row.	Read access only to the row.
NW* (Next Key Weak Exclusive)	None.	Row	Read access only to the row.	Read access only to the row.
X (Exclusive)	If an X lock is obtained on a table, no row locks are necessary.	Table, Row	Read and update access to the row (row lock) or table (table lock).	Read access only to the row or table, and only to UR applications.
W (Weak Exclusive)	None.	Row	Read and update access to the row.	Read access only to the row, and only to UR applications.
Z** (Super exclusive)	None.	Tablespace, Table	Read and update access to the object.	No access.

** The NW lock is acquired when a row is inserted into the index of a user (noncatalog) table. The lock is held on the next row to the inserted row in the index.*

*** The Z lock is acquired when special operations are being performed on the table. Some of these operations include* `alter table`, `drop table`, `create index`, *or* `drop index` *on the table, or table reorganization.*

The exam concentrates on table and row locks. Don't worry about understanding where tablespace locks come into play. Ensure that you're very familiar with Table 11-2 for the exam.

Lock compatibility

Lock compatibility deals with whether a lock request for a particular object will be granted to an application. The database manager must consider the lock mode being requested by the application as well as the locks currently held on the object. If the locks are compatible, the database manager will grant the application's lock request. If not, the database manager will force the application to wait until the current lock on the object is released or until a lock timeout is reached.

Lock timeout values specify the length of time an application is to wait to obtain a lock. This is set in the configuration file for the database. We discuss database configuration files in Chapter 9, "Database Building Blocks."

For example, say that application A currently holds a share lock on row 5 in table `test`. Application B comes along and also requires a share lock on row 5 in table test, because it wants to read only row 5. From Table 11-2, you can see that if a share lock is held, any other application can also read the row locked. So, the database manager would grant the S lock to application B in this case.

If application B wanted to update the row, it might request an X lock to do this. In this case, the database manager would not grant the request for an X lock on the row to application B. Instead, application B would have to wait until the S lock was released on the row by application A.

A held S lock and a requested X lock are incompatible locks. A held S lock and a requested S lock are compatible locks. Figure 11-1 summarizes whether the database manager would grant a specific lock request based on the current lock held. This table shows all possible lock combinations.

What locks do for fun

As you can probably imagine, this locking stuff can get pretty interesting. In addition to granting and denying lock requests, the database manager must also complete the work required to assign and release the locks on the various objects. Assigning and releasing many locks can cause a performance hit on the database. As locks and lock requests accumulate on any given object, the database manager must make decisions on whether a better locking strategy should be used. This is where lock escalation and conversion come into play.

Lock Mode	Lock Mode of Held Resource												
Requested	none	IN	IS	NS	S	IX	SIX	U	NX	X	Z	NW	W
none	granted	granted	granted	granted	granted	granted	granted	granted	granted	granted	granted	granted	granted
IN	granted	granted	granted	granted	granted	granted	granted	granted	granted	granted	wait	granted	granted
IS	granted	granted	granted	granted	granted	granted	granted	granted	wait	wait	wait	wait	wait
NS	granted	granted	granted	granted	granted	wait	wait	granted	granted	wait	wait	granted	wait
S	granted	granted	granted	granted	granted	wait	wait	granted	wait	wait	wait	wait	wait
IX	granted	granted	granted	wait	wait	granted	wait	wait	wait	wait	wait	wait	wait
SIX	granted	granted	granted	wait	wait	wait	wait	wait	wait	wait	wait	wait	wait
U	granted	granted	granted	granted	granted	wait	wait	wait	wait	wait	wait	wait	wait
NX	granted	granted	wait	granted	wait	wait	wait	wait	wait	wait	wait	wait	wait
X	granted	granted	wait	wait	wait	wait	wait	wait	wait	wait	wait	wait	wait
Z	granted	wait	wait	wait	wait	wait	wait	wait	wait	wait	wait	wait	wait
NW	granted	granted	wait	granted	wait	wait	wait	wait	wait	wait	wait	wait	granted
W	granted	granted	wait	wait	wait	wait	wait	wait	wait	wait	wait	granted	wait

Figure 11-1: Lock compatibility.

Another result of having many applications requesting different types of locks on the same objects is that the possibility of a lock being granted in a short period of time might be lessened. If a lock request has not been granted, the lock request is said to be in lock wait state.

Lock escalation

Lock escalation occurs when too many row locks are held on a particular table. A lock escalation will cause the row locks to be replaced by a table lock. The intent is to reduce the number of locks held, thereby greatly reducing the number of locks that need to be managed by the database.

There are two database configuration parameters that determine when a lock escalation might occur: `LOCKLIST` and `MAXLOCKS`. The lock list used to store all locks held by all applications running on the database. When a lock is released, it is removed from the lock list. The `MAXLOCKS` parameter specifies a percentage of the used lock list storage that, when reached, will initiate lock escalations.

For example, say that the `LOCKLIST` parameter is set to 4K and `MAXLOCKS` is set to 50. While locks are acquired on the database objects, information related to these locks is stored in the lock list. After 50 percent of the lock list (2K in this case) is filled with lock information, the database manager will scan the lock list to determine which table has the most row locks held. This table's row locks will be escalated to one table lock, reducing the amount of locks held in the lock list. This will happen each time the lock list reaches 50 percent of its capacity.

It is not desirable for many lock escalations to occur because a table lock will greatly reduce the concurrency of a table, which can greatly reduce the performance of many applications. Database administrators should configure the database to avoid experiencing large numbers of lock escalations. One way of avoiding lock escalations is to frequently commit transactions. This increases the frequency in which locks are released. If frequently committing transactions doesn't decrease the number of lock escalations on tables, the overhead of these lock escalations can be avoided by forcing a table lock by using the `LOCK TABLE` command or the `ALTER TABLE` command. The "Explicit locks on tables" section later in this chapter discusses these two commands in detail.

Lock conversion

A transaction can hold only one lock on a given object, at any given time. Lock conversion takes place when a unit of work requires a more restrictive lock on an object in which it already has a lock held. In this case, the database manager will attempt to convert the current lock mode to the requested lock mode. This new lock request may or may not be granted.

Lock conversion is performed internally by the database manager.

We can go back to the airline reservation application example again to illustrate lock conversion. When Rachelle requests a seat on Flight 123, the travel agent initiates the "book a seat" transaction by querying the available seats on this flight. From a database standpoint, the read-only query caused S locks to be obtained on three rows within the seat table and an IS lock to be obtained on the seat table itself. Rachelle decides to book seat 12A from the available seats retrieved by the current transaction. The travel agent proceeds to book seat 12A, making it unavailable for booking by other agents. At this point, the "book a seat" transaction completes. However, in order to update the row containing information for seat 12A, the database manager had to convert the IS lock on the table to an IX lock and convert the S lock on this row to an X lock.

Lock wait

As mentioned in the "Lock compatibility" section, if the database manager cannot grant a lock request to an application, that application will wait for the lock request to be granted. The requested lock is said to be in a lock wait state. The following four actions can move a lock out of a lock wait state. If none of these actions takes place, the lock will remain in a lock wait state indefinitely:

- The lock that was held on the object is released. In this case, the new lock request is granted.
- The application that requested this lock, is forced off the database by the database administrator. Applications can be forced off the database with the `FORCE APPLICATION` command.

- The database manager detects that this lock is in a deadlock situation. The application receives a lock timeout error due to deadlock, which essentially cancels the lock request.
- The `LOCKTIMEOUT` parameter specified in the database configuration file is reached. The application receives a lock timeout error, which essentially cancels the lock request.

The `LOCKTIMEOUT` parameter specifies the maximum number of seconds that an application will wait to obtain a lock. If this parameter is set to @ms1, the application will wait until one of the other three actions mentioned previously occurs.

Deadlock

Deadlocks are mentioned in the previous section, "Lock wait." Deadlocks involve locks that are in a special lock wait state. In a deadlock situation, the locks remain in a lock wait state indefinitely because they are each holding a resource that the other one needs to continue.

We can use a simple example, involving a married couple with joint bank accounts, to illustrate how a deadlock might occur. Say that the husband tries to transfer money from checking to savings from one bank machine. At the same time, across town at another banking machine, his wife is trying to transfer money from savings to checking. The husband's transaction locks the checking account and won't release it until it gets a lock on the savings account. The wife's transaction locks savings and won't release it until it gets a lock on checking. Each transaction now tries to outwait the other. If either were allowed to proceed, the receipt granted at the time would not agree with the monthly statement mailed out later. Rather than wait forever, DB2's deadlock detector picks a victim, causing someone's transaction to get cancelled and the other's to proceed. Basically, DB2 looks at two transactions that are trying to happen simultaneously and forces them to happen serially.

The frequency, in milliseconds, by which the database manager checks for deadlocks is determined by the `DLCHKTIME` database configuration parameter.

Lab 11-1 gives you some practice in working with locks.

Lab 11-1 Playing with DB2 locks

1. **Bring up two DB2 Command Windows.**

   You should already have the sample database created from earlier chapters. If not, issue `db2sampl` from one of the windows to create the sample database. Issue `db2 connect to sample` to connect to the sample database. Make sure that you're connected to the sample database from both command windows.

2. **Issue the command** `db2 create table locktest(c1 smallint, c2 char(1))`.

3. **Populate the table using the following five insert commands:**

   ```
   db2 insert into locktest values(3,'C')
   db2 insert into locktest values(1,'A')
   db2 insert into locktest values(7,'G')
   db2 insert into locktest values(5,'E')
   db2 insert into locktest values(6,'F')
   ```

4. **From one window (window 1), issue** `db2 +c update locktest set c1=1 where c2='A'`.

   The `+c` indicates that the command will not be committed until an explicit `db2 commit` statement is issued.

5. **From the second window (window 2), issue** `db2 select * from locktest`.

   You'll notice that the command in the window 2 appears to be hanging. It is actually in a lock-wait state. It is waiting for the update to be committed from window 1. It must wait because the CS isolation level (default for the CLP) ensures that no uncommitted updates will be read.

6. **Issue** `db2 commit" in window 1`.

   You should see that the query in window 2 is removed from lock-wait state and the result set is returned.

Explicit locks on tables

A table can be explicitly locked using the `LOCK TABLE SQL` statement. The table can be locked in `SHARE` or `EXCLUSIVE` mode using this statement. `SHARE` mode limits concurrent transactions to read-only access to this table; `EXCLUSIVE` mode prevents concurrent transactions from any type of access to the table.

An example of this statement follows.

```
db2 lock table test in share mode
```

It is also possible to explicitly state what locking granularity is to be used on a table with the `LOCKSIZE` option of the `ALTER TABLE` command. The two lock size options, `TABLE` and `ROW`, are used as follows on a table called `test`.

```
db2 alter table test locksize table
```

```
db2 alter table test locksize row
```

```
A table lock size means that no row locks are to be held on
           this table. S or X table locks will be held as
           appropriate. No "intent" table locks will be held
           on the table.A row lock size is the default lock
           size used for all tables. This means that row
           locks will be used as appropriate.
```

Moving from Isolation to Lockdown

Now that you are familiar with isolation levels and locks, try tying the two concepts together to answer the question, "Based on an isolation level, what locks will be obtained?" The best way to answer this question is with examples. Assume that you have the following information stored in a table called `locktest`. The table has an ascending index on column C1.

Row Number	C1	C2
1	3	C
2	1	A
3	7	G
4	5	E
5	6	F

UR isolation

When a UR application reads a portion of this table, no rows will be locked! The `select` statement that follows will not acquire any locks on the table or rows.

```
db2 select * from locktest where C1 > 3 and C1 < 7
```

When the following command is issued to update the table, the update command will attempt to obtain an IX lock on the table and X locks on rows 1 and 4.

```
db2 update locktest set C1=2 where C2 > 'A' and C2 < 'E'
```

CS isolation

When a CS application reads a portion of this table, the rows that the cursor is positioned over are locked. After the cursor moves to a new row, the lock on the previous row is released. Over the duration of the `select` statement that follows, the database manager will have attempted to acquire an IS lock on the table and an NS lock on row 4 and then row 5.

```
db2 select * from locktest where C1 > 3 and C1 < 7
```

When the following command is issued to update the table, the `update` command will attempt to obtain an IX lock on the table and X locks on rows 1 and 4.

```
db2 update locktest set C1=2 where C2 > 'A' and C2 < 'E'
```

RS isolation

When an RS application reads a portion of this table, all the rows that are part of the result set are locked. The `select` statement that follows will attempt to acquire an IS lock on the table and NS locks on rows 4 and 5.

```
db2 select * from locktest where C1 > 3 and C1 < 7
```

When the following command is issued to update the table, the `update` command will attempt to obtain an IX lock on the table and X locks on rows 1 and 4.

```
db2 update locktest set C1=2 where C2 > 'A' and C2 < 'E'
```

RR isolation

When an RR application reads a portion of this table, all the rows that were scanned in order to return the correct result set must be locked. For example, the following query would attempt to get an IS lock on the table and three S locks on rows 3, 4, and 5.

```
db2 select * from locktest where C1 > 3 and C1 < 7
```

When an RR application issues the following command to update this table, the `update` command will attempt to acquire an SIX lock on the table and an X lock on the row being updated and the row that is the next key in the index. In this case, row 1 and row 4 would obtain X locks.

```
db2 update locktest set C1=2 where C2 > 'A' and C2 < 'E'
```

The exact lock mode selected by DB2 depends on a number of factors, including the number of indexes defined on a table and the number of row locks required to satisfy the request. The database manager might decide to obtain one table lock rather than several row locks, for example. Know which lock modes are specific to updates, which are specific to reads, and how many rows might be locked for a particular statement based on the isolation level.

Use Lab 11-2 to get some practice in dealing with isolation levels.

Lab 11-2 Playing with isolation levels

1. **Issue** `db2 terminate` **from both windows that were used in Lab 11-1.**
2. **Issue** `db2 change isolation to rr` **from both windows.**

   This will change the isolation level of the DB2 Command Window to repeatable read. Then issue `db2 connect to sample` from both windows.
3. **Issue** `db2 +c select * from locktest` **from window 1.**
4. **From window 2, issue** `db2 +c update locktest set c1=1 where c2='A'`**.**

   In this case, window 2 will appear to be hanging. Because RR isolation is active, the `select` statement has locked all rows in the table to ensure that if another `select` is issued, the result set will not change at all. These locks will not be released until window 1 commits its work.
5. **Issue** `db2 commit` **in window 1 to release the row locks on locktest, allowing the update to complete.**
6. **Issue the same** `select` **in window 1 as specified in Step 3.**

   This command is now hanging because the `update` command in window 2 has still not been committed. RR isolation ensures that uncommitted data will not be read by the application. Commit the `update` command in window 2 and the `select` will be processed.
7. **Repeat the instructions given in Steps 3 and 4. Then issue** `db2 +c update locktest set c1=1 where c2='A'` **from window 1.**

   We've created a deadlock situation! The `update` command in window 1 completes only because the database manager rolled back the `update` command in window 2. An SQL0911 error is returned to the `update statement` in window 2. It takes DB2 10 seconds (10000 ms) to detect the deadlock. This is because `DLCHKTIME` is set to 10000 in the database configuration file for the sample database.

Prep Test

1 **Which of the following isolation levels will allow an application to read updates that haven't yet been committed to the database?**

A ❍ UR
B ❍ CS
C ❍ RR
D ❍ RS

2 **Which of the following isolation levels will allow an application to update uncommitted changes made by other applications?**

A ❍ CS
B ❍ RS
C ❍ UR
D ❍ None of the above

3 **Which of the following isolation levels will allow the re-execution of a statement within an application to be affected by other applications?**

A ❑ UR
B ❑ CS
C ❑ RS
D ❑ RR

4 **Given an application bound with RR isolation, if the application is to read rows from a table (the table `LOCKSIZE` is set to `ROW`), which of the following locks will the database manager attempt to obtain on the table?**

A ❍ X
B ❍ IX
C ❍ S
D ❍ IS

5 **Given an application bound with UR isolation, if the application is to read rows from a table, which of the following row locks will be obtained?**

A ❍ S
B ❍ IS
C ❍ X
D ❍ None of the above

6 **Given the following table data, how many rows would be locked if an application bound with RS isolation issues** `db2 select * from locktest where c1 > 5`**?**

C1	*C2*
3	C
1	A
7	G
5	E
6	F

A ❍ 4
B ❍ 3
C ❍ 2
D ❍ None of the above

Answers

1 **A.** UR translates to Uncommitted Read. *Review "Isolating Data with Isolation Levels."*

2 **D.** DB2 won't allow an update to occur on uncommitted data regardless of the isolation level that is being used. *Review "Isolating Data with Isolation Levels."*

3 **A, B, and C.** Repeatable read is the only isolation level that guarantees that the result set will be identical if a query is issued twice within a unit of work. *Review "Isolating Data with Isolation Levels."*

4 **D.** IS translates to Intent Share lock. *Review "Moving from Isolation to Lockdown."*

5 **D.** No locks will be obtained when a UR application reads rows from a table. *Review "Moving from Isolation to Lockdown."*

6 **C.** Only the rows in the result set are locked with RS isolation. *Review "Moving from Isolation to Lockdown."*

Part IV

Talking to DB2 with Structured Query Language

"Our automated response policy to a large company-wide data crash is to notify management, back up existing data and sell 90% of my shares in the company."

In this part . . .

SQL is the language that's used to talk to relational databases. Though many databases have their own brand of SQL, the most basic concepts of SQL are the same for all relational database-management systems. Paying special attention to these chapters will help you talk to any database! Work through the examples in this chapter and experiment a little with the SAMPLE database. SQL accounts for most of the questions on the DB2 Family Fundamentals exam, and you're expected to know it. After reading the chapters in this section, make sure that you add the letters S-Q-L to your resume.

Chapter 12

SQL Boot Camp

Exam Objectives

- Given a DCL SQL statement, knowledge to identify results
- Given a DDL SQL statement, knowledge to identify results
- Given a DML SQL statement, knowledge to identify results
- Ability to use SQL to SELECT data from tables
- Ability to use SQL to SORT or GROUP data
- Ability to use SQL to INSERT, UPDATE, or DELETE data
- Ability to start/end a unit of work
- Knowledge to identify the scope of a COMMIT or ROLLBACK
- Knowledge to identify the effect of a COMMIT or ROLLBACK statement

SQL, Structured Query Language. You've probably heard this term many times, and may have wondered what it's all about. One official-sounding definition is that SQL is a standardized language for defining and manipulating data in a relational database. All that means is that SQL is a language that is used for getting data in and out of databases. SQL is an essential part of DB2 and any relational database management system (RDBMS). The good part is that SQL is a *standardized* language, meaning that it is basically the same, no matter what RDBMS you're using.

In this chapter, you learn the fundamentals of SQL, with a focus on SQL language elements. SQL is divided into three major categories:

- DCL: Data Control Language, used to provide access control to database objects
- DDL: Data Definition Language, used to create, modify, or drop database objects
- DML: Data Manipulation Language, used to select, insert, update, or delete data

Quick Assessment

Using DCL

1 To grant privileges on database objects, you must have _____ authority or _____ authority.

Working with DDL

2 The DECLARE statement is similar to the _____ statement, except that it is used to create temporary tables that are around for only the duration of a connection.

Introducing queries and DML

3 A _____ specifies something about a row that is either true or false.

4 Use the _____ clause to eliminate duplicate rows in a result set.

5 A _____ is a SELECT statement that queries two or more tables simultaneously.

6 LCASE or LOWER is an example of a _____ function.

7 The _____ statement can be used to remove all the rows in a table or view.

Understanding units of work

8 A unit of work (UOW) is also known as a _____.

Answers

1 `SYSADM` *authority or DBADM authority.* Review "Data Control Language (DCL)."

2 `CREATE`. Review "Data Definition Language (DDL)."

3 *predicate.* Review "The WHERE clause."

4 `DISTINCT`. Review "The DISTINCT clause."

5 *join.* Review "Joins."

6 *scalar.* Review "Functions."

7 `DELETE`. Review "The DELETE statement."

8 *transaction.* Review "Units of Work (Transactions)."

Data Control Language (DCL)

To understand how DCL is used to provide access to database objects, you need to know how access to a DB2 system is controlled. Two levels of security control such access.

With the first level, access to the instance is managed outside of DB2, normally by the operating system. *Authentication* involves verifying a user's identity through a valid user ID and password.

You can establish a connection (or attachment) between your DB2 client and an instance on the server using the DB2 ATTACH command. But before you can access a database on the server, you need to establish a connection between your DB2 client and the database using the SQL CONNECT statement. With each, you can specify a user ID and password, and DB2 will use them to authenticate you. You can also request a password change by supplying your user ID, old password, and new password twice. If you don't specify a user ID and password with the ATTACH command or the CONNECT statement, DB2 may use the user ID and password you logged on with at the client for authentication, or it may prompt you to supply a user ID and password. Here are some examples:

```
CONNECT TO SAMPLE USER melnyk USING mypassword
CONNECT TO SAMPLE USER melnyk USING mypassword
  NEW newpassword CONFIRM newpassword
```

The following message tells you that you have made a successful connection:

```
Database Connection Information
Database product       = DB2/NT 7.1.0
SQL authorization ID   = MELNYK
Local database alias   = SAMPLE
```

After you are connected, you can access the database.

With the second level of security, access to the database, its objects, and the data is managed by DB2, using authorities and privileges that are defined in the database. *Authorities* are high-level categories of user rights. They include SYSADM, SYSCTRL, SYSMAINT, DBADM, and LOAD (see Chapter 10). *Privileges* are specific rights that are normally granted to users, allowing them to work with specific objects in the database. A privilege is the right to create or access a database object. Privileges are stored in the system catalog tables for a database. The three types of privileges are the following

- CONTROL **privilege:** If you create an object, you usually have full access to that object. You can even give access to others and give others permission to *grant* privileges on the object. These users can grant or revoke privileges using two SQL statements, GRANT or REVOKE:

- The `GRANT` statement gives privileges to a user. For example

```
GRANT CONTROL ON TABLE staff TO Tallerico
```

- The `REVOKE` statement takes privileges away from a user. For example

```
REVOKE CONTROL ON TABLE staff FROM Tallerico
REVOKE ALL PRIVILEGES ON TABLE staff FROM Tallerico
```

- **Individual privileges:** These are privileges that allow you to perform a specific function, sometimes on a specific object. They include `SELECT`, `INSERT`, `DELETE`, and `UPDATE`.
- **Implicit privileges:** An implicit privilege is granted to you automatically when you are explicitly granted certain high-level privileges. These privileges are not revoked when the high-level privileges are explicitly revoked.

To grant privileges on database objects, you must have `SYSADM` authority, `DBADM` authority, `CONTROL` privilege, or have the `WITH GRANT OPTION` (a selectable option on the `GRANT` statement) on that object. You must have `SYSADM` or `DBADM` authority to grant `CONTROL` privilege to another user. You must have `SYSADM` authority to grant `DBADM` authority.

Data Definition Language (DDL)

DDL is used to create, modify, or drop (delete) database objects. DDL contains four main SQL statements:

- `CREATE`
- `DECLARE`
- `ALTER`
- `DROP`

The CREATE statement

The `CREATE` statement is used to create database objects, including:

- Tables
- Views
- Indexes
- Schemas

- User-defined functions (UDFs)
- User-defined (data) types (UDTs)
- Buffer pools
- Table spaces
- Stored procedures
- Triggers

The CREATE TABLE statement, which is one of the statements that DB2 runs when creating the SAMPLE database. The statement specifies the creation of an EMPLOYEE table under the schema MELNYK. The table consists of several columns with different data type definitions. Some of the columns cannot have null values. The table is to be created in the default table space USER-SPACE1. Here is an example:

```
CREATE TABLE "MELNYK"."EMPLOYEE" (
   "EMPNO" CHAR(6) NOT NULL ,
   "FIRSTNME" VARCHAR(12) NOT NULL ,
   "MIDINIT" CHAR(1) NOT NULL ,
   "LASTNAME" VARCHAR(15) NOT NULL ,
   "WORKDEPT" CHAR(3) ,
   "PHONENO" CHAR(4) ,
   "HIREDATE" DATE ,
   "JOB" CHAR(8) ,
   "EDLEVEL" SMALLINT NOT NULL ,
   "SEX" CHAR(1) ,
   "BIRTHDATE" DATE ,
   "SALARY" DECIMAL(9,2) ,
   "BONUS" DECIMAL(9,2) ,
   "COMM" DECIMAL(9,2) )
IN "USERSPACE1" ;
```

The system catalog tables are updated whenever you create a database object.

The DECLARE statement

The DECLARE statement is similar to the CREATE statement, except that it is used to create temporary tables that are around only for the duration of a connection. A table is the only object that can be declared, and it must be located in an existing user temporary table space. Temporary tables are really useful when you're working with intermediate results.

It's important to remember that if you want to reference a declared table in an SQL statement, the table must be explicitly or implicitly qualified by the schema name SESSION. This qualification is necessary because each session that defines a declared table has its own (possibly unique) description of that declared temporary table.

Declared tables can be altered or dropped, but no other database objects can be derived from or applied against them. Declared tables can be referenced like any other table.

The DECLARE GLOBAL TEMPORARY TABLE statement is a statement that specifies the declaration of a temporary table named TEMP1, located in an existing user temporary table space named MYTEMPSPACE. The columns in this table will have the same names and definitions as the columns in the EMPLOYEE table. The rows of the temporary table will be preserved (not deleted) whenever a COMMIT statement is processed. Finally, changes to the temporary table are not logged (this is the only option). Here is an example:

```
DECLARE GLOBAL TEMPORARY TABLE temp1
  LIKE employee
  ON COMMIT PRESERVE ROWS
  NOT LOGGED
IN mytempspace
```

The system catalog tables are *not* updated whenever you create a temporary table.

The ALTER statement

The ALTER statement lets you change some of the characteristics of an existing database object, including:

- Tables
- Table spaces
- Views
- Buffer pools

Following is an example of a CREATE TABLE statement, followed by an ALTER TABLE statement. These are two of the statements that DB2 runs when creating the SAMPLE database. The first statement specifies the creation of an EMP_RESUME table under the schema MELNYK. The table consists of three columns with different data type definitions. Two of the columns cannot have null values. The table is to be created in the default table space USERSPACE1. The second statement (ALTER TABLE) defines the two columns that cannot have null values to be a composite primary key for the table.

```
CREATE TABLE "MELNYK"."EMP_RESUME" (
  "EMPNO" CHAR(6) NOT NULL ,
  "RESUME_FORMAT" VARCHAR(10) NOT NULL ,
  "RESUME" CLOB(5120) LOGGED NOT COMPACT )
IN "USERSPACE1" ;
```

```
ALTER TABLE "MELNYK"."EMP_RESUME"
  ADD PRIMARY KEY
  ("EMPNO",
   "RESUME_FORMAT");
```

An ALTER TABLE statement will fail if you try to add a check constraint that is incompatible with table rows that already exist. A *check constraint* is a rule that specifies allowable values for a column in a table.

You cannot alter an index. If you want to change an index, you must drop it and then create a new one with a different definition.

Store the DDL statements for a database in a script file that can be run from the DB2 command-line processor or from the DB2 Command Center. Get the DDL statements for an existing DB2 database by invoking the db2look utility.

The DROP statement

You can drop any object that was created through an SQL CREATE or DECLARE statement, including:

- Aliases
- Buffer pools
- Event monitors
- Functions
- Indexes
- Nodegroups
- Schemas
- Tables
- Table spaces
- Triggers
- Views

The DROP statement removes object definitions from the system catalog tables and therefore from the database itself.

Here is an example of the DROP TABLE statement:

```
DROP TABLE melnyk.employee
```

Because database objects can be dependent on other database objects, dropping an object can result in a related object becoming invalid.

Data Manipulation Language (DML)

DML is used to retrieve or modify table data. DML contains four main SQL statements:

- SELECT
- INSERT
- UPDATE
- DELETE

The SELECT statement

The SELECT statement is used to retrieve table data. In the simplest case, you can use the SELECT statement to retrieve all the data in a table. For example, to retrieve all the STAFF data from the SAMPLE database, issue

```
"SELECT * FROM staff"
```

Following is the result set that is returned to you:

```
ID     NAME      DEPT   JOB   YEARS  SALARY    COMM
------ --------- ------ ----- ------ --------- ---------
    10 Sanders       20 Mgr        7  18357.50         -
    20 Pernal        20 Sales      8  18171.25    612.45
    30 Marenghi      38 Mgr        5  17506.75         -
    40 O'Brien       38 Sales      6  18006.00    846.55
    50 Hanes         15 Mgr       10  20659.80         -
    60 Quigley       38 Sales      -  16808.30    650.25
    70 Rothman       15 Sales      7  16502.83   1152.00
    80 James         20 Clerk      -  13504.60    128.20
    90 Koonitz       42 Sales      6  18001.75   1386.70
   100 Plotz         42 Mgr        7  18352.80         -
   110 Ngan          15 Clerk      5  12508.20    206.60
   120 Naughton      38 Clerk      -  12954.75    180.00
   130 Yamaguchi     42 Clerk      6  10505.90     75.60
   140 Fraye         51 Mgr        6  21150.00         -
   150 Williams      51 Sales      6  19456.50    637.65
   160 Molinare      10 Mgr        7  22959.20         -
   170 Kermisch      15 Clerk      4  12258.50    110.10
   180 Abrahams      38 Clerk      3  12009.75    236.50
```

```
 190 Sneider        20 Clerk       8  14252.75     126.50
 200 Scoutten       42 Clerk       -  11508.60      84.20
 210 Lu             10 Mgr        10  20010.00          -
 220 Smith          51 Sales       7  17654.50     992.80
 230 Lundquist      51 Clerk       3  13369.80     189.65
 240 Daniels        10 Mgr         5  19260.25          -
 250 Wheeler        51 Clerk       6  14460.00     513.30
 260 Jones          10 Mgr        12  21234.00          -
 270 Lea            66 Mgr         9  18555.50          -
 280 Wilson         66 Sales       9  18674.50     811.50
 290 Quill          84 Mgr        10  19818.00          -
 300 Davis          84 Sales       5  15454.50     806.10
 310 Graham         66 Sales      13  21000.00     200.30
 320 Gonzales       66 Sales       4  16858.20     844.00
 330 Burke          66 Clerk       1  10988.00      55.50
 340 Edwards        84 Sales       7  17844.00    1285.00
 350 Gafney         84 Clerk       5  13030.50     188.00

35 record(s) selected.
```

If you use SELECT * from two or more tables, for example

```
"SELECT * FROM staff, employee"
```

the result set will contain a number of rows equivalent to the product of the number of rows in each specified table. In this case, that would be 35 * 32 = 1120 rows!

To restrict the number of rows in a result set, use the FETCH FIRST clause. For example

```
"SELECT * FROM staff, employee FETCH FIRST 2 ROWS ONLY"
```

You can use the SELECT statement to retrieve specific columns from a table by specifying a *select list* of column names (or column position numbers) separated by commas. For example:

```
"SELECT name, salary FROM staff"
```

This statement returns

```
NAME       SALARY
--------- ---------
Sanders    18357.50
Pernal     18171.25
Marenghi   17506.75
O'Brien    18006.00
Hanes      20659.80
Quigley    16808.30
Rothman    16502.83
James      13504.60
```

```
Koonitz    18001.75
Plotz      18352.80
Ngan       12508.20
Naughton   12954.75
Yamaguchi  10505.90
Fraye      21150.00
Williams   19456.50
Molinare   22959.20
Kermisch   12258.50
Abrahams   12009.75
Sneider    14252.75
Scoutten   11508.60
Lu         20010.00
Smith      17654.50
Lundquist  13369.80
Daniels    19260.25
Wheeler    14460.00
Jones      21234.00
Lea        18555.50
Wilson     18674.50
Quill      19818.00
Davis      15454.50
Graham     21000.00
Gonzales   16858.20
Burke      10988.00
Edwards    17844.00
Gafney     13030.50

  35 record(s) selected.
```

The WHERE clause

Use the `WHERE` clause to select specific rows from a table by specifying one or more selection criteria, or search conditions. A *search condition* consists of one or more predicates. A *predicate* specifies something about a row that is either true or false. Here are some predicates that you can use in a `WHERE` clause:

```
Predicate                      Function
x = y                          x is equal to y
x <> y                         x is not equal to y
x < y                          x is less than y
x > y                          x is greater than y
x <= y                         x is less than or equal to y
x >= y                         x is greater than or equal to y
IS NULL / IS NOT NULL          tests for null values
IN / NOT IN                    compares a value to a set of
                               values
BETWEEN / NOT BETWEEN          compares a value to a range of
                               values
LIKE / NOT LIKE                searches for strings having a
                               specified pattern
EXISTS / NOT EXISTS            tests for the existence of a row
                               that satisfies some condition
```

When building search conditions, be sure to do the following:

- Apply arithmetic operations only on numeric data types.
- Make comparisons only among compatible data types.
- Enclose character values within single quotation marks.
- Specify character values exactly as they appear in the database and be sure to match the case.

Example 1

Find the names of staff members whose salaries are greater than $20,000.

```
 "SELECT name, salary FROM staff
WHERE salary > 20000"
```

This statement returns

```
NAME      SALARY
--------- ---------
Hanes      20659.80
Fraye      21150.00
Molinare   22959.20
Lu         20010.00
Jones      21234.00
Graham     21000.00

  6 record(s) selected.
```

Enclosing the statement within double quotation marks keeps your operating system from misinterpreting certain characters, such as >. The greater-than symbol could be interpreted as an output redirection request.

Example 2

List the name and salary of staff members who are managers.

```
 "SELECT name, salary FROM staff
WHERE job = 'Mgr'"
```

This statement returns

```
NAME      SALARY
--------- ---------
Sanders    18357.50
Marenghi   17506.75
Hanes      20659.80
Plotz      18352.80
Fraye      21150.00
Molinare   22959.20
```

```
Lu          20010.00
Daniels     19260.25
Jones       21234.00
Lea         18555.50
Quill       19818.00

  11 record(s) selected.
```

You can specify more than one condition in a single query.

Example 3

List the name, job title, and salary of staff members who are managers and whose salary is greater than $20,000.

```
 "SELECT name, job, salary FROM staff
WHERE job <> 'Mgr'
AND salary > 20000"
```

This statement returns

```
NAME       JOB   SALARY
--------- ----- ---------
Graham     Sales  21000.00

  1 record(s) selected.
```

Example 4

List the name and years of service of staff members who have been employed for fewer than four years.

```
"SELECT name, years FROM staff
WHERE years IN (1, 2, 3)"
```

This statement is equivalent to

```
"SELECT name, years FROM staff
WHERE years = 1
OR years = 2
OR years = 3"
```

Either statement returns

```
NAME      YEARS
--------- ------
Abrahams       3
Lundquist      3
Burke          1

  3 record(s) selected.
```

Example 5

List the name and years of service of staff members who have been employed for fewer than three or for more than eight years.

```
"SELECT name, years FROM staff
WHERE years NOT BETWEEN 3 AND 8"
```

This statement returns

```
NAME      YEARS
--------- ------
Hanes         10
Lu            10
Jones         12
Lea            9
Wilson         9
Quill         10
Graham        13
Burke          1

  8 record(s) selected.
```

Example 6

Find names that are seven characters long and that start with the letter *S*.

```
"SELECT name FROM staff
WHERE name LIKE 'S______'"
```

This statement returns

```
NAME
---------
Sanders
Sneider

  2 record(s) selected.
```

Find all names that start with the letter *S*.

```
"SELECT name FROM staff
WHERE name LIKE 'S%'"
```

This statement returns

```
NAME
---------
Sanders
Sneider
Scoutten
Smith

  4 record(s) selected.
```

The ORDER BY clause

Use the ORDER BY clause to sort the result set by values in one or more columns. For example:

```
"SELECT name, salary FROM staff
WHERE salary > 20000
ORDER BY salary"
```

This statement returns

```
NAME       SALARY
--------- ---------
Lu          20010.00
Hanes       20659.80
Graham      21000.00
Fraye       21150.00
Jones       21234.00
Molinare    22959.20

  6 record(s) selected.
```

The column names in the ORDER BY clause do not have to be specified in the select list.

You can sort the result set in *descending order* by specifying DESC in the ORDER BY clause. For example

```
"SELECT name, salary FROM staff
WHERE salary > 20000
ORDER BY salary DESC"
```

This statement returns

```
NAME       SALARY
--------- ---------
Molinare    22959.20
Jones       21234.00
Fraye       21150.00
Graham      21000.00
Hanes       20659.80
Lu          20010.00

  6 record(s) selected.
```

The DISTINCT clause

Use the DISTINCT clause to eliminate duplicate rows in a result set. For example

```
"SELECT DISTINCT dept, job FROM staff
WHERE dept < 30
ORDER BY dept, job"
```

This statement returns

```
DEPT   JOB
------ -----
    10 Mgr
    15 Clerk
    15 Mgr
    15 Sales
    20 Clerk
    20 Mgr
    20 Sales

  7 record(s) selected.
```

The AS clause

Use the AS clause to assign a meaningful name to an expression or to any item in the select list. For example

```
"SELECT name, salary + comm AS pay FROM staff
WHERE (salary + comm) < 12000
ORDER BY name"
```

This statement returns

```
NAME      PAY
--------- ----------
Burke       11043.50
Scoutten    11592.80
Yamaguchi   10581.50

  3 record(s) selected.
```

Without the AS clause, the column name would have been 2, meaning that the derived column is the second column in the result set.

PAY cannot be used in the predicate because the WHERE clause is processed before (SALARY + COMM) is labeled as PAY.

Joins

You can construct a SELECT statement to query two or more tables simultaneously. This type of statement is known as a join. For example, to get a list of departments and their managers, you must select information from two tables, because no one table contains all the required information:

```
"SELECT deptname, name AS manager FROM org, staff
WHERE manager = id
ORDER BY deptname"
```

This statement returns

```
DEPTNAME        MANAGER
--------------- ---------
Great Lakes     Plotz
Head Office     Molinare
Mid Atlantic    Sanders
Mountain        Quill
New England     Hanes
Pacific         Lea
Plains          Fraye
South Atlantic Marenghi

  8 record(s) selected.
```

Note that the column name `MANAGER` in the `ORG` table is *not* the same as the column name `MANAGER` in the result set. The context is quite different. In the first case, `MANAGER` is an actual table column name; in the second case, it is a label that you can affix to an output column to make it easier to interpret.

Subqueries

A subquery is a `SELECT` statement that appears within a `WHERE` clause and feeds its result set to that `WHERE` clause. A subquery can itself include another subquery. A `WHERE` clause can include different subqueries for more than one search condition. Moreover, a subquery often refers to tables and columns that are different than the ones used in the main query. For example

```
"SELECT lastname FROM employee
WHERE lastname IN
(SELECT sales_person FROM sales
WHERE sales_date < '01/01/1996')"
```

```
LASTNAME
---------------
GOUNOT
LEE
LUCCHESSI

  3 record(s) selected.
```

Functions

A database function is a relationship between a set of input data values and a single result value. DB2 Universal Database provides many built-in functions, including column functions and scalar functions. These are explained in the following sections.

Column functions

Column functions operate on a set of values in a column. Here are some examples of column functions:

- SUM returns the sum of the values in a set.
- AVG returns the sum of the values in a set divided by the number of values in that set.
- MIN returns the smallest value in a set of values.
- MAX returns the largest value in a set of values.
- COUNT returns the number of rows or values in a set of rows or values.

Do not try to specify column functions in a WHERE clause. Because of the order of operations, this won't work. (Remember: The WHERE clause is evaluated before the SELECT clause.)

You can use the DISTINCT clause in a column function to get rid of duplicate values before a function is applied. For example,

```
"SELECT COUNT(DISTINCT workdept) AS total_no_depts FROM
          employee"
```

returns the total number of different departments:

```
TOTAL_NO_DEPTS
--------------
             8

  1 record(s) selected.
```

A *scalar fullselect* is a fullselect (a statement that generates a result table), enclosed in parentheses, that returns a single row consisting of a single column value. Scalar fullselects are useful for computing data values from the database for use in an expression. For example, the following statement:

```
"SELECT lastname, firstnme, salary FROM employee
WHERE salary > (SELECT AVG(salary) FROM employee)
ORDER BY salary DESC"
```

returns the names of employees whose salary is greater than the average salary for all employees:

```
LASTNAME        FIRSTNME     SALARY
--------------- ------------ -----------
HAAS            CHRISTINE       52750.00
LUCCHESSI       VINCENZO        46500.00
THOMPSON        MICHAEL         41250.00
GEYER           JOHN            40175.00
KWAN            SALLY           38250.00
PULASKI         EVA             36170.00
STERN           IRVING          32250.00
LUTZ            JENNIFER        29840.00
HENDERSON       EILEEN          29750.00
O'CONNELL       SEAN            29250.00
MARINO          SALVATORE       28760.00
```

```
NICHOLLS          HEATHER           28420.00
BROWN             DAVID             27740.00
PEREZ             MARIA             27380.00

  14 record(s) selected.
```

Scalar functions

Scalar functions operate on a single value to return another single value. Here are some examples of scalar functions:

- ABS returns the absolute value of a number.
- HEX returns the hexadecimal representation of a value.
- LENGTH returns the number of bytes in an argument; for a GRAPHIC string, it returns the number of double-byte characters.
- YEAR extracts the year portion of a DATETIME value.
- MONTH extracts the month portion of a DATETIME value.
- DAY extracts the day portion of a DATETIME value.
- LCASE or LOWER returns a string in which all the characters have been converted to lowercase characters.
- UCASE or UPPER returns a string in which all the characters have been converted to uppercase characters.

Example 1

```
 "SELECT MIN(LENGTH (deptname)) AS min,
MAX(LENGTH(deptname)) AS max,
AVG(LENGTH(deptname)) AS avg_length_of_deptname
FROM department"
```

This statement returns

```
MIN         MAX         AVG_LENGTH_OF_DEPTNAME
----------- ----------- ----------------------
          8          28                     17

  1 record(s) selected.
```

Example 2

```
"SELECT DISTINCT YEAR(sales_date) AS sales_year FROM sales"
```

This statement returns

```
SALES_YEAR
-----------
       1995
       1996

  2 record(s) selected.
```

The GROUP BY clause

Use the `GROUP BY` clause to organize rows in a result set. Each group is represented by a single row in the result set. For example

```
"SELECT sales_date, MAX(sales) AS max_sales FROM sales
GROUP BY sales_date"
```

This statement returns

```
SALES_DATE MAX_SALES
---------- -----------
12/31/1995           3
03/29/1996           7
03/30/1996          18
03/31/1996          14
04/01/1996           9

  5 record(s) selected.
```

You can eliminate nonqualifying rows before groups are formed and column functions are computed by specifying a `WHERE` clause before the `GROUP BY` clause. For example

```
"SELECT sales_date, MAX(sales) AS max_sales FROM sales
WHERE YEAR(sales_date) < 1996
GROUP BY sales_date"
```

This statement returns

```
SALES_DATE MAX_SALES
---------- -----------
12/31/1995           3

  1 record(s) selected.
```

The HAVING clause

Use the `HAVING` clause to retrieve results for groups that satisfy only a specific condition. A `HAVING` clause can contain one or more predicates that compare some property of the group with

- Another property of the group
- A constant

For example

```
"SELECT sales_person, SUM(sales) AS total_sales FROM sales
GROUP BY sales_person
HAVING SUM(sales) > 25"
```

This statement returns

```
SALES_PERSON    TOTAL_SALES
--------------- -----------
GOUNOT                   50
LEE                      91

  2 record(s) selected.
```

Correlation names

A correlation name is an identifier that is usually associated with a table and defined in the FROM clause of a query. You can use a correlation name as a convenient short name for a table. Correlation names also eliminate ambiguous references to identical column names from different tables. For example

```
"SELECT e.salary FROM employee e
WHERE e.salary < (SELECT AVG(s.salary) FROM staff s)"
```

This statement returns

```
SALARY
-----------
   15340.00
   15900.00

  2 record(s) selected.
```

After you have defined a correlation name, you can use this name only to qualify the table.

Use correlation names when you need to compare a table with itself. In the following example, the EMPLOYEE table is compared with itself to find the managers of all employees. It displays the name of the employees who are not designers, the name of their manager, and the department number.

```
"SELECT e2.lastname, e2.job, e1.lastname AS mgr_lastname,
         e1.WORKDEPT
FROM employee e1, employee e2
WHERE e1.workdept = e2.workdept
AND e1.job = 'MANAGER'
AND e2.job <> 'MANAGER'
AND e2.job <> 'DESIGNER'"
```

This statement returns

```
LASTNAME        JOB      MGR_LASTNAME    WORKDEPT
--------------- -------- --------------- --------
QUINTANA        ANALYST  KWAN            C01
NICHOLLS        ANALYST  KWAN            C01
JEFFERSON       CLERK    PULASKI         D21
```

```
 MARINO          CLERK    PULASKI         D21
SMITH           CLERK    PULASKI         D21
JOHNSON         CLERK    PULASKI         D21
PEREZ           CLERK    PULASKI         D21
SCHNEIDER       OPERATOR HENDERSON       E11
PARKER          OPERATOR HENDERSON       E11
SMITH           OPERATOR HENDERSON       E11
SETRIGHT        OPERATOR HENDERSON       E11
MEHTA           FIELDREP SPENSER         E21
LEE             FIELDREP SPENSER         E21
GOUNOT          FIELDREP SPENSER         E21

  14 record(s) selected.
```

The UNION set operator

You can combine two or more outer-level queries into a single query by using the `UNION` set operator, which generates a result table by combining two other result tables. For example

```
"SELECT sales_person FROM sales
WHERE region = 'Ontario-South'
UNION
SELECT sales_person FROM sales
WHERE sales > 3"
```

The first statement returns

```
SALES_PERSON
---------------
LUCCHESSI
LEE
LUCCHESSI
LEE
GOUNOT
LUCCHESSI
LEE
GOUNOT
LEE
GOUNOT
LUCCHESSI
LEE
GOUNOT

  13 record(s) selected.
```

The second statement returns

```
SALES_PERSON
---------------
LEE
```

```
GOUNOT
LEE
LEE
LEE
GOUNOT
LEE
LEE
LEE
LEE
LEE
GOUNOT

  12 record(s) selected.
```

The UNION set operator processes the results of both queries, *eliminates duplicates*, and returns the final result set

```
SALES_PERSON
---------------
GOUNOT
LEE
LUCCHESSI

  3 record(s) selected.
```

The EXCEPT set operator

You can combine two or more outer-level queries into a single query by using the EXCEPT set operator, which generates a result table by including all rows that are returned by the first query, but not by the second and any subsequent queries. For example

```
"SELECT sales_person FROM sales
WHERE region = 'Ontario-South'
EXCEPT
SELECT sales_person FROM sales
WHERE sales > 3"
```

The EXCEPT set operator processes the results of both queries, *eliminates duplicates*, and returns the final result set

```
SALES_PERSON
---------------
LUCCHESSI

  1 record(s) selected.
```

The INTERSECT set operator

You can combine two or more outer-level queries into a single query by using the INTERSECT set operator, which generates a result table by including only rows that are returned by all the queries. For example

```
"SELECT sales_person FROM sales
WHERE region = 'Ontario-South'
INTERSECT
SELECT sales_person FROM sales
WHERE sales > 3"
```

The INTERSECT set operator processes the results of both queries, *eliminates duplicates*, and returns the final result set

```
SALES_PERSON
---------------
GOUNOT
LEE

  2 record(s) selected.
```

The INSERT statement

The INSERT statement is used to add new rows to a table or view. Inserting a row into a view also inserts the row into the table on which the view is based. When assembling an INSERT statement, you can use one of the following options:

- Use a VALUES clause to specify column data for one or more rows. For example

```
"INSERT INTO staff
VALUES (999,'Tallerico',20,'Sales',7,75000.00,24000.00)"

"INSERT INTO staff (id, name, dept)
VALUES (666,'Bailey',66),
(750,'Cerny',38)"
```

- Specify a fullselect to identify data contained in other tables or views. Remember that a fullselect is a statement that generates a result table. This form of the INSERT statement is useful for populating a table with values from rows in other tables. For example

```
"CREATE TABLE pers LIKE staff"

"INSERT INTO pers (id, name, dept, job, years, salary)
SELECT id, name, dept, job, years, salary FROM staff
WHERE dept = 38"

"INSERT INTO pers
SELECT id, name, dept, job, years, salary, comm
FROM staff

WHERE dept = 38"
```

The UPDATE statement

The UPDATE statement is used to change the data in a table or view. You can change the value of one or more columns for each row that satisfies the conditions specified by a WHERE clause. For example

```
 "UPDATE staff
SET dept = 51, salary = 70000
WHERE id = 750"

"UPDATE staff
SET (dept, salary) = (51, 70000)
WHERE id = 750"
```

If the WHERE clause is omitted, DB2 *updates each row* in the table or view with the values you supply.

The DELETE statement

The DELETE statement is used to delete entire rows of data from a table. You can delete each row that satisfies the conditions specified by a WHERE clause. For example:

```
"DELETE FROM staff
WHERE id IN (666, 750, 999)"
```

If you omit the WHERE clause in a DELETE statement, DB2 deletes all the rows in the table or view!

Units of Work (Transactions)

A UOW and a transaction are the same thing: one or more SQL statements that are processed together. A transaction succeeds or fails as a whole; therefore it is an example of an *atomic* operation (see Chapter 4, "An Introduction to DB2 Products and Packaging"). It starts during the processing of the first SQL statement in a session or program. It completes when a COMMIT (WORK), ROLLBACK (WORK), TERMINATE or a CONNECT RESET statement is issued, either explicitly or implicitly. Locks are released following completion of a unit of work. Data that is modified by SQL statements is tracked by DB2 and either permanently changed (committed) or returned to its original state (rolled back). If a program ends abnormally during an active unit of work, that unit of work is rolled back. DB2 ensures that all committed transactions are physically applied to the database.

To practice some of the things that you learned in this chapter, try the exercises in Lab 12-1.

Lab 12-1 Exploring SQL

1. **On Windows NT/2000, issue** `db2cmd` **from a command prompt to open a DB2 command window and initialize the DB2 command-line environment.**
2. **If the database manager is not already running, issue** `db2start`.
3. **Create a simple database, MYDATABASE, under your default instance (most likely** `DB2`**).**

   Use all the default settings. To connect to your database, issue `db2 connect to mydatabase`.
4. **Create a table, MYTABLE, with several columns having different data type definitions.**
5. **Using the ALTER TABLE statement, add a new column to MYTABLE.**
6. **Insert some rows into MYTABLE.**
7. **Retrieve the rows.**

   Try to sort the rows. Depending on how many rows you have, try to group the results. Make up some interesting queries and test them.
8. **Update some of the rows in MYTABLE.**
9. **Delete a row.**
10. **Drop your table.**
11. **To break your connection to the database, issue** `db2 connect reset`.
12. **Using the** `DROP DATABASE` **command, drop your database.**
13. **To stop the command line processor, issue** `quit`.

Prep Test

1 **Given the tables**

EMPLOYEE		
emp_num	*emp_name*	*dept*
1	Adams	1
2	Jones	1
3	Smith	2
4	Williams	1

DEPT	
dept_id	*dept_name*
1	Planning
2	Support

and the statement

```
ALTER TABLE employee
ADD FOREIGN KEY (dept) REFERENCES (dept_id)
ON DELETE CASCADE
```

How many units of work will be needed to process this statement?

```
DELETE FROM dept WHERE dept_id=1
```

A ❍ 0
B ❍ 1
C ❍ 2
D ❍ 3
E ❍ 4
F ❍

2 **Given the tables**

COUNTRY

ID	*NAME*	*PERSON*	*CITIES*
1	Argentina	1	10
2	Canada	2	20
3	Cuba	2	10
4	Germany	1	0
5	France	7	5

STAFF

ID	*LASTNAME*
1	Jones
2	Smith

The statement

```
INSERT INTO staff
SELECT person, 'Greyson' FROM country WHERE person > 1
```

will insert how many rows into the STAFF table?

A ❍ 0
B ❍ 1
C ❍ 2
D ❍ 3

3 **Which of the following statements eliminates all but one of each set of duplicate rows in the final result table?**

A ❍ SELECT UNIQUE * FROM t1
B ❍ SELECT DISTINCT * FROM t1
C ❍ SELECT * FROM DISTINCT T1
D ❍ SELECT UNIQUE (*) FROM t1
E ❍ SELECT DISTINCT (*) FROM t1

4 **Given the following table definition and SQL statements:**

```
CREATE TABLE table1 (col1 INT, col2 CHAR(40), col3 INT)
GRANT INSERT, UPDATE, SELECT, REFERENCES ON TABLE
            table1
TO USER usera
```

Which of the following SQL statements will revoke privileges for user USERA on COL1 and COL2?

A ❍ REVOKE UPDATE ON TABLE table1 FROM USER usera

B ❍ REVOKE ALL PRIVILEGES ON TABLE table1 FROM USER usera

C ❍ REVOKE ALL PRIVILEGES ON TABLE table1 COLUMNS (col1, col2) FROM USER usera

D ❍ REVOKE REFERENCES ON TABLE table1 COLUMNS (col1, col2) FROM USER usera

5 **Given the two table definitions**

```
ORG

deptnumb INTEGER
deptname CHAR(30)
manager INTEGER
division CHAR(30)
location CHAR(30)
```

```
STAFF

id INTEGER
name CHAR(30)
dept INTEGER
job CHAR(20)
years INTEGER
salary DECIMAL(10,2)
comm DECIMAL(10,2)
```

Which of the following statements will display each department alphabetically by name, and the name of the manager of the department?

A ❍ SELECT a.deptname, b.name FROM org a, staff b WHERE a.manager=b.id

B ❍ SELECT a.deptname, b.name FROM org a, staff b WHERE b.manager=a.id

C ❍ SELECT a.deptname, b.name FROM org a, staff b WHERE a.manager=b.id GROUP BY a.deptname, b.name

D ❍ SELECT a.deptname, b.name FROM org a, staff b, WHERE b.manager=a.id GROUP BY a.deptname, b.name

6 **Given the table**

STAFF	
ID	***LASTNAME***
1	Jones
2	Smith

When issuing the query SELECT * FROM staff, the row return order will be based on which of the following?

A ❍ An ambiguous order
B ❍ The primary key order
C ❍ The order that the rows were inserted into the table
D ❍ The values for the ID column, then the LASTNAME column

7 **Given the table**

STAFF	
ID	***LASTNAME***
1	Jones
2	Smith
1	<null>

Which of the following statements removes all rows from the table where there is a null value for LASTNAME?

A ❍ DELETE FROM staff WHERE lastname IS NULL
B ❍ DELETE FROM staff WHERE lastname = 'NULL'
C ❍ DELETE ALL FROM staff WHERE lastname IS NULL
D ❍ DELETE ALL FROM staff WHERE lastname = 'NULL'

8 **Given the tables**

COUNTRY			
ID	***NAME***	***PERSON***	***CITIES***
1	Argentina	1	10
2	Canada	2	20

ID	NAME	PERSON	CITIES
3	Cuba	2	10
4	Germany	1	0
5	France	7	5

STAFF	
ID	*LASTNAME*
1	Jones
2	Smith

Which of the following statements removes the rows from the COUNTRY table that have PERSONS in the STAFF table?

A ❍ DELETE FROM country WHERE id IN (SELECT id FROM staff)

B ❍ DELETE FROM country WHERE id IN (SELECT person FROM staff)

C ❍ DELETE FROM country WHERE person IN (SELECT id FROM staff)

D ❍ DELETE FROM country WHERE person IN (SELECT person FROM staff)

9 **The table STOCK has the following column definitions:**

```
type CHAR(1)
status CHAR(1)
quantity INTEGER
price DEC(7,2)
```

Items are indicated to be out-of-stock by setting STATUS to null and QUANTITY and PRICE to zero. Which of the following statements updates the STOCK table to indicate that all the items except for those with TYPE of "S" are temporarily out of stock?

A ❍ UPDATE stock SET status = 'NULL', quantity = 0, price = 0 WHERE type <> 'S'

B ❍ UPDATE stock SET (status, quantity, price) = (NULL, 0, 0) WHERE type <> 'S'

C ❍ UPDATE stock SET (status, quantity, price) = ('NULL', 0, 0) WHERE type <> 'S'

D ❍ UPDATE stock SET status = NULL, SET quantity = 0, SET price = 0 WHERE type <> 'S'

10 **Given the successfully executed embedded SQL**

```
INSERT INTO staff VALUES (1, 'Colbert', 'Dorchester', 1)
COMMIT
INSERT INTO staff VALUES (6, 'Anders', 'Cary', 6)
INSERT INTO staff VALUES (3, 'Gaylord', 'Geneva', 8)
ROLLBACK WORK
```

Which of the following indicates the number of new rows that would be in the STAFF table?

A ❍ 0
B ❍ 1
C ❍ 2
D ❍ 3

11 **Given CREATE TABLE t1 (c1 CHAR(4) NOT NULL), which of the following can be inserted into this table?**

A ❍ 4
B ❍ NULL
C ❍ 'abc'
D ❍ 'abcde'

12 **Which of the following DDL statements creates a table where employee IDs are unique?**

A ❍ CREATE TABLE t1 (employid INTEGER)
B ❍ CREATE TABLE t1 (employid UNIQUE INTEGER)
C ❍ CREATE TABLE t1 (employid INTEGER NOT NULL)
D ❍ CREATE TABLE t1 (employid INTEGER NOT NULL, PRIMARY KEY (employid))

13 **Given the transaction**

```
"CREATE TABLE t1 (id INTEGER, CONSTRAINT chkid CHECK
          (id<100))"
"INSERT INTO t1 VALUES (100)"
"COMMIT"
```

Which of the following is the result from the transaction?

A ❍ The row is inserted with a null value.
B ❍ The row is inserted with a value of 100.
C ❍ The row insertion with a value of 100 is rejected.
D ❍ The trigger called chkid is fired to validate the data.

14 **Given the statement**

```
CREATE VIEW v1 AS
SELECT c1 FROM t1 WHERE c1='a'
WITH CHECK OPTION
```

Which of the following SQL statements will insert data into the table?

A ❍ INSERT INTO v1 VALUES (a)

B ❍ INSERT INTO v1 VALUES (b)

C ❍ INSERT INTO v1 VALUES ('b')

D ❍ INSERT INTO v1 VALUES ('a')

E ❍ INSERT INTO v1 VALUES ('ab')

Answers

1 **B.** A unit of work is one or more SQL statements that are processed together. *See "Units of Work (Transactions)."*

2 **D.** Hint: Selecting a delimited string or a number from a table returns that string or the number. *Review "The SELECT statement."*

3 **B.** The DISTINCT clause is used to eliminate duplicate rows in a result set. *See "The DISTINCT clause."*

4 **B.** Hint: Privileges are revoked at the table level, not at the column level. *Review "Data Control Language (DCL)."*

5 **C.** Correlation names eliminate ambiguous references to column names from different tables. *Review "Correlation names."*

6 **A.** Hint: The rows in a result set are returned in an arbitrary order. (This may or may not be ambiguous to you.) *Review "The SELECT statement."*

7 **A.** The DELETE statement is used to delete entire rows of data from a table; a WHERE clause can be used to identify the rows that are to be deleted. *See "The DELETE statement."*

8 **C.** The DELETE statement is used to delete entire rows of data from a table; a WHERE clause can be used to identify the rows that are to be deleted. The IN predicate compares a value to a set of values. *See "The DELETE statement" and "The WHERE clause."*

9 **B.** Hint: Using double quotation mark delimiters or no delimiters with the null string (specified in upper, lower, or mixed case) in an UPDATE statement places a null value in the row; using single quotation mark delimiters updates the row with the string itself, exactly as specified. *Review "The UPDATE statement."*

10 **B.** A unit of work is one or more SQL statements that are processed together. In this example, only the first unit of work (the first statement) is committed; the second unit of work (the other two statements) gets rolled back. *See "Units of Work (Transactions)."*

11 **C.** Based on the column definition provided, the correct value cannot be a numeric value, a null value, or a character value with a length greater than 4. *Review "The INSERT statement."*

12 **D.** The primary key constraint ensures that the primary key is unique. *Review "Data Definition Language (DDL)."*

13 **C.** A check constraint is a rule that specifies allowable values for a column in a table. *Review "The ALTER statement."*

14 **D.** Inserting a row into a view also inserts the row into the table on which the view is based. *Review "The INSERT statement."*

Chapter 13

The Rest of the SQL Story

Exam Objectives

- Given a DML SQL statement, knowledge to identify results
- Ability to use SQL to SELECT data from tables

Now for the tough stuff! It's not that bad, actually. This chapter covers

- Correlated subqueries
- Recursive queries
- Joins
- ROLLUP groupings
- CUBE groupings
- Other OLAP features

These are some advanced concepts in SQL that facilitate data analysis, helping you to extract useful information from a database.

To understand the topics in this chapter, make sure that you thoroughly understand Chapter 12.

Quick Assessment

Constructing more complex queries

1 A subquery that can refer to a previously identified table is known as a _____ subquery.

2 A common table expression is like a temporary _____ inside a complex query.

3 _____ return rows that are generated by an inner join operation, plus rows that would not be returned by the inner join operation.

4 Although `ROLLUP` and `CUBE` groupings both generate result sets that show different aggregates, or data groupings, in a single pass, _____ groupings enable a finer degree of analysis.

Answers

1 *correlated*. Review "Correlated Subqueries."

2 *view*. Review "Recursive Queries."

3 *Outer joins*. Review "Joins Revisited."

4 *CUBE*. Review "ROLLUP Groupings" and "CUBE Groupings."

Correlated Subqueries

A *correlated subquery* is a subquery that can refer to a previously identified table; the subquery is said to have a *correlated reference* to a table in the main query.

Suppose that you want to know the average salary for every department listed in the EMPLOYEE table. You can get this information by running the following query:

```
SELECT workdept, CAST(ROUND(AVG(salary),2) AS DECIMAL(9,2))
AS AVERAGE_SALARY
FROM employee
GROUP BY workdept
ORDER BY workdept
```

Casting (or converting) the result to the same data type (decimal) with a different precision or scale cleans up the output. Without the CAST specification, the result set is shown with a high level of precision (the number of digits excluding the sign) and scale (the number of digits in the fractional part of the number), which is quite a bit more than you need in this case! (Remember, when DB2 computes an average, if the data type of the argument values is decimal with precision *p* and scale *s*, the precision of the result is 31 and the scale is 31-*p*+*s*.)

The statement returns

```
WORKDEPT AVERAGE_SALARY
-------- --------------
A00            42833.33
B01            41250.00
C01            30156.66
D11            24677.77
D21            25153.33
E01            40175.00
E11            20998.00
E21            23827.50

  8 record(s) selected.
```

Now, suppose that you want to list all the employees whose salary is greater than the average salary of their department. You can do this with a correlated subquery running once for each row identified in the main query

```
"SELECT e1.lastname, e1.workdept, e1.salary FROM employee e1
WHERE salary >
(SELECT AVG(salary) FROM employee e2
WHERE e2.workdept = e1.workdept)
ORDER BY e1.workdept"
```

The subquery contains column references that are qualified by a correlation name that you have defined in the outer query. In this example, E1 is the correlation name, and E1.WORKDEPT refers to the WORKDEPT value of the *current* table row in the outer query.

The statement returns

```
LASTNAME        WORKDEPT SALARY
--------------- -------- -----------
HAAS            A00         52750.00
LUCCHESSI       A00         46500.00
KWAN            C01         38250.00
STERN           D11         32250.00
ADAMSON         D11         25280.00
YOSHIMURA       D11         24680.00
BROWN           D11         27740.00
LUTZ            D11         29840.00
PULASKI         D21         36170.00
MARINO          D21         28760.00
PEREZ           D21         27380.00
HENDERSON       E11         29750.00
SCHNEIDER       E11         26250.00
SPENSER         E21         26150.00
LEE             E21         25370.00
GOUNOT          E21         23840.00

  16 record(s) selected.
```

Recursive Queries

A *recursive query* is a query that uses result sets to get additional results; it contains a common table expression that includes a reference to itself. A *common table expression* is like a temporary view inside a complex query.

Wow! What's that about, you ask? We admit that this topic is not easy and that it will probably take some effort to wrap your mind around it, but go for it! We use an example based on the SAMPLE database to figure this out.

The SAMPLE database contains a table called ORG with the following records:

```
DEPTNUMB DEPTNAME       MANAGER DIVISION   LOCATION
-------- -------------- ------- ---------- -------------
      10 Head Office        160 Corporate  New York
      15 New England         50 Eastern    Boston
      20 Mid Atlantic        10 Eastern    Washington
      38 South Atlantic      30 Eastern    Atlanta
      42 Great Lakes        100 Midwest    Chicago
```

```
     51 Plains                 140 Midwest     Dallas
     66 Pacific                270 Western     San Francisco
     84 Mountain               290 Western     Denver

  8 record(s) selected.
```

The table contains information about a corporation's offices located in various cities; the head office is located in New York. Suppose that you need to know what options are available for traveling between the head office and the other offices belonging to the corporation. For example, to get from New York to San Francisco, you could fly direct or transfer at one or more intermediate locations, such as Dallas. You could construct a recursive query to determine what your options are.

You begin by creating a new table that contains information about the distances between cities. For example

```
CREATE TABLE distances (
  start VARCHAR(15) NOT NULL,
  end VARCHAR(15) NOT NULL,
  distance SMALLINT NOT NULL)
IN userspace1
```

You can create this table in the SAMPLE database. Don't worry: You can just as easily drop (delete) the table later when you're finished with it!

The table needs to be populated with data. Here is an example of some INSERT statements that will do just that. (These figures are approximate.) The cities referenced in this example are cities in which the corporation's offices are located. The first record specifies that the distance between New York and Chicago is 719 (miles), the second record specifies that the distance between New York and Denver is 1629 (miles), and so on.

```
INSERT INTO distances VALUES('New York','Chicago',719)
INSERT INTO distances VALUES('New York','Denver',1629)
INSERT INTO distances VALUES('New York','Atlanta',748)
INSERT INTO distances VALUES('Denver','San Francisco',963)
INSERT INTO distances VALUES('Washington','Atlanta',544)
INSERT INTO distances VALUES('Dallas','San Francisco',1493)
INSERT INTO distances VALUES('Atlanta','Denver',1204)
INSERT INTO distances VALUES('Washington','Boston',394)
INSERT INTO distances VALUES('Boston','Chicago',856)
INSERT INTO distances VALUES('Chicago','Dallas',798)
INSERT INTO distances VALUES('Chicago','Atlanta',585)
INSERT INTO distances VALUES('New York','Boston',190)
INSERT INTO distances VALUES('New York','Washington',204)
```

You need to design a query that will generate a list showing the distances between New York City (Head Office) and the other cities in which corporate offices are located. The trick here is that the query must be able to figure out, for example, that the distance between New York and Denver is 1,629 miles if you fly direct, but that it is 1,952 miles if you stop in Atlanta. In this example, recursive SQL treats each end point as a potential start point for another distance calculation, and it does this until all the records have been processed.

Here is the query that solves the problem; note that it starts with the word *WITH* — this identifies it as a common table expression (one of the few SQL statements that does not begin with a verb):

```
WITH path (start, end, distance) AS
  (SELECT d.start, d.end, d.distance FROM distances d
  WHERE start = 'New York'
  UNION ALL
  SELECT p.start, d.end, p.distance + d.distance
  FROM distances d, path p
  WHERE p.end = d.start)
SELECT DISTINCT start, end, distance FROM path
ORDER BY end, distance;
```

The heart of the recursive query is the common table expression, which in this case is called `path`:

```
(SELECT d.start, d.end, d.distance FROM distances d
WHERE start = 'New York'
UNION ALL
SELECT p.start, d.end, p.distance + d.distance
FROM distances d, path p
WHERE p.end = d.start)
```

The first part of this expression simply returns the *direct* distances between New York City and other cities:

```
SELECT d.start, d.end, d.distance FROM distances d
WHERE start = 'New York'
```

Notice the correlation name `d`. (For more information about correlation names, see Chapter 12.

The second part of the common table expression references itself:

```
SELECT p.start, d.end, p.distance + d.distance
FROM distances d, path p
WHERE p.end = d.start
```

In this part, the common table expression and the base table are joined to create the recursion. Total distances are also calculated. Notice the `UNION ALL` clause, which is a required part of a recursive query.

The main query retrieves all the possible routes from New York City:

```
SELECT DISTINCT start, end, distance FROM path
ORDER BY end, distance;
```

Here is the final result set

```
START           END             DISTANCE
--------------- --------------- --------
SQL0347W  The recursive common table expression "MELNYK.PATH"
            may
contain an infinite loop.  SQLSTATE=01605

New York        Atlanta              748
New York        Atlanta             1304
New York        Atlanta             1631
New York        Atlanta             2039
New York        Boston               190
New York        Boston               598
New York        Chicago              719
New York        Chicago             1046
New York        Chicago             1454
New York        Dallas              1517
New York        Dallas              1844
New York        Dallas              2252
New York        Denver              1629
New York        Denver              1952
New York        Denver              2508
New York        Denver              2835
New York        Denver              3243
New York        San Francisco       2592
New York        San Francisco       2915
New York        San Francisco       3010
New York        San Francisco       3337
New York        San Francisco       3471
New York        San Francisco       3745
New York        San Francisco       3798
New York        San Francisco       4206
New York        Washington           204

  26 record(s) selected with 1 warning messages printed.
```

Watch out for infinite loops when building recursive queries! If you have an infinite loop in your query, you'll have to manually terminate it by killing the thread or process; this can be as simple as Ctrl+Break or Control+C for the command-line processor. A query killed in this manner will not return any results. Remember that recursive algorithms need a defined end point. That's what a `WHERE` clause in the main query can do for you: To avoid infinite loops, consider including a restrictive `WHERE` clause in the main query. A warning is returned by all recursive queries, whether or not they include protection against the possibility of infinite loops.

Joins Revisited

We talk a bit about joins in Chapter 12. In SQL land, a *join* is a query that combines data from two or more tables.

A UNION also combines data from two or more tables (see Chapter 12). Distinguish them as follows: A UNION combines rows from both tables, without adding columns. (A UNION ALL of two three-row tables, for example, produces a result set of six rows.) A join adds columns to the result set. (A full join of two three-column tables produces a result set with six columns.) A join may add or subtract rows from the result set, depending on whether the join is an inner or outer join, and depending on the evaluation of any WHERE predicate used as a join condition.

Joins are quite common because relational tables contain information about the attributes of *discrete* entities, and if you want a result set that contains attribute information about several related entities, you will need to construct a query that joins several related tables.

The simplest join is one in which there are no specified conditions. For example

```
SELECT deptnumb, deptname, manager, id, name, dept, job
FROM org, staff
```

This statement returns 280 records, representing all combinations of rows from the ORG table and the STAFF table. Such a result set, referred to as the *cross product* of the two tables, may not make a lot of sense. For example, here are the first ten records returned by this statement:

```
DEPTNUMB DEPTNAME       MANAGER ID     NAME      DEPT   JOB
-------- -------------- ------- ------ --------- ------ -----
      10 Head Office        160     10 Sanders       20 Mgr
      10 Head Office        160     20 Pernal        20 Sales
      10 Head Office        160     30 Marenghi      38 Mgr
      10 Head Office        160     40 O'Brien       38 Sales
      10 Head Office        160     50 Hanes         15 Mgr
      10 Head Office        160     60 Quigley       38 Sales
      10 Head Office        160     70 Rothman       15 Sales
      10 Head Office        160     80 James         20 Clerk
      10 Head Office        160     90 Koonitz       42 Sales
      10 Head Office        160    100 Plotz         42 Mgr
```

What you need is a *join condition* to refine the result set. For example

```
SELECT deptnumb, deptname, id AS manager_id, name AS manager
FROM org, staff
WHERE manager = id
ORDER BY deptnumb
```

This statement returns

```
DEPTNUMB DEPTNAME       MANAGER_ID MANAGER
-------- -------------- ---------- ---------
      10 Head Office           160 Molinare
      15 New England            50 Hanes
      20 Mid Atlantic           10 Sanders
      38 South Atlantic         30 Marenghi
      42 Great Lakes           100 Plotz
      51 Plains                140 Fraye
      66 Pacific               270 Lea
      84 Mountain              290 Quill

  8 record(s) selected.
```

Here, the result set is short and to the point, and much more useful than the previous one.

The two main types of joins are *inner joins* and *outer joins*; these are discussed in the following sections.

Inner joins

The previous statement is an example of an inner join. *Inner joins* return only rows from the cross product that meet the join condition. If a row exists in one table but not the other, it is not included in the result set. To explicitly specify an inner join, the previous query can be rewritten with an `INNER JOIN` operator in the `FROM` clause, as follows:

```
SELECT deptnumb, deptname, id AS manager_id, name AS manager
FROM org INNER JOIN staff
ON manager = id
ORDER BY deptnumb
```

This statement returns the identical result set

```
DEPTNUMB DEPTNAME       MANAGER_ID MANAGER
-------- -------------- ---------- ---------
      10 Head Office           160 Molinare
      15 New England            50 Hanes
      20 Mid Atlantic           10 Sanders
      38 South Atlantic         30 Marenghi
      42 Great Lakes           100 Plotz
      51 Plains                140 Fraye
      66 Pacific               270 Lea
      84 Mountain              290 Quill

  8 record(s) selected.
```

The INNER JOIN operator specifies that an inner join operation should be used when processing the statement. The keyword ON is used to specify the join conditions for the tables being joined.

Remember that DEPTNUMB and DEPTNAME are columns in the ORG table, and that MANAGER_ID and MANAGER are based on columns (ID and NAME) in the STAFF table. The result set for the inner join consists of rows that have matching values for the MANAGER and ID columns in the left table (ORG) and the right table (STAFF), respectively.

Outer joins

Outer joins return rows that are generated by an inner join operation, plus rows that would not be returned by the inner join operation.

When you perform an outer join on two tables, you arbitrarily designate one table to be the left table and the other one to be the right table. There are three types of outer joins:

- A *left outer join* includes the inner join and the rows from the *left* table that are not returned by the inner join.
- A *right outer join* includes the inner join and the rows from the *right* table that are not returned by the inner join.
- A *full outer join* includes the inner join and the rows from *both the left table and the right table* that are not returned by the inner join.

Left outer join

If a left outer join includes the inner join plus the rows from the left table that are not returned by the inner join, how many records do you think the previous query will return if it is rewritten as a left outer join? Right! The query returns the same eight records that were returned by the inner join query, because the inner join query returned *all* the rows contained in the ORG table.

```
SELECT deptnumb, deptname, id AS manager_id, name AS manager
FROM org LEFT OUTER JOIN staff
ON manager = id
ORDER BY deptnumb
```

This statement returns

```
DEPTNUMB DEPTNAME       MANAGER_ID MANAGER
-------- -------------- ---------- ---------
      10 Head Office           160 Molinare
      15 New England            50 Hanes
      20 Mid Atlantic           10 Sanders
      38 South Atlantic         30 Marenghi
```

```
      42 Great Lakes                100 Plotz
      51 Plains                     140 Fraye
      66 Pacific                    270 Lea
      84 Mountain                   290 Quill

  8 record(s) selected.
```

The `LEFT OUTER JOIN` (or `LEFT JOIN`) operator specifies that a left outer join operation should be used when processing the statement. The keyword `ON` is used to specify the join conditions for the tables being joined.

Compare this result with the result set generated by `SELECT * FROM org`:

```
DEPTNUMB DEPTNAME       MANAGER DIVISION   LOCATION
-------- -------------- ------- ---------- -------------
      10 Head Office        160 Corporate  New York
      15 New England         50 Eastern    Boston
      20 Mid Atlantic        10 Eastern    Washington
      38 South Atlantic      30 Eastern    Atlanta
      42 Great Lakes        100 Midwest    Chicago
      51 Plains             140 Midwest    Dallas
      66 Pacific            270 Western    San Francisco
      84 Mountain           290 Western    Denver

  8 record(s) selected.
```

Right outer join

A right outer join includes the inner join plus the rows from the right table that are not returned by the inner join. Here is our example rewritten as a right outer join:

```
SELECT deptnumb, deptname, id AS manager_id, name AS manager
FROM org RIGHT OUTER JOIN staff
ON manager = id
ORDER BY deptnumb
```

This statement returns

```
DEPTNUMB DEPTNAME       MANAGER_ID MANAGER
-------- -------------- ---------- ---------
      10 Head Office           160 Molinare
      15 New England            50 Hanes
      20 Mid Atlantic           10 Sanders
      38 South Atlantic         30 Marenghi
      42 Great Lakes           100 Plotz
      51 Plains                140 Fraye
      66 Pacific               270 Lea
      84 Mountain              290 Quill
       - -                      20 Pernal
       - -                      40 O'Brien
       - -                      60 Quigley
```

```
      - -                              70 Rothman
      - -                              80 James
      - -                              90 Koonitz
      - -                             110 Ngan
      - -                             120 Naughton
      - -                             130 Yamaguchi
      - -                             150 Williams
      - -                             170 Kermisch
      - -                             180 Abrahams
      - -                             190 Sneider
      - -                             200 Scoutten
      - -                             210 Lu
      - -                             220 Smith
      - -                             230 Lundquist
      - -                             240 Daniels
      - -                             250 Wheeler
      - -                             260 Jones
      - -                             280 Wilson
      - -                             300 Davis
      - -                             310 Graham
      - -                             320 Gonzales
      - -                             330 Burke
      - -                             340 Edwards
      - -                             350 Gafney

  35 record(s) selected.
```

The RIGHT OUTER JOIN (or RIGHT JOIN) operator specifies that a right outer join operation should be used when processing the statement. The keyword ON is used to specify the join conditions for the tables being joined.

In this example, we are requesting all the names in the STAFF table and identifying all the staff members who are managers. Not all staff members are managers. (Otherwise, nothing much would get done!) Those records contain null values in the left table portion of the result set. The right table portion of the result set has assigned column names (MANAGER_ID and MANAGER) that are misleading, again because not all of these staff members are managers.

Full outer join

A full outer join includes the inner join plus the rows from both the left table and the right table that are not returned by the inner join. Here is our example rewritten as a full outer join:

```
SELECT deptnumb, deptname, id AS manager_id, name AS manager
FROM org FULL OUTER JOIN staff
ON manager = id
ORDER BY deptnumb
```

This statement returns the same result set that was returned by the right outer join, because the right outer join in this example already accounts for all the records in both tables.

The FULL OUTER JOIN (or FULL JOIN) operator specifies that a full outer join operation should be used when processing the statement. The keyword ON is used to specify the join conditions for the tables being joined.

Combining outer joins

How would you combine two outer joins in a single query? Suppose that you wanted a list of employees who are responsible for projects, identifying those employees who are also managers by listing the departments that they manage. The following query satisfies your request:

```
SELECT empno, deptname, projname
FROM (employee
LEFT OUTER JOIN project
ON respemp = empno)
LEFT OUTER JOIN department
ON mgrno = empno
```

The first outer join gets the name of the project for which the employee is responsible, if applicable. If an employee is responsible for two projects, the employee is represented by two records in the result set. If an employee is not responsible for any project, that employee shows a null value in the PROJNAME column. The first outer join is enclosed by parentheses and is resolved first. The second outer join gets the name of the employee's department if that employee is a manager. Because these are both outer join operations, all employees are represented in the result set, even if the DEPTNAME column and the PROJNAME column contain null values.

The statement returns

```
EMPNO  DEPTNAME                       PROJNAME
------ ------------------------------ -----------------------
000010 SPIFFY COMPUTER SERVICE DIV.   ADMIN SERVICES
000010 SPIFFY COMPUTER SERVICE DIV.   WELD LINE AUTOMATION
000020 PLANNING                       WELD LINE PLANNING
000030 INFORMATION CENTER             QUERY SERVICES
000030 INFORMATION CENTER             USER EDUCATION
000050 SUPPORT SERVICES               OPERATION SUPPORT
000050 SUPPORT SERVICES               GEN SYSTEMS SERVICES
000060 MANUFACTURING SYSTEMS          W L PROGRAMMING
000070 ADMINISTRATION SYSTEMS         GENERAL ADMIN SYSTEMS
000090 OPERATIONS                     OPERATION
000100 SOFTWARE SUPPORT               SYSTEMS SUPPORT
000110 -                              -
000120 -                              -
000130 -                              -
000140 -                              -
000150 -                              W L ROBOT DESIGN
000160 -                              W L PROD CONT PROGS
000170 -                              -
000180 -                              -
000190 -                              -
```

```
000200 -                                    -
000210 -                                    -
000220 -                                    W L PROGRAM DESIGN
000230 -                                    PAYROLL PROGRAMMING
000240 -                                    -
000250 -                                    PERSONNEL PROGRAMMING
000260 -                                    -
000270 -                                    ACCOUNT PROGRAMMING
000280 -                                    -
000290 -                                    -
000300 -                                    -
000310 -                                    -
000320 -                                    SCP SYSTEMS SUPPORT
000330 -                                    APPLICATIONS SUPPORT
000340 -                                    DB/DC SUPPORT

  35 record(s) selected.
```

Records with values in all columns are the result of the inner join operation. Records in which the join condition is not satisfied contain the null value in columns representing the right table. All rows from the left table are included in the result set.

Star joins

Star joins are typically used in queries against databases with a star schema design. (If you've forgotten what a star schema design is, review the material in Chapter 8.) A star join contains *local predicates* referencing values in the dimension tables, and *join predicates* connecting the dimension tables to the fact table. For example

```
SELECT empno, firstnme, lastname, SUM(sales) AS tot_sales,
(salary + bonus + comm) AS compensation
FROM employee, sales
WHERE sex = 'M' AND
YEAR(sales_date) = 1996 AND
lastname = sales_person
GROUP BY empno, firstnme, lastname,
(salary + bonus + comm)
```

This example uses the SAMPLE database, which does not really have a star schema design but is close enough to illustrate the point. The fact table in this case is the SALES table, and there is one relevant dimension table, EMPLOYEE. Normally, there would be more dimension tables, but none of the other tables in the SAMPLE database qualify. There are two local predicates in this example: WHERE sex = 'M' AND.YEAR(sales_date) = 1996, and there is one join predicate: WHERE lastname = sales_person (LASTNAME is a column in the EMPLOYEE table and SALES_PERSON is a column in the SALES table). The query identifies all male salespersons that completed sales in

1996, and it returns the total number of sales completed by that person in that year; it also shows the total annual compensation for each salesperson. (Compensation being the sum of salary, bonuses, and commissions.)

The statement returns

```
EMPNO  FIRSTNME     LASTNAME        TOT_SALES   COMPENSATION
------ ------------ --------------- ----------- -------------
000110 VINCENZO     LUCCHESSI                13      51120.00
000330 WING         LEE                      85      27900.00
000340 JASON        GOUNOT                   49      26247.00

  3 record(s) selected.
```

The result set shows that in this corporation, there appears to be an almost inverse relationship between performance and compensation, at least in the Sales area. Lee and Gounot closed many more sales in 1996 than did Lucchessi, but they were paid much less. Time to move on, boys!

ROLLUP Groupings

The ROLLUP operator generates a result set that shows different *aggregates*, or data groupings, in a single pass. This gives you the opportunity to analyze the results from a more general to a more specific perspective.

Here we examine a simple example, based on the SALES table in the SAMPLE database. Suppose that you want to see the total number of sales by year:

```
SELECT YEAR(sales_date) AS year, COUNT(*) AS tot_sales
FROM sales GROUP BY ROLLUP (YEAR(sales_date))
```

The statement returns

```
YEAR        TOT_SALES
----------- -----------
          -          41
       1995           5
       1996          36

  3 record(s) selected.
```

The result set shows the grand total number of sales (41), followed by the totals for each year.

Suppose that you want to see the results broken down by sales region. The following statement is identical to the previous one, except for the specification of the REGION column in two places:

```
SELECT YEAR(sales_date) AS year, region, COUNT(*) AS tot_sales
FROM sales GROUP BY ROLLUP (YEAR(sales_date), region)
```

The statement returns

```
YEAR        REGION          TOT_SALES
----------- --------------- -----------
          - -                        41
       1995 -                         5
       1996 -                        36
       1995 Manitoba                  1
       1995 Ontario-South             2
       1995 Quebec                    2
       1996 Manitoba                 10
       1996 Ontario-North             5
       1996 Ontario-South            11
       1996 Quebec                   10

  10 record(s) selected.
```

The result set has become more complex. In addition to the previous totals, you now have regional totals for each year.

Let's take it a step further. Suppose that you want to see these results broken down by salesperson. The following statement is identical to the previous one, except for the specification of the SALES_PERSON column in two places:

```
SELECT YEAR(sales_date) AS year, region, sales_person,
COUNT(*) AS tot_sales
FROM sales GROUP BY ROLLUP (YEAR(sales_date), region,
          sales_person)
```

The statement returns

```
YEAR        REGION          SALES_PERSON    TOT_SALES
----------- --------------- --------------- -----------
          - -               -                        41
       1995 -               -                         5
       1996 -               -                        36
       1995 Manitoba        -                         1
       1995 Ontario-South   -                         2
       1995 Quebec          -                         2
       1996 Manitoba        -                        10
       1996 Ontario-North   -                         5
       1996 Ontario-South   -                        11
       1996 Quebec          -                        10
       1995 Manitoba        LEE                       1
       1995 Ontario-South   LEE                       1
       1995 Ontario-South   LUCCHESSI                 1
       1995 Quebec          GOUNOT                    1
       1995 Quebec          LEE                       1
```

```
        1996 Manitoba         GOUNOT                     3
        1996 Manitoba         LEE                        4
        1996 Manitoba         LUCCHESSI                  3
        1996 Ontario-North    GOUNOT                     1
        1996 Ontario-North    LEE                        4
        1996 Ontario-South    GOUNOT                     4
        1996 Ontario-South    LEE                        4
        1996 Ontario-South    LUCCHESSI                  3
        1996 Quebec           GOUNOT                     4
        1996 Quebec           LEE                        4
        1996 Quebec           LUCCHESSI                  2

  26 record(s) selected.
```

The result set has become even more complex. In addition to the previous totals, you now have totals for each salesperson by region by year.

The ROLLUP operator is easy to use yet provides a substantial degree of analytical power.

CUBE Groupings

The CUBE operator also generates a result set that shows different aggregates, or data groupings, in a single pass. Why is it called a *cube*? A table is essentially a two-dimensional view of data (a square or rectangle, with the two dimensions represented by rows and columns). A cube adds a third dimension, typically for data summarized over time, although summaries by location are also quite common (sales by region, for example). The CUBE operator extends the output from the ROLLUP operator by generating even more useful data groupings. For example

```
SELECT YEAR(sales_date) AS year, region, COUNT(*) AS tot_sales
FROM sales GROUP BY CUBE (YEAR(sales_date), region)
```

The statement returns

```
YEAR        REGION          TOT_SALES
----------- --------------- -----------
          - Manitoba                 11
          - Ontario-North             5
          - Ontario-South            13
          - Quebec                   12
          - -                        41
       1995 -                         5
       1996 -                        36
       1995 Manitoba                  1
       1995 Ontario-South             2
       1995 Quebec                    2
```

```
      1996 Manitoba                   10
      1996 Ontario-North               5
      1996 Ontario-South              11
      1996 Quebec                     10

  14 record(s) selected.
```

This result set is identical to the result set that would have been generated by specifying ROLLUP rather than CUBE, except for four new records that summarize the sales data by region collapsed across years.

Now we introduce "salesperson" into the mix

```
SELECT YEAR(sales_date) AS year, region, sales_person,
COUNT(*) AS tot_sales
FROM sales GROUP BY CUBE (YEAR(sales_date), region,
             sales_person)
```

The statement returns

```
YEAR        REGION          SALES_PERSON    TOT_SALES
----------- --------------- --------------- -----------
          - Manitoba        GOUNOT                    3
          - Manitoba        LEE                       5
          - Manitoba        LUCCHESSI                 3
          - Manitoba        -                        11
          - Ontario-North   GOUNOT                    1
          - Ontario-North   LEE                       4
          - Ontario-North   -                         5
          - Ontario-South   GOUNOT                    4
          - Ontario-South   LEE                       5
          - Ontario-South   LUCCHESSI                 4
          - Ontario-South   -                        13
          - Quebec          GOUNOT                    5
          - Quebec          LEE                       5
          - Quebec          LUCCHESSI                 2
          - Quebec          -                        12
          - -               GOUNOT                   13
          - -               LEE                      19
          - -               LUCCHESSI                 9
          - -               -                        41

       1995 Manitoba        -                         1
       1996 Manitoba        -                        10
       1996 Ontario-North   -                         5
       1995 Ontario-South   -                         2
       1996 Ontario-South   -                        11
       1995 Quebec          -                         2
       1996 Quebec          -                        10
       1995 -               -                         5
       1996 -               -                        36
       1995 -               GOUNOT                    1
```

```
       1996 -                GOUNOT                     12
       1995 -                LEE                         3
       1996 -                LEE                        16
       1995 -                LUCCHESSI                   1
       1996 -                LUCCHESSI                   8
       1995 Quebec           GOUNOT                      1
       1996 Manitoba         GOUNOT                      3
       1996 Ontario-North    GOUNOT                      1
       1996 Ontario-South    GOUNOT                      4
       1996 Quebec           GOUNOT                      4
       1995 Manitoba         LEE                         1
       1995 Ontario-South    LEE                         1
       1995 Quebec           LEE                         1
       1996 Manitoba         LEE                         4
       1996 Ontario-North    LEE                         4
       1996 Ontario-South    LEE                         4
       1996 Quebec           LEE                         4
       1995 Ontario-South    LUCCHESSI                   1
       1996 Manitoba         LUCCHESSI                   3
       1996 Ontario-South    LUCCHESSI                   3
       1996 Quebec           LUCCHESSI                   2

  50 record(s) selected.
```

In comparison to the same query, specifying ROLLUP rather than CUBE, this query returns a lot more information. You now have data groupings that represent every possible permutation of YEAR, REGION, and SALES_PERSON.

The CUBE operator is easy to use yet provides a tremendous degree of analytical power.

Other OLAP Features

SQL has other useful Online Analytical Processing (OLAP) features, in addition to star joins and ROLLUP or CUBE operators. OLAP functions operate over a "window" (or subset) of the data. A window can be defined on the basis of how the data should be partitioned, sorted, or aggregated during calculations.

One such OLAP function is a ranking function called RANK(). Suppose you want to see a table of staff salaries, ranked by department. You can get that information by issuing the following query:

```
SELECT name, dept, salary, RANK() OVER
(PARTITION BY dept ORDER BY salary DESC) AS salary_rank
FROM staff
ORDER BY dept, salary_rank
```

The window in this case is defined on the basis of a partition by department, in which staff salaries are sorted in descending order.

The statement returns

```
NAME        DEPT   SALARY     SALARY_RANK
---------  ------ --------- --------------------
Molinare       10  22959.20                    1
Jones          10  21234.00                    2
Lu             10  20010.00                    3
Daniels        10  19260.25                    4
Hanes          15  20659.80                    1
Rothman        15  16502.83                    2
Ngan           15  12508.20                    3
Kermisch       15  12258.50                    4
Sanders        20  18357.50                    1
Pernal         20  18171.25                    2
Sneider        20  14252.75                    3
James          20  13504.60                    4
O'Brien        38  18006.00                    1
Marenghi       38  17506.75                    2
Quigley        38  16808.30                    3
Naughton       38  12954.75                    4
Abrahams       38  12009.75                    5
Plotz          42  18352.80                    1
Koonitz        42  18001.75                    2
Scoutten       42  11508.60                    3
Yamaguchi      42  10505.90                    4
Fraye          51  21150.00                    1
Williams       51  19456.50                    2
Smith          51  17654.50                    3
Wheeler        51  14460.00                    4
Lundquist      51  13369.80                    5
Graham         66  21000.00                    1
Wilson         66  18674.50                    2
Lea            66  18555.50                    3
Gonzales       66  16858.20                    4
Burke          66  10988.00                    5
Quill          84  19818.00                    1
Edwards        84  17844.00                    2
Davis          84  15454.50                    3
Gafney         84  13030.50                    4

  35 record(s) selected.
```

RANK( )correctly accounts for ties. For example, if two values are tied for first place, the next position is third place.

An OLAP function can also be used to calculate moving (or "smoothed") averages. To illustrate this using an existing table in the SAMPLE database, we temporarily insert some new data into the SALES table:

```
INSERT INTO sales VALUES('04/02/1996','LEE','Ontario-
            South',20);
INSERT INTO sales VALUES('04/03/1996','LEE','Ontario-
            South',9);
```

```
INSERT INTO sales VALUES('04/04/1996','LEE','Ontario-
            South',18);
INSERT INTO sales VALUES('04/05/1996','LEE','Ontario-
            South',17);
INSERT INTO sales VALUES('04/06/1996','LEE','Ontario-
            South',12);
INSERT INTO sales VALUES('04/07/1996','LEE','Ontario-
            South',5);
INSERT INTO sales VALUES('04/08/1996','LEE','Ontario-
            South',14);
INSERT INTO sales VALUES('04/09/1996','LEE','Ontario-
            South',11);
INSERT INTO sales VALUES('04/10/1996','LEE','Ontario-
            South',24);
INSERT INTO sales VALUES('04/11/1996','LEE','Ontario-
            South',10);
```

We need this extra data to calculate a moving average on a significant number of Lee's sales figures for the Ontario-South region.

Here is our query:

```
"SELECT sales_date, AVG(sales) OVER
(ORDER BY sales_date ROWS BETWEEN 1 PRECEDING AND 1 FOLLOWING)
AS smoothed_sales
FROM sales
WHERE sales_date > '03/28/1996' AND sales_person = 'LEE'
AND region = 'Ontario-South'"
```

The statement returns

```
SALES_DATE SMOOTHED_SALES
---------- --------------
03/29/1996              4
03/30/1996              7
03/31/1996              9
04/01/1996             14
04/02/1996             12
04/03/1996             15
04/04/1996             14
04/05/1996             15
04/06/1996             11
04/07/1996             10
04/08/1996             10
04/09/1996             16
04/10/1996             15
04/11/1996             17

  14 record(s) selected.
```

The simple average of Lee's Ontario-South data for this period is 12, a number that conveys much less information about what is going on as a function of time than does the moving average. By the way, to get rid of the inserted rows and restore the SALES table to its previous state, issue "DELETE FROM sales WHERE sales_date > '04/01/1996'".

Another useful OLAP feature is *grouping sets*, which are related to ROLLUP and CUBE groupings. ROLLUP and CUBE groupings can be thought of as a series of grouping sets that don't require you to specify column permutations. Grouping sets are also used to analyze data in multiple dimensions — or different levels of data aggregation — in a single pass. To do this, use the GROUPING SETS specification in the GROUP BY clause. For example

```
"SELECT YEAR(sales_date) AS year, region, sales_person,
COUNT(*) AS tot_sales
FROM sales GROUP BY GROUPING SETS (YEAR(sales_date),
region, sales_person, ())"
```

To get a grand total in your result set, add the grand total group — () — to the grouping sets list.

The statement returns

```
YEAR        REGION          SALES_PERSON    TOT_SALES
----------- --------------- --------------- -----------
          - -               -                        41
          - -               GOUNOT                   13
          - -               LEE                      19
          - -               LUCCHESSI                 9
          - Manitoba        -                        11
          - Ontario-North   -                         5
          - Ontario-South   -                        13
          - Quebec          -                        12
       1995 -               -                         5
       1996 -               -                        36

  10 record(s) selected.
```

Did you notice that this statement is identical to one of the queries we explored in the "CUBE Groupings" section earlier in this chapter? You can get remarkably different summaries of your data simply by changing what you specify in the GROUP BY clause.

You can also modify the granularity of the summaries by specifying multiple columns enclosed by parentheses in the GROUPING SETS list. For example

```
"SELECT YEAR(sales_date) AS year, region, sales_person,
COUNT(*) AS tot_sales
FROM sales
GROUP BY GROUPING SETS (YEAR(sales_date), region,
              sales_person,
(YEAR(sales_date), region, sales_person), ())
ORDER BY YEAR(sales_date), region, sales_person"
```

The statement returns

```
YEAR        REGION          SALES_PERSON    TOT_SALES
----------- --------------- --------------- -----------
       1995 Manitoba        LEE                       1
       1995 Ontario-South   LEE                       1
       1995 Ontario-South   LUCCHESSI                 1
       1995 Quebec          GOUNOT                    1
       1995 Quebec          LEE                       1
       1995 -               -                         5
       1996 Manitoba        GOUNOT                    3
       1996 Manitoba        LEE                       4
       1996 Manitoba        LUCCHESSI                 3
       1996 Ontario-North   GOUNOT                    1
       1996 Ontario-North   LEE                       4
       1996 Ontario-South   GOUNOT                    4
       1996 Ontario-South   LEE                       4
       1996 Ontario-South   LUCCHESSI                 3
       1996 Quebec          GOUNOT                    4
       1996 Quebec          LEE                       4
       1996 Quebec          LUCCHESSI                 2
       1996 -               -                        36
          - Manitoba        -                        11
          - Ontario-North   -                         5
          - Ontario-South   -                        13
          - Quebec          -                        12
          - -               GOUNOT                   13
          - -               LEE                      19
          - -               LUCCHESSI                 9
          - -               -                        41

  26 record(s) selected.
```

The data is summarized clearly, with subtotals for each possible aggregation and a grand total at the bottom of the list.

To practice some of the things that you learned in this chapter, try the exercises in Lab 13-1.

Lab 13-1 Exploring SQL

1. **On Windows NT/2000, issue** `db2cmd` **from a command prompt to open a DB2 command window and initialize the DB2 command-line environment.**
2. **If the database manager is not already running, issue** `db2start`.
3. **To connect to the SAMPLE database, issue** `db2 connect to sample`.
4. **Create one or more tables, such as CUSTOMER or PRODUCT, to complete a star schema for the SAMPLE database.**

5. **Populate your new tables with some data.**
6. **Make up some interesting queries containing star joins and test them.**
7. **Using the SALES table, explore the differences between GROUP BY, GROUP BY ROLLUP, and GROUP BY CUBE.**
8. **Drop the tables that you created for this exercise.**
9. **To break your connection to the database, issue** `db2 connect reset`**.**
10. **To stop the command-line processor, issue** `quit`**.**

Prep Test

1 **Given the following tables**

NAMES

NAME	*NUMBER*
Wayne Gretzky	99
Jaromir Jagr	68
Bobby Orr	4
Bobby Hull	23
Brett Hull	16
Mario Lemieux	66
Steve Yzerman	19
Claude Lemieux	19
Mark Messier	11
Mats Sundin	13

POINTS

NAME	*POINTS*
Wayne Gretzky	244
Jaromir Jagr	168
Bobby Orr	129
Bobby Hull	93
Brett Hull	121
Mario Lemieux	189

PIM	
NAME	***PIM***
Mats Sundin	14
Jaromir Jagr	18
Bobby Orr	12
Mark Messier	32
Brett Hull	66
Mario Lemieux	23
Joe Sakic	94

Which of the following statements will display the players' names, numbers, points, and PIMs for all players with an entry in all three tables?

A ❍ SELECT names.name, names.number, points.points, pim.pim
FROM names
INNER JOIN points ON names.name=points.name
INNER JOIN pim ON pim.name=names.name

B ❍ SELECT names.name, names.number, points.points, pim.pim
FROM names
OUTER JOIN points ON names.name=points.name
OUTER JOIN pim ON pim.name=names.name

C ❍ SELECT names.name, names.number, points.points, pim.pim
FROM names
LEFT OUTER JOIN points ON names.name=points.name
LEFT OUTER JOIN pim ON pim.name=names.name

D ❍ SELECT names.name, names.number, points.points, pim.pim
FROM names
RIGHT OUTER JOIN points ON names.name=points.name
RIGHT OUTER JOIN pim ON pim.name=names.name

2 Given the following table definitions

```
DEPARTMENT
deptno              CHAR(3)
deptname            CHAR(30)
mgrno               INTEGER
admrdept            CHAR(3)
```

```
EMPLOYEE
empno               INTEGER
firstname           CHAR(30)
midinit             CHAR
lastname            CHAR(30)
workdept            CHAR(3)
```

Which of the following statements will list every employee's number and last name with the employee number and last name of their manager, including employees without a manager?

A ❍ SELECT e.empno, e.lastname, m.empno, m.lastname FROM employee e
LEFT INNER JOIN department
INNER JOIN employee m
ON mgrno = m.empno
ON e.workdept = deptno

B ❍ SELECT e.empno, e.lastname, m.empno, m.lastname FROM employee e
LEFT OUTER JOIN department
INNER JOIN employee m
ON mgrno = m.empno
ON e.workdept = deptno

C ❍ SELECT e.empno, e.lastname, m.empno, m.lastname FROM employee e
RIGHT OUTER JOIN department
INNER JOIN employee m
ON mgrno = m.empno
ON e.workdept = deptno

D ❍ SELECT e.empno, e.lastname, m.empno, m.lastname FROM employee e
RIGHT INNER JOIN department
INNER JOIN employee m
ON mgrno = m.empno
ON e.workdept = deptno

Answers

1 **A.** Hint: You're looking for *all players* with an entry in *all three tables*. Only an inner join will give you that. *Review "Joins Revisited."*

2 **B.** Hint: There is no such thing as a *left inner* join, or a *right inner* join. That automatically eliminates A and D. Look for the small difference between the remaining two answers; it is the small difference that makes one answer right and the other answer wrong. Don't be overwhelmed by the complexity of the queries. The parts that are identical are usually irrelevant to the point of the question. *Review "Joins Revisited."*

Part V
The Part of Tens

"Oh, Scarecrow! Without the database in your laptop, how will we ever find anything in Oz?"

In this part . . .

The *For Dummies* old reliable: "The Part of Tens." You will find The Part of Tens in every *For Dummies* book, no matter what the topic. You won't find any of this information on David Letterman's top ten lists, but you will be able to check out:

- SQL questions that you should look over ten times
- Ten sources for DB2 information

Chapter 14

SQL Questions That You'll Need to Read Ten Times

In This Chapter

- Using the `CREATE` vs. the `DECLARE` statement
- Using the `ORDER BY` vs. the `GROUP BY` clause
- Using the `SELECT` statement to echo specified values
- Using the `DROP` vs. the `DELETE` statement
- Using the `HAVING` clause with the `COUNT()` function
- Identifying tables with correlation names
- Choosing names that help you distinguish separate expressions
- Distinguishing `NULL` from a value that is null
- Staying on top of your joins
- Searching when there is case sensitivity

Remember that SQL questions make up the largest part of the DB2 Family Fundamentals Certification Exam. After having read and understood Chapters 12 and 13, you're right on top of things, it's true, but some things about SQL can be tricky or confusing, and are worth revisiting. That's what we do here.

CREATE versus DECLARE

Both the `CREATE` statement and the `DECLARE` statement are part of that subset of SQL called Data Definition Language (DDL), and both are used to create database objects. However, whereas the `CREATE` statement is used to create a large variety of database objects, such as tables, views, indexes, and so on, you can use the `DECLARE` statement only to create *temporary* tables, which are useful for handling intermediate results.

ORDER BY versus GROUP BY

It's easy to confuse the ORDER BY clause and the GROUP BY clause. They look similar. Each is followed by one or more column names.

Remember, however, that the ORDER BY clause is used simply to *sort* the result set returned by a SELECT statement. In this case, the column names represent the sort key that you want to specify. The only other thing that you can specify with the ORDER BY clause is sort order, using either ASC (the default value) or DESC, for ascending or descending order, respectively. For example:

```
SELECT name, salary FROM staff
ORDER BY salary DESC
```

The GROUP BY clause, on the other hand, is used to *summarize* the results returned by a SELECT statement. In its simplest form, a group consists of identical column values for a column that you've specified. For example:

```
SELECT sales_date, MAX(sales) AS max_sales FROM sales
GROUP BY sales_date
```

In this example, the query examines all the records in the SALES table, which may have more than one record for a given sales date. The GROUP BY clause organizes the records by sales date, and the query returns the maximum number of sales recorded for each sales date.

Of course, you also know that the GROUP BY clause can be followed by a GROUPING SETS specification, or by the ROLLUP or the CUBE operator (see Chapter 13, "The Rest of the SQL Story"), and this alone may help you to differentiate the ORDER BY clause and the GROUP BY clause!

"I Love Barney!"

What do you suppose would be returned by the following statement?

```
SELECT 'I love Barney!' FROM staff
```

That's right! The statement returns 35 lines of "I love Barney!" It returns 35 lines because that's the number of records in the STAFF table that's part of the SAMPLE database. If the statement were

```
SELECT 'I love Barney!' FROM staff
WHERE name = 'Plotz'
```

only one record would be returned.

In fact, *what you specify is exactly what is returned*. How can this feature be useful? Suppose that you wanted to insert a record into the STAFF table. This new record is for a certain Mr. Crunch, whose ID number is 360. However, all other column values for Mr. Crunch happen to be identical to those of Ms. Gafney (ID number 350). Here is the statement that will do the trick:

```
INSERT INTO staff
SELECT 360, 'Crunch', dept, job, years, salary, comm
FROM staff WHERE id = 350
```

Here are the two records in question:

```
ID     NAME      DEPT   JOB   YEARS  SALARY    COMM
------ --------- ------ ----- ------ --------- ---------
350     Gafney      84    Clerk     5    13030.50     188.00
360     Crunch      84    Clerk     5    13030.50     188.00
```

DROP versus DELETE

The DROP statement (part of Data Definition Language, or DDL) is used to get rid of *any object* that was created through a CREATE or DECLARE statement, such as a table or a view. The DELETE statement (part of Data Manipulation Language, or DML) is used to get rid of *one or more rows* of data from a table or view. Now, if you leave out the WHERE clause in a DELETE statement, *all the rows* are deleted, but the table still exists. To really get rid of the table, you must use the DROP statement, which removes the table definition from the system catalog tables and therefore from the database itself.

HAVING with COUNT()

Consider the following statement:

```
"SELECT deptno FROM project GROUP BY deptno HAVING
          COUNT(*) > 1"
```

This statement returns:

```
DEPTNO
------
C01
D01
D11
D21
E01
E21
  6 record(s) selected.
```

The result set is a list of all departments that have more than one row in the PROJECT table; it's a list, in fact, of all departments that are responsible for more than one project.

A bit of experimentation shows that you could replace the asterisk with any valid column name from the PROJECT table and still get the same result. Although the COUNT function requires an argument, the function is interpreted in the context of the GROUP BY clause that precedes it.

When Can a Table Have More Than One Correlation Name?

Remember that a correlation name is a table identifier that is defined in a query's FROM clause. For example:

```
"SELECT e.salary FROM employee e
WHERE e.salary < (SELECT AVG(s.salary) FROM staff s)"
```

In this case, the correlation names e and s are used to differentiate the SALARY column in the EMPLOYEE table from the SALARY column in the STAFF table.

You can use two or more correlation names for the same table when building a correlated subquery. For example:

```
"SELECT e1.lastname, e1.workdept, e1.salary FROM employee e1
WHERE salary >
(SELECT AVG(salary) FROM employee e2
WHERE e2.workdept = e1.workdept)
ORDER BY e1.workdept"
```

In this case, the EMPLOYEE table (indicated by e2) is used to calculate departmental salary averages that are compared to employee salaries taken from the EMPLOYEE table (indicated by e1).

When Is a Manager Not a Manager?

When using the AS clause to assign a meaningful name to an expression, try not to pick a name that is identical to a column name in some table that you're using in the same query: DB2 will have no trouble keeping them apart, but you might, and you may find yourself looking at that query more than ten times for reasons that are completely avoidable!

When Is a Null Not a Null?

Quotation marks can be tricky! If you're trying to specify a null value for some column in an UPDATE or an INSERT statement, remember that putting *single* quotation marks around the word NULL will insert the word NULL, *not a null value,* into the row.

Joins: Innies and Outies

Beware the query that sports a left or a right *inner* join — there's no such thing! There is only one kind of inner join, and it joins two tables by returning only those rows from each table that meet the join condition. A *left outer* join, on the other hand, combines the results of the inner join with the rows from one of the tables (the left table) that are not returned by the inner join. And (you guessed it), a *right outer* join combines the results of the inner join with the rows from the other table (the right table) that are not returned by the inner join. For more information about inner and outer joins, see Chapter 13.

Get Off My Case!

You'll probably quite often construct queries that include some search condition that is to be applied to string values. And you'll find that those queries sometimes come back empty-handed! Because character data is stored exactly as specified, the predicates that are part of such search conditions must be case sensitive. Aha, you say, I don't always know the case of the string for which I search! Of course, there is a way around that problem, and it involves a pair of handy scalar functions: UCASE (or UPPER) and LCASE (or LOWER). These functions return a string in which all the characters have been converted to uppercase or lowercase characters, respectively. For example:

```
SELECT * FROM staff WHERE name = 'wheeler'
```

returns zero records, but:

```
SELECT * FROM staff WHERE LCASE(name) = 'wheeler'
```

returns:

```
ID     NAME      DEPT   JOB   YEARS  SALARY    COMM
------ --------- ------ ----- ------ --------- ---------
   250 Wheeler       51 Clerk      6  14460.00    513.30

  1 record(s) selected.
```

What do you do if there is an apostrophe in the name you're trying to retrieve? In this case, put another apostrophe (effectively, a single quotation mark) in front of it, as in the following example:

```
SELECT * FROM staff WHERE LCASE(name) = 'o''brien'
```

This statement returns:

```
ID     NAME      DEPT   JOB   YEARS  SALARY    COMM
------ --------- ------ ----- ------ --------- ---------
    40 O'Brien       38 Sales      6  18006.00    846.55

  1 record(s) selected.

6
```

Chapter 15

Ten Sources of DB2 Information

In This Chapter

- DB2 for Dummies
- DB2 High Performance Design and Tuning
- DB2 Magazine
- DB2 Performance Journal
- DB2 Product Documentation
- DB2 Product Family Web Page
- DB2 Update
- DB2 Technical Conference
- IDUG
- Internet newsgroups

Outlined in this chapter are some quick ways to get more information on DB2 Universal Database, with sources ranging from technical books and magazines to newsgroups and Web sites that give insight to other users' experiences with DB2.

DB2 For Dummies

by Paul Zikopoulos, Lily Lugomirski, and Roman Melnyk

This book contains introductory information to DB2 and not just what you need to know for the DB2 Family Fundamentals Exam, either! If you're looking for a great source of basic DB2 information, including administration tasks, such as backup, recovery, performance tuning, troubleshooting, and so on, then this book is for you.

DB2 High Performance Design and Tuning

by Richard Yevich and Susan Lawson

This book teaches you more than you'll ever need to know about tuning performance for an IBM DB2 database with expert tuning techniques. It's an all-in-one, start-to-finish guide to maximizing DB2 performance — definitely reserved for the gurus of DB2.

DB2 Magazine

DB2 Magazine is a quarterly publication that contains user-driven articles written by DB2 experts like us! The material is always practical and the topics timely. *DB2 Magazine* targets database administrators, analysts, and programmers and covers topics for all DB2 platforms. You can find this publication on the Web and subscribe to receive a hard copy as well at `www.db2mag.com`.

DB2 Performance Journal

Yevich, Lawson & Associates, Inc. (`www.ylassoc.com`) is a firm headed by Richard Yevich and Susan Lawson. They specialize in all areas of database performance. Its consultants are among the most notable in the industry in terms of experience and depth of knowledge. They have a performance journal that is read by thousands around the world. We know Susan and Richard personally, and they're world-renowned DB2 experts *and* noted IBM Gold consultants.

DB2 Education and Skills Web Page

This Web page offers users all sorts of extracurricular DB2 activities, including downloadable courses, pointers to more DB2 learning tools, quizzes, and other useful aids. You can view this page at `www-4.ibm.com/software/data/education.html`.

DB2 Product Family Web Page

The DB2 product Web site keeps you informed about new versions and maintenance FixPacks. It also offers free demo downloads and describes how some companies are using DB2. You can view this Web site at `www.ibm.com/software/data/db2`.

DB2 Update

This is a monthly publication that's definitely packed with information on DB2 across all platforms and topics. You can subscribe to a hard copy version of this publication or view it online at `www.xephon.com`.

DB2 Technical Conference

Every year, IBM sponsors a DB2 technical conference for vendors and users. The conference boasts that it lets you "thoroughly examine advances across the entire family of DB2 products and discover faster, more efficient, and cost-effective ways to access data, manage it, and share it with anyone, anywhere in the world."

Check out `www.ibm.com/services/learning/conf/db2` for more information. IBM often makes the presentations available on the Web as well. Watch out, though — this stuff gets pretty technical!

IDUG

IDUG is the International DB2 Users Group. IDUG defines itself as "an independent, not-for-profit, user-run organization whose mission is to support and strengthen the information systems community by providing the highest quality education and services designed to promote the effective utilization of the DB2 family of products."

The IDUG Web site, `www.idug.org`, has a wealth of useful information, ranging from upcoming conferences and discussion forums to links to other DB2 resources. The site offers user group memberships and provides links to regional user groups and their activities.

IDUG holds conferences around the world each year. If you ever get a chance to go to an IDUG conference, take the opportunity — your DB2 knowledge will be changed forever!

Internet Newsgroups

Check out the following newsgroups, where DB2 users discuss their experiences with IBM DB2 products:

- `bit.listserv.db2-l` (To subscribe to this newsgroup, send an e-mail to `listserv@american.edu` with the text "Subscribe db2-1".)
- `comp.databases.ibm-db2`

You can put your DB2 skills to good use in a job market that is begging for certified people like yourself! Though the exam you write after reading this book is the first step to becoming an IBM Certified Professional, check out the following Web sites for DB2-related jobs:

- `www.justdb2jobs.com` — The URL says it all!
- `www.idug.org` (follow the Career link) — A world-recognized site to advertise for DB2 talent!
- `www.job-hunt.com` (SoftSearch Executive Recruiters) — Specializes in recruitment and placement of DB2 Information Systems Professionals.
- `www.workopolis.com` (No relation to Paul) — This Web site is a Canadian-based job board; however, you can substitute it with any nationally recognized job board in your area (such as `www.hotjobs.com`). Recruiters are always looking at these Web sites for people with DB2 skills. They search on the keyword DB2 and, believe us, if you post your resume there, you'll get a call for a DB2 job.
- `www.ibm.com` — Perhaps you love DB2 so much that you want to come and work with us! DB2 is developed around the world. DB2 on the distributed platform and DB2 for VM/VSE are developed mainly in Toronto, Canada (that's where we are), with some development in the Silicon Valley (such as the Extenders, Data Warehouse Manager, and some others). DB2 for OS/390 is developed in the Silicon Valley lab, whereas DB2 for AS/400 is developed in Rochester, New York.

Appendix

About the CD-ROMs

On the CD-ROMs

- DB2 Universal Database Workgroup Edition, Version 7.1
- DB2 OLAP Starter Kit
- The Dummies Test Engine for Hungry Minds

Disk #1 of the *DB2 Fundamentals Certification For Dummies* CD contains a trial version of DB2 Universal Database Workgroup Edition, Version 7.1 for Windows NT/2000. The software is fully functional but becomes disabled after 60 days. The *DB2 OLAP Starter Kit* CD (Disk #2) contains an OLAP engine that you can use to discover the features and functions of OLAP. The licensing for this software is limited to three concurrent users and does not expire. Disk #2 also contains the Dummies Test Engine for Hungry Minds. You will need to use both of these CDs to complete the exercises in this book and prepare for your exam.

This appendix describes what's on the CDs, how to install DB2, and what you need to run it.

System Requirements

Make sure that your computer meets the minimum system requirements in the following list. If your computer doesn't match up to most of these requirements, you may have problems using the contents of the CD.

- A PC with an Intel-based 586 (Pentium II) or faster processor.
- Microsoft Windows NT 4.0 with Service Pack 5 or later or Windows 2000 (recommended).
- At least 64MB of total RAM installed on your computer. For best performance, we recommend at least 128MB of RAM installed. You can make do with less RAM, but you may end up with memory errors or yawn-inspiring performance.

- At least 300MB of hard drive space available to install all the software from the two CDs. This amount of space will not be sufficient to install all the DB2 tools and to perform all the tasks that are referenced throughout this book. If you are serious about preparing for the exam, we recommend that you have at least 500MB of free disk space so that you can load and explore all the functions and features that will be covered on your test.
- A CD-ROM or DVD drive (we refer to both here as a CD-ROM drive).

If you need more information on the basics, check out *PCs For Dummies,* 7th Edition, by Dan Gookin (published by Hungry Minds).

Using the CD

To install DB2 Universal Database Workgroup Edition, Version 7.1 from the CD labeled Disk 1 of 2 that comes with this book, insert the CD into your computer's CD-ROM drive and let the installation program walk you through the process of setting up your new software. Of course, we recommend that you install DB2 alongside the instructions in Chapter 5, "Installing a DB2 Server."

When you insert the CD-ROM, the auto-run feature automatically starts the installation program for DB2 server. Even if the CD-ROM is in the drive, when you double-click the icon for the CD-ROM drive, the CD should auto-run before looking at the drive's contents. If for some odd reason the auto-run feature fails to start the DB2 installation program, enter ***x*:\setup**, where *x*:\ is the letter assigned to your CD-ROM drive.

After you install DB2, you can eject the CD. Carefully place it back in the plastic jacket of the book for safekeeping.

If you want to install a DB2 client, use the same CD that you use to install a DB2 server. The DB2 installation program will prompt you for the OLAP Starter Kit CD-ROM during the installation process.

Finally, there is testing software on the OLAP Starter Kit CD. This software contains all sorts of sample DB2 questions and will allow you to quiz yourself to gauge your progress. The testing software, can be run directly from the CD. Insert the CD into your CD-ROM drive, wait for the Autorun feature to bring up a simple interface, this interface will allow you to browse the CD, run the self-assessment test or practice test, and exit.

What You Find

- **DB2 Universal Database Workgroup Edition, Version 7.1** from International Business Machines Corporation. Disk #1 of the CD-ROMs that come with this book offers a "try and buy" version of DB2. This version of DB2 is fully functional but becomes disabled after 60 days. You can find out more at: `www.ibm.com/software/data/db2/`. If you decide to purchase this version of DB2, you can upgrade the license without uninstalling DB2.
- **DB2 OLAP Starter Kit** from International Business Machines Corporation. Disk #2 of the CD-ROMs that come with this book offers the DB2 OLAP Starter Kit, limited to three concurrent users. You can find out more at: `www.ibm.com/software/data/db2/`. If you decide to purchase the upgrade to this product (DB2 OLAP Server), you can upgrade the license without uninstalling DB2.
- **Dummies Test Engine from Hungry Minds.** A testing program designed to test your knowledge on the topics that are covered on the exam is on the OLAP Starter Kit CD. To start this program, use the AutoRun feature of the CD. The testing program will challenge you with more than 250 questions written to fully prepare you for your exam.

If You've Got Problems (Of the CD Kind)

We tried our best to create examples that work on most computers with the minimum system requirements. Alas, your computer may differ, and some programs may not work properly for some reason.

The two likeliest problems are that you don't have enough memory (RAM) for the programs you want to use, or you have other programs running that are affecting installation or running of a program. If you get error messages such as `Not enough memory` or `Setup cannot continue`, try one or more of these methods and then try using the software again:

- **Turn off any antivirus software that you have on your computer.** Installers sometimes mimic virus activity and may make your computer incorrectly believe that it's being infected by a virus. Fear not! No such monkey business is going on, so temporarily turn off your antivirus software.
- **Close all running programs.** The more programs you're running, the less memory is available to other programs. Installers typically update files and programs. So if you keep other programs running, installation may not work properly. Close them!

- **Have your local computer store add more RAM to your computer.** This is, admittedly, a drastic and somewhat expensive step. But adding more memory can really help the speed of your computer and allow more programs to run at the same time. If you add more RAM to your computer, you should ensure that the amount of "paging space" is equal to the amount of RAM on your system. Paging space is virtual RAM that your computer uses instead of the physical RAM; it helps computers run faster. Contact your administrator for more information, or refer to *Windows NT 4 For Dummies* by Andy Rathbone and Sharon Crawford (published by Hungry Minds, Inc.).

If you still have trouble with installing the items from the CDs, please call the Hungry Minds, Inc., Customer Service phone number: 800-762-2974 (outside the U.S.: 317-572-3342).

Index

• A •

• B •

• C •

• D •

• E •

• I •

• J •

• K •

• L •

• M •

• N •

• O •

• Q •

• R •

• S •

• U •

• V •

• W •

• Z •

Notes

Hungry Minds, Inc., End-User License Agreement

READ THIS. You should carefully read these terms and conditions before opening the software packet(s) included with this book ("Book"). This is a license agreement ("Agreement") between you and Hungry Minds, Inc. ("HUNGRY MINDS"). By opening the accompanying software packet(s), you acknowledge that you have read and accept the following terms and conditions. If you do not agree and do not want to be bound by such terms and conditions, promptly return the Book and the unopened software packet(s) to the place you obtained them for a full refund.

1. **License Grant.** HUNGRY MINDS grants to you (either an individual or entity) a nonexclusive license to use one copy of the enclosed software program(s) (collectively, the "Software") solely for your own personal or business purposes on a single computer (whether a standard computer or a workstation component of a multiuser network). The Software is in use on a computer when it is loaded into temporary memory (RAM) or installed into permanent memory (hard disk, CD-ROM, or other storage device). HUNGRY MINDS reserves all rights not expressly granted herein.

2. **Ownership.** HUNGRY MINDS is the owner of all right, title, and interest, including copyright, in and to the compilation of the Software recorded on the disk(s) or CD-ROM ("Software Media"). Copyright to the individual programs recorded on the Software Media is owned by the author or other authorized copyright owner of each program. Ownership of the Software and all proprietary rights relating thereto remain with HUNGRY MINDS and its licensers.

3. **Restrictions on Use and Transfer.**

   (a) You may only (i) make one copy of the Software for backup or archival purposes, or (ii) transfer the Software to a single hard disk, provided that you keep the original for backup or archival purposes. You may not (i) rent or lease the Software, (ii) copy or reproduce the Software through a LAN or other network system or through any computer subscriber system or bulletin-board system, or (iii) modify, adapt, or create derivative works based on the Software.

   (b) You may not reverse engineer, decompile, or disassemble the Software. You may transfer the Software and user documentation on a permanent basis, provided that the transferee agrees to accept the terms and conditions of this Agreement and you retain no copies. If the Software is an update or has been updated, any transfer must include the most recent update and all prior versions.

4. **Restrictions on Use of Individual Programs.** You must follow the individual requirements and restrictions detailed for each individual program in the "About the CD-ROMs" appendix of this Book. These limitations are also contained in the individual license agreements recorded on the Software Media. These limitations may include a requirement that after using the program for a specified period of time, the user must pay a registration fee or discontinue use. By opening the Software packet(s), you will be agreeing to abide by the licenses and restrictions for these individual programs that are detailed in the "About the CD-ROMs" appendix and on the Software Media. None of the material on this Software Media or listed in this Book may ever be redistributed, in original or modified form, for commercial purposes.

5. **Limited Warranty.**

HUNGRY MINDS warrants that the Software and Software Media are free from defects in materials and workmanship under normal use for a period of sixty (60) days from the date of purchase of this Book. If HUNGRY MINDS receives notification within the warranty period of defects in materials or workmanship, HUNGRY MINDS will replace the defective Software Media.

(b) **HUNGRY MINDS AND THE AUTHOR OF THE BOOK DISCLAIM ALL OTHER WARRANTIES, EXPRESS OR IMPLIED, INCLUDING WITHOUT LIMITATION IMPLIED WARRANTIES OF MERCHANTABILITY AND FITNESS FOR A PARTICULAR PURPOSE, WITH RESPECT TO THE SOFTWARE, THE PROGRAMS, THE SOURCE CODE CONTAINED THEREIN, AND/OR THE TECHNIQUES DESCRIBED IN THIS BOOK. HUNGRY MINDS DOES NOT WARRANT THAT THE FUNCTIONS CONTAINED IN THE SOFTWARE WILL MEET YOUR REQUIREMENTS OR THAT THE OPERATION OF THE SOFTWARE WILL BE ERROR FREE.**

(c) This limited warranty gives you specific legal rights, and you may have other rights that vary from jurisdiction to jurisdiction.

6. **Remedies.**

(a) HUNGRY MINDS's entire liability and your exclusive remedy for defects in materials and workmanship shall be limited to replacement of the Software Media, which may be returned to HUNGRY MINDS with a copy of your receipt at the following address: Software Media Fulfillment Department, Attn.: *DB2 Fundamentals Certification For Dummies*, Hungry Minds, Inc., 10475 Crosspoint Blvd., Indianapolis, IN 46256, or call 800-762-2974. Please allow three to four weeks for delivery. This Limited Warranty is void if failure of the Software Media has resulted from accident, abuse, or misapplication. Any replacement Software Media will be warranted for the remainder of the original warranty period or thirty (30) days, whichever is longer.

(b) In no event shall HUNGRY MINDS or the author be liable for any damages whatsoever (including without limitation damages for loss of business profits, business interruption, loss of business information, or any other pecuniary loss) arising from the use of or inability to use the Book or the Software, even if HUNGRY MINDS has been advised of the possibility of such damages.

(c) Because some jurisdictions do not allow the exclusion or limitation of liability for consequential or incidental damages, the above limitation or exclusion may not apply to you.

7. **U.S. Government Restricted Rights.** Use, duplication, or disclosure of the Software for or on behalf of the United States of America, its agencies and/or instrumentalities (the "U.S. Government") is subject to restrictions as stated in paragraph (c)(1)(ii) of the Rights in Technical Data and Computer Software clause of DFARS 252.227-7013, or subparagraphs (c) (1) and (2) of the Commercial Computer Software - Restricted Rights clause at FAR 52.227-19, and in similar clauses in the NASA FAR supplement, as applicable.

8. **General.** This Agreement constitutes the entire understanding of the parties and revokes and supersedes all prior agreements, oral or written, between them and may not be modified or amended except in a writing signed by both parties hereto that specifically refers to this Agreement. This Agreement shall take precedence over any other documents that may be in conflict herewith. If any one or more provisions contained in this Agreement are held by any court or tribunal to be invalid, illegal, or otherwise unenforceable, each and every other provision shall remain in full force and effect.

Installation Instructions

To install the items from the CD to your hard drive, follow these steps.

To install DB2 Universal Database Workgroup Edition, Version 7.1 from the CD that comes with this book, insert the CD into your computer's CD-ROM drive and let the installation program walk you through the process of setting up your new software. Of course, we recommend that you install DB2 alongside the instructions in Chapter 5, "Installing a DB2 Server."

When you insert the CD-ROM, the auto-run feature automatically starts the installation program for DB2 server. Even if the CD-ROM is in the drive, when you double-click the icon for the CD-ROM drive, the CD should auto-run before looking at the drive's contents. If for some odd reason the auto-run feature fails to start the DB2 installation program, enter ***x*:\setup**, where *x*:\ is the letter assigned to your CD-ROM drive.

After you install DB2, you can eject the CD. Carefully place it back in the plastic jacket of the book for safekeeping.

If you want to install a DB2 client, use the same CD that you use to install a DB2 server. The DB2 installation program will prompt you for the OLAP Starter Kit CD-ROM during the installation process.

Finally, there is testing software on the OLAP Starter Kit CD. This software contains all sorts of sample DB2 questions and will allow you to quiz yourself to gauge your progress. The testing software, can be run directly from the CD. Insert the CD into your CD-ROM drive, wait for the Autorun feature to bring up a simple interface, this interface will allow you to Browse the CD, Run the Assessment test or Self Test, and Exit.

For more information, see the "About the CD-ROMs" appendix.

FOR DUMMIES BOOK REGISTRATION

Register This Book and Win!

We want to hear from you!

Visit **dummies.com** to register this book and tell us how you liked it!

- Get entered in our monthly prize giveaway.
- Give us feedback about this book — tell us what you like best, what you like least, or maybe what you'd like to ask the author and us to change!
- Let us know any other *For Dummies* topics that interest you.

Your feedback helps us determine what books to publish, tells us what coverage to add as we revise our books, and lets us know whether we're meeting your needs as a *For Dummies* reader. You're our most valuable resource, and what you have to say is important to us!

Not on the Web yet? It's easy to get started with *Dummies 101: The Internet For Windows 98* or *The Internet For Dummies* at local retailers everywhere.

Or let us know what you think by sending us a letter at the following address:

For Dummies Book Registration
Dummies Press
10475 Crosspoint Blvd.
Indianapolis, IN 46256

BESTSELLING BOOK SERIES